T. E. Lawrence: an Arab

T. E. LAWRENCE

AN ARAB VIEW

Suleiman Mousa

Translated by Albert Butros

1966
OXFORD UNIVERSITY PRESS
LONDON AND NEW YORK

B
Lawrence

Printed in the United States of America

Contents

Preface

Publisher's Note

Chapter I FIRST STEPS   1
1. Lawrence's Upbringing. 2. Archaeology and History. 3.
Crusader Castles in Syria. 4. Excavations at Carchemish.
5. Wilderness of Zin. 6. Intelligence Officer.

Chapter II REVOLT IN ARABIA   13
1. The First World War. 2. The Arab Revolt. 3. Fighting
in Hejaz. 4. Lawrence on Leave. 5. Feisal's Camp. 6. New
Plans. 7. From Yanbo' to Wejh. 8. Wadi Ais. 9. Organizing
the Arab Armies. 10. The Seige of Medina.

Chapter III WEJH TO AQABA   64
1. Auda Abu Tayeh. 2. The Occupation of Aqaba. 3.
Between Fact and Fancy. 4. Allenby and Lawrence. 5. The
Northern Army at Aqaba. 6. 'How to treat the Arabs.'

Chapter IV PUNCHING THE TURK   93
1. Gueira and Wadi Musa. 2. Two Raids on the Railway
Line. 3. Tell Shehab Bridge. 4. The Munifa Train. 5. The
Legend of Dera'a.

Chapter V REGULAR AND IRREGULAR   121
1. The Attacks by the Beni Atiyeh. 2. The Battle of the
Wadi Musa. 3. The Capture of Tafileh. 4. Tell al-Shahm. 5.
The Battle of Tafileh. 6. Al-Mazra'a and Mudowwara. 7.
The Storm. 8. Claims and Contradictions.

Chapter VI ADVANCE AND RETREAT   152
1. Lawrence at British Headquarters. 2. The Raid on Fassua'. 3. The Turks regain Tafileh. 4. The British at Salt and Amman. 5. The Battles of Ma'an. 6. Attacks on the Stations. 7. The Destruction of Mudowwara.. 8. War and Politics. 9. The Turks offer Peace.

Chapter VII THE FINAL CAMPAIGN   185
1. The Final Campaign.. 2. Demolition around Dera'a. 3. Attack and Defence. 4. The Capture of Dera'a. 5. The Liberation of Damascus. 6. First days in Damascus. 7. Aleppo and Medina.

Chapter VIII WAR AND PEACE   213
1. Lawrence leaves Damascus. 2. Arabs invited to Peace Conference. 3. Feisal in France and England. 4. The Peace Conference and the Arabs. 5. Zionist Endeavours. 6. The King-Crane Commission.. 7. The Petroleum Policy. 8. National Rule in Iraq and Transjordan. 9. Lawrence Negotiates with King Hussein. 10. Lawrence later on. 11. Friend of the Arabs?

Chapter IX SUMMING UP   257
1. The Expenses of the Revolt. 2. The Arab Military Effort. 3. The Hero in the East. 4. Lawrence's Views and his Role.. 5. Lawrence's Zionist leanings. 6. Lawrence's Personality. 7. Lawrence's Complex

Comment by A. W. Lawrence   279
Bibliography   288
Index   291

MAPS

1 The Arab Revolt Southern Theatre   48
2 The Arab Revolt Northern Theatre   94
3 The Battle of Tafileh   134

PREFACE

The principal motive for writing this book was a sense of what one might call 'cultural obligation' towards the Arab people on the one hand and the western world on the other. An interest in modern Arab history from early youth has led me to study the successive books on Lawrence. This revealed to me that there was a serious gap in information about the life of a man who had become one of the world's celebrated figures. This gap was not only apparent in the writings and attitude of westerners but also in the Arab world itself, where views on Lawrence conflicted sharply.

Western encomiums of Lawrence abounded. To westerners Lawrence's name became inextricably coupled with that of the Arabs, to the extent that he became widely known as 'Lawrence of Arabia'. Examples of western exaggeration are to be found in General Allenby's claim that Lawrence was 'the mainspring of the Arab movement', in Sir Basil Liddell Hart's statement that but for Lawrence 'the Arab Revolt would have remained a collection of slight and passing incidents', and in Sir Ronald Storrs' description of Lawrence as 'kingmaker'. There were, of course, some Western writers—Aldington was one—who attempted to belittle Lawrence and reveal the rather unsavoury aspects of the Lawrence legend. But in the works of Lawrence's admirers and detractors alike one seeks in vain for a semblance of justice to the Arabs. Those who praised Lawrence put in a good word for the Arabs not as a tribute to Arab achievement but as a means of clarifying the background against which Lawrence's 'genius' flourished and to ensure that he was duly in the limelight. Lawrence's detractors criticized both him and the Arabs, and thus deprecated the achievements of the Revolt. In both cases, the Arabs were treated unfairly. Arab history was coloured and distorted in a way that no Arab could possibly accept.

Lawrence's resounding fame was viewed by the Arabs with a mixture of amazement and disbelief. This was because they understood the Revolt to be a purely Arab endeavour, carried out by Arabs to achieve Arab objectives. The participation of the two British and French military missions in the Revolt mainly took the form of technical advice and demolition work. The Arabs certainly appreciated the work done by members of these missions and its contribution to the Revolt, but they never expected that its success would be attributed largely to these missions or to any of their officers. It therefore surprises the Arabs that western writers should have described Lawrence as the leader, the genius and the driving force of the Arab Revolt. In fact, with the exception of Lawrence, none of the British or French officers ever claimed to be instrumental in bringing the Revolt to a successful conclusion or to have actually led the Arabs. Yet in his memoirs King Abdullah goes to the extent of saying that some of these officers rendered greater services than Lawrence. Many Arabs, therefore, view the Lawrence legend as a western fabrication. Some of them even consider that Lawrence was a spy or intelligence officer.

Another important point is that all Lawrence's biographers, from Lowell Thomas in 1924 to Anthony Nutting in 1961, relied heavily on Lawrence's own statements and writings. In general, they analysed Lawrence's own claims as they liked, rejecting some and accepting others. None of them, however, took the trouble to come to this part of the world and investigate the Arab viewpoint. On the other hand the Arabs themselves have not attempted to put forward their side of the argument. This in itself is further evidence that there is a gap which must be bridged.

So it was that I felt impelled to attempt this task. I have tried to be as thorough and objective as I could. Knowing that the material published on the subject in English and Arabic was incomplete, I made contact with several persons who knew Lawrence personally at the time of fighting or in the days of peace and political settlement after the War. Through them I obtained much more information than I had expected at the time I started my research. I had not, for instance, previously doubted the truth of Lawrence's alleged journey in June 1917 to Ba'albek, Palmyra, Damascus and Jebel Druze. And many other of his statements which I had not doubted I discovered to be untrue. I feel fully satisfied with the conclusions at which I have arrived, and I have confidence in the correctness of the material I have uncovered and in the integrity of the persons from whom I have obtained it.

I would like here to express my gratitude to those people who answered my queries whether by correspondence or in personal interviews. The information I obtained from them contributed much to clarifying the role that Colonel Lawrence played in Arab affairs. I would particularly like to express my sincere thanks to: H. H. Emir Zeid ibn al-Hussein; H. E. Sherif Hussein ibn Nassir; Naseeb al-Bekri; Awni Abdul Hadi; Faiz al-Ghussein; Emir Mohammed Sa'id al-Jezairi; Sherif Hussein al-Shaqrani; Subhi al-'Umari; General Mohammed Ali al-Ajluni; Adhoub al-Zebn and Turki al-Mifleh of the Beni Sakhr Tribe; Mohammed Abu Tayeh and Feisal ibn Jazi of the Huweitat Tribe; Mohammed Pasha al-Shureiqi and Mohammed al-Asbali al-Shahri. My thanks are also due to Fayek Janho who helped in various ways.

This book answers many hitherto unresolved questions. When the Arabic version appeared in 1962, it was received with approbation by Arab readers, who were relieved to find explanations of several matters that had, until then, been uncertain. I hope that I have succeeded in elucidating the Arab viewpoint and that English readers, like my own countrymen, will appreciate my endeavour. Since Lawrence's fame rests on his work with the Arabs, it is the duty of Arab writers to investigate his life in the same way as western writers have done.

In the introduction to the Arabic edition of my book, I did not fail to give due credit to the extraordinary work done by Lawrence and some of his countrymen who worked with the Arabs, like St. John Philby, General Glubb and Gertrude Bell. They acted according to the advice of the Arab poet, Ubaid ibn al-Abras: 'Give help in whichever country you are and do not say "I am a stranger." ' They did in fact encounter many difficulties for the sake of their country. I say this to remove any doubt about my fairness to Lawrence. I hope that those readers who may disagree with any of my conclusions will find in my sincerity and good faith an acceptable excuse.

Amman, Jordan, April 1965   SULEIMAN MOUSA

PUBLISHER'S NOTE

Mr. Mousa's book, the first full-length study of T. E. Lawrence by an Arab, is in places critical of certain of Lawrence's statements about the Arab Revolt. Mr. A. W. Lawrence, T. E.'s brother, was therefore invited, with Mr. Mousa's approval, to read the work and to comment on it, if he wished. Mr. Lawrence accepted this invitation and his comments will be found on page 279.

We are also asked to state that permission to quote from *The Seven Pillars of Wisdom*, the letters of T. E. Lawrence, and *T. E. Lawrence by his Friends* was given by the Trustees of the T. E. Lawrence Estate because they felt that direct quotation was preferable to the use of summaries. The quotations from *The Arab Bulletin* and *Military Operations in Egypt and Palestine* are made by permission of the Controller of Her Majesty's Stationery Office.

T. E. Lawrence: an Arab view

1

FIRST STEPS

1. LAWRENCE'S UPBRINGING

THOMAS EDWARD LAWRENCE was born on 15 August 1888 in the village of Tremadoc, County Carnarvon in North Wales. His father's family had emigrated from England to Ireland and acquired Irish blood through marriage. Lawrence's father was originally named Sir Thomas Chapman. He married an Irish woman, who gave birth to four daughters in their seven years of marriage. Eventually he left her and his family and went to England with Sarah Maden, his daughters' Scottish governess, with whom he lived for the rest of his life. He never formally married her because his wife refused to grant him a divorce. Sarah was still alive when he died in 1919.

It was after eloping with Sarah Maden that Chapman changed his name to Lawrence. He owned some property that yielded a yearly income of £300 on which the new family survived until the sons grew up. The life they lived was not out of the ordinary and they never attained a degree of prosperity that would allow lavish spending. Thomas Lawrence, the subject of this book, was the second of five brothers.

The family spent over twelve years wandering from one place to another. From Wales they moved to Scotland, the Isle of Man, Brittany, and later to the Channel Islands, finally settling down in Oxford with a view to educating the children. This wandering was prompted, it seems, by the lack of a fixed home. One may also conjecture that it resulted from a preference for the economical life of remoter parts.

The mother personally supervised the upbringing of her children. She was a remarkable woman: strict, intelligent, endowed with an iron will and a strong physique and possessed of an excessive piety which was perhaps an act of expiation for her illicit love. She gave her children a religious upbringing, and lived with her family in a state of semi-isolation, never allowing her sons to mix with the neighbours' children.

The young Lawrence was able-bodied, agile and intelligent. He displayed in early childhood the characteristics that were to distinguish him in later life: a strong constitution, a good memory, and an adventurous disposition. By the age of eight he was skilled in tree-climbing, swimming and horse-riding, and showed remarkable stoicism and fortitude. It has been said that he inherited his will-power and vigour from his mother, who died in 1959 at the great age of ninety-eight.

The story goes that Lawrence learned his alphabet at three and the fundamentals of reading and writing at five. One of his biographers declared that he started reading newspapers and books when he was four years old, but this, of course, is part of the stock of exaggeration that was to be built up round the whole of Lawrence's career. He studied French in a village school in France. He was about eight years old when the family made their home in Oxford, and his regular education began there. From the time he was twelve until the end of his university education his work was outstanding and gained him many prizes and scholarships.

2. ARCHAEOLOGY AND HISTORY

Lawrence's interest in archaeology and history showed itself early in life. At ten he began to collect pieces of pottery and Roman coins. When he was thirteen he embarked upon a series of strenuous bicycle tours of different parts of England no doubt to quench his archaeological thirst. It is said that he sometimes did as much as a hundred miles a day. In the summers of 1906, 1907 and 1908 he went on cycle tours of France, visiting the castles, particularly those of the twelfth century. At sixteen he was studying siege techniques of the Middle Ages. He was always a voracious reader,[1] though the accounts of his reading given by some of his biographers must be greatly exaggerated.

1. A book that he read at some time during his student years was Charles Doughty's *Arabia Deserta*. It was a book to which he took an instant liking, and it is possible that his desire to live among the bedouin had its origins in this literary experience.

For instance, it is difficult to credit the claim by Robert Graves that Lawrence read fifty thousand volumes in three years. As for languages, he had a fluent knowledge of French, Latin and Greek by the time he graduated. Arabic he learnt later on.

As a sixteen-year-old lad he engaged in a scuffle with an older student at his school and emerged with a broken leg. It has been claimed that the accident retarded his physical growth, causing him to remain short and boyish-looking. Be that as it may, he certainly profited from the ambitious reading he did during the long months of recuperation. It has been reported that round about this time he abstained from eating meat for three years, and he himself claimed that during his university years he worked for forty-five hours at a stretch without food, in order to test his powers of endurance. Occasionally he would fast for three whole days.

In 1907 he won a history scholarship to Jesus College, Oxford, his entry being facilitated by the fact that he was born in Wales, which made him eligible to sit for a Welsh Exhibition.

In the interval between school and university we find that, unknown to his parents, he served as a private in the Royal Artillery for a period of six months. It is believed that this was prompted by his discovery of the nature of his birth. On the other hand, we know that Lawrence told some of his associates that he had known of his illegitimacy as early as his tenth year.

3. CRUSADER CASTLES IN SYRIA

As a subject for his graduation thesis on a special historical topic, Lawrence chose 'The influence of the Crusades on Medieval European military architecture', probably because of the extensive information he had already gathered on twelfth-century castles in England and France. He decided to visit the castles of the Crusaders in Syria, and therefore took a few lessons in colloquial Arabic from the Reverend N. Odeh, a Syrian clergyman who lived in Oxford. Through Lord Curzon, the Master of Jesus College succeeded in obtaining for Lawrence a written permit from the Turkish Government which helped him to overcome the many difficulties he had to face during his wanderings in Syria. It is worth mentioning here that he embarked upon this journey against the advice of Hogarth and Doughty, both of whom pointed out its dangers. Dr. Hogarth, who was keeper of the Ashmolean Museum, had become interested in Lawrence because of Lawrence's frequent visits to the Museum and his special interest in medieval pottery. Lawrence once said that it was to Hogarth, archaeologist, orientalist, and author, that he owed every good job (except the R.A.F.) he had ever had in his life and he described him as the best friend he ever had.[2]

In June 1909, Lawrence left England equipped with a revolver, a camera and some clothes. As soon as he arrived in Beirut, he headed south, passing by Sidon, Banias, Safad, Lake Huleh, Tiberias, Nazareth and Haifa, and returned to Beirut by way of Acre, Tyre and Sidon. In the letters he wrote to his mother he described how he travelled on foot, depending upon the hospitality of the local population for his food *(leben, burghul,* bread and fruit) and lodging. He assured her that his digestion was not affected by his new diet.

After his return to Beirut, he headed north to Tripoli, Latakieh, Antioch, Aleppo, Urfa and Harran, returning through Damascus. In all, he spent four months in Syria, and he claimed that during this time he visited and thoroughly examined fifty Crusader castles. On one of his trips he was attacked by a Turkoman, who, in addition to giving him a sound beating, robbed him of his watch, his money and his revolver. These were eventually returned to him by the Turkish authorities.

In one of his letters to his mother, he asserted that he had become Arab in habits',[3] adding that he had tramped 1,100 miles, averaging twenty miles a day. In another letter he said:

I have had a most delightful tour . . . on foot and alone all the time, so that I have perhaps, living as an Arab with the Arabs, got a better insight into the daily life of the people than those who travel with caravan and dragoman . . .[4]

He had no time left to visit the castles of Shobek and Kerak in the Transjordan area but declared that the castle of Hosn was 'the finest castle in the world'.

Lawrence had ample opportunity during his sojourn in Syria to experience the ruggedness of Bedouin life. He seems to have

2. *T. E. Lawrence to his Biographers, Robert Graves and Liddell Hart* (1936) Part I, p. 50, Part II, p. 160.
3. *Selected Letters of T. E. Lawrence* (ed. Garnett) (1938), p. 29.
4. *Letters,* no. 17.

emancipated himself from the conventions of civilized living, never caring what sort of food he ate nor what sort of mattress he slept on. It did not matter whether he spent the night in a village guest house or in the open with the poorest of bedouin. The sight of a fair-haired young Englishman wandering alone through an expanse of country which knew no peace or security must have been very strange to the bedouin.

His thesis was presented at Oxford shortly after his return from Syria. In it he concluded that the Crusaders had brought more to the architecture of Syria than they had learned from it, and that their castles were not greatly influenced by Byzantine art. This thesis earned him a First Class Honours degree in modern History, with the result that, through the good offices of Hogarth, he was awarded a senior demyship at Magdalen College and a hundred pounds a year for four years to allow him to join the British Museum's expedition, which was to carry out excavations at Jerablus (Carchemish, the fortress city of the Hittite Empire), by the Euphrates.

4. EXCAVATIONS AT CARCHEMISH

Thus Lawrence returned to the Middle East towards the end of 1910. He spent nearly two months at the American Mission School in Jebail, Lebanon, taking lessons in Arabic from Miss Fareedah al-Akle. In February 1911 Hogarth arrived in Lebanon and he and Lawrence sailed from Beirut to Haifa, and from there travelled by train to Damascus, Aleppo and Carchemish. But although Hogarth was in charge of the excavations he did not stay long at Carchemish. He was replaced by another archaeologist, R. Campbell Thompson and Lawrence was given charge of the pottery work, the photography and the keeping of some of the archaeological records. He also supervised the actual diggings. In 1913 Leonard Woolley replaced Thompson.

During this period Lawrence had ample opportunity to meet the Arabs, study their customs, and acquire a greater fluency in Arabic. He was later to describe this period as 'the best life I ever lived', and attributed this contentment to his poverty, which forced him to mix with the people and learn from them. One of the secrets of his later success was his ability to penetrate the inner self of the Arab individual. In this connexion he wrote:

Among the Arabs there were no distinctions, traditional or natural, except the unconscious power given a famous sheikh by virtue of his accomplishment; and they taught me that no man could be their leader except he ate the ranks' food, wore their clothes, lived level with them, and yet appeared better in himself.[5]

At Carchemish Lawrence began to wear Arab clothes and around his waist he wrapped a multi-coloured belt with red tassels bunched over the left hip. He had his hair cut only when it got in the way of his food. He struck up a friendship with two of the workers at the site, Sheikh Hammoudi, the foreman, and Sheikh Ahmed (Dahoum), the water-boy, whom Lawrence later took on as companion and assistant.

Sir Leonard Woolley has said that the Arabs in Carchemish believed that Lawrence was a homosexual because of his close friendship with Dahoum, but Woolley goes on to say that this was a mistake. So immersed was Lawrence in fraternizing with the Arabs that, during short breaks in his work, he would take trips with Dahoum and Hammoudi to visit those in the neighbouring villages. This provided him with the opportunity of learning a great deal about the customs of the people, of adapting himself to their way of life and of learning their language. Apparently he found this more rewarding than returning to England, for, during the whole period of his stay in the Middle East, he went to England only twice. On the second occasion (July 1913) he took Hammoudi and Dahoum with him for a two-week visit. It has been said that the purpose of this visit was to reward Hammoudi for his loyalty, for on one occasion when Lawrence had been extremely ill Hammoudi had taken him to his home and done all he could to help him until he recovered, in spite of the warnings of the villagers that Hammoudi would be held responsible if Lawrence died.

5. WILDERNESS OF ZIN

Towards the end of 1913, while Lawrence and Woolley were spending a holiday in Aleppo, they received a telegram from London instructing them to join a surveying party in the Sinai Peninsula. Lord Kitchener, British Representative in Egypt, had approved a plan to be accomplished by Captain (later Colonel) S. F. Newcombe for conducting a survey of the Sinai Peninsula

5. T. E. Lawrence, *Seven Pillars of Wisdom* (1935), p. 157.

and thoroughly mapping the area. But in order to cover up this military plan, the British announced that they were merely engaged in archaeological investigations. In 1906 a dispute had arisen between Britain and the Ottoman Government over the determination of the Egyptian–Palestinian border, particularly with regard to Sinai. Kitchener, however, succeeded in procuring a permit from the Ottoman authorities for this party to travel between Beersheba and Aqaba.

It took the party two months, January and February 1914, to complete their mission. Lawrence and Dahoum, who had accompanied him, then walked from Aqaba to Petra which, as Lawrence wrote to a friend, was

> . . . the most wonderful place in the world, not for the sake of its ruins . . . but for the colour of its rocks, all red and black and grey with streaks of green and blue, in little wriggly lines . . . and for the shape of its cliffs and crags and pinnacles, and for the wonderful gorge it has . . . Only be assured that till you have seen it you have not the glimmering of an idea how beautiful a place can be.[6]

In Petra he was met by two English ladies who later reported that they had given him sufficient money to make his way to Damascus, since they thought he was a 'half-starved young compatriot in dire straits'.

In one of his letters Lawrence wrote that he reached the Hejaz Railway

> . . . after arresting three policemen at Ma'an, and marching them disarmed through the streets to the Serial, while my camels which they had arrested, escaped.[7]

but this is one of the many stories that Lawrence fabricated. It is scarcely credible that three Turkish gendarmes would have surrendered to a destitute foreign youth and handed their arms over to him. It has, in fact, been reported that he tried to reach Faraun Island (facing Aqaba), against the orders of the Turkish governor, and that he was forcibly ejected from the place.

From Ma'an he returned to Damascus by train and then left for Carchemish, where he spent some time on the excavation site. He and Woolley left for England in the summer to present their report on the Sinai mission. This report, which later ap-

6. *Selected Letters*, p. 69.   7. *Ibid.*

peared in a booklet entitled *Wilderness of Zin*, was still in preparation in June 1914 when the shot which triggered off the First World War was fired at Sarajevo.

6. INTELLIGENCE OFFICER

When the war broke out, Lawrence tried to enlist or to secure military employment. In September 1914, through his friend Dr. Hogarth, he obtained a job at the Geographical Section of the War Office. It was Lawrence's good fortune that most of the officers in this department had already been called to active service and the one remaining officer was preparing to leave for the front in France. The first thing Lawrence did in his new job was to prepare a detailed map of the Sinai Peninsula. This he accomplished alone, because his colleagues Newcombe and Woolley were away at the front.

Lawrence remained a civilian until the occasion when he was requested to present some maps to a general, who refused to talk to him, complaining furiously, 'I want to speak to an officer'. As a result, in October, his superiors arranged for him to be commissioned as a Second Lieutenant, without his obtaining a medical certificate and before his name appeared in the official gazette.

Lawrence had his golden opportunity when the Ottoman Government joined forces with Germany on 30 October 1914, for it was immediately felt that the Intelligence Service in Egypt had to be strengthened. General Headquarters therefore called a number of officers with experience in the Middle East to work with General Clayton, head of Military and Political Intelligence in Egypt. Among these were Newcombe, Woolley and Lawrence. In addition to these three, the Intelligence branch included two M.P.s, George Lloyd and Aubrey Herbert; also Ronald Storrs, who played an important part in bringing Britain and Sherif Hussein ibn Ali to an agreement. Later the group was joined by Miss Gertrude Bell and Dr. Hogarth. Thus Lawrence left England for the Nile Valley in November 1914, after having been promoted to the rank of Captain. For this promotion, which he obtained in seven weeks, he had his friends and his happy stars to thank—in normal circumstances it would have taken him some years.

Lawrence was engaged in his new work for two years. His

duties were many and varied. There is no doubt that the three years he had spent at Carchemish and his trips in Syria, Lebanon, Palestine and Sinai together with his Arabic, provided him with a good knowlege of the area and its people. He began his work by preparing maps of Syria and cataloguing information relevant to these maps. He interviewed prisoners of war, deserters from the Ottoman army and new arrivals from Arab territory. He extracted information from these as well as from spies, local Intelligence Service men and others, and passed on the bits of information he gleaned to his colleagues, who profited from them in studying Ottoman military tactics and dispositions. His work once took him to the Western Desert, where the Sanussi forces, under Ja'afar al-Askari, were engaged in raids against the Italians and the British. On another occasion he travelled to Greece and made contact with British Intelligence there.

He also worked as liaison officer between the Survey Department of Egypt on one side, and the British Department of Military Intelligence and (after February 1916) the Arab Bureau on the other. In another capacity, he provided the link between General Headquarters and the Egyptian Government Press. Those who knew him during this period attested to his intelligence, capability, wit and perseverance. But the fact remains that Lawrence's job was no more important than those of his colleagues; his work was certainly not beyond the capabilities of any educated and experienced young officer.

Dr. Shahbender has recalled in a series of articles how he arrived in Cairo in March 1916, having fled from the Turkish atrocities in Syria, and was requested to report to the British Army Headquarters, which he did in company with his friend Tawfiq al-Halabi. This is how he describes his meeting with Lawrence:

When we knocked at the door of the room, we were received by an officer, who was short, fair-haired, with a large head and a small body, a rectangular face and blue fiery eyes in constant motion. When he walked he barely touched the ground. As he talked to us we noticed that he looked at our faces only furtively, and that he spoke in near-whispers, with a reticence that aroused our caution; but his conversation was precise, profound and searching, which indicated a subtle mind and a thorough grasp of the subject.
The questions he asked us were many. They had to do, in part, with the reasons why we left Syria and the conditions in the country

when we left it, especially its economic situation at a time when famine had started devouring its meat and bone. He was also particularly interested in the secret societies which were working for the liberation of the Arabs.[8]

In April 1916 Lawrence had the opportunity of taking part in a strange enterprise. The Turks had succeeded in surrounding the forces of General Townshend at Kut al-Amara in Iraq, and all the efforts of the British to raise the siege were unsuccessful. Townshend persuaded the British cabinet to approve a plan aimed at bribing the Turkish commander, Khalil Pasha, with the sum of one million pounds sterling (the sum was later raised to two million) in return for lifting the siege. Three persons were chosen to make the offer to Khalil Pasha: Aubrey Herbert, M.P., Colonel Beach of the Iraq command and Captain Lawrence of the Intelligence Bureau in Egypt. But the mission failed because Khalil Pasha refused the bribe and Townshend's forces surrendered to the Turks. Sir Hubert Young met Lawrence at Basrah and remarked that 'He seemed to me thoroughly spoilt, and posing in a way that was quite unlike what I remembered of him at Carchemish'.[9]

In February 1916, the Arab Bureau had been established in Cairo. This was a department attached to the Foreign Office for 'the study and development of British policy in Arab affairs and the collection of information'. Dr. Hogarth was appointed director of the Bureau and granted the rank of naval commander. The Bureau issued the *Arab Bulletin,* starting from the spring of 1916, and Lawrence became a contributor.

Lawrence was still attached to Military Intelligence in Egypt, where the army was completing its preparations and bolstering up its reinforcements with the ultimate intention of marching east on Palestine. It is clear that after his return from Iraq Lawrence had begun to have serious difficulties, for it seems that he had developed the habit of criticizing his colleagues and superiors, and that his experience in Syria was encouraging him to make a parade of his knowledge. Colonel Holdich, who replaced General Clayton as head of Military Intelligence, found 'Lawrence's cheek intolerable'.

But Lawrence was as adept at winning the friendship and

8. 'Lawrence in the Balance', *Al-Muqtataf,* March–July, 1931.
9. *T. E. Lawrence by his Friends* (ed. A. W. Lawrence) (1937), p. 104.

securing the patronage of some influential people as he was at managing to invoke the wrath of many others. Thus he succeeded in securing the patronage of General Clayton, as well as of Commander Hogarth; and Ronald Storrs, Oriental Secretary to the High Commissioner, with whom he shared several cultural interests—particularly Arab life, history and language—was a staunch supporter and friend.

Lawrence profited from the patronage of these important people. Clayton and Hogarth, for instance, arranged for his transfer from the War Office to the Arab Bureau. This transfer was very well timed, because it thwarted the efforts at General Headquarters to transfer him to the front, where he could have met the fate of two of his brothers, who were killed on the Western Front. It has been reported that a reason for the indignation directed at Lawrence was his open support for the Arab Revolt at a time when the prevailing impression at Headquarters was that the Revolt constituted a blunder on the part of the Foreign Office.

Thus we see that Lawrence went through two of the war years in the same way as any other officer under similar circumstances, and that no salient feature distinguished him from his colleagues in the huge army that Britain was preparing for its major offensive against the Ottoman Empire. In fact, Lawrence's achievements during these two years are dwarfed by the heroic deeds carried out by many others on the front or even in the Intelligence Service.

Lawrence makes the incredible claim that he had had a hand in the capture of Erzerum in the spring of 1916, for in *T. E. Lawrence to His Biographers* it is recorded (p. 61) that he told Liddell Hart that he had arranged contact between Duke Nicholas, the Russian commander in the Caucasus, and a number of Arab officers serving in the Turkish army at Erzerum. It seems almost superfluous to assert that Lawrence's claim cannot have been grounded in fact, since the capture of Erzerum was a purely military operation. We must not forget that the Arab officers in the Turkish Army who had not deserted remained loyal until the last moment, in spite of the connexion some of them had with the leaders of the Arab Revolt. This can be proved by the fact that Ali Rida el-Rikabi and Yasin el-Hashimi remained in their military posts as high-ranking officers in the

Turkish army until the final defeat of 1918, despite their avowed belief in the Revolt. They always kept a clear distinction between nationalism and military honour.

His biographers claim that Lawrence worked diligently for a British landing in Alexandretta in order to disrupt communications between Anatolia and Syria and deliver a fatal blow to the Ottoman Empire, especially after the failure of the Allies in Gallipoli. Lawrence himself made the claim that he had talked Lord Kitchener into this, even before the war, and that he continuously belaboured the British commanders with this idea, but that the French refused to consider it. It is a fact that the landing in Alexandretta had been discussed in high British circles and that Lord Kitchener, Secretary of State for War, had supported such a move. We know from Arab records that Sherif Hussein was urging such an action, and we are given to understand that it was discussed between him and Sir Henry McMahon.

Nobody, including Lawrence's detractors, would doubt his intelligence or diligence; but the suspicions of many have been aroused regarding the truth of stories such as those we have outlined, and we shall come across more of the same kind as we proceed. On the other hand, those who believe in luck will find much evidence of it in Lawrence's life: he spent three years at Carchemish because of Hogarth's friendship; he explored Sinai because he happened to be at Carchemish when the need for this trip arose; and he obtained a commission because he had spent some years in Syria. At a time when thousands were being killed at the front, he held a clerical post away from the battle-field for two full years. When the time came when he would have either to be transferred to the front or, at least, to remain in Cairo until the end of the war, the Arab Revolt broke out in Hejaz, and Lawrence, through a series of lucky strokes, became involved in its operations. Indeed, the Revolt provided him with opportunities beyond his wildest dreams and opened wide for him the gates of fame.

2

REVOLT IN ARABIA

1. THE FIRST WORLD WAR

WAR broke out between the Allies and the Ottoman Empire, on 30 October 1914. On the following day, Lord Kitchener, Secretary for War, telegraphed Ronald Storrs, Oriental Secretary to the British High Commissioner in Egypt, requesting him to convey the following message to Sherif Hussein ibn Ali:

> Germany has now bought the Turkish Government with gold, notwithstanding that England, France and Russia guaranteed integrity of Ottoman Empire if Turkey remained neutral in the War. Turkish Government have against will of Sultan committed acts of aggression by invading the frontiers of Egypt with bands of Turkish soldiers. If Arab nation assist England in this war England will guarantee that no intervention takes place in Arabia and will give Arabs every assistance against external foreign aggression.

Preliminary exchanges had been made between the Arabs and the British in February 1914 during a visit that Sherif Abdullah ibn al-Hussein paid to the Khedive Abbas Hilmi in Cairo—six months before the outbreak of the war. These exchanges were a result of the silent struggle that was going on between Sherif Hussein on the one side and the Committee of Union and Progress, which was fanatical in its Turkish racial leanings, on the other. At the time, the British had not evinced much enthusiasm for the idea of supporting the Sherif and supplying him with arms. But soon after the outbreak of war and especially when it became apparent that the Turks wished to join forces with Germany, they hastened to establish contact with him. The Sherif, however, preferred to wait, mainly because of his loyalty to the Ottoman Empire of which the Arabs formed an important part and also because of his hopes that the Arabs would obtain self-rule, so that all races in the Empire might co-operate in augmenting the military effort. In addition, the Sherif, who was an extremely pious man, did not relish the idea of taking up arms against the Muslim Caliph unless he was absolutely obliged to do so.

Early in February 1915, Jemal Pasha, Commander of the Fourth Army in Syria, attempted to cross the Suez Canal. Failing in his attempt, he returned to Damascus and began to seek a pretext for his failure. It dawned upon him that his best chance lay in levelling accusations against Arab political and cultural leaders. Towards the end of June he had a number of Syrian, Lebanese and Palestinian leaders arrested and brought before a court martial. When the news of the arrests reached the Sherif, he realized that the Unionists harboured no good intentions towards the Arabs, and that they were using the war as a pretext to rid themselves of Arab nationalists and to teach them a lesson they would not easily forget. He also realized that this policy would eventually lead the Turks to do likewise with other Arab leaders, including himself. He therefore thought it wisest to proceed with the plan he had hoped to avoid: that of negotiating with the British with a view to co-operation between them and the Arabs. Once the Turks had openly displayed their hostility to the Arabs and closed the door in the face of an amicable settlement, he had no option.

Consequently, on 14 June 1915, Sherif Hussein sent his well-known memorandum to Sir Henry McMahon, British High Commissioner in Egypt, declaring the desire of the Arabs to win full freedom and unity for their territories, and asking the British to recognize this freedom and unity and to help the Arabs to achieve them, by force of arms. As is well known, this correspondence was protracted until March 1916. Sherif Hussein set no date for commencing military operations against the Turks, having left this for a more opportune moment, particularly as he had suggested that the British should land troops in Alexandretta. Also, he was expecting that the Arabs would soon be able to start their revolt in Syria and the Hejaz to coincide with the British landing, in order to achieve significant results in the shortest possible time. These plans, however, were not followed through because the British were not prepared for a landing after their failure in Gallipoli, and because ruthless Turkish measures had disorganized the secret Arab movement in Syria. The French, for their part, were against a British landing in Alexandretta. Events had taken place in Syria which proved that Arabs and Turks had reached the cross-roads: the Turks had publicly hanged, in Damascus and Beirut, two groups of prominent Arabs, on 21 August 1915 and 6 May 1916 respectively. Hussein's earnest pleas for the lives of these men had passed completely unheeded.

To begin with, Sherif Hussein was not in haste to declare the revolt: he knew that his military resources would not allow him to meet the regular troops, armed with the lethal modern weapons which the Turks could command. Suddenly, however, a new factor emerged that forced the Sherif to precipitate the action. A Turkish force of three thousand five hundred strong under Kheiri Bey arrived in Damascus in April 1916, accompanied by a German military mission led by Baron Von Stotzingen.[1] This force then moved from Damascus towards Medina, ostensibly on its way to Yemen. The Sherif, being cognizant of the Turkish methods of deceit, immediately became suspicious. He conjectured that the military situation in Arabia did not require such massive reinforcements, which were sorely needed by the Turks in other areas, and he feared that the Turks' real intention was to depose him and put an end to all Arab aspirations. Another factor which had driven the Sherif to act had been the arrival of Emir Feisal in Medina. For some months Feisal had been in Damascus under semi-arrest, but he had succeeded in deceiving Jemal Pasha and obtaining his permission to go to Medina, on the pretext that he would return at the head of a large volunteer force to fight the British in Palestine.

2. THE ARAB REVOLT

The date originally set by the Sherif for the declaration of the Revolt was August, 1916, but it had to be brought forward because of these new developments, for fear that the opportunity might be lost completely. Since Medina was the centre of gravity from which the Turks were expected to direct their major attacks, the Emirs Ali and Feisal notified Fakhri Pasha, O.C. Turkish forces at Medina, on 5 June, that the Arabs were

1. *Memoirs of King Abdullah of Transjordan* (ed Graves) (1950), pp. 165–166.

severing relations with the Turks. They immediately followed this up with military activities. As early as 10 June the Revolt had spread to important areas in Hejaz. In Mecca the Sherif personally supervised the fighting against Turkish military strongholds, while Emir Abdullah laid seige to the Turkish Division in Taif under Ghalib Pasha, *Wali* of Hejaz and commander-in-chief of the armed forces in the area. In the port of Jedda, Arab forces launched an offensive under Sherif Muhsin Mansur.

The Revolt registered immediate victories. On 16 June Jedda surrendered; the last Turkish fort in Mecca yielded on 9 July; on 27 July the Arabs captured Yanbo' and Rabegh, and on 15 August Leith, Um lejj and Kunufdeh; on 22 September the Taif garrison surrendered. Three and a half months after the outbreak of the Revolt, the situation in Hejaz had developed along the following lines:

1. Arab forces had taken six thousand prisoners-of-war of all ranks, in addition to weapons and military equipment for a division and a number of garrisons.

2. Turkish forces at Medina were brought up to fourteen thousand strong.

3. The three Turkish divisions stationed in Asir and Yemen were completely isolated, their only means of contact with the central Turkish forces through Hejaz being disrupted.

4. Arab military activities prevented the spread of hostilities against the Allies to Africa, which was the objective of the Stotzingen mission and the forces of Kheiri Bey. We can assess the importance of this joint expedition from an article published by Dr. Hogarth after the war, in which he says:

Had the Revolt never done anything else than frustrate the combined march of Turks and Germans to Southern Arabia in 1916, we should owe it much more than we have paid to this day.[2]

The Sherif had no regular forces. He depended for the success of his Revolt on tribesmen armed with nothing but obsolete rifles which were useless for modern warfare. He had no artillery or machine-guns. He therefore sought the help of his allies, and on 28 June there arrived from Port Sudan two mountain batteries and four machine-guns, under Egyptian officers headed by General Sayyid Ali. The guns were soon transported from

2. George Antonius, *The Arab Awakening*, p. 210.

Jedda to Taif, where they were used in applying pressure on the besieged Turkish garrison. The British fleet bombarded Turkish strongholds in Jedda and other Hejazi ports, thus helping to bring about their rapid surrender.

In the middle of July a contingent of seven hundred Iraqi soldiers and officers, who had been detained as prisoners-of-war by the British and had subsequently volunteered to serve in the Revolt, left Egypt for Hejaz under Nuri as-Said. On the same ship the British despatched a 4.5-howitzer battery, four mountain screw-guns, eight machine-guns and about four thousand rifles. These statistics would indicate that the British were quick in fulfilling their obligations to the Revolt; but, as it turned out, most of these weapons had been rejected by the British army as too old to be effective.

Nuri as-Said stated that the greatest difficulties he faced upon joining the Revolt grew from 'the suspicions with which the Allies viewed us'. Upon receiving instructions to begin preparations for his departure as commander of the Iraqi contingent, he had requested that the officers be permitted to leave camp to obtain certain necessaries at Suez, but the British turned down his request. After several attempts, permission was granted to a small number of officers to leave camp and purchase uniforms for the rest of the contingent. Nuri as-Said claimed also that he did not actually meet the volunteers until they were on board ship. Upon reaching Jedda, he supervised the opening of the cases which were expected to hold a number of guns only to discover that the guns had been sent in pieces, several of which were missing. Sights, for instance, were not available; there were no written instructions on the method of use, nor did the British send any experts or instructors. Nuri and his companions had had some experience with German harness but none at all with British equipment. Finally, with the help of Colonel Wilson, British Representative at Jeddah, the guns were made serviceable. The Sherif returned the sticks of dynamite (which had also been sent along) because his men had had no previous training in handling explosives.

We know well enough today that the Arab Revolt was not received with enthusiasm at Army Headquarters in Egypt. General Murray and his staff regarded it as a political matter, of which military men are usually wary. They disapproved of all side shows, being of the opinion that better results could be obtained if all forces available were used in a single theatre of war.

It is worth noting that France sent a military mission to Hejaz, made up of Moroccans and Algerians under Colonel Brémond, who had spent several years in North Africa and spoke Arabic fluently. This mission arrived at Jedda on 20 September and was accompanied by a political deputation headed by Qaddour ibn Ghabrit.

In a statement describing the attitude of General Headquarters to the Arab Revolt, Dr. Shahbender shed light from his own experience on the obstacles that were being placed in the way of the Revolt:

One of the mysterious problems that faced us during the Arab Revolt was the attitude of the British towards our national awakening, an attitude which was a mixture of encouragement and discouragement at the same time. I will illustrate from my own experience; I did not leave Syria until it had become a tenet of my faith and that of my brethren that we were to fight the Turks with all fervour. When I contacted the Arab prisoners-of-war camp at Ma'adi, near Cairo, I took it upon myself to instil into them the national spirit. My aim was to form them up into a nucleus of a regular army which would be the country's vanguard in its renaissance and support in its difficulties. In this way I won over the brave officer Ja'afar al-Askari. We pursued this plan of enlightenment, and succeeded in winning over a considerable number of men, whom we persuaded to volunteer in the Arab army. But every time our efforts were about to bear fruit, they were dealt an almost fatal blow by British army personnel. Every encouragement that came from the Arab Bureau was opposed by Colonel Simpson of Ma'adi Camp.[3]

After the declaration of the Revolt, however, the British Government tried to co-ordinate relations with Sherif Hussein. Sir Henry McMahon, High Commissioner in Egypt, was given the task of directing the political side, while control of military affairs was vested in Sir Reginald Wingate, Governor of the Sudan. Colonel Wilson was appointed Representative at Jedda.

Until this date and all through these events, Lawrence was still attached to Intelligence Service as an ordinary officer, in no way distinguished from several other colleagues.

In his military activities against the Turks the Sherif apparently depended upon the co-operation of the British. As he saw it,

3. *Al-Muqtataf* (Cairo), March–July, 1931.

ements. The Turks would not be able to inflict heavy losses on
ecause it could move at will north or south, and return to its
s for reinforcements and supplies. Emir Feisal liked the idea,
asked that this force be placed under his command, while the
regular army was to be commanded by his brother Emir Ali.
der to ensure the success of this plan, it was decided that Maulud
hlis should be Feisal's military adviser.

is was the strategy that guided the operations of the Arab
s, though the northern army made more use of it owing to
eater resources. It was this plan, formulated by Aziz, that
ence later claimed to have devised and carried out. Aziz
elf, however, did not remain in the Hejaz long enough
e it through. He and Sherif Hussein had a difference of
on, mainly because each held firm to his own views, but
s a result of a false charge made by an officer, who accused
of having established secret contact with the Turks.

e understand from the *Memoirs of King Abdullah* that
llah was the originator of the plan to march eastward from
a to Henakiyeh and Wadi Ais—a move which thwarted the
ish intention of marching on Mecca. The memoirs state
bdullah left Mecca for Juheina territory, leading his army
direction of Medina. On his way, however, he heard that
urks were applying pressure on the armies of Ali and
; so he sent Sherif Fawzan al-Harith at the head of one
nd five hundred camel men to occupy Hejr (east of
h) and eliminate Hussein ibn Mbeirik who was siding
he Turks.[7] He also sent Sherif Abdullah ibn Thawab al-
i with a similar force to Medina in order to conduct raids
Turkish strongholds in the mountains of Waira and Uhud
read panic and chaos along the path leading to Medina.
himself, he continued his march through Henakiyeh west-
n the direction of the railway line, where he succeeded in
lating a Turkish force under Eshref Bey on 13 January
He then crossed the line after damaging part of it and
ng a number of rails.

earing of this success, Fakhri Pasha withdrew his right flank,
had been pressing on Feisal, from Yanbo' al-Nakhl, Wadi

ssein's memoirs lead us to believe that a large force of Emir Abdullah's
ived at Rabegh towards the end of October, and that in the middle of
r Fawzan al-Harith attacked Ibn Mbeirik and defeated him.

the purpose of this co-operation should have been for the
British to engage the Turks in Syria to an extent that would
prevent them from reinforcing their troops in Hejaz. The Sherif
evidently imagined that the British would make a landing on
the Syrian coast or at Aqaba, or at least register important victories on the Palestine front, thus easing the pressure that the
Turks were applying on his own forces.

In his account of the first trip he made to the Hejazi coast on
6 June 1916, Sir Ronald Storrs stated that he and his two companions, Commander Hogarth and Captain Cornwallis, held a
meeting with Emir Zeid and Sherif Shakir. Zeid handed him a
letter from Emir Abdullah which said, 'My only request of you
is to start operations in Syria to the best of your ability'. Storrs
added that Zeid discussed with him the question of effecting a
diversion in Syria to relieve the pressure on Hejaz, insisting that
his father 'felt very strongly on this point'.[4]

We find further evidence of this in the correspondence between Sherif Hussein and his representative Faruki in Egypt.
In a telegram to Hussein dated 20 July 1916, Faruki asked if
Hussein would approve of a British attack on the Hejazi Railway
in the Ma'an area, aimed at technically damaging the line.
Hussein immediately agreed and urged 'the expediting of this
essential move'. Faruki telegraphed again, 'The cutting of the
line by a British force has been finally decided upon by the
British', requesting that this decision be treated as top secret. On
1 January 1917 Hussein telegraphed to Faruki:

Inform His Excellency the King's Viceroy that the Turks have
despatched new forces from Sinai to our front. Owing to our realization of a natural weakness in our preparations, we had made the
damaging of the line at the beginning of the movement a main
article of our agreement, because it would be the most important
factor in driving the Turks out of the whole country. We actually
organized our government on this basis. Had we known that (the
British) were not going to fulfil the said agreement, we would have
devised a different plan for the movement.[5]

3. FIGHTING IN HEJAZ

The fighting in Medina was not decisive, not only because of the

4. Ronald Storrs, *Orientations* (1939), pp. 182–185.
5. Mohammed Taher Al-Umari, *Tarikh Muqaddarat al' Iraq al-Siyasyyah*
(History of Political Destinies of Iraq) (1924), Vol. I, pp. 285–290; Vol. II, pp. 61
and 187.

Hejazi railway which linked Medina with the centre of Turkish military supplies in Damascus, but also because of the considerable strength of the Turkish forces in the area. Here, General Fakhri Pasha, famous for his stubbornness and persistence, was appointed Commander-in-Chief and his army was considerably reinforced by the column of Kheri Bey and by artillery and various equipment.

The first clash between the two sides occurred on 5 June, when the brothers Ali and Feisal attacked the railway line and removed a number of rails. On the next day they attacked 'Muhit' station. Fakhri Pasha led a counter attack and fighting continued from dawn to noon, when the Arabs withdrew to Bir Mashi because of Turkish superiority in the field. The Arabs then returned to Ghadir, where Ali and Feisal parted, each trying to rally the tribes and supply them with weapons. In the middle of June Fakhri Pasha attacked Feisal's forces and captured Alawa and Bir Mashi, which he proceeded to fortify together with Mejezz. Emir Ali camped in Wadi Itheb, about fifty km. to the south-west of Medina, while Emir Feisal set up camp at Yanbo' al-Nakhl, north-west of Medina. Ali's force numbered just over four thousand, including a camel unit of Ageyl, led by Ibn Dakhil. This was the same unit Sherif Hussein had previously organized to fight on the side of the Turks in Palestine.

Late in July, Nuri as-Said joined Emir Ali and started organizing his forces and co-ordinating his military activities. He was thus able to launch a surprise attack on Rabegh, where the pro-Turk Ibn Mbeirik was camping. Nuri as-Said captured Rabegh and Ibn Mbeirik took to flight. This successful operation solved the grave problem of supplies; equipment started reaching Ali by sea, whereas earlier it had had to come by way of Mecca over a long rugged road that took two weeks to traverse. Ali made his headquarters at Rabegh, where Nuri as-Said and his officers embarked on the organization of a regular battalion. In the meantime Emir Zeid arrived at the head of another force.

In September Aziz Ali al-Misri arrived in Hejaz, where he was appointed chief of staff by Sherif Hussein. Aziz vigorously started the work of establishing a regular Arab Army. On 16 November a very important conference was held at Rabegh, attended by Ali, Feisal, Aziz Ali, Nuri as-Said and British and French representatives, at which they decided upon future plans

for further activities against the Turks. Nu[...] Ali insisted that the Arabs should be suppli[...] tain guns, since the old big guns that the Brit[...] were valueless in the rugged fighting area, e[...] the difficulties of watering and feeding th[...] that were used to pull them.

This conference became especially import[...] massed a huge force in Medina with ample i[...] planned to march on Mecca. There were [...] Mecca: one in the interior which was ru[...] generally impenetrable by a regular force, [...] the coast, which could be taken only if the [...] Rabegh for water. Thus the defence of Rah[...] tive. The decisions arrived at at the confere[...] agreed that Abdullah should lead his forces [...] miles north-east of Medina. Here he would [...] disrupt all communications between the [...] Ibn Rasheed Emir of Hail. It was also decid[...] strengthen his front at Yanbo', then march [...] he was to capture before moving east to at[...] Ali, on the other hand, was to march from [...] tion of Medina and engage the enemy, us[...] and the Egyptian guns which were then o[...] to Rabegh. The plan aimed primarily at [...] from all sides to prevent their march on M[...] Medina closely, forcing it to surrender. F[...] in his memoirs that after the fall of Ta[...] sulted his sons and decided that Ali and [...] up the siege of Medina until it surrender[...] push north to Syria.[6]

In his lectures on Arab military tacti[...] Said had this to say:

Aziz Ali urged that the army should be di[...] first and more important was to be devel[...] lines: the second was to be developed in [...] equipped with light weapons with the t[...] Turkish lines in Arabia, right up to Syria. [...] to terrify the Turks, disrupt their communi[...]

6. Faiz al-Ghussein *Muthakkarati 'an al-Thawre*[...] the Arab Revolt) (1956), p. 255-6.

Safra and Bir Said to Bir Darwish. He also withdrew his left flank, which had been engaging Emir Ali's forces, from Bir Kadi, Sath al-Ghair, Bram and Abud to Mejezz and Majzan brook thence to Abar Ali. I took up a position at Wadi Ais and ordered continuous attacks on the railway to be pushed by day and by night. Feisal's force thus relieved, it advanced along the coast to Wejh. . . . In this way the Arab movement registered a success because I chose the eastern road. The siege of Medina was gradually perfected after that.[8]

However, the last three months of 1916 were the most critical for the Revolt. The Turks in Medina had gathered a large force, equipped with modern weapons. All indications showed that they were preparing to march towards Mecca and wipe out the rebels. During this period, Sherif Hussein was becoming extremely worried and he requested the British to send urgent help. So worried was he that he asked the British to land a force in Rabegh to defend it and forestall the impending Turkish attack. Hurried telegrams were exchanged between Mecca, Cairo and London, and the subject was discussed at a meeting of the British Cabinet and in General Army Headquarters. What the British mainly feared was exposing themselves to hostile propaganda by landing a Christian force in Hejaz. In spite of all their misgivings, however, they had a brigade in Suez ready to leave for Hejaz, and they asked Hussein to make an official request in writing for the landing of the troops and to declare that he would shoulder all consequences. At first Hussein hesitated, then he refused to sign such a statement. But he persisted in demanding effective modern weapons and aircraft to withstand the brunt of Turkish arms and German aeroplanes.

Nuri as-Said stated that two Turkish columns marched from Medina in October. Feisal and his forces at Yanbo' al-Nakhl had to retreat under pressure from the first, while the second moved in the direction of Rabegh. At King Hussein's instructions both the regular and the irregular forces of Emir Ali set out to hinder the Turkish offensive. Aziz Ali joined these forces and personally supervised the fighting. While preparations were being made for the major encounter with the Turks, Emir Ali insisted that his forces should withdraw to Rabegh, because an officer had

8. In translating Abdullah's memoirs I have made use of *Memoirs of King Abdullah of Transjordan* (ed. P. P. Graves) (1950), although I differ from this translation in several significant ways. This passage comes from pp. 135, 136 and 138 of the Arabic edition.

intimated to him that Aziz was in collusion with the Turks. The Turks continued their march but it was hindered by the Hejazi tribes, who impaired their communications and robbed their convoys. In vain the Turks tried to preserve their communication lines with Medina. The tribes brought their booty and prisoners either to Rabegh or to Yanbo. Two month later, the Turks had to make a gradual retreat *'because they despaired of overcoming the tribes and preserving their communication lines'*.

Hussein's telegrams to his representative Faruki in Egypt give a clear picture of the critical juncture which the fighting had reached. When, at the request of the British, his representative inquired about the probability of peace between him and the Turks, he cabled on 23 Ramadan (July):

Peace is contingent upon our allies. I will never accept separate peace with the Turks. Inform the British that they should take this as a final decision, even if only my sons remain with me.

Towards the end of July, he cabled:

The situation in our camp at Medina has begun to improve after arming [our soldiers] with the guns despatched. [This improvement came about] after the weakness resulting from the lack of military equipment, especially rifle cartridges.

He demanded that the British supply him with aircraft to meet the Turkish planes that were terrifying the bedouin and giving them cause for panic. In this we see the reasons for Hussein's insistence on quick action. If rifles could do so much for the morale of the bedouin, modern artillery, in place of the huge old guns, would work wonders. A month later, in August, we see Hussein pleading again for the despatch of field guns and aircraft to Yanbo 'in order to resist enemy attacks on our armies, *which are deprived of all equipment*, and withstand their superiority'.

The Turks on their side were faced with equally difficult problems. They were operating in hostile territory, with its rough terrain, unpaved roads and lack of water. In spite of their technical superiority and their trained army, they were hampered on every side. The Arabs on the other hand derived their strength from the ruggedness of the terrain, so suited to the bedouin, who could carry on his camel his whole week's ration of food and water. Their familiarity with the whole territory enabled them to move in small lightly-equipped parties that would launch a surprise attack, inflict losses and generally demoralize the enemy. The very absence of conventional military tactics among the bedouin played havoc with Turkish plans and forced the Turks into sudden changes of movement. Fakhri Pasha could not have done more than he actually did, as he was fighting an unknown enemy under very uneven circumstances. He never managed to meet the Arabs in an open decisive battle—the bedouin were masters at their desert game of hit-and-run. They attacked and plundered at every turn; then, at the first sign of enemy retaliation, they slipped away as suddenly as they had appeared. Hindered by their heavy equipment and their fear of ambush, the Turks had no chance of chasing the bedouin. They tried to employ the tactics of their Arab opponents; they brought Sherif Ali Heidar to Medina and announced the deposition of Sherif Hussein; they gave the new Sherif a large sum of money with which to woo the Arab tribes. But their attempt failed, because the Arabs put their independence and unity above all other considerations. Furthermore, Ali and Feisal had parted as soon as skirmishes began, with the result that the Turks could not follow the army of the one without being subject to a sudden attack from the forces of the other. The two brothers depended upon reinforcements from the coast and took refuge, when necessary, in Rabegh and Yanbo', to which the Turks dared not advance for fear of the long-range guns of British warships.

A letter from Feisal to Ali, dated 26 October 1916, stated that the three leaders planned to strengthen the siege of Medina in the following way: Abdullah was to march east of the city; Ali was to march on Mejezz with the objective of cutting enemy communications in Ghair; Feisal was to march north and cut the railway line at Buwat station.[9]

On 26 November Feisal arrived in Rabegh to discuss the situation with Ali; they decided that Zeid should hold Bir Said with the Harb, Juheina and Ageyl, and that Feisal should move in stages to Wejh. The plan was actually implemented, but the Turks attacked Zeid in Bir Said and Wadi Safra and forced him to retreat to Yanbo. Feisal thus had to postpone his northward march until the outlook improved.

9. *Arab Bulletin*, 8 November 1916.

Nuri as-Said's lectures provide clear information on the activities of Emir Ali in this critical period. In November the Turks abandoned their southward march, while Ali was preparing to attack them with the help of Egyptian artillery. Early in December, he advanced to Badr and Wadi Safra. The Turks were in force at Bir Derwish, with three battalions, artillery and some machine-guns. The attacking Arab force consisted of four battalions, a mountain battery, 18-pounders and three thousand bedouin volunteers. Regulars and bedouin co-operated to the full: the bedouin began by making a series of sudden raids and capturing Turkish positions immediately overlooking Wadi Safra. This forced the Turks to abandon their main positions at Bir Derwish before the regulars began their own attack. The Turks' losses amounted to 500 killed or taken prisoner and a large quantity of weapons and equipment. Nuri as-Said says that this victory had a marked effect upon the course of the war in the Hejaz.

Three weeks after the capture of Bir Derwish, Emir Ali marched upon the Turkish strongholds at Bir Mashi, where the Turks had about one brigade; they had an ample water supply and they could count upon Medina for reinforcements. In this attack, the regulars joined forces with bedouin volunteers under Ali and Zeid. The Arabs at first registered some success, but Turkish reinforcements were immediately dispatched and the Turkish guns had a range longer than that of the Arab guns. The bedouin were afraid of attacking Turkish entrenchments and Ali had to withdraw to Bir Derwish. Feisal's army was also on the move. In September it had to retreat to Yanbo' in the face of continued pressure from Fakhri Pasha. However, Fakhri ordered a sudden retreat and Feisal followed the Turks to Bir Abbas, where they renewed their attack in October. On the night of the 31st of that month, Feisal surrounded the enemy forces at Masialeh; the Turks were thus compelled to abandon their front lines.

In January 1917, the siege of Medina was tightened: Abdullah arrived at Wadi Ais, Ali moved to Abu Auf brook and Feisal defeated the Turkish forces in Kharza. It then became clear that the Turks were in no position to march on Mecca. The British High Commissioner in Egypt congratulated Hussein on these victories.

At this time also, Feisal sent a report to his father outlining his future military plans. From this report dated 21st Rabi Awwal (13 January 1917), we can piece together the situation as it really was. The report said:

(1) The arrival of Sidi Abdullah at Wadi Ais *has enabled me to march on Wejh,* which we will capture within the next two days.

(2) After the arrival of Shakir [Abdullah's delegate], we shall decide whether I should move close to Ala, unite our activities and engage the Turks in a decisive battle, since we should have no fewer than 25,000 men, or whether I should head north and cut the railway line between Muadhdham and Tebuk stations.

(3) I am upset about the shortage of camels [because of the three-year old drought in the area] to transport heavy equipment. I therefore request 2,000 camels and 20,000 rifles.

From this we can arrive at two conclusions:

1. The Arabs, in the last three months of 1916, were afraid that Fakhri Pasha might march on Mecca. For this reason Sherif Hussein was clamouring for artillery, modern weapons, experts and aircraft. When the danger was greatest he had requested the landing of British forces for the defence of Rabegh, but he soon withdrew this request. The Arabs' position was improving because of Abdullah's activities east of Medina and his presence at Wadi Ais.

2. British aid to the Revolt was not until that date satisfactory. Most of the weapons the British had sent were obsolete. They did not send experts or instructors for several months. Aircraft did not arrive until after some months.

Lawrence said of this:

Things in the Hejaz went from bad to worse. No proper liaison was provided for the Arab forces in the field, no military information was given the Sherifs, no tactical advice or strategy was suggested, no attempt made to find out the local conditions and adapt existing Allied resources in material to suit their needs.[10]

4. LAWRENCE ON LEAVE

We left Lawrence working in the Intelligence Service. *Seven Pillars of Wisdom* indicates that he was not happy because his inclination towards the Arabs was making him extremely unpopular. He says that when his request for a transfer was turned

10. *Seven Pillars,* p. 62.

down, he had to resort to other tactics, such as capitalizing on his superiors' mistakes, exposing their ignorance and inefficiency, and even revealing their grammatical errors and ridiculing the style of their reports. Their decision to get rid of him stands witness to the success of his manoeuvres. Grasping an opportune moment, he asked for ten days' leave so that he could join Ronald Storrs on a trip to Jedda, where Storrs was scheduled to meet Sherif Hussein.

What concerns us here is that Lawrence was granted leave to make the trip and that, after sensing the hostility of his colleagues and superiors, he went to Clayton and put the state of affairs to him. Clayton arranged for the Residency to make application to the Foreign Office for his transfer to the Arab Bureau. On this occasion Lawrence said:

> But I justified myself by my confidence in the final success of the Arab Revolt if properly advised. I had been a mover in its beginning; my hopes lay in it.[11]

This was Storrs's third visit to Hejaz. His first had been in June when the Revolt was declared; the second was in September. He and Lawrence reached Jedda on 16 October, at the same time that Abdullah arrived at the town coming from Mecca. A meeting was held between Storrs, Wilson, and Lawrence on one side, and Emir Abdullah and Aziz Ali on the other. The Emir, whose intention was to explain the need of the Arabs for arms and equipment, was shocked at Storrs's announcement that the promised British brigade was not going to be sent to Hejaz and that the aircraft, which had arrived a few days earlier, were to be withdrawn. Storrs further announced that he was not empowered to give any views on military affairs. Wilson then read a telegram he had received to this effect. In his *Memoirs* Abdullah describes the news as 'a great shock to me and to Aziz Ali, for we were in need of aircraft, artillery, machine guns and engineers; such could only be handled by trained men and we had none of them'.

Angered, the Emir withdrew from the meeting and went to Colonel Brémond, head of the French military mission, to whom

---

11. *Seven Pillars*, p. 63. But on p. 552 Lawrence says 'I had had no concern with the Arab Revolt in the beginning.'

he declared that, because of the British attitude, the Arabs had no alternative but to contract peace with Turkey. Brémond hurriedly carried the news to the three Englishmen, who instantly followed the Emir to his camp, requesting that he remain in Jedda long enough for them to make representations to their superiors. The Emir, however, insisted on leaving for Mecca, where on arrival Sherif Hussein informed him that the British Representative in Jedda had cabled saying that all the demands of the fighting forces would be attended to without delay.

One finds some discrepancy in the writings of Abdullah, Storrs and Lawrence about these meetings.[12] Storrs, for instance, states that Wilson read the telegram in English, that he himself translated it to the Emir and that they then proceeded to debate its contents. All he says about Lawrence is that the latter could understand the Emir's flowery Arabic more readily than Wilson. The two parties, he further states, held a meeting next day in which Aziz Ali voiced the opinion that there was no real need for the British brigade. Storrs does not make any mention of Lawrence in writing about the second meeting.

Lawrence's account is a lengthy one. He gives a picture of Abdullah as a charming and easy conversationalist, but one who, when they fell into serious talk 'chose his words, and argued shrewdly'.[13] Describing Abdullah as 'astute', he goes on to say,

His object was, of course, the winning of Arab independence and the building up of Arab nations, but he meant to keep the direction of the new states in the family.[14]

Lawrence also says that he began at the time to form his opinion about the Revolt and its progress.

My suspicion was that its lack was leadership: not intellect, nor judgement, nor political wisdom, but the flame of enthusiasm, that would set the desert on fire. My visit was mainly to find the yet unknown master-spirit of the affair, and measure his capacity to carry the revolt to the goal I had conceived for it. As our conversation continued, I became more and more sure that Abdulla was too balanced, too cool, too humorous to be a prophet. . . . His value would come perhaps in the peace after success.[15]

12. This is perhaps explained by the fact that, writing several years after the event, they were all influenced by the subsequent history of the Revolt.
13. *Seven Pillars*, p. 67.
14. *Ibid.*
15. *Ibid.*

Lawrence goes on to say that, when asked to give his views
on the state of the campaign, 'Abdulla at once grew serious' [16]
and laid the blame on the British for neglecting to cut the
Hejaz railway, which fed Medina, and for neglecting to send
supplies, machine-guns and artillery to the Arabs. At this point,
Lawrence claims, he was the one who replied, answering Abdullah point by point, especially with regard to the British
brigade under discussion. The Emir replied that 'The ear-
marking of a brigade and transports need be only temporary;
for he was taking his victorious Taif troops up the eastern road
from Mecca to Medina'.[17] Lawrence said that he would represent
his views to Egypt but that he would also like to see Feisal to
discuss his needs with him. He added:

Storrs then came in and supported me with all his might, urging
the vital importance of full and early information from a trained
observer for the British Commander-in-Chief in Egypt, and showing
that his sending down me, his best qualified and most indispensable
staff officer, proved the serious consideration being given to Arabian
affairs by Sir Archibald Murray.[18]

The Emir conveyed this wish to his father by telephone,
but Hussein, who did not hide his suspicions, was hesitant. Storrs
pleaded with Hussein, who finally agreed. Abdullah then wrote
a letter to his brother Ali, recommending Lawrence and requesting that he be granted safe conduct to Feisal's camp.

This account of Lawrence's raises several questions, for all
other sources agree that the discussion was of the highest serious-
ness, and that Wilson and Storrs were officially informing the
Emir of the views of the British Government. The telegram was
produced as a document. How is one to believe that Lawrence
played such a role in these discussions, when he had no official
capacity? And how is one to believe Lawrence's claim to be a
mover of the Revolt in the beginning? How could Lawrence
speak about the Revolt's lack of leadership and the 'flame of
enthusiasm' when the facts clearly show that the Revolt started
with defined leadership? The declaration of the Revolt itself
was sufficient proof of the flame of enthusiasm in Arabia. Storrs
could not possibly have said that the Commander-in-Chief in
Egypt had sent Lawrence especially to visit the battle-field and
report to him, and that the 'serious consideration' he gave the

16. *Seven Pillars*, p. 69.   17. *Ibid.*, p. 70.   18. *Ibid.*, pp. 70–71.

Arab Revolt had prompted him to send his 'best qualified . . . officer', because we have already been told that for Lawrence this trip was to be a vacation. Surely Lawrence was not telling the whole truth. Furthermore, I doubt the truth of Storrs's statement in his book that Abdullah so admired Lawrence's precise information about Turkish dispositions that he ex-claimed, 'Is this man God, to know everything?' [19] Abdullah may have complimented Lawrence in some way, but I think it im-probable that he ever used these very words.

From the correspondence between Hussein and McMahon about the withdrawal of the British aircraft from Rabegh, we get a glimpse of the serious Arab concern for obtaining effective military aid. On 20 October Hussein sent the following cable to McMahon:

> The fact that our Bedouin troops have resisted Turkey and its ally, withstood their pressure and retained their own positions for the last four months—does not dissuade me from requesting mili-tary reinforcements from Great Britain in accordance with our agreement. We have met with great grief and despair because Britain also withdrew the aircraft after they reached Rabegh . . . I demand that the aircraft be returned without delay. The lives of our sons Ali, Feisal and Zeid would guarantee their protection.

On the following day Hussein telegraphed McMahon saying:

> Wishing to clarify further what ought to be done, and to remove the possibility of misunderstanding, we are of the opinion to have our son Abdullah meet your Excellency, provided that the period covering his departure, stay and return does not exceed ten days, because his task of attacking the strongholds to the north east of Medina does not permit longer absence. If your Excellency agrees, please be so kind as to fix a day for the arrival of the ship which is to carry him from Jedda.

This telegram makes it quite clear that Abdullah's decision to attack Medina from the north-east had been taken before the arrival of Lawrence in the Hejaz. Meanwhile, Faruki telegraphed to Hussein stating that McMahon had asserted Britain's willing-ness to aid the Revolt in all possible ways. [20]

It is important for us to remember that Hussein 'directed the administrative, political and military affairs of the Revolt by himself. He held all the reins: it was from him that military

19. *Orientations*, p. 221.
20. Al-Umari, *op. cit.*, Vol. I, pp. 296–298.

orders went out to his sons, directing them as to the manner military activities were to be conducted.'[21]

It is apt at this point to present the text of a telegram that Lawrence sent to his chief, Clayton, on 17 October 1916, which was the day following his arrival in Jedda with Ronald Storrs:

> Meeting to-day. Wilson, Storrs, Sherif Abdulla, Aziz Ali al-Misri, myself. Nobody knew real situation Rabegh. So much time wasted. Aziz Ali al-Misri going Rabegh with me tomorrow. Sherif Abdulla apparently wanted foreign force at Rabegh as rallying point if combined attack on Medina ended badly. Aziz Ali al-Misri hopes to prevent any decisive risk now and thinks English Brigade neither necessary nor prudent. He says only way to bring sense and continuity into operation is to have English staff at Rabegh dealing direct with Sherif Ali and Sherif Feisal without referring detail to Sherif of Mecca of whom they are all respectfully afraid. Unfortunately withdrawal of aeroplanes coincided with appearance of Turkish machines, but Aziz Ali al-Misri attaches little weight to them personally. He is cheerful and speaks well of Sherif's troops.[22]

This telegram shows how Lawrence later distorted the opinions of the leaders of the Revolt and attributed them to himself; for the telegram refers to the combined attack on Medina, which is clarified by King Abdullah's statement in his *Memoirs* that he was preparing to travel to Medina and co-operate with his brothers in launching a combined attack on the city and that he had suggested this to his father King Hussein, who approved it. This, of course, had been planned without consultation with Lawrence. The telegram further refers to Aziz Ali's opinion with regard to the British brigade, which is the same opinion Lawrence later carried to his superiors in Egypt and took great pride in having proposed. The same applies to Aziz Ali's views on the presence of British staff officers in Rabegh. Storrs, Aziz and Lawrence sailed on the third day from Jedda to Rabegh, Ali's headquarters, where they held talks with Ali and Zeid, after which Storrs left Rabegh for Egypt. Lawrence stayed on and met Colonel Parker, British liaison officer and Nuri as-Said. Faiz al-Ghussein had travelled on the same ship from Jedda to Rabegh and met Storrs and Lawrence on this trip.

Lawrence did not write anything significant about his stay at

Rabegh, but he did express his opinion of Ali and Zeid; an opinion which is disturbingly superficial. Take, for example, his slur on Zeid whom he describes as 'no zealot for the Revolt' because his mother was Turkish, when he himself on other occasions attested to Zeid's daring and courage. We know also that, at eighteen, Zeid had led Arab troops in the field starting from the Hejaz in the south to Damascus in the north, facing all the dangers that confronted any other soldier in the Revolt.

The Arab observer might well feel sorry because Ali, Feisal, Zeid and Aziz Ali al-Misri did not furnish us with their memoirs, which would have been invaluable in guiding us to a better understanding of the situation. In the absence of such memoirs, the opinions of Nuri as-Said assume great significance. In his introduction to the Arabic translation (1927) of Lawrence's *Revolt in the Desert*, Nuri as-Said mentioned his first meeting with Lawrence:

In the autumn of 1915, I moved from my prison-camp in India to Egypt, where I frequently visited my friend Cornwallis, of the Arab Bureau. There I met Lieutenant Lawrence for the first time. I was neither interested in the young man nor did I notice in him any distinguishing trait which might have enabled me to foresee the important part he was destined to play in the future.
Time passed. In July, 1916, I left for Hejaz with a number of officers, then I moved to Rabegh . . . In October, Lt. Lawrence arrived and had the honour of meeting Emir Ali. When I gathered from him that he had come to study the conditions in Feisal's army and our own in order to present a report upon his return, I seized the opportunity and explained to him our difficulties. . . . I also explained how little we were helped by the British, especially as regards guns. I never hoped my words would have the effect which they had afterwards. I remember now Lawrence's words when we parted. 'I shall do my best to help you; and insha'llah (God willing) it will be all right. Do not worry.' [23]

In a nutshell, then, here is a Britisher wearing the badge of a staff officer visiting the camp of the rebels, claiming that he had been sent down by the British Commander-in-Chief in Egypt to study the situation on the Hejaz front and write a report about it. The leaders of the Revolt make use of the opportunity to complain about the dearth of British aid, and Lawrence promises to carry their complaint to Egypt and do everything he can for them.

23. *Baghdad Times*, 24 March 1927.

In spite of all this, Emir Ali took all possible measures to ensure the safety of this 'delegate'. At first he hesitated about sending Lawrence to Feisal's camp; perhaps he saw no need for it, since the British knew full well the position and the needs of the Arabs. Notwithstanding, he preferred to act according to the letter he had received from Abdullah. So he chose a dependable bedouin guide and ordered a camel to be prepared for Lawrence, but he did not allow him to leave camp until after dark in an effort to conceal his identity; he gave him an *aba*, a *kefiyyeh* and an *egal* as a further precaution. Ali feared that, should the bedouin discover Lawrence's true identity, they might be tempted to waylay and perhaps murder him. He did not reveal Lawrence's identity even to his slaves, and he instructed the guide and his son to see to his safety at all costs. As for Lawrence's claim that Ali gave him his own camel and his own saddle, we could with impunity add it to the long list of sayings with which, for the whole of his life, Lawrence embellished his stories. The Emir no doubt kept a number of camels in readiness for his transport, and he understandably allowed his guest the use of one of them, but Lawrence's love for self-aggrandizement transformed it into the Prince's 'own splendid riding-camel, saddled with his own saddle'.[24]

5. FEISAL'S CAMP

On the evening of 21 October, Lawrence and his two guides started their northbound journey from Ali's camp, and reached Feisal's camp in Wadi Safra on the third day. This is how Lawrence describes his first meeting with Feisal:

Hamra opened on our left . . . Tafas said something to a slave who stood there with silver-hilted sword in hand. He led me to an inner court, on whose further side, framed between the uprights of a black doorway, stood a white figure waiting tensely for me. I felt at first glance that this was the man I had come to Arabia to seek —the leader who would bring the Arab Revolt to full glory.[25]

After greetings, Feisal invited him to sit, and inquired about his trip from Rabegh. He then asked:
'And do you like our place here in Wadi Safra?'
'Well; but it is far from Damascus.'

24. *Seven Pillars*, p. 76.　　25. *Ibid*, pp. 90–91.

The word [Lawrence goes on to inform us] had fallen like a sword in their midst. There was a quiver. Then everybody present stiffened where he sat, and held his breath for a silent minute . . . Feisal at length lifted his eyes, smiling at me, and said 'Praise be to God, there are Turks nearer us that that'. We all smiled with him; and I rose and excused myself for the moment.[26]

Lawrence's descriptive powers and his dramatic and imaginative tendencies were real assets to him. This is something we understand in the Arab world, but many of those who wrote about Lawrence in the west took his sayings at their face value and accepted his book as an authentic history of the Arab Revolt. By so doing, they were being less than fair to Lawrence, for they were reading more into his remarks and actions than he had intended by them.

Lawrence met Feisal once again and this time Maulud Mukhlis, who attended Feisal, complained bitterly about the lack of weapons, which was the main reason for Arab weakness. Maulud said that Feisal's army was receiving only thirty thousand pounds a month from the Sherif, 'but little flour and rice, little barley, few rifles, insufficient ammunition, no machine guns, no mountain guns, no technical help, no information'. Feisal then outlined for Lawrence the initial activities around Medina and told him how Fakhri Pasha had surrounded the Awali suburb and ordered his soldiers to massacre the entire population, including women and children. He added that Fakhri's measures had aroused deep indignation among the bedouin, convincing them beyond all doubt that there could be no peace between them and the Turks. He then told Lawrence of Colonel Wilson's visit in August, during which Wilson, after surveying the situation, arranged for the dispatch of a battery of mountain guns and some maxims, to be handled by men and officers of the Egyptian Army garrison in the Sudan. When the four guns arrived the Arabs discovered that they were twenty-year-old krupps with a range of only three thousand yards, while the Turkish guns had a range of about nine thousand.

It was inevitable that the conversation should be a lengthy one, because Feisal was glad of the opportunity to explain matters to a British officer and to emphasize the harsh and unequal conditions under which the Arabs were operating. It was perfectly

26. *Seven Pillars*, p. 91.

natural that Feisal should want to do this, but it is doubtful if he openly declared, as Lawrence would have us believe, that he was 'carrying the whole war upon his neck while Abdullah delayed in Mecca, and Ali and Zeid at Rabegh'. No one who appreciated the strictness of the Sherifs' training and the respect of the younger for the elder would readily believe that Feisal would have spoken in this way.

It seems that Lawrence kept a diary of his impressions and of the information he was gathering; it also appears that he expressed a desire to write something about the Revolt, for he says that Maulud cried out:

> Don't write a history of us. The needful thing is to fight and fight and kill them. Give me a battery of Schneider mountain guns, and machine-guns, and I will finish this off for you. We talk and talk and do nothing.[27]

Lawrence's identity, however, was still kept secret from many of Feisal's associates. Perhaps nobody beyond Maulud and Feisal himself knew who he was. The others were told that he was a Syrian officer who had deserted from the Ottoman army.

During his stay with Feisal Lawrence went about among the bedouin volunteers in the Emir's army, on the pretext that he wished to familiarize himself with their military life so that he could include as much information as possible in his forthcoming report. Although Lawrence's views originated with Abdullah, Ali, Feisal and their officers in Jedda, Rabegh and Wadi Safra, they contain flights of fancy that are both incorrect and misleading. We may take, for example, his assumption that the bedouin tribes were good for defence only, which shows that he is forgetting the need for a balance in arms and equipment between attackers and defenders. How could a Bedouin, armed with nothing more than an ancient rifle, attack fortified entrenchments, defended by regular troops carrying the most modern weapons? Yet, despite this handicap, the bedouin proved their effectiveness in attack on more than one occasion—the battle of Abu al-Lissan, for instance. The leaders of the Revolt made excellent use of available means and resources. The bedouin, after all, are masters of the desert, and as such they helped to bring off some spectacular victories. Their foremost achievement lay in jeopardizing enemy communications, thus forcing the enemy to restrict their

27. *Seven Pillars*, p. 96.

activities to areas within their own lines. Had it not been for the Hejaz Railway, the Medina garrison would not have held out for very long.

Lawrence believed that it was impossible for the Turks to cross the rugged hills and rocky barren mountains that stood between Medina and the coast unless treachery was perpetrated by one of the tribes; the Turks might not risk it even then, since the tribes were liable to switch to the Arab side at any time. Lawrence said that the bedouin were terrified by the powerful Turkish guns, supposing that the destructive power of the guns was directly proportionate to their sound. This explains why, from the magnificent Feisal down to the most naked stripling in the army, the insistence was upon—artillery, artillery, artillery.

Lawrence met Feisal once again, and again he promised to do everything he could for the Revolt. He then left Wadi Safra for Yanbo'. He claimed that Feisal detailed fourteen Juheina Sherifs to escort him; but we know that Juheina had no connexion whatever with the Sherifs—Lawrence's imagination must have carried him away. His generous promises must have been more wishful thinking than anything else. He had come to Hejaz on a vacation (or perhaps out of curiosity) and had then forced this visit of his, through Storrs, who had an old acquaintance with the leaders of the Revolt. Actually he was not acting in any official capacity and he had no sort of authority, though he could, of course, volunteer to submit a report about what he had seen and heard in Hejaz.

Lawrence spent only one day in Feisal's camp, followed by five days at Yanbo', and it was there that he wrote his report on his findings in Hejaz. In it he said:

In June, Feisal's first attack on Medina failed, partly because he was met by Kheiri Bey's troops, but more because his own men were short of arms and ammunition . . . The Egyptian artillery had come up, and the Arabs had recovered confidence, but lost it again when they saw it was quite useless against the Turkish guns. . . . Partly to prevent their utter demoralization, but more, I think, because he was faced with his own obvious impotence, Feisal withdrew to Hamra, leaving only a covering force to act on the defence in the hills. The Turks made no attempt to push forward after him. . . .

Feisal from Hamra proposes to retire to Bir Said for a few days, and then devote his personal attention to the Hejaz railway, the primary importance of which he is beginning to recognize. . . . He will . . . make a grand assault on Buwat and Bir Nasif. He does not

want to do this till Abdulla is approaching Medina on the eastern
road, and till Ali or Zeid, or Sherif Shakir has reinforced Sharif
Ahmed el Mansur. . . . This idea is to distribute the Arab forces—each
of which is available for service only in its own tribal district—as
widely as possible, partly so as to raise the concentration of almost all
their force at Bir Derwish, which as a common point of the Ghayir
(Fura), Gaha and Sultani roads, threatens Rabegh unpleasantly. The
difficulty is the faulty intercommunication, inevitable till we supply
field wireless sets. It is, of course, hardly safe to prophesy, but I
think that if the scheme works out, the Turks may have to retire from
Bir Derwish to Medina . . . and if the railway is cut, and kept cut,
Medina may fall more quickly than is expected, as its civil population is reported to be already short of food. If the plan fails, the next
move is with the Turks. After what I have seen of the hills between
Bir Abbas and Bir ibn Hassani, I do not see how . . . the Turks here
can risk forcing their way through. . . . Looked at locally the bigness
of the Revolt impresses me. We have here a well-peopled province,
extending from Um Lejj to Kunfida, more than a fortnight long in
camel journeys, whose whole nomad and semi-nomad population
have been suddenly changed from casual pilferers to deadly enemies
of the Turks, fighting them . . . effectively enough in their own way,
in the name of the religion. . . . They are definitely looking North
towards Syria and Bagdad. . . . They want to add an autonomous
Syria to the Arab estate.[28]

In addition to this, in another report, which he wrote on 26
November 1916, he said that the forces of the Sherif numbered
between fifteen and twenty thousand warriors, and that the Turkish force was estimated at fourteen thousand, three hundred
men, stationed at Medina, Bir Derwish, Ala and Wejh. He said
of Sherif Hussein that his gentle appearance hid a deep policy,
wide ambitions and foresight, strength of character and
persistence.

We understand from all this—including Lawrence's own
statements—that the leaders of the Revolt had made up their
minds to besiege Medina on all sides well before Lawrence
arrived in Hejaz.

The captain of the ship on which Lawrence sailed did not
approve of his wearing an Arab head-dress. But he did give him
passage from Yanbo' to Jedda, where he met Admiral Wemyss,
commander of the British fleet in the Red Sea, who was about
to sail to Port Sudan *en route* for Khartoum, and a meeting with
Sir Reginald Wingate. Lawrence asked Wemyss if he could

accompany him, saying that he wished to inform Wingate of his impressions about the Revolt. After a lengthy cross-questioning, Wemyss agreed.

While in Port Sudan Lawrence met two British officers, Joyce and Davenport, who were waiting to embark for Rabegh in order to take charge of the Egyptian forces there, and to co-operate in organizing and training the regular Arab troops. Davenport remained with Ali's army, while Joyce was later attached to Feisal. These two officers performed services in the Revolt which were not inferior to those of Lawrence, but for reasons we shall outline later they had no similar share in the glory.

In Khartoum Lawrence met Wingate and presented to him the reports he had written at Yanbo'. He was of the opinion that 'the situation seemed full of promise'.[29] The main need, Lawrence insisted, was 'skilled assistance', and all should go well 'if some regular British officers, professionally competent and speaking Arabic, were attached to the Arab leaders as technical advisers'.[30] During Lawrence's stay in Khartoum, the British Government issued orders for the recall of Sir Henry McMahon and named Sir Reginald Wingate as his successor.

Wingate had telegraphed to England on 7 November, suggesting the dispatch to Rabegh of a British brigade or an Arab force of 5,000 strong, with artillery. Lawrence had opposed this measure for fear that the tribes might rise against the Sherif. It thus seems that Wingate had paid little attention to Lawrence's opinions. The British Chief of Staff, however, did not approve Wingate's proposal, and it stopped at that—although General Murray had actually concentrated two brigades at Suez in anticipation of definite orders from London. (These two brigades remained at Suez until the end of January 1917, when it was decided that there was no further need for them.)

Upon his arrival in Egypt, Lawrence was transferred to the Intelligence branch under General Clayton, to whom he presented his report, which, he claimed, was enthusiastically received at General Headquarters, because it voiced the views they already held. He added that, although he had formerly been regarded as 'a disrespectful and eccentric young civilian in uniform', there was now a change in their opinion of him. In fact, there was no novelty in Lawrence's views, for Sherif Hussein, his

29. *Seven Pillars*, p. 110.   30. *Ibid.*

sons and commanders had grown hoarse with crying out for
military aid, new weapons and experts.[31] All that Lawrence did
was to present these views as if they were his own. He stated that
he opposed the suggestion of Colonel Brémond, head of the
French military mission, to send foreign forces to Hejaz. The
truth is that the idea of landing troops at Hejaz had come first
from Sherif Hussein. When indications showed that the Turks
were intending to march on Mecca, Hussein had requested the
dispatch of a force of Muslim regular troops whether Arab,
Indian or African. Lawrence and Brémond had very little to do
with the final decision because the whole matter was discussed
at the highest level between the British cabinet, its chief of staff
and the High Commissioner in Egypt on one side and Sherif Hussein on the other. Consultations took so long that Sherif Hussein
of his own accord withdrew his request.

Lawrence magnified his quarrel with Brémond and accused
him of not caring for the Arab cause or for the success of the
Arab Revolt. Lawrence's hostility to France was of long standing and Brémond, a professional soldier, did not conceal his dis-
taste for Lawrence's cheek and insolence. In turn, Lawrence took
it upon himself to smear Brémond's reputation; and although
I do not claim that Brémond was the Arab's friend, I have serious
doubts of the truth of Lawrence's accusations. It is an established
fact that Lawrence's hatred for France was prompted, not by love
for the Arabs, but by a desire to reserve all influence in Arab
affairs to his own country. It might be added that Lawrence did
a great deal to widen the chasm between France and the Arabs.

It was natural that General Clayton should ask Lawrence to
return to Yanbo' to put his experience at the disposal of the
Arabs and to work for the implementation of the views that he
had presented. He was to act both as liaison-officer and counsel-
lor to Feisal. Expressing his reaction to this, Lawrence said:

> This being much against my grain I urged my complete unfitness
> for the job: said I hated responsibility , . . and that in all my life
> objects had been gladder to me than persons, and ideas than objects
> . . . I was unlike a soldier: hated soldiering.[32]

31. On 7 November, four British aircraft, under Major Ross, had arrived at
Rabegh to operate against German aeroplanes. Lawrence says that over a long
period, 23 guns came into Rabegh, 'mostly obsolete, and of fourteen patterns'.
(*Seven Pillars*, p. 115.)
32. *Seven Pillars*, p. 114.

Wingate had telegraphed to London for regular officers competent to work with the Arabs and when Lawrence mentioned this so that he might be excused, Clayton replied that

. . . they might be months arriving, and meanwhile Feisal must be linked to us, and his needs promptly notified to Egypt. So I had to go; leaving to others the Arab Bulletin I had founded, the maps I wished to draw, and the file of the war-changes of the Turkish Army . . . to take up a role for which I felt no inclination.[33]

Thus on 2 December, Lawrence returned to Yanbo', where the British had set up a supply base for Feisal's army and where a nucleus for this army was being organized. Captain Garland, an expert in the art of demolition, had arrived earlier. His knowledge of Arabic helped him to train the bedouin in the methods of using explosives. Lawrence himself was trained by him in these methods. Garland had 'derailed the first train and broken the first culvert in Arabia'.[34]

From Yanbo' Lawrence travelled inland to Nakhl Mubarak, where he found Feisal's army assembling as a result of a sudden Turkish attack on Zeid's forces in Wadi Safra. Arriving soon after dusk, he found Feisal seated between Sherif Sharaf and Maulud, reading reports, issuing orders and running the affairs of the army. Feisal stayed up until 4.30 a.m. to settle some urgent matters, then took an hour's nap on his carpet.

Lawrence spent two days in Feisal's camp, studying and investigating the situation. His regard for the Emir was increasing, particularly after he had come to understand Feisal's methods of leadership, his patience, forbearance and self-control and his manner of handling tribal sheikhs. Lawrence said, 'I never saw an Arab leave him dissatisfied or hurt'.[35] He went on to describe Feisal's life in camp, with all its activity, ruggedness and lack of comfort.

Suddenly, Feisal asked Lawrence if he thought he should wear Arab clothes while at camp. He explained that it was a 'comfortable dress in which to live Arab-fashion', and that the tribesmen would then understand how to take Lawrence. Furthermore, he could 'slip in and out of Feisal's tent without making a sensation which he (Feisal) had to explain away each time to stran-

33. *Seven Pillars*, p. 114.
34. *Ibid.*, p. 115. In the memoirs of Faiz al-Ghussein, mention is made of Garland as the man to whom much credit goes for training bedouin and others in the use of dynamite.   35. *Ibid.*, p. 124.

gers'.[36] Lawrence gladly agreed, because he was already used to wearing Arab clothes. Higris, Feisal's private servant, fitted him out in white silk, but Lawrence's imagination later moved him to claim that the clothes given to him were 'gold-embroidered wedding garments which had been sent to Feisal lately by his great-aunt in Mecca'.[37]

It would be as well to say a word here about Lawrence's Arab clothes. From an Arab viewpoint, these clothes were nothing but a means of facilitating life among the bedouin for a foreign officer who had declared his goodwill towards the Arabs and his desire to be one of Feisal's retinue. In any case, Lawrence was not the only foreigner to whom this privilege was extended; photographs of the period indicate that several others in the company of Feisal and his brothers wore Arab clothes. It is an old custom among the Arabs to present clothes to guests and supporters. But Lawrence's exaggerated fondness for the exotic and romantic, combined with the imaginative efforts of Western writers with their heads full of *The Arabian Nights,* gradually built up a legend round Lawrence, depicting him as one of the Emirs or Sherifs of Mecca—a far cry from the truth. A glance at the picture of Joyce in *Seven Pillars* reveals that he also wore the *aba, keffiyeh* and embroidered *egal*—which indicates that colourful Arab clothes were not a mark of distinction for Lawrence but were available to any foreigner who worked directly with Ali, Abdullah and Feisal.

Lawrence returned to Yanbo' and telegraphed on 6 December to Colonel Wilson, British Agent in Jedda, saying '. . . the only thing urgent is for an air reconnaissace of Bir Said and Bir Jabir and Wadi Safra. . . .'[38] He also said, 'Feisal treats me very well and lets me ask, hear and see everything, including his agents. Of course I still pass as a Syrian officer. . . .'[39] But Feisal himself retreated to Yanbo' after the Turks applied pressure on his forces in Nakhl Mubarak. The Turks had three battalions of mounted infantry which had marched from Bir Said and were now firing their seven guns at Nakhl Mubarak. Feisal threw out the Juheina on his left to work down Wadi Yanbo', and he sent the Egyptian artillery to engage the enemy, while Rasim Sardast was to fire his two guns in the direction of the marching

---

36. *Seven Pillars,* p. 126.   37. *Ibid.*
38. *Selected Letters,* p. 96.   39. *Ibid.*

Turks. Encouraged, the bedouin attacked and kept up steady pressure on the Turkish line of communications. But the Juheina retreated and Feisal feared the Turks might surround his camp, so he ordered Rasim and the Egyptians to retreat to Yanbo', after they had come so close to victory. It was later discovered that the Juheina had retired for a meal after a whole day of fighting and had then returned to engage the enemy throughout the night.

In an effort to consolidate his forces for the defence of Yanbo', Feisal sent the Juheina once again to Wadi Yanbo' to engage the enemy. He also set up defences against a possible Turkish attack on the town. While Captain Garland worked on the defence preparations, Lawrence was spending the night on board one of the five battleships which the British had brought over to protect the town. The Turks, however, made no move, and Lawrence believed that their failure to make use of this opportunity cost them the war. But was he right? We know that the Turks could not have kept Yanbo', mainly because they had no fleet, but also because the armies of Ali and Abdullah at Rabegh and Henakiyeh respectively were in a position to threaten any intended march on Mecca. Fakhri Pasha could not seriously have entertained the notion of marching on Mecca with only three battalions operating in such adverse circumstances.

A further interesting aspect of Lawrence reveals itself at this point, for he had now begun to use an unreserved 'we' for Feisal and himself. Lawrence said that when Abdul Kerim Beidawi related to Feisal the story of the Juheina's retreat at Yanbo':

. . . Feisal and I lay back and laughed: then we went to see what could be done to save the town.
The first step was simple. We sent all the Juheina back to Wadi Yanbo with orders to mass at Kheif. . . .[40]

But it is certain that Lawrence was in no position, then or later, to issue orders to Bedouin tribes. However, by placing himself at Feisal's elbow he could mislead foreign readers into believing that he was at least the force behind Feisal.

As we have stated, the Turks did not attack Yanbo'. After a few days the ships dispersed and the tribes spread out inland and entered into sporadic fighting with the enemy. At this time

40. *Seven Pillars*, p. 129.

Lawrence went to Rabegh, where he had a discussion about future Arab moves with Colonel Brémond. Lawrence was of the opinion that the Arabs should occupy Medina, then march north to Damascus, while Brémond insisted that it would be much better to restrict the Arab Revolt to Hejaz until the end of the war, for fear that Arab expansion might jeopardize French ambitions in Syria.

Fakhri Pasha retreated from Yanbo' to Bir Said, then turned south to meet the advance of Ali, who had marched from Rabegh with the object of attacking Turkish positions, and relieving the pressure on Yanbo'. This plan was so successful that Zeid was able to occupy Bir Said, from which the Turkish march had started. Ali's attack, however, did not last long because of his suspicion that some of the tribes were insufficiently loyal.

6. NEW PLANS

But Feisal's plan was to move northward to Wejh in order to cut the railway line and thus cut off Turkish reinforcements and supplies from Syria. Feisal had been waiting since October for an opportune moment to put his plan into effect. Some months earlier, as a preliminary step, he had detailed Sherif Nassir to proceed north as a vanguard. Nassir began rallying the tribes, and after capturing Um Lejj, he surrounded Wejh and cut all communications between it and Medina. Early in January 1917 Colonel Wilson came to Yanbo' and discussed with Feisal the plan to attack Wejh. Feisal expressed his fear of a Turkish attack on Yanbo' and Rabegh while he was engaged on his northbound move. But Wilson assured him that the army of Emir Ali was capable of defending Rabegh and that the British Fleet would take part in defending both Rabegh and Yanbo'. He also assured him that the Fleet would give him all possible help during his march on Wejh. After Wilson returned, Feisal received written orders from his father King Hussein to march on Wejh with all the forces at his disposal. An indication of Hussein's intention to capture Wejh and his preparation for it from the beginning is found in the cable he sent to his representative in Egypt on 30 July, requesting that a warship, accompanied by three aeroplanes, should be based at Yanbo' in order to demoralize the Turks. This ship was to sail later to Wejh, and co-operate with the Arabs, who were fighting the Turks all around it.

Colonel Brémond, trying in his turn to take some credit, claims that on 14 December 1916 he held a meeting in Khartoum with Sir Reginald Wingate and George Lloyd in which they decided to conquer Wejh and Aqaba and to delay the major offensive against Medina until a junction had been effected between the armies of Egypt and Iraq because, if taken earlier, the capture would 'cause a development of Pan-Arabism harmful to the Allies'.[41] The tendency of the British and French to put their own political ambitions above all military considerations in their dealings with the Arabs is thus only too clearly revealed.

Ali's retreat had encouraged the Turks, who early in January 1917 had advanced in the direction of Rabegh. The Turks, however, did not press their advance because their communication lines were being subjected to continuous bedouin onslaughts. During the first half of the month they daily lost an average of forty camels and twenty soldiers, dead or wounded, in addition to losses in stores and equipment. The Turks' troubles increased with every mile they put between themselves and Medina. Fakhri Pasha found himself in a dilemma because his communications were being threatened from the west and his army was seriously threatened by Abdullah from the east; so on 18 January he ordered a retreat, evacuated the whole of Wadi Safra and returned to his defensive positions and trenches close to Medina. There he and his forces remained until the end of the war. All that the Turks reaped from this was the morale-boosting claim that they were still holding this Holy City.

Lawrence stated that, on 2 January 1917 while preparations were being made at Yanbo' for the northward march to Wejh, he went with a party of thirty-five Mahamid towards Turkish positions in order to gain experience in raiding. They marched during the night, and at daybreak they came across some Turkish tents, opened fire and returned hurriedly to Yanbo'. It is interesting to note that this was Lawrence's first participation in a military operation—even a minor skirmish—*and this was a full seven months after the outbreak of the Arab Revolt.*

He was quick to claim credit for the move of Emir Abdullah from Henakiyeh to Wadi Ais, which had taken place in December. He wrote:

41. Edouard Brémond, *Le Hedjaz dans la Guerre Mondiale (Paris 1931),* p. 96.

. . . we suddenly remembered Sidi Abdulla in Henakiyeh. He had some five thousand irregulars, and a few guns and machine-guns. . . . It seemed a shame to leave him wasting in the middle of the wilderness. A first idea was that he might come to Kheibar, to threaten the railway north of Medina: but Feisal improved my plan vastly, by remembering Wadi Ais. . . . It lay just one hundred kilometres north of Medina, a direct threat on Fakhri's railway communications with Damascus. From it Abdulla could keep up his arranged blockade of Medina from the east, against caravans from the Persian Gulf. Also it was near Yenbo, which could easily feed him there with munitions and supplies.

The proposal was obviously an inspiration and we sent off Raja el Khuluwi at once to put it to Abdulla.[42]

This was only one of a long series of similar claims which Lawrence made. It was enough for him to be sitting in Feisal's Diwan, hear part of the conversation, familiarize himself with the decisions made and perhaps make a few remarks himself, to claim at the end of the war that he was the man who directed the Revolt. His style in his later writings is full of equivocations, half-truths, hints and clues which are difficult to refute even for those who knew the whole story. However, Lawrence's version of events successfully captured the imaginations of those who knew nothing about the Revolt, and they took his half-truths and hints at their face value, even inventing some stories of their own and attributing them to Lawrence.

It is necessary for us here to return to King Abdullah's *Memoirs,* from which we understand that Abdullah moved towards Medina with a full knowledge of his aim and purpose. His stay in Henakiyeh did not exceed three days:

I moved with my original force in the direction of Henakiyah where I stayed three days; then I moved to the west and crossed the Hejaz Railway between Abu al-Na'am and Hadiyya stations.

It is quite obvious that Emir Abdullah could not possibly have stayed in Henakiyeh longer owing to the difficulty of supplying his army along the Jedda–Mecca road, and all the way to Henakiyeh east of Medina.

Upon the request of King Hussein, Storrs arrived in Hejaz for the fourth time.[43] He reached Jedda on 11 December and

---

42. *Seven Pillars,* pp. 138–139.
43. It is worth mentioning here that Storrs, in writing about this journey, makes no reference to Lawrence. His excuse in later days was that he did not at the time anticipate that Lawrence would attain such fame.

met Hussein at a time when the situation in Rabegh was still critical. Two days later, Storrs sailed to Yanbo' where he met Feisal, who complained that the guns he had requested four months earlier had not arrived and insisted on British warships defending Rabegh and Yanbo' so that the Arab forces might retire to them in case they were defeated by the Turks. He wanted to make certain of being able to march northwards from Yanbo' to Wejh, and he explained that what he feared most was the possibility of his communication lines being cut during his absence. Zeid attended this meeting, but although Lawrence was present in Yanbo' he was not invited.

7. FROM YANBO' TO WEJH

Finally, Feisal decided to move northward towards Wejh, 180 miles from Yanbo'. He began his march on 3 January 1917 with an army that consisted of ten thousand warriors, most of whom were bedouin including one thousand two hundred Ageyl whom the Turks had conscripted at Kasim in Nejd and who later joined the Revolt. The army had a battery of Egyptian field guns, which the Arabs had been trained to operate in place of the Egyptians. It was at this point that Feisal began to make use of Lawrence's services. He was acting as liaison officer between Feisal and the British ships which were helping the Arabs in their march along the coast towards Wejh and transporting supplies to them. Feisal's Army set out from Yanbo', while Lawrence boarded a ship for Um Lejj which he reached at the same time as Major Vickery,[44] member of the British Military Mission under Colonel Newcombe. The Commander of the British Fleet met Emir Feisal in a place close to Um Lejj and the two worked out their plans for the attack on Wejh. The ships carried five hundred bedouin volunteers under Saleh ibn Shefia intending to land them at the appointed time north of Wejh. The main attack was to be carried out at dawn on 23 January, as the climax to a series of preliminary operations which had started as early as Novem-

---

44. Lawrence informs us that he had quarrelled with Vickery on the first day. Vickery was a professional officer and senior to him in rank. He also, according to Lawrence, had ten years service in the Sudan behind him and spoke Arabic fluently. He felt that, as a liaison officer, Lawrence had a political rather than a military task and he was irritated by Lawrence's constant bragging and interference in everything. It does seem that Lawrence was afraid Vickery might prove an obstacle; so he worked in his own secret way, which has never been fully revealed, to have Vickery transferred to another front.

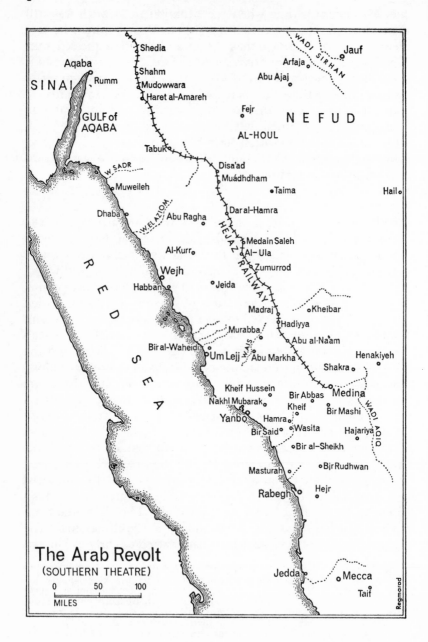

Shedia

Shahm

Rumm

Aqaba

SINAI

GULF of
AQABA

Mudowwara

Haret al-Amareh

Jauf

WADI SIRHAN

Arfaja

Abu Ajaj

Fejr

N E F U D

AL-HOUL

Tabuk

W. SADR

Muweileh

Dhaba

W. EL AZLOM.

Abu Ragha

Al-Kurr

Disa'ad

Muádhdham

Taima

Hail

Dar al-Hamra

HEJAZ RAILWAY

Medain Saleh

Al-Ula

Zumurrod

Wejh

Habban

Jeida

R E D

S E A

Madraj

Kheibar

Hadiyya

Murabba

Abu al-Na'am

Bir al-Waheidi

Um Lejj

Abu Markha

Henakiyeh

Shakra

Kheif Hussein

Nakhl Mubarak

Yanbo

Bir Said

Hamra

Wasita

Bir Abbas

Kheif

Bir Mashi

Medina

WADI AQIQ

Hajariya

Bir al-Sheikh

Masturah

Bir Rudhwan

Rabegh

Hejr

The Arab Revolt

(SOUTHERN THEATRE)

Jedda

Mecca

Taif

0　　50　　100

MILES

Regmarod

ber 1916. Since that time Sherif Nassir, in conjunction with the tribe of Billi, had been attacking Turkish communication lines, and in December had seized a caravan of seventy camels.

Feisal resumed his march from Um Lejj on 18 January, being soon overtaken by Colonel Newcombe, who had arrived from Egypt.[45] Heavy rain, which fell at the time, delayed the army, so that the Emir was not able to reach Wejh on the appointed day. As a result, the six British ships disembarked their load of bedouin volunteers together with Major Vickery at a point close to Wejh, well before the main force arrived. The ships had also landed a detachment of British marines and proceeded to bombard the town. The Turkish garrison, which was made up of two hundred officers and men, surrendered after a short battle. Feisal reached Wejh on the following day, and Sherif Nassir participated so actively in capturing Wejh that Faiz al-Ghussein was moved to say that Wejh actually surrendered to him 'for he had surrounded it on land while the ships held siege on the sea'.

The capture of Wejh was part of the overall Arab plan of harrassing the Turkish Army in Medina. Feisal's march from Yanbo' was closely co-ordinated with the activities of other Arab armies. Ali for instance had gone out with his army from Rabegh and advanced for forty miles, while the British aeroplanes were bombing Turkish positions. Encouraged by his success, Ali sent detachments to attack Turkish communication lines and some of them reached the suburbs of Medina. At the same time Abdullah had camped at Wadi Ais. The Turks had no option but to retreat from their front lines. As for Zeid, he was commanding the forces at Yanbo'. These forces were made up of eight thousand warriors with Sherif Sharaf acting as second in command. Zeid advanced in conjunction with Ali's army in the direction of Wadi Safra and Bir Said and followed the retreating Turkish forces as far as Mejezz and Ghair.

The capture of Wejh is considered an important turning point in the Revolt. Emir Abdullah's advance to Wadi Ais, referred to before, and his immediate threat to the railway line close by, enabled Feisal's army to extricate itself from the Medina area and move to other fields. Wejh itself had not figured greatly

45. It is interesting to note that Lawrence had no differences of opinion with Newcombe, perhaps because he never dared to, or perhaps because Newcombe himself never paid any attention to formalities. During his service with Feisal's army Newcombe wore Arab dress.

in Turkish plans because it was 150 miles from the railway line; but the presence or Feisal just outside the sphere of contact with Turks in Medina, and the probability that he might any day launch an attack on new Turkish positions, was in itself sufficient to worry the Turks and force them to alter their plans. The combined military activities of the Arabs further helped in finally removing the threat to Mecca. The position was radically changed and the initiative really passed to the Arabs. Lawrence himself said:

It was pointed out to Feisal how effective Abdulla might be made if he was moved to Wadi Ais. . . . He would there be astride the Medina Lines of Communication, and no Turkish advance towards Mecca, Yanbo', or even Rabegh would be possible till he had been dislodged.

He added:

Sherif Abdulla's occupation of Wadi Ais rendered possible Feisal's move north to Wejh. . . .' [46]

Gradually, the Turkish forces established themselves north of Medina to defend the railway line. The Second Composite Force, made up of five thousand men, was formed at Tebuk, three hundred miles north of Medina. The First Composite Force was formed at Ma'an from some of the battalions of the Seventh Division, which was brought from Northern Syria. The Ma'an force was thus raised from three thousand to seven thousand strong. The Turks were no longer able to join these two forces to Fakhri Pasha's army in Medina with the purpose of launching a combined attack, because the main objective of these three forces had to be directed to the defence of their main communication lines; so they divided into several small garrisons along the railway line, across spaces of dry desert.

At this point it is as well to mention the report that Feisal sent to his father on 15 January 1917, ten days before entering Wejh. In this report he said: 'The arrival of Abdullah at Wadi Ais has enabled me to march on Wejh.' Feisal also referred to his expected meeting with Sherif Shakir, who had been sent by Abdullah to discuss the co-ordination of military activities; it indicates that future activities aimed either at launching an attack on Medina and engaging the Turks in a decisive battle or,

46. *Arab Bulletin* (6 February 1917), No. 41, p. 62.

tribesmen, a mule-mounted unit and a gun, were to proceed to a position north of Wadi Ais, to hold up the first section of railway from Abdullah's area northward. Ali ibn al-Hussein al-Harithi would attack the next section of line northward from Mastur. Ibn Muhanna was to stand watch over Al-Ula, while Sherif Nassir was to stay near Muadhdham. Feisal also requested Sherif Muhammad Ali Beidawi to move from Dhaba to an oasis near Tebuk.

8. WADI AIS

Lawrence says that his part was to go to Abdullah in Wadi Ais, 'to find out why he had done nothing for two months'.[51] At this point we must pause a little and contemplate Lawrence's impudence and conceit—characteristics which were not to appear in him until after the war, or which, at least, had not yet become obvious to the Arabs. It is certain that Lawrence did not dare set himself up as 'Inspector General' over the Arab armies, and Feisal certainly never thought of sending him off to Wadi Ais in this capacity. Feisal considered Lawrence an ordinary British officer who liked the Arabs, worked for their good, provided easy contact with the British Command and was always ready with advice. In Feisal's presence, Lawrence behaved as a member of his retinue in a democratic bedouin atmosphere, where Feisal's followers were free to express any opinion which purported to be in the interest of the Arabs. The observer would immediately notice this from a comparison of Lawrence's style in the reports he sent to the *Arab Bulletin,* and his style in *Seven Pillars,* which he wrote after the end of the war and after his participation, with Feisal, in the Peace Conference. It also came, one must remember, after Lawrence had established contact with the British Foreign Office, and had become a famous man.

On 10 March Lawrence left Wejh 'ill and unfit for a long march, while Feisal in his haste and many preoccupations had chosen me a travelling party of queer fellows'.[52] This is near to the truth, for it shows that Feisal did not pay Lawrence special attention beyond the requirements of propriety and the necessity for security, which—as a foreigner—Lawrence needed. It is interesting that here Lawrence does not claim that Feisal gave

51. *Seven Pillars,* p. 178.   52. *Ibid.,* p. 178.

at damaging the railway line between Muadhdham and Tabuk in order to force the Turks to evacuate Medina or get out of their entrenchments and fight. Feisal states that he had submitted the same suggestion two months ago. He added that he intended to contact the northern tribes, particularly the Ruwalla Huweitat, and Beni Atiyeh, and get them to participate in military operations and that he also intended to send some money to Nuri as-Sha'alan and Auda Abu Tayeh. He went on to say that nothing remained in the hands of the Turks on the Hejazi coast except Dhaba and Muweileh, 'and therefore all that remains for us to do is capture Aqaba and effect a junction with the British army there'.[47]

This report makes it clear that the Arabs had always co-ordinated their plans in advance and that Hussein's sons were in the habit of presenting suggestions to him concerning actual operations. It also shows that the Arabs were concerned mainly with tightening the siege on Medina until it surrendered, and then spreading northwards into Syria (that constant preoccupation of the leaders of the Revolt). It is important to note that Feisal's reference to Aqaba and Auda Abu Tayeh indicates that at that early date he was preparing to seek the co-operation of the northern tribes in occupying Aqaba and joining up with the British army marching in Sinai.

This is another example of the way in which Lawrence transformed evidence to his own advantage, for, in his report about the capture of Wejh, he said: 'Feisal decided to carry out the northern expedition to Wejh, and to do it himself'.[48] He made no mention of having expressed an opinion to Feisal or anybody else. But in October 1920, when he had become famous after the war, he published an article entitled 'The Evolution of a Revolt', in which, after discussing the Turkish threat to Rabegh and Yanbo', he said:

> . . . it occurred to me that . . . if we moved towards the Hejaz railway behind Medina, we . . . would force the Turks to the defensive, and we might regain the initiative. Anyhow, it seemed our only chance, and so, in January, 1917, we took all Feisal's tribesmen, turned our backs on Mecca, Rabegh and the Turks, and marched away north two hundred miles to Wejh . . . our march recalled the

47. *Al-Umari, op. cit.,* Vol. 2, pp. 198–200.
48. *Arab Bulletin* (6 February 1917), p. 60.

Turks (who were almost into Rabegh) all the way back to Medina, and there they halved their force. One half took up the entrenched position about the city, which they held until after the Armistice. The other half was distributed along the railway to defend it against our threat. For the rest of the war the Turks stood on the defensive against us....[49]

Feisal entered Wejh on 25 January and began making contact with the northern tribes, while detachments of his army started attacking the railway line in repeated raids. Two days later Lawrence left for Egypt, where he spent ten days, ostensibly to seek more aid for the Arab forces. This is doubtful, for it is more likely that his trip to Egypt had an ulterior motive, namely, to air his grievances against Major Vickery. The Arabs had lost twenty men in the battle of Wejh, at a time when Lawrence believed that the bedouin were in no position to suffer so many casualties, and that the capture of Wejh could have been accomplished without this loss. Vickery's mistake, according to Lawrence, was his premature landing of the bedouin before the arrival of Feisal. In any case, it seems that Lawrence's efforts were successful, because before long Vickery was removed from the Hejazi scene.

Lawrence's stay in Wejh did not exceed two weeks; on 20 February he returned for another ten-day visit to Cairo, where he claims to have persuaded General Murray to leave Aqaba alone and put the brigade that had been earmarked for this purpose to better use. At about this time two armoured cars with two British officers and a number of men arrived at Wejh following the despatch of a wireless set that would facilitate army communications.

Meanwhile Feisal's letters to the chiefs of the northern tribes were beginning to bear fruit. The Billi tribe, because of its proximity to Wejh, was the first to respond, offering its services to the Revolt, with the exception of Sheikh Suleiman ibn Rafada, who was a friend of the Turks. Then the Sheikh of Beni Atiyeh arrived at Wejh and declared the allegiance of his tribe. Feisal himself sent a delegation to Ibn Sa'ud and despatched his private secretary Faiz al-Ghussein with a letter to Nuri as-Sha'alan and his son Nawwaf in Jauf (Nuri was in control of Jauf and Wadi Sirhan). In this letter he requested Nuri not to lend a

49. T. E. Lawrence, *Oriental Assembly* (1939), pp. 107–108.

helping hand to the Turks and to co-operate with the Revolt, whose forces had begun their march on Syria.[5 Dughmi, a Ruwalla chieftain, was the next arrival, follow ibn Za'al and Deifalla Abu Skour from the Huweitat c Transjordan area. Soon after that Abu Tageiga, Sheikh coastal Huweitat, announced that on 11 February he had pied Dhaba and Muweileh, which were the last Turkish c outposts between Wejh and Aqaba. Soon Wejh started rec an endless stream of tribal chiefs, who partook of Feisal's tality and declared their allegiance to the Revolt and thei ingness to join the Arab forces. Feisal, for his part, was m continuous efforts to rally the tribes, join them togetl amity, conclude peace among them and arbitrate in quarrels, in the hope that all their efforts would be di towards accomplishing the noble end for which the Arab had been declared. There is no doubt that Feisal's brought him to the realization that his next step would be the occupation of Aqaba.

In the first week of March Lawrence received a lette General Clayton in Egypt advising him that the Turkish Command had ordered Fakhri Pasha to effect an imm withdrawal from Medina to the north. Lawrence says tha ton ordered the capture of Medina or the interception Turkish forces in the initial stages of their retreat. La held the opinion that the retreat of the Turks suited the very well but that British Headquarters did not relish tl of having twenty-five thousand Anatolian warriors added force that was facing the British in Sinai. While Newcom accompanying a unit of the Northern Army on a raid the railway line, Lawrence took the matter up with Fei explained frankly that the higher interests of the Allies re that the Arabs temporarily sacrifice their own. He re that Feisal rose to this 'proposition of honour' and prom do anything he could to destroy the line and prevent the from retreating. Accordingly, Sherif Mastur and Rasin

50. Faiz al-Ghussein told me that, when he went to Jauf he was af Nuri as Sha'alan might hand him over to the Turks, because rumour him of being a party to the arrest by the Turks of two Syrian leaders fled from Damascus to Hejaz. Contrary to his fears, Nuri welcomed hir because he had heard the news that the British had occupied Baghda 1917). Nevertheless, Nuri did not take part in the operations of the Re September, 1918, when the attack on Damascus took place.

him his own riding-camel or that he sent with him any Sheikhs or Sherifs.

He reached Wadi Ais on 15 March and had a meeting with Emir Abdullah. Here is his account of his encounter with Abdullah:

> I gave him the documents from Feisal, explaining the situation in Medina, and the need we had of haste to block the railway. I thought he took it coolly; but, without argument, went on to say that I was a little tired after my journey, and with his permission would lie down and sleep a while. He pitched me a tent next his great marquee, and I went into it and rested myself at last. It had been a struggle against faintness day-long in the saddle to get here at all: and now the strain was ended with the delivery of my message. . . .[53]

Here Lawrence admits that he had gone to Wadi Ais to deliver Feisal's documents, not to 'find out why [Abdulla] had done nothing for two months'.

King Abdullah, however, mentions Lawrence's arrival at Wadi Ais very briefly in his *Memoirs*. It is unfortunate that Arabic sources are rather reticent about Lawrence—a fact which makes the task of the Arab observer a most difficult one. The excuse of the Arab writers might well be that Lawrence was merely one of several foreign officers working with the Arabs and merited no special attention. King Abdullah's statements, however, have a special significance.

> A week after we had established ourselves in Wadi Ais,[54] there arrived a Northern Army unit, accompanied by Captain Lawrence, whom King Feisal had sent to supervise the technical aspects of wrecking the railway. I was not happy with his arrival because I knew of his adverse influence on the fanatical tribes. Ibn Luayy, a Whahhabi, said to me, 'You are fighting the Turks because they have fallen under the influence of Germany. And this man—who is he? If the Germans are the friends of the Turks, then these are your friends. What is all the fighting about then?' . . . Nahis al-Dhuweibi said, 'Who is this "red" newcomer, and what does he want?' I explained that he had come to blow up the railway, that he was an engineer, that he represented our friend and ally Great Britain and that things were not as they imagined. I said that the British and ourselves had joined forces against their and our enemies: their enemies were the Germans, ours the Turks! 'Do you think,' I asked 'that the British would supply us with arms, ammunition and money

53. *Seven Pillars*, p. 187.
54. In fact, Lawrence reached Wadi Ais two months after Emir Abdullah had established himself there.

unless they saw what losses we were inflicting on our enemies?' But
although these words made some impression, the general dislike of
Lawrence's presence was quite clear. He tried to get in touch with
the tribes, but he could not do so because of the guard that was
placed over him, to prevent any Turkish spies from killing him and
thus causing ill-feeling between us and the British. . . . We then sent
a force to wreck the line and oust the Turks from Abu al-Na'am,
Jeda'aeh Al-Wakir and Hadiyya; Lawrence was one of several others
who accompanied the force to do demolition work. He returned dissatisfied, criticized the force and claimed that they could have done
an effective job, had they been willing to wait long enough. Actually,
a locomotive was blown up, a whole train damaged and eleven kilometres of line put out of action. But all this did not please Lawrence
because things did not go the way he wished. Sherif Heidar left
Medina for the Lebanon a week after this attack. As for Lawrence,
he fell ill with boils and swellings, begged leave and departed. I
treated him with kindness and generosity, acknowledged his valuable
services but did not like his interference in things that were no
business of his.[55]

Lawrence spent nearly twenty-five days in Wadi Ais. For the
first ten he was bed-ridden in his tent with dysentery and fever.
He later devoted a whole chapter in Seven Pillars to an account
of these ten days. In this chapter he explained his views on the
Revolt and on the best methods of conducting its operations.
He stated that he concentrated his mind on the theories of great
military men, such as Napoleon, Clausewitz, Moltke, Foch and
Von der Goltz, in the hope of applying their theories to the
exigencies and circumstances of the Arab Revolt. Lawrence's
views do not concern us much here, not only because they amount
to no more than ink on paper, but also because they were written
down five full years after the date of his stay at Wadi Ais. Lawrence was of course free to dwell on any kind of thoughts that
occurred to him before or after, but attention ought to be drawn
to the following statement: 'As I have shown, I was unfortunately as much in command of the campaign as I pleased . . .'.[56]
The observer, no matter how objectively he views this, is at a
loss to comprehend in what way Lawrence could command as he
pleased, particularly during the period under discussion. Surely
this is an example of Lawrence's conceit and impudence, or perhaps of his deception both of himself and others. Or could it be
a combination of all these? Furthermore, Lawrence labelled the
Turks 'stupid', but several war leaders have borne witness to the

55. Memoirs of King Abdullah, pp.139–141.   56. Seven Pillars, p. 188.

courage and sagacity of the Turks, and have resented Lawrence's verdict.

After his recovery, Lawrence went to Abdullah and expressed his willingness to assist in dynamiting the railway line. The Emir appointed Sherif Shakir to command a fresh expedition, and asked him to take Lawrence with him. Shakir selected a number of men from Uteiba, and, in addition to Lawrence, Captain Rahu, an Algerian officer who was a member of the French military mission, and Sherif Fawzan al-Harith. On 26 March, this force—three hundred in all—moved in the direction of Abu al-Na'am station. On the following day they shelled the station with their mountain guns, dynamited the railway line and captured two front-line outposts, with the result that the losses inflicted on the Turks amounted to one hundred men, killed, wounded and captured. In addition, some of the station installations were damaged and a train and one locomotive were derailed. The party then returned to Wadi Ais, leaving a small unit behind to remove part of the line. This was the first time Lawrence took part in a military operation; he planted the mine that slightly damaged the locomotive and cut the telephone lines off one pole. It is worth noting that *this participation on the part of Lawrence came ten months after the outbreak of The Arab Revolt.* We should also remember that a number of British and French officers, among whom were Newcombe, Garland, Hornby and Rahu, preceded Lawrence in the business of planting mines and blowing up trains.

On 22 April, another party under Dakhil Allah al-Kadi, and accompanied by Lawrence, left camp for the railway line between the Hadiyya and Madraj stations. With Lawrence's help they attacked the line, derailed a train, damaged a bridge, removed some rails and cut telephone lines. Lawrence admitted that on this raid he prayed with the Juheina as a Muslim, but he added, 'This was the first and last time I ever prayed in Arabia as a Moslem'.[57] This fact indicates that his real identity had not been revealed to everybody. Perhaps—in circumstances like these—he claimed that he was an Arab with a Turkish mother and that he had lived in Istanbul (Storrs says something in his book to this effect). The reader, of course, may draw his own conclusions.

57. *Seven Pillars*, p. 209.

Lawrence did not have a lengthy stay in Wadi Ais because, he said, military activity in Abdullah's army fell short of the high standard he desired, although he did admit that 'there were now two parties on the railway, with reliefs enough to do a demolition of some sort every day or so'.[58] No doubt this daily work of demolition was no easy task, particularly when we realize with King Abdullah that 'as for armaments, the Eastern Army was not given anything except weapons used by infantrymen. The Eastern Army was not supplied with any guns or other machinery suitable for use against forts and fortifications'.

Lawrence thus returned to Wejh about the middle of April. During his absence the situation had become more settled. Supplies and equipment had been brought on from Yanbo'; new armoured cars had arrived from Egypt; regular units had been formed; aircraft had been transferred fom Rabegh to Wejh, and Colonel Joyce had come to assist in organizing the camp and in training and arming the regular troops.

9. ORGANIZING THE ARAB ARMIES

During this period the Arab armies were organized as follows:

1. The Southern Army under Emir Ali, assisted by Emir Zeid, stationed at Rabegh.
2. The Eastern Army under Emir Abdullah, stationed at Wadi Ais.
3. The Northern Army under Emir Feisal, stationed at Wejh and Jeida.

In February and March, the Southern Army made a formidable effort to engage the Turks and divert their attention from the movements of the Northern Army. On 27 February Emir Ali organized a force of five thousand regulars and irregulars, supported by seven guns and seven machine guns. Ali advanced with this force from Rabegh along the Sultani road. Four British aeroplanes under Major Ross provided air-cover for the expedition, which continued its advance until Bir Abbas was captured on 10 March. The bedouin penetrated as far as the gates of Medina and returned with several prisoners of war, while the Turks concentrated at Bir Mashi and Bir Derwish for the protection of the railway line. This battle continued for eleven

58. *Seven Pillars*, p. 216.

days and registered the most important victory the Arabs had gained around Medina until then. Turkish losses were estimated at one hundred and fifty men. After this the Turks kept to their trenches and settled down to purely defensive measures. The bedouin used to lie in wait for them behind the cliffs and keep up morning-to-evening sniping. On 27 March Emir Ali struck camp at Bir Derwish. No important battles were fought after that, because the Arabs did not have sufficient regular forces or heavy artillery to attack Turkish defences and break the resistance of their troops. The Arabs, nevertheless, tried to capture the entrenchments at Bir Mashi which formed part of the Medina defensive line. But Fakhri Pasha assembled all his forces and counter-attacked. As a result Emir Zeid had to retreat to Mejezz, while Emir Ali fought his way back to the Sultani road.

When the Eastern and Northern Armies began to blow up the line, the Turks had to resort to new methods of defence. They divided the line into three sections: the Ula Section, commanded By Basri Pasha; the Tebuk Section, commanded by 'Atef Bey; and the Ma'an Section, commanded by Mehmed Jemal Pasha. The Eighth Corps, under Jemal Pasha the lesser was charged with guarding the stretch from Ma'an to Dera'a.

10. THE SIEGE OF MEDINA

The army of Emir Abdullah was the first to damage the railway line while marching from Henakiyeh to Wadi Ais. The Northern Army did not start its attacks on the line until a month later. On 12 February a force made up of fifty bedouin and accompanied by Captain Garland marched from Wejh in a south-easterly direction until they reached the line near Tuweira, eight days later. At night the party divided into two groups: the first, with Garland, planted the mine under the line, south of Tuweira, while the other mined a bridge. A train was soon derailed and the bridge was brought down by a bedouin, in spite of a volley of fire from an approaching Turkish patrol.

The party of Sherif Sharaf consisted of a mounted unit, two mountain guns and four machine guns, together with a demolition group, supported by a thousand bedouin camelmen. Early in March this party raided Muadhdham, whose garrison consisted of an infantry battalion, six machine guns, two guns and some cavalry. The Turks were in readiness to meet the Arab attack. After an exchange of fire the regular forces under Maulud advanced and forced the enemy to retire from their front-line trenches and seek refuge inside the fort, while the demolition group proceeded to blow up the line. The bedouin did not take part in this attack, nor did Arab artillery get the chance to destroy the fort, with the result that after a few hours fighting the regulars had to withdraw in the face of heavy enemy fire. Arab losses amounted to a hundred and twenty-five, killed or wounded, while Maulud emerged with two wounds and a broken arm. The Turks incurred thirty casualties.

On the night of 3 March, a force led by Sherif Nassir launched a successful attack on Dar al-Hamra station north of Medain Saleh, took fifteen Turkish prisoners and removed two thousand eight hundred yards of line. Colonel Newcombe accompanied this force and supervised demolition work. After a series of successful Arab attacks on the line and the railway stations, the Turks set up a vigilant watch.. Towards the end of March, a Northern Army unit attacked the railway south of Al-Ula station, destroying three bridges and removing part of the line.

At the same time, army morale was boosted considerably by the arrival of Ja'afar Pasha al-Askari from Egypt to take up the command of the regular forces in Feisal's army. Ja'afar had earlier led the Sanussi forces against the British, who eventually succeeded in taking him prisoner; he had remained in a prison-camp until he heard of the atrocities that Jemal Pasha was committing in Syria, especially the public hanging of Ja'afar's officer friends. He then vowed revenge and requested King Hussein's permission to join the Revolt. After some hesitation Hussein allowed him to go to Feisal's army in Wejh. He arrived about the middle of June and proceeded to train and organize the regular forces, remaining with Feisal until the end of the war.

At the end of July a big battle was fought at Zumurrod station. This battle can be considered as an example of the kind of fighting in which the Arabs engaged during their war of liberation. A large force commanded by Ja'afar marched from Wejh. It comprised Maulud's Hashimi Brigade, two mountain guns, two machine-gun companies, an infantry battalion and a demolition party under Colonel Newcombe.. The Arabs reached the station shortly after midnight on 30 July. The Turks had despatched a party to engage Colonel Newcombe's unit, which had preceded Ja'afar and occupied a position close to the water wells, three miles from Zumurrod. While the Turkish force was engaged with Newcombe the regulars attacked the station, which was strongly defended by the Turkish garrison. The water wells came within the range of fire from Turkish reinforcements and the right flank of the Arab force was held at bay while the left flank, comprising Maulud's brigade, stood its ground and actually forced the enemy to retreat. On the arrival of more Turkish reinforcements, the enemy tried to surround the Brigade but Maulud manoeuvred his way out and the attempt failed. Fighting continued until sunset, when Ja'afar gave the signal to retreat because the Arabs had consumed all their water. Maulud, however, suggested that an attempt be made to regain control of the hills overlooking the water wells. He argued that if they returned without water for themselves and their animals, they would meet with certain destruction. Ja'afar agreed and the Arabs were able to occupy the hills; soldiers and animals drank their fill. At midnight the Arabs withdrew to Jeida, which was the Northern Army headquarters, instead of Wejh. In all, they had suffered fifty casualties.

Foreign sources have habitually attributed any Arab military success to the British or French officers on the scene. Even if the Arab party consisted of a thousand men led by senior Arab officers, these sources would only mention them as a marginal appendage to the heroics of the foreign officer, whose task could have been nothing more than advising the party on planting or exploding mines. An echo of all this came in November 1917 from the Iraqi officers serving with Abdullah. According to General Brémond, Colonel Wilson was sent to urge Abdullah to capture Medina. He was met with various excuses: 'If we fail it will be said that the fault was ours; and if there is a success, all the merits will go to the English.' [59] The Arab observer would not deny the achievements, daring and fortitude of these officers, but he would feel in duty bound to clarify the whole issue, for none of these officers could have accomplished anything in the Arabian peninsula on their own. In response to several questions I once put to Sherif Hussein Shakrani about Lawrence, he exclaimed with obvious impatience, 'Lawrence. I saw much of him during the Revolt, but never did I see him fire a revolver or a rifle. By Allah,

59. *Le Hedjaz dans la Guerre Mondiale*, pp. 209–210.

had it not been for the Sherifs, he would not have managed to live among the bedouin for a single day.'

Western sources, of course, have ample excuse for their partiality, for they obtained their information from the detailed reports which the British and French officers habitually made about the activities in which they had taken part.. The extensive details of Lawrence's own *Seven Pillars of Wisdom* are based in many cases on the reports that he himself wrote during the Revolt. It is indeed unfortunate that Arab leaders and officers left nothing but a few sporadic references, mostly based on memory, thus leaving the door wide open to Lawrence, Brémond and other westerners.

Lawrence has placed on record that, at about this time, he changed his views and his military plans regarding the conduct of the Revolt operations. Previous to this he had endorsed the view of those who believed that the ideal plan, after the capture of Wejh, would be for the three Arab armies to launch a decisive combined attack on Medina. Feisal's report to his father just before the capture of Wejh indicates that this plan was foremost in the minds of Arab leaders. Lawrence's new outlook was based on his belief that the capture of Medina would bring more harm than good to the allies, because the twelve-thousand-strong garrison of Medina would then have no alternative but to retreat or surrender. Its retreat would strengthen the Turkish armies in Palestine and give them a better chance of withstanding the British. On the other hand, their surrender would become a heavy and expensive burden on the British. According to him, the advantages of Medina remaining in the hands of the Turks could be summed up as follows: the Medina garrison would be paralysed for the duration of the war; it would consume large quantities of food; it would be a drain on the Turkish resources; and it would increase the burden of the Turkish war effort. Lawrence, therefore, held the view that the Arabs should not inflict permanent damage on the railway line, so that the Turks might be encouraged to stay where they were.

There is no doubt that Lawrence's view held water, but it is doubtful whether this was a view that he actually developed at Wejh in April 1917. In any case, Lawrence's opinions are more plausible from a British than from an Arab standpoint. Lawrence seems to have forgotten that the siege of Medina would require a large Arab force, while its early surrender would have enabled the three Arab armies to make a combined advance on the countries of the Fertile Crescent (Iraq, Syria, and the Jordan Area) and to carry the war to Jebel Druze and Damascus at a time when Gaza and Beersheba were still in the hands of the Turks. In contrast with Lawrence's views, King Abdullah's opinions are outlined in his *Memoirs* in the following way:

It was my idea to occupy the railway line and then storm Medina with all three armies together. But unfortunately we dissipated our strength by trying to exert pressure on the Turks at too many points along the line. Feisal's army advanced later to capture Aqaba and from there started to press on Ma'an. Had Medina been taken in 1917, the three armies could have united for the conquest of Syria and could have participated in the war in Iraq. But others inclined to this plan.[60]

60. *Op cit.*, p. 143.

3

WEJH TO AQABA

1. AUDA ABU TAYEH

DR. ABDUL RAHMAN SHAHBENDER once described Lawrence as a man of dramatic leanings, whose life was characterized by vagabondage, exaggeration and unorthodoxy, one who loved adventure for its own sake. Awni Abdul Hadi told me personally that Lawrence was fond of adventure, of exploring unknown paths and of attempting things his colleagues did not think of doing. Lawrence's behaviour lives up to this description, particularly his refusal to cling to accepted conventions. His deportment in the Arab countries certainly differed from that of other foreign officers; he was so uninhibited in his relation with the bedouin that they regarded him as one of themselves, or at least had more confidence in him than they did in other officers. But his love for bedouin and his lack of inhibition were not sufficient for the role that he played with the Arabs; he was aided immeasurably by his intelligence, by his bodily strength and by luck, or, for those who do not believe in luck, by coincidence.

The *Arab Bulletin* of 21 April 1917 said that Auda Abu Tayeh arrived in Wejh 'on or about 9 April', while Lawrence got there from Wadi Ais on the fourteenth, but Lawrence claimed that Auda walked in whilst he was in Feisal's tent. Feisal, in a telegram that he sent to his father on 1 April, said that there arrived at Wejh two thousand camelmen including 242 sheikhs of the Ruwalla, Shararat, Huweitat, Beni Sakhr and Imran—northeastern tribes living in Jauf, Kerak and Ma'an—and he asked for an increase of his financial allocations so that he could give them generous gifts. Hussein in turn telegraphed to his deputy in Egypt, who notified him that the British were sending thirty thousand pounds to Feisal. It is probable that Auda Abu Tayeh was among this group. From the Turkish viewpoint, Auda Abu Tayeh was an outlaw, because he had refused to pay some taxes on the ground that they were not just. The Turkish authorities had sent a party of soldiers to collect these taxes, and one of them fired at Auda missing him but mortally wounding one of his slaves. Auda fired back and killed two soldiers. Since then he had carefully avoided Government centres.. In addition Auda's enmity to his relative Hammad ibn Jazi, Sheikh of the Huweitat west of Ma'an, had led him to move east of the railway line near Wadi Sirhan.

Lawrence has given us a detailed account of Auda's life and characteristics,[1] and there is no doubt that Auda fully deserved the praise that Lawrence showered upon him. We find, however, that later Lawrence also cast some aspersions upon him. Since Lawrence admitted that he owed a great deal to Dr. Hogarth for sending him to Carchemish, he should also have admitted that he owed his great reputation to Auda Abu Tayeh. Had it not been for Auda, the Aqaba expedition, which opened wide the doors of fame for Lawrence, would never have taken place. Without Auda Lawrence would have stayed in Feisal's camp with no definite assignment. While Newcombe, Garland and Hornby[2] spent most of the time in February, March and April, conducting attacks on the railway line, Lawrence was doing comparatively little. The fact that he accompanied Auda proves that he was not responsible for the campaign, as he claimed, for how could a responsible commander allow himself to leave his headquarters and throw himself into a mysterious and dangerous adventure? We sense something of this in his book where he has admitted that he decided to go with Auda 'with or without orders' and that he wrote a letter of apology to Clayton.. His love of the sensational, however, prompted him to claim that he opposed the efforts to occupy Medina and that this opposition on his part had led him to go north with Auda. Strange to say, Lawrence's many contributions to the *Arab Bulletin* make no reference whatsoever to these suggestions.

It might be useful to mention here that Sir Mark Sykes and Colonel Leachman visited Wejh on 3 May. During this visit

1. The first mention of Auda by Lawrence appeared in the *Arab Bulletin* of 24 July 1917.
2. The bedouin called Lawrence 'Orens', Newcombe 'Nekoom' and Hornby 'Hanbi'.

Sykes discussed the future of Syria with Feisal, without acquaint-
ing him with the agreement he had signed on behalf of his
Government with Monsieur George Picot. Lawrence did not
take any part in the Sykes–Feisal talks. This gives a clear picture
of Lawrence's position in Feisal's army, and shows that he did
not enjoy any special privileges at the time.

2. THE OCCUPATION OF AQABA

Information available from Arab sources indicates quite clearly
that the plan for capturing Aqaba was devised by Feisal and
Auda in Wejh. After the occupation of Wejh Feisal had sent
letters to the sheikhs of the northern tribes. As already stated,
Auda was an enemy of the Turks, and at first he sent one of
his cousins, but early in April he came himself with a number of
Tawaiha Sheikhs.[3]

It was only natural that Feisal should welcome Auda's arrival,
because Auda's enlistment in the Revolt would facilitate Feisal's
progress northwards and make possible a surprise attack on the
Turks. Auda spent more than three weeks in Feisal's camp and it
was he who suggested that the Revolt be carried to the Ma'an
area, emphasizing that he was capable of occupying Aqaba and
perhaps Ma'an itself with external military aid, provided he had
the money and the arms. This suggestion accorded with the wishes
of Feisal, who appointed Sherif Nassir to accompany Auda as his
personal representative. Preparations immediately began for
this expedition.[4] Sir Mark Sykes, M. Picot, Col. Leachman and
George Lloyd came via Wejh, where they took Feisal and Newcombe aboard, to Jedda on 19 May 1917.

Fortunately, we can make use of the information supplied by
Naseeb al-Bekri, who witnessed these events, being one of
Feisal's closest associates and one of the first participants in
the Revolt.[5] Naseeb emphasized the fact that Feisal intended to

3. General Brémond stated that he met Feisal in Wejh on 31 January 1917, in
the presence of Newcombe, and that Feisal informed them that he intended to
occupy Aqaba. (Lawrence was in Cairo at the time.)
4. Lawrence has to say about Sherif Nassir: 'He was the opener of roads,
the fore-runner of Feisal's movement, the man who had fired his first shot in
Medina, and who was to fire our last shot at Muslimieh beyond Aleppo on the
day that Turkey asked for an armistice . . .' *Seven Pillars*, p. 160.
5. Naseeb was born in 1888. He was one of the pioneers of Arab Nationalism, a
member of the 'Fetat' secret society and a personal friend and adviser to Feisal.
When it was decided to declare the Arab revolt Feisal sent him a coded telegram:
'Send the grey mare.' He immediately sent his family by train to Hejaz. Then

push the Revolt north to Syria, and was in touch for this purpose with Nuri as-Sha'alan, Auda Abu Tayeh and some military and civilian Syrian leaders. All Feisal was waiting for was the opportune moment before raising the banner of the Revolt in Syria. The arrival of the famous desert warrior Auda, well known for his courage and qualities of leadership, was the opportunity Feisal had lacked for so long. Auda, in his turn, was warmly enthusiastic about Feisal's plan of campaign. Though Auda was in a position to fight the Turks, he could not bear all the political implications. Consequently Sherif Nassir was selected to declare the Revolt in the name of King Hussein and to rally the tribes and various sections of the population, so that all might sink their private quarrels. Naseeb al-Bekri, on the other hand, was despatched as a political emissary to the leaders of the Jebel Druze and of Syria, to prepare their minds, to explain the purpose of the revolution and to explore possible chances. The fact that Naseeb came from a distinguished Syrian family made him especially qualified to play this important role.

Discussions concerning the occupation of Aqaba had been in progress for quite a while between the British and King Hussein, because of its important strategic position. The Turks were using it as a base for planting mines in the Red Sea, and the allies were afraid that the Germans might use it as a submarine base. The British Navy had bombarded Aqaba twice. On the second occasion (20 April 1917), a unit of British marines actually landed and forced the Turkish garrison to withdraw after suffering some casualties. The Turks, however, took positions in the hills overlooking the town and set up fortifications from which they were able to command the Gulf. As a result, the British were not able to stay there for long or advance up the rugged hills.

The whole expedition was thus planned with no reference to Lawrence, despite his post-war claims that he had been its leader and its inspiration. However, led by his love of adventure on one hand and by his dissatisfaction with his work on the other, Lawrence asked Feisal to let him go along with the party, saying that he could help in planting mines. Feisal agreed. Law-

he left Damascus with Feisal's fifty men, including Sharif Ali ibn Areid. Taking the desert route they were barely missed by Jemal Pasha's men. They reached the Arab army near Medina three months later, after a difficult journey. He took part in the Syrian revolt against the French and became a minister after independence.

rence, we might add, was not the only foreign volunteer. Naseeb al-Bekri assured me that a French officer also requested permission from Feisal to join the expedition, but Feisal did not agree in view of French ambitions in Syria.

We observe that up to 14 June the *Arab Bulletin* made no mention of this expedition. At this date the *Bulletin* reported that information was received by Feisal indicating 'that there has been fighting at Akaba between Turks and Arabs, resulting in the evacuation of the place by the Turks, who retired to Maan'. There was no mention of Lawrence in this issue. The *Bulletin* of 9 July contained information from Hejaz to the effect that the Huweitat in the neighbourhood of Ma'an had recently broken into active revolt at Fuweila and other places. Here again we find no mention of Lawrence. But another item stated that many Arabs had come to Auda to submit loyalty and to fight under the flag which was given to him by Feisal. It went on to say that Nassir, Naseeb, and Lawrence were with Auda.

The *Bulletin* of 24 July furnishes us with more adequate information, obviously obtained from Lawrence. It referred to his arrival at Cairo, and stated that he had 'left Wejh on 9 May with Sherif Nasir ibn Hussein as O.C. Expedition, and Nasib Bey el-Bakri as Political Officer'. It then went on to say that the Arab concentration took place at Bair 'under the general command of Sherif Nasir'.

We can now summarize the story of this expedition as follows:

When Sherif Nassir had completed his preparations and obtained twenty thousand pounds for future expenses, he started from Wejh on 9 May with Auda Abu Tayeh, Naseeb al-Bekri, Captain Lawrence, Major Zaki Drubi and thirty-five Ageyl under Nassir ibn Dghaithir. With a number of rifles, some equipment and a few sticks of dynamite, this small party passed through the oasis of Al-Kurr and Abu Ragha, then headed in a north-easterly direction through the desert and crossed the railway line near Disa'ad station, where they blew up part of the railway and cut some telephone lines. They then entered Al-Houl Plain, Wadi Fejr, Basita Plain and reached Arfaja in Wadi Sirhan. Finally, they arrived at Isawiya, where they were hospitably received by a Huweitat tribe after crossing this dangerous stretch of country. From Isawiya, which they reached on 27 May, Auda departed, carrying with him six thousand pounds as a

present from Feisal to Nuri as-Sha'alan. Sherif Nassir and his
other companions left for Nebk in Wadi Sirhan, where they were
soon joined by Auda, accompanied by some Ruwalla horsemen.
The bedouin started gathering to declare their allegiance to the
Revolt and the process of recruiting and arming volunteers began. While Auda was busily massing recruits, Naseeb sent a
messenger to his old Druze friend Hussein al-Atrash, Sheikh of
Anz. Hussein duly arrived at Nebk accompanied by a sheikh of
the Serdyeh tribe. There they discussed the possibility of carrying out rebel activities in Jebel Druze. They agreed to return
together to Jebel Druze so that Naseeb could begin to make
contact with Syrian leaders sympathizing with the Revolt. Accordingly Naseeb left Sherif Nassir and went to Jebel Druze
together with Hussein al-Atrash and Zaki Drubi. He had with
him seven thousand pounds in gold, which he was to spend in
connexion with his mission. Once there he contacted Sultan al-
Atrash and, although his efforts were not successful at the time,
they did eventually result in the enlistment of the Druze in
Feisal's final campaign of September 1918.[6]

As for Sherif Nassir and Auda Abu Tayeh, they succeeded in
recruiting more than five hundred volunteers, whom they led
on 19 June from Nebk westward towards Bair, where they
discovered that the Turks had damaged the water wells, which
forced them to stay there for a week to open up the wells and obtain water. In an effort to blind the Turks to the activities of his
force, Auda sent his nephew Za'al at the head of a hundred men
to raid in the north. The party reached Wadi Dhuleil, north of
Zerka, where Lawrence, who had accompanied them, dynamited
a culvert, and the men removed some rails. On their way back
to Bair they came close to Tway station where they captured
twenty-five head of sheep belonging to the station garrison and
exchanged fire with the Turks, with no casualties on either side.
According to Sheikh Qasim ibn Eid,[7] they spent three days

6. Emir Hasan al-Atrash has confirmed this information. He told me 'that
most of the Druzes, especially their chieftain Salim al-Atrash, were completely
loyal to the Turks, who had exempted them from military service and from
taxes. A volunteer Druze unit continued to serve with the Turks until the end
of the war. At the same time, Jebel Druze became a shelter for deserters from the
Turkish Army during the war, and supporters of the Arab Revolt were able
to operate there without restriction. Sultan al-Atrash was the Druze chieftain
who led the Syrian revolt against the French in 1925–1927.

7. Qasim ibn Eid is Auda's first cousin. He accompanied Auda to Wejh and
took part in the Aqaba expedition. He is now about seventy.

waiting in vain for the train at Munifa; when no train passed they removed the rails. Then they spotted a detachment of seventy Turkish cavalry. The bedouin wanted to attack, but Lawrence convinced Za'al that the derailing of a train was more important, so the Turks were left to pass by unmolested.

On 28 June, after receiving promises of support from the Dumaniyeh, Darawsheh, Dhiabat, and Huweitat clans, the expedition left Bair for Jefer, arriving there two days later. After watering, they moved in a south-westerly direction and hurriedly crossed the railway line at a point close to Ghadir al-Haj station. At the same time the Dumaniyeh, together with a few of Auda's men, attacked and annihilated a Turkish garrison at Fuweila. In the evening the Arabs withdrew a few miles from the railway line to pass the night, but upon hearing that a Turkish infantry battalion under Niazi Bey had arrived at Abu al-Lissan to oppose them, they hurried to the hills overlooking the place, where, with the help of other Huweitat clans, they divided into several little groups and completely surrounded the Turks. At daybreak they started firing at the Turks and cut the telephone lines to Ma'an. Exchange of fire continued for the whole morning of 2 July, the Turks making highly inaccurate use of a mountain gun. The Turks had not been too wise in their choice of the water stream as their camping site, for it stood in a low position surrounded by hills. In the afternoon, Auda launched a two-pronged attack on the exhausted enemy; fifty horsemen descended on them from one side, while four hundred camelry charged at top speed from the other. The Turks started to flee in panic only to discover that they were completely surrounded. Soon the battle was over, the defeated Turks having suffered 300 casualties in addition to 160 prisoners. The few who had horses or mules managed to escape but they were pursued as far as Mreigha by Mohammed Dheilan (Auda's cousin). The Arabs lost only two men.

What part did Lawrence play in this battle? He admitted that when he charged and started firing his revolver his camel fell down killed by one of his own bullets. He himself remained unconscious until the end of the battle. As for Auda, he emerged unscatched although his horse was killed under him and his clothes were riddled with shots in six different places.

Auda insisted on leaving Abu al-Lissan at night. So the Arabs and their prisoners marched to a point a few miles away, from which they sent several messages to Huweitat Sheikhs camping near the coast. They also sent messages to the commanders of the Turkish garrisons in Gueira, Kethara and Khadra, the Turkish positions overlooking Aqaba, warning them to surrender lest they should meet the fate of their brothers-in-arms.

The Arabs resumed their march on the following day until they arrived at Naqab Ashtar. On 4 July they surrounded Gueira, forcing the garrison of 120 to surrender. On the following night they attacked and captured the garrison of Kethara, whose resistance broke after an initial refusal to capitulate. On the morning of 5 July the Arab force descended the Wadi Itm gorge and discovered that the Turks had evacuated all their minor positions and gathered their forces at Khadra, a fortified position at the mouth of the valley commanding the Gulf of Aqaba. From this position the Turks were trying to prevent the landing of forces in Aqaba from the sea. It is worthy of note that the Turks had set up their entrenchments to face the sea, since they never expected an inland attack from their rear.

In the evening the Arabs approached Khadra, which was defended by over three hundred officers and men; but at that point the number of Arab warriors had multiplied, owing to the arrival of some neighbouring clans. At first the Turks refused to surrender, but they soon realized that they were incapable of defending their positions for long because of scarcity of supplies and lack of communications with Ma'an. Therefore, for fear of meeting the fate of their comrades in Abu al-Lissan, they surrendered on the following morning. Shortly afterwards the Arabs descended upon Aqaba, whose inhabitants had already been evacuated. Thus they achieved the aim for which they had set out from Wejh two months earlier. As a result of this operation, the enemy suffered not less than six hundred casualties with seven hundred taken prisoner, including forty-two officers.

After sending his messengers to notify Feisal of this victory, Sherif Nassir set up headquarters at Aqaba. It was arranged that Auda should stay at Gueira and send some of his men to set up front-line posts at Abu al-Lissan, Mreigha, al-Wahida and Delagha. As for Lawrence, it was agreed that he should leave Aqaba on the same day with eight Huweitat in order to contact the British in Suez, because Arab supplies were running short and Sherif Nassir was in need of money. It was much easier and shorter to reach the British in Suez than to reach Feisal in Wejh. Also, Feisal was not in a position to lend a quick helping hand because he had no ships or other means at his disposal. Lawrence and his friends reached Suez in fifty hours and informed General Headquarters of the capture of this important strategic position. The *Dufferin* was at once dispatched loaded with food and supplies. She reached Aqaba on 13 July.

3. BETWEEN FACT AND FANCY

It is best to pause at this point to examine the secret report which Lawrence wrote after his arrival in Suez and submitted to General Clayton on 10 July 1917. A comparison of its contents with what Lawrence wrote in the *Arab Bulletin* and *Seven Pillars of Wisdom* soon reveals that it contained a startling conglomeration of lies and fabrications.

Here is a summary of the report:

. . . I left Wejh on 9 May 1917 with Sherif Nassir . . . as O.C. Expedition . . . Sherif Feisal's instructions were to open Aqaba for use as a base of supply for the Arab forces. . . . We . . . marched to Nebk (near Kaf) on 2 June. . . . Sherif Nassir stayed in Kaf to enrol Rualla, Shererat and Huweitat for the Aqaba expedition.

I rode on 4 June with two men into Wald Ali country via Burga and Seba' Biar to Ain al Barrida near Tudmor on 8 June. Here I met Sheikh Dhami of the Kawakiba Aneza. . . . I . . . went west with Dhami and his 35 men (whom I enrolled) to Ras Ba'albek on 10 June and dynamited a small girder bridge there. From Ras Ba'albek we rode south to El Gabbon, in the Ghuta 3 miles from Damascus where on 13 June I met Ali Rida al-Rikabi, G.O.C. Damascus. Thence I rode to El Rudeine where I met Sheikh Saad Ed Din Ibn Ali of the Leja, and passed on to Salkhad to see Hussein Bey al Atrash. From Salkhad we went to Azrak and saw Nuri and Nawwaf, and returned to Nebk on 18 June.

I found the enrolment finished. Naseeb Bey al-Bekri went to Salkhad with Hussein al Atrash with the instructions attached, and with Nassir I marched on 19 June to Bair where we re-opened the dynamited wells. From Bair I rode to Ziza and saw Fawaz Ibn Faiz, and thence West of Amman to Um Keis on 23 June where I looked at railway bridge Z in the Yarmuk valley and saw Shererat and Beni Hassan Sheikhs. From Um Keis I went to Ifdein (Mafrak) the first station below Deraa, and destroyed a stretch of curved rails at km. 173. From Ifdein we rode to Zerga, and thence to Atwi,[8] where we

8. (Tway) no longer used, situated between Khan al-Zebib and Kutrani station.

failed to take the station, but killed three out of the five of the garrison, captured a large flock of sheep and destroyed a telegraph party of four men repairing the wire. We also dynamited a stretch of line. From Atwi I rode back to Bair, and rejoined Sherif Nassir who had meantime prepared the Western Huweitat. On 30 June we moved to el Jefer, clearing one well, and then to km. 479 which we destroyed on a large scale, while a column was attacking N. of Ma'an near Aneyza. We then marched towards Fuweileh, where the gendarmes' post had been destroyed by an advance column. They met us with the news of the re-occupation of Fuweileh by the belated relief expedition of 4/174/59 from Ma'an. We wiped out the battalion on 2 July (taking the O.C., a mountain gun and 160 prisoners) at Abu al-Lissan, and sent a flying column North which defeated the Turkish post at Hisha (railhead 5 miles East of Shobek), occupied Wadi Musa, Shobek, Tafileh, and is now near Kerak to take action there.

Lawrence then proceeded to describe the occupation of Aqaba, stating that as a result of his journeys and interviews he believed in the possibility of forming seven Arab fighting groups between Ma'an and Aleppo, to attack Turkish lines of communication. At the end of his report he stated that Sherif Nassir had asked him to discuss the general situation, his needs and the possibility of joint action against the Turkish forces in Palestine.

In the several footnotes to his report, Lawrence states that he tried to compose the feud between the Bishr and Huweitat and that Hussein al-Atrash told him the terms on which the Druze were prepared to rise. He also says that the mine he had planted at km. 173 blew up a train which fell off a fifteen-foot-high culvert into the valley. Fawaz al-Faiz was apparently friendly, but pro-Turk at heart. As for the instructions which he claimed to have given to Naseeb al-Bekri, they consisted of ten items requiring Naseeb to set up an Intelligence Service, to reconcile the Druze leaders with one another, to get in touch with the Druzes of the Lebanon and Matawala, to reassure the Maronites and to get in touch with the population of the Lake Huleh, Lejah and Ba'albek areas.

We find some interesting details about the use of dynamite by the Ageyl and about the extent of the demolition, in an article by Lawrence published soon after the occupation of Aqaba:

Circumstances forced us to stay in Bair till Thursday 28 June. The time was spent in negotiations with Ibn Jazi . . . we also carried out demolitions against the railway at Atwi, Sultani, Minifir, and elsewhere. The Ageyl dynamiters were inefficient, and our supply of dynamite small, so that the demolitions were of a pin-prick character, meant only to distract the Turks, and advertise our coming to the Arabs, The staffs of two stations were killed, to the same intent.[9]

It is to be noted that in his report to Clayton, Lawrence said that his alleged trip to Palmyra (Tudmor) and Damascus took place before the departure of Naseeb al-Bekri for Jebel Druze, and that he gave Naseeb the 'instructions' on 18 June, while in *Seven Pillars of Wisdom* he said that this trip took place after Naseeb's departure, without giving any details. He also said in the report that he went as far as Um Keis and the railway line in the Yarmuk Valley, while, in *Seven Pillars*, he is satisfied with reaching Munifa (km. 173) only and returning straight to Bair via Khau and Dhaba. He also said in *Seven Pillars* that ten bridges south of Ma'an (km. 479) were destroyed, though nothing of this had appeared in his report. The real facts are that when the Arabs crossed the railway line in the direction of Aqaba they had no time to blow up a single bridge. Had they actually damaged as many as ten bridges, Lawrence's report could not have ignored such an important feat.

We can see from the above the contradiction in Lawrence's two statements about the alleged trip. We also note that in *Seven Pillars* there is no reference to Um Keis, Yarmuk and Zizia; nor is there any mention of the Arab attack on Uneiza station. The occupation of Wadi Musa, Shobek and Tafileh is also ignored. All this was omitted because it never happened at all. Lawrence knew this very well and therefore avoided exposing himself in *Seven Pillars* but he could do nothing to change the contents of his report to Clayton.

In an effort to arrive at the truth I have carried out extensive investigations; Lawrence's trip to Tudmor (Palmyra) and Ba'albek was strongly denied by Naseeb al-Bekri, who assured me that Lawrence remained all the time with the Arabs in Wadi Sirhan (Nebk and Kaf). They parted ways only when Naseeb left for Jebel Druze and Nassir, Auda and Lawrence for Aqaba. This story was confirmed by Qasim ibn Eid and Mohammed Abu Tayeh.[10] It was also confirmed by Faiz al-Ghussein, who told me

9. *Arab Bulletin*, 12 August 1917, No. 59.
10. Son of Auda.

that he never heard of this story from his son-in-law, Zaki Drubi [11] or his brother-in-law, Sa'ad al-Din Abu Suleiman, Sheikh of the Lejah. We can assert here that this story was entirely fabricated by Lawrence. Furthermore, Lawrence's trip to Wadi Yarmuk was virtually impossible because that area, besides being densely populated, was the scene of hostilities between the local people and the bedouin. Moreover, Lawrence's claim that he attacked the Sultani (Manzil) Station it patently untrue because Sultani lies at a distance of seventy kilometres from Dhaba Station. A further error is his reference to the Shararat as a northern tribe. This tribe has always lived south of Ma'an. The tribe of Beni Hassan was as loyal to the Turks as the rest of the Balqa District and remained so until the last days of the war. The Beni Hassan Sheikhs, with whom I discussed this matter, denied any knowledge of this incident. A further fabrication is Lawrence's claim that the Arabs brought supplies to Bair from Tafileh and conducted negotiations with Ibn Jazi.

Naseeb al-Bekri has informed me that, at the request of Sherif Nassir and Auda, he spent about twenty days at Nebk and Kaf in order to assist in reconciling the tribes with each other and encouraging them to join the Revolt. Furthermore, his presence was a proof that Damascus, the heart of Syria, was ready to fight the Turks.

As for Lawrence's claim [wrote Naseeb] that he went in disguise to Damascus, Ba'albek and Tudmor, it strikes me as very strange indeed, because it is far from the truth. I am certain Lawrence did not leave us for a single day, and we were not separated until after he left for Aqaba, with Auda and Nassir, while I left for Jebel Druze. Similarly, Lawrence's strange claims about his leading the Revolt indicate a complete ignorance of those Arab activities since 1908 that aimed at independence and a forgetfulness of the martyrs which the Arab nation had to offer in hundreds and thousands. I must also mention the fact that Lawrence was inclined to double-dealing, slander and dissemination of discord and that he urged Auda and Nassir to take the 7,000 pounds which Feisal had allotted to me to spend in Syria and Jebel Druze. They actually asked for the money on the grounds that their own allotment had run out; in spite of much argument I insisted on keeping the money. Sherif Nassir informed me confidentially that Lawrence was the instigator. Nassir

11. Naseeb al-Bekri's close friend and companion on the trip from Wejh to Kaf and Jebel Druze. Lawrence refers to him by his first name only.

said that to prevent a misunderstanding, he would inform Auda and Lawrence that I had passed the money on to him. I believe that until he died Lawrence thought that I had actually surrendered the money. In fact I did not part with a single pound. In spite of all Lawrence's claims and fabrications I can still say that he was a brilliant adventurer who got used to ruggedness of life.

On the other hand, Sheikh Adhoub al-Zebn states that he and a number of Beni Sakhr tribesmen went out to meet Sherif Nassir. When they reached Jarajer (close to Nebk in Wadi Sirhan) they discovered that Nassir and Auda had left for Bair and they followed them there. As for Rafe' al-Khreisheh, whom Lawrence mentions as his companion to Um Keis, the truth is that he had had a difference with the Sheikh of his tribe and was living with the Zebn, so he never met Lawrence during that period at all.

It is clear from all this that Lawrence's story that he passed through Zizia, visited the tents of Beni Sakhr and spent the night as a guest of Fawaz al-Faiz was completely untrue; for in his report to Clayton he said: 'From Bair I rode to Ziza and saw Fawaz Ibn Faiz, and thence west of Amman to Um Keis', while in *Seven Pillars* he claims that his visit to Beni Sakhr took place on his way back from Um Keis. In *Seven Pillars* Lawrence says that Nawaf al-Faiz 'led out his mare, and guided us, loaded rifle across his thigh, to the railway and beyond it into the desert. There he gave us the star-direction of our supposed goal in Bair.'[12] Lawrence's story of an attempt by Fawaz to betray him and his two companions by handing them over to the Turks seems both absurd and incredible. I have asked Mithqal al-Faiz, paramount Sheikh of Beni Sakhr and brother to Fawaz and Nawaf, about this. He denied that Lawrence had ever visited their tents during the war, secretly or openly, and added that Lawrence's story is certainly untrue because bedouin traditions do not permit the host to surrender his guest to anybody. Furthermore, Fawaz, as a member of the Fetat secret society would never have made such an attempt.[13]

In an article by Lawrence about this same expedition, he made a quaint statement about the enmity of the Transjordan people towards the Turks, which he said was the result of the

12. *Op. cit.*, p. 532.
13. The Zebn, Khreishen and Faiz are clans of the Beni Sakhr tribe.

murder by the Turks of women and children in a bedouin encampment and

the previous execution of Sheikh Abd el-Rahman, a Belgawiya from Kerak. He was popular, and anti-Turk, but the Government caught him, and harnessing him between four wild mules tore him to death. This was the culmination of a series of executions by torture in Kerak, and the memory of them has embittered local opinion.[14]

Lawrence might well have heard about the well-known Kerak revolt of 1910 under Sheikh Qader al-Majali and about the ruthless methods that the Turks used in quelling it, but the name Abdul Rahman was certainly a figment of his imagination, and so was the execution through harnessing men between wild animals, a European practice of the Middle Ages which never found its way to the East. Nobody else, in fact, has ever mentioned that the Turks applied this method. In this one sees evidence of Lawrence's dependence on his imagination in distorting information which had reached him through hearsay.

I asked Akram al-Rikabi, son of Ali Rida al-Rikabi, if he could give me any information about the alleged meeting between his father and Lawrence at Qabun. He replied: 'I have heard from my father that in the early days of Military Government in Syria (late 1918) a number of British officers visited him at Government House, Damascus. One of them stood up in front of my late father and asked if my father remembered him. He looked at him and said, "Are you not the archaeologist I met at Carchemish before the war?" (my father was then Commander of the 6th division at Aleppo). He answered, "Yes." My father asked "What do you do now?" He said, "I am Colonel Lawrence, and I work with Emir Feisal." This proves that that was the first time my father saw him after Carchemish. It also refutes Lawrence's claim that he met my father at Qabun during the war.'[15]

Lawrence came near to confessing that the story of his alleged trip was pure fiction in the notes he sent on 22 July 1927 to Robert Graves who was engaged at the time in writing his biography:

14. *Arab Bulletin*, No. 59., 12 August 1917, p. 338.
15. It is worthy of note that in 1917 Ali Rida al-Rikabi was Mayor of Damascus and not G.O.C. Damascus as Lawrence alleges. Liman von Sanders appointed him i/c fortifications west of Damascus in the last months of the war.

In my report to Clayton after Akaba I gave a short account of my excursion from Nebk northward. It was part of the truth. During it some things happened, and I do not want the whole story to be made traceable. So on this point I have since darkened counsel. You'll have to say something, but you'll not be able to be right in what you say. So hedge yourself, and me, if you can, by cautionary phrases. Some such thing as the following:

'From Nebk during the Akaba expedition's halt there, "L" went off on a solitary excursion northward. On this ride he was said to have been convoyed by relays of local tribesmen, beginning with the Rualla and changing them at each tribal boundary. Apparently none of his own, nor of Sherif Nasir's men completed the journey with him. He is said to have been franked by private letters of Emir Feisal, but nothing certain is known of his purpose, his route, and the results of his journey. . . .'

He adds:

You may make public if you like the fact that my reticence upon this northward raid is deliberate, and based on private reasons: and record your opinion that I have found mystification, and perhaps statements deliberately misleading or contradictory, the best way to hide the truth of what really occurred, *if anything did occur*.[16]

In addition to all this, Lawrence admitted in *Seven Pillars* that he resorted to intrigue in order to separate Naseeb al-Bekri on the one side from Nassir and Auda on the other. He also claims that Naseeb offered to launch a revolt in Syria, provided that it was independent of the Arab Revolt led by Sherif Hussein, and that he—Lawrence—promised to help Naseeb if he succeeded. Needless to say, Naseeb had denied this, because he was one of the most enthusiastic supporters of Sherif Hussein and because his family's friendship with the Sherif was of long standing. He and his elder brother played an honourable part in the Arab Revolt.

It is to be noted that in his writings immediately following the occupation of Aqaba, Lawrence did not claim that he was the leader of the expedition nor did he allege that he was the originator of the idea. In fact he stated more than once that Sherif Nassir was the leader of the expedition and that Auda Abu Tayeh was the actual commander of the fighting force. We might add here that, in its obituary notice of Auda Abu Tayeh in 1924, the Transjordan official Gazette described him as 'the

16. *T. E. Lawrence to his Biographers*, Part I, pp. 88–90 (*my italics*).

conqueror of Aqaba'. No Arab can ever believe that a foreign officer could have led such an expedition. It is strange that Lawrence should have later claimed all credit for this,[17] and that several American and British writers should have accepted this claim, added to it and influenced their many readers as well as public opinion in their countries. Lawrence was fortunate in that the Arab leaders of the Revolt did not leave detailed memoirs about these events and the part that foreign officers played in them. Further, it is certain that important documents of great historical value were lost as a result of the termination of the Hashemite rule in Hejaz and the hasty departure of the Hashemites from Mecca in 1924. Sheikh Hafez Wahbeh states that his attention was drawn at the time to piles of neglected papers in the courtyard of Government House in Mecca. Upon examining them, he found the administrative records of the Hashemite Government and several other important documents relating to the Arab Revolt and the whole Arab movement in its various phases.[18]

4. ALLENBY AND LAWRENCE

On his trip to Cairo, Lawrence proved his proficiency in acting and his love for arousing the surprise and admiration of others and his indulgence in unconventional methods. On the train he wore the white robes which Feisal had given him. Arriving at Ismailia, he spotted General Allenby with three other high ranking British officers and seized the opportunity to approach one of them. Writing of the conversation, he said:

I explained the history of our unannounced raid on Akaba. It excited him. I asked that the admiral send a storeship there at once. Burmester said the *Dufferin*, which came in that day, should load all the food in Suez, go straight to Akaba, and bring back the prisoners. . . . . He would order it himself, not to interrupt the Admiral and Allenby.[19]

Lawrence's immediate superior, Clayton, whom in normal military discipline he should not have by-passed, was in Cairo,

17. General Wingate has also claimed that the occupation of Aqaba was a result of his own strategic plan and that 'he achieved what he had planned for the Arab Revolt'. Cited by Zeine N. Zeine in *The Struggle for Arab Independence* (Beirut 1960), p. 23.

18. Hafeth Wahba, *Jazairel al-Arab fi al-Qarn al-'Ishrin* (Arab Peninsula in the 20th Century) (Cairo 1934) Preface. Hafeth Wahba is now Saudi Ambassador in London.

19. *Seven Pillars*, pp. 319-320.

where Lawrence could have arrived in two hours' time. But had he intended to behave normally he would not have stood on the station platform gesticulating with his hands and shuffling his feet in order to attract the attention of those senior officers, with his white silk robes and his sunburned face.

Once in Cairo, Lawrence met General Clayton in his office. Clayton, of course, welcomed the news Lawrence was carrying and got in touch with Admiral Wemyss requesting that the Arabs be supplied with immediate aid. Wemyss said that a ship was being loaded with sacks of flour. And since money is usually a decisive factor in war, Clayton despatched £16,000 in gold to Suez with instructions that it be shipped to Sherif Nassir, who had spent all he had before leaving Wadi Sirhan, and had been promising the tribes that payment would be effected at Aqaba.

Allenby then called Lawrence in for a meeting, thus fulfilling in great measure Lawrence's wish to establish connexion with high circles. Lawrence summoned up all his courage, cleverness and cunning to influence Allenby and to convince him of his ability to spark off trouble in the whole of Syria in order to facilitate the advance of the British army on Gaza and Beersheba. He did not forget to request a special fund which he could use independently of the leaders of the Arab Revolt. Describing this meeting, Lawrence wrote:

. . . the Commander-in-Chief sent for me, curiously. In my report, thinking of Saladin and Abu Obeida, I had stressed the strategic importance of the eastern tribes of Syria, and their proper use as a threat to the communications of Jerusalem. This jumped with his ambitions, and he wanted to weigh me.

It was a comic interview, for Allenby was physically large and confident, and morally so great that the comprehension of our littleness came slow to him. He sat in his chair looking at me—not straight, as his custom was, but sideways, puzzled. He was newly from France, where for years he had been a tooth of the great machine grinding the enemy. He was full of Western ideas of gun power and weight . . . , yet he was hardly prepared for anything so odd as myself—a little bare-footed silk-skirted man offering to hobble the enemy by his preaching if given stores and arms and a fund of two hundred thousand sovereigns to convince and control his converts.

Allenby could not make out how much was genuine performer and how much charlatan. The problem was working behind his eyes, and I left him unhelped to solve it. He did not ask many questions, nor talk much, but studied the map and listened to my unfolding of

Eastern Syria and its inhabitants. At the end he put up his chin and said quite directly, 'Well, I will do for you what I can', and that ended it. I was not sure how far I had caught him; but we learned gradually that he meant exactly what he said; and that what General Allenby could do was enough for his very greediest servant.[20]

Lawrence thus won half the battle through a series of co-incidences compounded by lies, daring and impudence. He made direct contact with the Commander-in-Chief and proposed that he—Lawrence—assume the responsibility of arousing the tribes in Eastern Syria from Aleppo in the north to Ma'an and Amman in the south. The question is: Where did the Arabs and the Arab Revolt stand in relation to Lawrence's plan? Of course Lawrence was in no position to ignore the idea upon which the Revolt was built, but he intended to use this idea as a bait for his own propaganda. As for money, equipment and arms, these were his means of persuasion. Instead of remaining an unknown officer in a military mission, he could—if his request were granted—become the actual leader of a wide movement which drew its moral support from the Revolt, without being completely tied down to the principles of this Revolt.

At this stage, he began his real game between the Arabs and the British. It was an act played on two different platforms:

Lawrence addresses Allenby: Sir, give me money and arms, and I will pave the road for your army. I will mass the tribes, and lead them in surprise attacks on enemy communications and positions. Arms and money do wonders in Arab countries. I know their language, and habits and traditions, I know how to get what I want from them, and I can be of great help to you.

Lawrence addresses Feisal: Sidi, I have informed General Allenby of your wish to march upon Syria and unfold the banner of the Revolt there. I have convinced the General that the Arabs can contribute effectively to the defeat of Turkey if only they had money and arms. The General is very pleased, and has promised to help your Highness and provide all your needs. I can get from Allenby whatever you want.

Lawrence was determined to improve his position. A man of his intelligence knew full well that such an opportunity might not present itself more than once. Having taken full advantage of

20. *Seven Pillars*, p. 322.

it, he left Allenby with renewed vigour. He had persuaded the Commander-in-Chief to deal with him directly without reference to Clayton and Feisal. It was not difficult, therefore, to convince these two men of his worth and of his right to reap the fruits of his own labour.

Upon Clayton I opened myself completely. Akaba had been taken on my plan by my effort. The cost of it had fallen on my brains and nerves. There was much more I felt inclined to do, and capable of doing—if he thought I had earned the right to be my own master. The Arabs said that each man believed his ticks to be gazelles: I did, fervently.

Clayton agreed they were spirited and profitable ticks; but objected that actual command could not be given to an officer junior to the rest. He suggested Joyce as commanding officer at Akaba: a notion which suited me perfectly.[21]

This is quite clear. Encouraged by Allenby, Lawrence went to his direct superior and told him openly: I have captured Aqaba and I have opened up a whole new front against the enemy. I have given of my soul and nerves to this great enterprise and I demand my reward. I want to be the officer in charge, so that I may put all my genius at the disposal of the war effort, and you shall find that I shall not disappoint you and that the whole of Syria shall be the theatre of my activities. Clayton agreed with kind expressions of approval, and apologized for the fact that army regulations do not permit a captain to shoulder the responsibility for action, and to overstep his superior who holds the rank of colonel. But he promised to keep Lawrence as the intermediary between General Headquarters and Feisal. The other officers would not have the authority to interfere in his actions. However, as an immediate reward, he was promoted to the rank of Major and was made Companion of the Bath.

Thus we see that within a mere two months Lawrence's position had changed radically. He had left Wejh from sheer adventurousness, as a companion to a purely Arab expedition that succeeded in accomplishing its predetermined plan. When the aim was attained, Lawrence left Aqaba to carry the requests of Sherif Nassir to British Headquarters. But he suddenly transformed himself from an emissary to a responsible leader, and found ready ears. One can find an excuse for this: for how could the British believe that bedouin bands were capable of perform-

21. *Seven Pillars*, p. 323.

ing such a great feat without the guidance of this officer, who made use of the theories of Saxe, Foch and Napoleon?

5. THE NORTHERN ARMY AT AQABA

When Feisal sent Sherif Nassir north to Aqaba, he declared his intention of moving his army there as soon as the Arabs had captured it and firmly established themselves. Aqaba was the northern key to Syria and the leaders of the Revolt were very anxious to spread military activities beyond the boundaries of Hejaz. Lawrence stated that Feisal had previously told him at Wejh of his intention to move to Aqaba, but the impression the reader gains on reading *Seven Pillars* is that Lawrence was directing these affairs on his own initiative. We are told that he arranged the transfer of the armoured cars from Wejh to Aqaba and also arranged with Admiral Wemyss to post one of his warships in the Gulf to protect Aqaba from possible Turkish attacks during this first stage. Lawrence alleged that he asked for the transfer of Feisal's army from Wejh to Aqaba, and for the transfer also of the regulars serving with Abdullah and Ali. He explained that Aqaba had now become the right wing for Allenby's army because it was only a hundred miles from Suez, while it was eight hundred miles from Mecca. It was thus reasonable and logical, he argued, that Allenby, rather than King Hussein should take charge of Feisal's army. General Clayton obtained the approval of Sir Reginald Wingate, the High Commissioner. It remained to persuade King Hussein and obtain his consent for the proposed plan. Lawrence as the political officer concerned was entrusted with the mission.

Lawrence thus left Cairo with messages from Wingate to King Hussein. In these messages he requested Hussein's approval for the transfer of Feisal's army and pointed out the benefits that would accrue to the Arab cause from this strengthening of the army, so that it could participate effectively in the projected campaign in Syria. He sailed to Wejh, then flew to Jeida, midway between Wejh and the railway, where Feisal was directing operations against the Turks. He managed to procure a further message to the King in which Feisal recommended this move to Aqaba. Then he returned to Wejh and sailed to Jedda, 'where things became easy for me with Wilson's powerful help'.[22]

22. *Seven Pillars*, p. 325.

The king came from Mecca to Jedda on 28 July 1917. After examining the letters of Wingate and Feisal and listening to the arguments of Wilson and Lawrence, he could do nothing but agree to the transfer of Feisal's army and declare his satisfaction with Britain's attitude and his confidence in her wisdom and good intentions towards the Arab nation.

It is unfortunate that we possess only Lawrence's story and that of his friends. In *Seven Pillars* Lawrence claims that all these suggestions were of his own making. Official British sources, however, do not attribute them to Lawrence but rather say:

In the spring of 1918, when the railway was destroyed near Ma'an so thoroughly that the Turks were unable to withdraw from Medina whether or not they desired to do so, one of the reasons for the attack was the news that Turkish G.H.Q. was seriously considering the evacuation of the Hejaz. At least it was recognized from the moment of Sir Edmund Allenby's arrival that the Hejaz was a secondary theatre of the Arab campaign.

Aqaba was only 130 miles from the British position on the Wadi Ghazze, but it was 700 miles from Mecca, also it was to be the base for expeditions which would bring Arab forces still more closely in touch with the British and remove them still further from the control of King Hussein. . . . It was therefore decided that the Emir Feisal should become, in effect, an army commander under Sir Edmund Allenby's orders. All Arab operations north of Ma'an were to be carried out by him under the direction of the British commander in chief. South of Ma'an the High Commissioner, Sir Reginald Wingate, was still to act as adviser to the Emirs Ali and Abdulla and to be responsible for their supplies.[23]

At this point we may ask whether King Hussein was right in agreeing to transfer the responsibility of the Northern Army to Allenby. Information available to us indicates that King Hussein was personally distrustful of Lawrence, as if he intuitively sensed an unhealthy attitude in this double-dealing, bragging officer. But Lawrence did not lay all his cards on the table, for he came to the King as a messenger from the High Commissioner and the British Command. The King was told that higher policy required the transfer, that things were going according to plan and that Feisal would officially remain under him. It was also pointed out that the distance between Aqaba and Mecca made it necessary for Feisal's army to be attached to Allenby, so that

23. *Military Operations: Egypt and Palestine* (London, H.M.S.O., 1930), Vol. 2, Part II, pp. 396–397.

military plans could be more easily co-ordinated. In Storrs's *Orientations*, one finds that the British were hoping that the King would leave military matters to professional officers. Storrs himself suggested to the King that he should bestow his confidence on Aziz Ali al-Misri and turn over to him the task of organizing the army and its activities according to the best military methods. The King agreed and appointed Aziz Chief of Staff and Minister for War. It was not long, however, before he terminated his service.

What concerns us here is that Lawrence succeeded in his mission. Of course Wilson Pasha [24] was the main instrument in convincing the King, but Lawrence succeeded in becoming the liaison officer between British H.Q. and the Northern Army on the one hand, and the personal emissary between Feisal and Allenby on the other.

Lawrence's imagination, however, was so fertile that it could not rest until it had fabricated a new story. He stated that during his stay at Jedda he received two telegrams from Cairo indicating that the Huweitat were in touch with the Turks at Ma'an and that Auda was an accomplice in the plot. Be that as it may, Lawrence returned to Aqaba on 4 August, nearly one month after he had left it. We do not know how the news of this 'plot' reached Egypt, but we do know that Lawrence's story was a far cry from the truth.

What had actually happened was that the Turks were greatly disturbed by the fall of Aqaba. They realized that it was Auda Abu Tayeh who had done them the greatest harm and that it was he who was really responsible for this surprise attack. Since they did not have sufficient forces or supplies to recapture the positions they had lost, they tried to contact Auda and lure him with bribes and promises of a high position to shift his allegiance from Sherif Hussein and the Arab Revolt to their side. For this purpose, Mehmed Jemal Pasha, O.C. Eighth Corps, sent three of Auda's personal friends to Gueira (Hussein Kreishan, a Ma'an Sheikh, Dhiab al-Auran, paramount Sheikh of Tafileh, and Deifalla Abur Skour, a Huweitat Sheikh). The emissaries offered him a large sum of money and the position of Emir of Shara' if he would sever his relations with the Revolt and fight on the side of the Turks. But Auda refused these tempting offers and

24. King Hussein conferred the title of 'Pasha' on Colonel Wilson.

declared that he would not break his promise nor go back on his word. He affirmed that he was an Arab patriot, whose duty was to fight for Arab independence. The three men returned to the Turkish general with Auda's reply and the matter stopped at that. Had Auda wished to betray the Revolt, the Turks would have returned to the positions they had lost, including Aqaba, because Sherif Nassir had no more than 30 Ageyl volunteers. But Auda preferred honour, and defended the liberated areas for over a month and a half, until the Northern Army was transferred from Wejh to Aqaba.

It is worth mentioning that this Turkish attempt to woo Auda had been preceded by a military operation. In his unpublished memoirs, Auda Qusus[25] states that Mehmad Jemal Pasha succeeded in enlisting 500 Kerak horsemen whom he despatched under three Turkish officers from Ma'an to Wahida and Fuweila on 17 July. They engaged a tribe loyal to the Revolt and captured their cattle. But the Kerak men soon realized that Jemal Pasha's purpose was to spark off enmity among the tribes. To the surprise of the Pasha, they suddenly returned to Ma'an and informed him that it was impossible for them to comply with his wishes. He realized that there was nothing he could do. A week later he led his forces to Wahida, and advanced to Abu al-Lissan. It is certain that this was the same attack which Lawrence referred to as preceding the Arab assault on Abu al-Lissan. The Turks, Lawrence claimed, murdered an old man, six women and seven children. All the people I contacted, Ma'an Sheikhs and tribes alike, have denied that the Turks killed any women or children.

Auda's position emerges more clearly if we refer to the *Arab Bulletin* of 12 August where there is an account of the situation in Aqaba. Here is a summary of the article (the italics are mine):

The Turkish force that occupied Fuweilah (strength about two battalions with some hundreds of mounted men) has not attempted any forward move. As far as Aba el-Lissan and Fuweilah, the road from Maan to Akaba runs over open rolling country, affording little opportunity for the exercise of Arab tactics, and the water supply at Aba el-Lissan is enough for perhaps 5,000 men. After Fuweilah the

25. Auda Qusus (1877–1943) was a Kerak notable. After Feisal's arrival at Aqaba, Auda Qusus was exiled by the Turks to Anatolia together with several Transjordanian leaders. He later held several important positions in Jordan, including membership of the Legislative Council and the Executive Council (Attorney-General). He was one of the leaders of the force he speaks of.

road descends the steep Nagb el-Star . . . and then runs over the
sandy plain of el-Hisma, which is studded with precipitous rock-
pinnacles of red sandstone. Behind one of these, at Guweira (twenty
miles from Fuweilah) are the present headquarters of Auda Abu
Tayi, who has about 600 Huweitat with him. The water at Guweira
. . . is sufficient for about 2,000 men .ı. . The Akaba road . . . then
runs for twenty miles through the gorge of Wadi Itm. . . .[26]
    The Arab tactics are to allow the Turks to advance to Guweira
and beyond, sniping them when possible. . . . In Wadi Itm itself they
would hold all the water sources strongly and occupy the hills each
side of the main valley. The Turkish problem is to carry enough
water from Aba el-Lissan to Akaba (55 miles) to support the relatively considerable body of troops necessary to force Wadi Itm, and
maintain itself before Akaba. . . . A hurried Turkish advance on
Aqaba is therefore hardly to be looked for, as it is impossible *unless
the Turks can persuade a sufficient number of the Sherifian Arabs to
cease fighting, and gather quantities of camels from the Turcophil
Arabs. They have made efforts in both directions, but so far without
much success.* Auda Abu Tayi remains unshakeably Arab, and he
commands a following so long as he remains in the field. He has
lately sent Mohammed el-Dheilan to near Ghadir el-Haj (a bridge
and about forty rails cut), Auda ibn Zaal to near Batn el Ghul (two
bridges blown up), and Zaal ibn Motlog to Aneze (a bridge destroyed). These raids were to distract the Turkish attention from the
Fuweilah district. . . . Turkish aeroplanes have made many short
flights over Auda's forces (inflicting one casualty and causing
panics). . . .
    From this we understand that the Turks tried to entice Auda.
But a mere attempt on the part of the Turks—with which Auda
did not concur—was transformed in Lawrence's book into a most
important event, which is not alluded to in any other available
sources. Here is Lawrence's story :
    While we played so interestingly at Jidda, two abrupt telegrams
from Egypt shattered our peace. The first reported that the Howeitat
were in treasonable correspondence with Maan. The second con-
nected Auda with the plot. This dismayed us. Wilson had travelled
with Auda, and formed the inevitable judgement of his perfect
sincerity: yet Mohammed el Dheilan was capable of double play,
and ibn Jad and his friends were still uncertain. We prepared to
leave at once for Akaba. Treachery had not been taken into account
when Nasir and I had built our plan for the town's defence.
    Fortunately the *Hardinge* was in the harbour for us. On the third
afternoon we were in Akaba, where Nasir had no notion that anything was wrong. I told him only of my wish to greet Auda: he lent

26. Sir Hubert Young states that there is a place in the gorge of Wadi Itm
where 'one company with two or three machine-guns could have stopped an army
corps.' (*The Independent Arab*, p. 147).

me a swift camel and a guide; and at dawn we found Auda and Mohammed and Zaal all in a tent at Guweira. They were confused when I dropped in on them, unheralded; but protested that all was well. We fed together as friends.

Others of the Howeitat came in, and there was gay talk about the war. I distributed the King's presents; and told them, to their laughter, that Nasir had got his month's leave to Mecca. The King, an enthusiast for the revolt, believed that his servants should work as manfully. So he would not allow visits to Mecca, and the poor men found continual military service heavy banishment from their wives. We had jested a hundred times that, *if he took Akaba, Nasir* would deserve a holiday; but he had not really believed in its coming until I gave him Hussein's letter the evening before. In gratitude he sold me Ghazala, the regal camel he won from the Howeitat. As her owner I became of new interest to the Abu Tayi.

After lunch, by pretence of sleep, I got rid of the visitors; and then abruptly asked Auda and Mohammed to walk with me to see the ruined fort and reservoir. When we were alone I touched on their present correspondence with the Turks. Auda began to laugh; Mohammed to look disgusted. At last they explained elaborately that Mohammed had taken Auda's seal and written to the Governor of Maan, offering to desert the Sherif's cause. The Turk had replied gladly, promising great rewards. Mohammed asked for something on account. Auda then heard of it, waited till the messenger with presents was on his way, caught him, robbed him to the skin: and was denying Mohammed a share of the spoils. A farcical story, and we laughed richly over it: but there was more behind.

They were angry that no guns or troops had yet come to their support; and that no rewards had been given them for taking Akaba. They were anxious to know how I had learnt of their secret dealings, and how much more I knew. We were on a slippery ledge. I played on their fear by my unnecessary amusement, quoting in careless laughter, as if they were my own words, actual phrases of the letters they had exchanged. This created the impression desired.

Parenthetically I told them Feisal's entire army was coming up; and how Allenby was sending rifles, guns, high explosive, food and money to Akaba. Finally I suggested that Auda's present expenses in hospitality must be great; would it help if I advanced something of the great gift Feisal would make him, personally, when he arrived? Auda saw that the immediate moment would not be unprofitable: that Feisal would be highly profitable: and that the Turks would be always with him if other resources failed. So he agreed, in a very good temper, to accept my advance; and with it to keep the Howeitat well-fed and cheerful.[27]

Lawrence's story reveals certain facts. Auda was, of course, interested in the arrival of Arab forces to oppose the Turks and

27. *Seven Pillars*, pp. 325–326.

there could be no doubt that his stand against the Turks for a
whole month and a half was a great achievement. It was natural,
however, that Auda would expect a reward for himself and his
men—it is proverbial that an army marches on its stomach. But
Auda did not know that the reward had actually gone to Lawrence, and that the victory which he and his men had registered
was transformed in Cairo, and that all credit had passed to someone else. As for the story on the contacts between Auda and the
Turks, we can only conclude that it is a further example of Lawrence's contempt for precision and truth in his writings and his
dependence on imagination and whim.

It might also be useful to refer to the *Arab Bulletin* of 5
August 1917, which, after discussing the military position of the
Arabs, goes on to say: '. . . there is no doubt that the Turks are
making great efforts to win over the tribes around Maan and
induce them to assist in an attack on Akaba, and are spending
considerable sums of money with this object. The G.O.C.
8th Army Corps is reported to have sent a messenger to Auda
Abu Tayi with the object of inducing the latter to rejoin the
Turks.' [28]

Nuri as-Said's lectures on the military operations of the Arab
Army furnish us with further information about the occupation
of Aqaba. He says, 'During my illness (in Egypt) I heard about
the capture of Aqaba by the tribes which were operating under
Emir Feisal and which were led by Sheikh Auda Abu Tayeh.
I was informed that Sheikh Auda Abu Tayeh, together with the
Huweitat tribes and a party of camel men accompanied by Lawrence moved from Wejh northwards. When they approached
Aqaba they discovered that its garrison was weak because it
was made up of one ineffective Turkish battalion; so they were
able to capture it by a surprise attack.'

6. 'HOW TO TREAT THE ARABS'

At this point I would like to put before the reader a summary
of the guide to the best methods of treating the Arabs, which
Lawrence wrote as soon as he reached the Hejaz for the benefit
of British officers working for the Revolt. Liddell Hart states that
Lawrence never paid much attention to the fact that the bedouin
treated him with scant respect when he first joined the Revolt,

28. *Op. cit.*, No. 58, p. 322.

and that the other British officers were perplexed at his indif-
ference to slights that made their blood boil. They were surprised to see him sharing the bedouin's humble food and attributed this to Lawrence's upbringing and his own 'street Arab'
past. There can be no doubt that Lawrence, in writing his guide,
had benefited greatly from his experience with the Arabs before
the war and from information compiled by Gertrude Bell on her
journeys in Arabia. The guide was first published in the *Arab
Bulletin* in the form of 'Twenty-seven Articles'.

Go easy just for the first few weeks. A bad start is difficult to
atone for, and the Arabs form their judgements on externals that
we ignore. When you have reached the inner circle in a tribe, you
can do as you please with yourself and them. Learn all you can about
your Ashraf and Bedu. Get to know their families, clans and tribes,
friends and enemies, wells, hills and roads. Do all this by listening
and by indirect inquiry. . . . In matters of business deal only with
the commander of the army, column, or party in which you serve.
Never give orders to anyone at all. . . . Win and keep the confidence
of your leader. Strengthen his prestige at your expense before others
when you can. Never refuse or quash schemes he may put forward;
but ensure that they are put forward in the first instance privately to
you. . . . Remain in touch with your leader as constantly and unob-
trusively as you can. Live with him, that at meal times and at
audiences you may be naturally with him in his tent. . . . Be shy of
too close relations with the subordinates of the expedition. . . .
Treat the leader, if a Sherif, with respect. He will return your
manner and you and he will then be alike, and above the rest. Precedence is a serious matter among the Arabs, and you must attain it.
Your ideal position is when you are present and not noticed. . . . To
do your work you must be above jealousies, and you lose prestige if
you are associated with a tribe or clan, and its inevitable feuds.
Sherifs are above all blood-feuds and local rivalries, and form the
only principle of unity among the Arabs. . . . Call your Sherif 'Sidi'
in public and in private. Call other people by their ordinary names,
without title. . . . Wave a Sherif in front of you like a banner and
hide your own mind and person. If you succeed, you will have hundreds of miles of country and thousands of men under your orders,
and for this it is worth bartering the outward show. Cling tight to
your sense of humour. . . . While very difficult to drive, the Bedu are
easy to lead, if you have the patience to bear with them. The less
apparent your interferences the more your influence. . . . Do not try
to do too much with your own hands. Better the Arabs do it tolerably
than you do it perfectly. It is their war, and you are to help them, not
to win it for them. . . . Never receive a present without giving a
liberal return. . . . Wear an Arab headcloth when with a tribe. . . .

If you wear Arab things, wear the best. . . . Dress like a Sherif, if they agree to it.[29] If you wear Arab things at all, go the whole way. Leave your English friends and customs on the coast, and fall back on Arab habits entirely. . . . But the strain of living and thinking in a foreign and half-understood language, the savage food, strange clothes, and stranger ways, with the complete loss of privacy and quiet, and the impossibility of ever relaxing your watchful imitation of the others for months on end, provide such an added stress to the ordinary difficulties of dealing with the Bedu, the climate, and the Turks, that this road should not be chosen without serious thought. Religious discussions will be frequent. Say what you like about your own side, and avoid criticism of theirs. . . . Do not think from their conduct that they are careless. Their conviction of the truth of their faith, and its share in every act and thought and principle of their daily life is so intimate and intense as to be unconscious, unless roused by opposition. . . . Learn the Bedu principles of war as thoroughly and as quickly as you can. . . . Don't play for safety. . . . Do not mix Bedu and Syrians, or trained men and tribesmen. You will get work out of neither, for they hate each other. . . . The beginning and ending of the secret of handling Arabs is unremitting study of them. Keep always on your guard; never say an unnecessary thing: watch yourself and your companions all the time: hear all that passes, search out what is going on beneath the surface, read their characters, discover their tastes and their weaknesses, and keep everything you find out to yourself.[30]

29. It should be noted that Lawrence used to dress like a Sherif and not as a bedouin.
30. *Arab Bulletin* (August 20 1917), No. 60.

4

PUNCHING THE TURK

1. GUEIRA AND WADI MUSA

LET us leave the other two Arab Armies—the Southern one led by Emir Ali and the Eastern one led by Emir Abdullah—perfecting the siege of Medina in a difficult and delicate operation, the full details of which are not generally known, and follow the movements of the Northern Army, with which Lawrence was mainly preoccupied, and through which he focused attention on himself and his activities.

As we have seen, Emir Abdullah favoured the union of the three armies in order to corner the Turkish forces, apply pressure on Medina and strengthen the siege on it until it surrendered. He believed that when this had been achieved, the three armies could march on the countries of the Fertile Crescent and take part in the battles of Iraq and Syria. But since this plan did not have sufficient support, Medina was left alone and all efforts went into strengthening the Northern Army with arms and regular volunteers. Ali and Abdullah had insufficient military resources to meet the Turks on equal terms and cut their communications for good. We have seen that bedouin volunteers, armed with rifles, were not capable of attacking permanent fortifications manned by regulars. In fact the reason that Medina held out for over two years was the lack of an Arab military force sufficient to capture it. It was not the result of a studied plan, as Lawrence later claimed. The Chief of Turkish Intelligence at Ma'an during the war has reported that the Turkish High Command detailed a high-ranking German Officer to meet Fakhri Pasha and discuss with him plans for the evacuation of Medina. Fakhri answered that he would not leave Medina alive and that

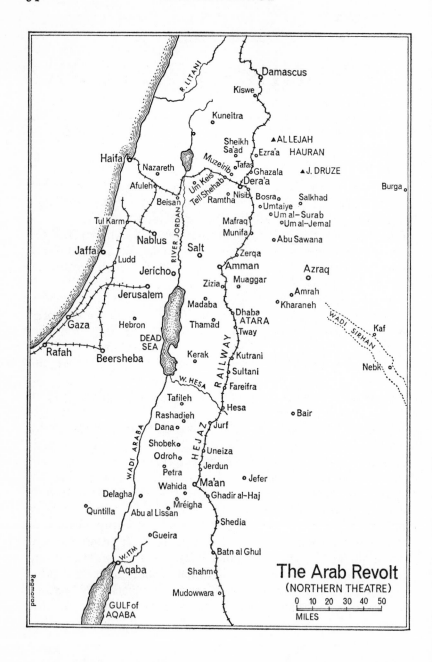

The Arab Revolt
(NORTHERN THEATRE)

0   10   20   30   40   50
MILES

he strongly opposed the idea of evacuation. It is not a secret that the Turks' decision to hold Medina till the bitter end was greatly influenced by this personal stand on the part of Fakhri.

As for the Northern Army, it moved back from Jeida to Wejh after King Hussein agreed to have it transferred to Aqaba. Army units began moving to Aqaba, the first to arrive being Sherif Sharaf and Colonel Rashid Madfa'i with 500 regulars. They were accompanied by Colonel Joyce and a small French contingent with two machine guns. This move took place on 7 August 1917, and the force immediately set up front-line position at Gueira. Ten days later a regular force made up of a thousand officers and men under Ja'afar al-Askari left Wejh accompanied by the rest of the French Detachment under Captain Pisani, with two mountain guns and four machine guns. Finally Feisal arrived at Aqaba on 23 August, with 400 soldiers and the Egyptian company. Following this, the remaining forces arrived at intervals and took up positions facing the Turks.

The Turks meanwhile had become seriously concerned about the approach of Arab forces. Marshal Falkenhayn arrived at Ma'an to supervise the defence plan. Mehmed Jemal Pasha, Commander of the Turkish forces at Ma'an,[1] had at his disposal a force of 6,000 infantry and a battalion of cavalry. The Turks set up strong fortifications at Ma'an, surrounded it with trenches and brought over some aircraft. As soon as they had completed their preparations they sent out a force of two thousand men, which settled first at Abu al-Lissan, then engaged the Arabs in a skirmish at Delagha. The Turks were stopped and they suffered some casualties. The Turkish march on Wadi Delagha took place in the middle of August, and there is no doubt that it was Auda Abu Tayeh and the bedouin at Gueira who stopped the advance of the Turks.

As a result, the Turks did not dare proceed towards Gueira. On 28 and 29 September British aircraft attacked Turkish positions at Ma'an, Fuweila and Abu al-Lissan and dropped a large number of bombs, in retaliation for Turkish air raids on Aqaba and Gueira. The British aeroplanes used a strip of landing-ground which had been hurriedly prepared for them at Quntilla, after their transfer from Wejh.

1. Lawrence claimed that the Commander at Ma'an was Behjat Pasha, while all other sources agree that Mehmed Jemal Pasha was the officer in charge.

It was decided to broaden the battle front against the Turks as a result of the transfer of the Northern Army to Aqaba. The Hashimi Brigade under Maulud Mukhlis moved towards the village of Wadi Musa, adjacent to Petra, and took up positions there. There was a special reason for this move, the inhabitants of Wadi Musa having supported the Revolt from its very beginning.

2. TWO RAIDS ON THE RAILWAY LINE

The military situation was thus beginning to take definite shape with respect to the two opposing sides. Tracing Lawrence's movements, we find that after his hurried visit to Auda's camp at Guiera on 4 August, he spent over two weeks in Egypt, then returned to participate in selecting and marking the landing-ground at Quntilla.

Lawrence wrote of how he spent the last week of August at Aqaba practising on a new method of demolition with the direct firing of the charge by electricity. Arab raids on the railway line around Ma'an had become more concentrated, and Lawrence wished to take part in them.

Here is a summary of Lawrence's detailed description [2] of the raid at the railway line near Haret al-Amareh station:

I left Aqaba on September 7, with the two British gun instructors, and two Sheikhs of the Ageilat Beni Atiyah, from Mudawarrah. . . . We rode gently to Gueira, where were a large camp, little water, and great tribal heartburnings. The three sub-tribes I was relying on were not yet paid, and Audah Abu Tayi was making trouble by his greediness and his attempt to assume authority over all the Huweitat. It was impossible to get either men or camels, so I moved to Rum, five hours S.S.E. of Gueira. . . .

At Rum the Dhumaniyah came in on September 12, mutinous. The situation became unpleasant, so I rode to Akaba, saw Feisal, and returned on the 13th with the promise of twenty baggage camels, and Sherif Abdullah ibn Hamza el Feir, who tried to smooth over the local friction.

On September 15th the camels arrived, and on the 16th we started for Mudowarrah with a force of 116 bedouins, made up of Toweiha, Zuweida, Darausha, Dhumaniyah, Togatga and Zelebani Huweitat, and Ageilat Beni Atiyah. Sheik Za'al was the only capable leader,

2. *Arab Bulletin* (8 October 1917), No. 65.

and Audah's pretensions had made the other sub-tribes determined not to accept his authority. This threw up on me a great deal of detailed work, for which I had no qualifications, and throughout the expedition I had more preoccupation with questions of supply and transport. . . . The Sherif with me, Nasir el-Harith, went blind the first day out and was useless.

We reached Mudowarrah well on September 17, in the afternoon, after thirteen hours march and went down at dusk to the station about three miles further east. We got within 300 yards of it, but could find no position for a Stokes gun. The station is large and the garrison seemed to be between 200 and 300 men, and I was doubtful whether it would be wise to take it on with the rather mixed force I had; so in the end I went back to the well and on 18th moved southward into sandy country. . . .

In the afternoon of September 18, I laid an electric mine, . . . over a culvert at kilo 587 . . . on the 19th about forty men were sent from Haret Ammar . . . to attack us from the south. . . . We detached thirty men to check them, and waited till noon, when a force of about 100 men moved out from Mudowarrah and came slowly down the line, to outflank us on the north. At 1 p.m. a train of two engines and two box-wagons came up slowly from the south, shooting hard at us from loopholes and positions on the carriage roofs. As it passed I exploded the mine under the second engine. . . . The mine derailed the front engine, smashing its cab and tender, destroyed the second engine altogether, and blew in the culvert. . . . The shock affected the Turks, and the Arabs promptly charged up to within twenty yards, and fired at the wagons, which were not armoured. The Turks got out on the far side, and took refuge in the hollow of the bank . . . and fired between the wheels at us. Two Stokes bombs at once fell among them there, and turned them out towards some rough country 200 yards N.E. of the line. On their way there the Lewis gun killed all but about twenty of them, and the survivors threw away their rifles and fled towards Mudowarrah. The action took ten minutes.

The Arabs now plundered the train, while I fired a box of guncotton on the front engine and damaged it more extensively . . . the Turks from the south opened fire on us at long range just as the train surrendered. . . . The baggage in the train was very large and the Arabs went mad over it. . . . I was therefore left with the two British N.C.O.'s and Zaal and Howeimil of the Arabs. . . . The north and south Turkish forces were both coming up fast. . . . I abandoned my own baggage and got away the men and guns to a safe position in the rear. Zaal was there able to collect thirteen men, and at 3 p.m. we counter-attacked the hills and regained our camping ground. We then managed to clear off most of the kit . . . and we retired ridge by ridge from 4.30 p.m. with no losses except four camels.

The Turkish killed amounted to about seventy men, with about thirty wounded. . . . We took . . . sixty-eight . . . prisoners.

We left the same evening, and got to Rum on the night of September
20. . . . The Arab casualties were one killed and four wounded.

Lawrence's description of this raid in the *Arab Bulletin* took
three pages, but in *Seven Pillars* the account filled thirty-two
pages, containing fourteen thousand words in all. In this latter
account he claimed that he looked after 'an ancient and very
tremulous Arab dame' and assured her that she would not be
harmed, and that months later he received from Damascus 'a
letter and a pleasant little Baluchi carpet from the lady Ayesha,
daughter of Jellal el Lel, of Medina, in memory of an odd meeting'.[3] I believe this story to be a fabrication and that the carpet
was part of the booty plundered from the train. Lawrence may
have fabricated the episode to forestall the charge that he shared
with the bedouin this primitive custom of plundering the
enemy, and to endow his story with something of a romantic
flavour. At this point we find Lawrence referring to Za'al as 'our
Leader' and describing him as a first-class horseman and a mar-
vellous shot. In the *Arab Bulletin* Lawrence says that it was he
who exploded the mine, while in *Seven Pillars* he admits that
this was the work of Salem, one of the loyal followers whom
Feisal had sent along with him. He also admits that his part was
to give a signal to Salem. Sherif Nasir in the *Arab Bulletin* becomes Sherif Aid in *Seven Pillars*. But the final proof that the
carpet story was a mere invention is supplied by a letter that
Lawrence himself wrote 'to a friend' on 24 September 1917, two
days after his return from the raid. Having informed his friend
of the part he had played in this raid he went on to say: 'The
Turks then nearly cut us off as we looted the train, and I lost some
baggage, and nearly myself. My loot was a superfine red Baluchi
prayer-rug.' Lawrence later gave this carpet as a present to Lady
Allenby.

Lawrence stayed only a few days at Aqaba, during which time
he prepared a fresh attack on the railway line. The following is
a summary of his description of this new raid, which was directed
against the railway to the south of Shedia station:[4]

I left Akaba on September 27. . . . I took with me Lieutenant
Pisani . . . and three educated Syrians (Faiz and Bedri el-Moayyad,
and Lutfi el Asali), in order to train them in anti-railway tactics. We

3. *Seven Pillars*, p. 371.
4. *Arab Bulletin* (21 October 1917), No. 66.

marched to Rum . . . where we stopped three days. . . . I spent the
time...arranging with Sherif Hashim, a Shenabra, who is O.C., Rum,
details of the Bedouin force required. Feisal's orders to him were to
go where, when, and as I wanted. . . . I appointed Sheikh Salem
Alayan (Dumaniyah) to be O.C. Bedouins, and asked for only
Dumaniyah and Derausha tribesmen . . . I accepted nearly 100
Darausha, and fifty Dumaniyah....

We marched up . . . till midnight, when we found a good place,
and buried an automatic mine at kilo. 500.4. . . . The mine-laying
took the five of us two hours, and then we retired 1,500 yards from the
line and camped. On the 4th no train passed. On the 5th a water-
train came down from Maan at 10 a.m. and went over the mine
without firing it. I waited till mid-day and then, in two hours, laid
an electric mine over the automatic. . . . On the 6th a train (twelve
wagons) came down from Maan. . . . I was sitting to give the signal
for firing. . . . The explosion shattered the fire-box of the locomotive . . .[5] the couplings and the last four wagons drifted backwards
downhill out of fire. I was too late to stop them with a stone. A
Kaimmakam, General Staff, appeared at one window, and fired at us
with a Mauser pistol, but a Bedouin blazed into him at twenty
yards, and he fell back out of sight and I hope damaged. . . . The
eight remaining wagons were captured in six minutes. They contained about seventy tons of foodstuffs. . . . We carried off about a
third of this. . . . The Turkish killed amount to about twenty . . . and
four officers taken prisoner.

The plundering occupied all the energies of our Bedouins, and
Turkish counter-attacks came up unopposed from N. and S. I rolled
up the electric cables first of all, and as they are very heavy and I was
single-handed, it took nearly three-quarters of an hour to do this.
Then two chiefs of the Darausha came to look for me. . . . I felt that
it would be foolish to delay longer alone on the spot, and so rode
off with the two Arabs who had come back for me. We all reached
Rum safely on the 7th, and Akaba on the 8th, where I found telegrams asking me to go to Suez and on to G.H.Q., E.E.F.

The raid was intended as an experiment only, and was most
successful. . . . The Lewis gunners on this occasion were two of my
Arab servants, trained by me in one day at Rum. They killed
twelve of the enemy's casualties, but of course went off to get booty
immediately afterwards.

M. Pisani, Faiz el-Moayyad, and Lutfi El-Asali, are now, I think,
competent to lay mines by themselves.

In his account of this raid Lawrence says, 'during the six
days' trip I had to adjudicate in twelve cases of assault with
weapons, four camel-thefts, one marriage-settlement, fourteen
feuds, two evil eyes, and a bewitchment. These affairs take up all

5. It was Faiz al-Moayyed who fired the mine.

one's spare time.'[6] In the account of the same incident given in
Seven Pillars, a Turkish Colonel fired at Lawrence, cutting the
flesh of his hip. Here a divorce case and two thefts are added. No
mention occurs of the danger that threatened Lawrence because
of the bedouin's pre-occupation with plunder, robbery and escape
with the loot. On the contrary Lawrence says, 'Farraj held my
camel, while Salem and Dheilan helped with the exploder and
the too-heavy wire. Rescue parties of Turks were four hundred
yards away when we had finished, but we rode off without a
man killed or wounded.'[7] We note here that the two Darawsheh
Sheikhs who returned to look for Lawrence have become in *Seven
·Pillars* three persons, who do not seem to be Sheikhs at all.

3. TELL SHEHAB BRIDGE

The Azraq oasis lies on the northern edge of Wadi Sirhan. At
that time it was part of the territory ruled by Nuri as-Sha'alan,
over which the Turks held no jurisdiction, like the rest of the
area east of the railway line. After the forces of the Revolt moved
to Aqaba the importance of Azraq was enhanced, for it became
a vital base and station for the commercial caravans between
Jebel Druze on one side and Feisal's army on the other, carrying
sugar, rice, coffee and textiles, which were not available in Syria
at that time. Azraq also became the main point of contact between Feisal and his Syrian and Druze supporters, particularly
since Arab nationalists were beginning to leave Syria in order
to join the Arab Forces. Accordingly, Feisal began preparations
for the establishment of a front-line position there to serve his
political and military objectives, among which was the task of
encouraging Nuri as-Sha'alan to join the Revolt openly. For this
mission Feisal chose a brave young Sherif, Ali ibn al-Hussein
al-Harithi.

It so happened that Lawrence was then ordered by Allenby
to report immediately to General Headquarters. Lawrence left
Aqaba for Egypt, where Allenby informed him that he was preparing a fresh attack on the Turkish defence line extending
from Gaza to Beersheba, after the failure of two previous attacks
that the British Army had launched on this line. Allenby wanted
to know what the Arabs could do to help his army in his impending attack. Lawrence said:

6. *Arab Bulletin*, No. 66, p. 413.   7. *Op. cit.*, p. 380.

He asked what our railway efforts meant; or rather if they meant anything beyond the melodramatic advertisement they gave Feisal's cause.

I explained my hope to leave the line just working, but only just, to Medina; where Fakhri's corps fed itself at less cost than if in prison at Cairo. The surest way to limit the line without killing it was by attacking trains. The Arabs put into mining a zest absent from their pure demolitions. We could not yet break the line, since railhead was the strongest point of a railway, and we preferred weakness in the nearest enemy neighbour till our regular army was trained and equipped and numerous enough to invest Maan.[8]

Lawrence then spoke of Allenby's plan for attack in October and said:

We [the Arabs] knew, better than Allenby, the enemy hollowness, and the magnitude of the British resources. We under-estimated the crippling effect of Allenby's too plentiful artillery, and the cumbrous intricacy of his infantry and cavalry, which moved only with rheumatic slowness. We hoped Allenby would be given a month's fine weather; and, in that case, expected to see him take, not merely Jerusalem, but Haifa too, sweeping the Turks in ruin through the hills.

Such would be our moment, and we needed to be ready for it in the spot where our weight and tactics would be least expected and most damaging. For my eyes, the centre of attraction was Deraa, the junction of the Jerusalem–Haifa–Damascus–Medina railways, the navel of the Turkish Armies in Syria, the common point of all their fronts; and, by chance, an area in which lay great untouched reserves of Arab fighting men, educated and armed by Feisal from Akaba. We could there use Rualla, Serahin, Serdiyeh, Khoreisha; and, far stronger than tribes, the settled peoples of Huaran and Jebel Druze.

I pondered for a while whether we should not call up all these adherents and tackle the Turkish communications in force. We were certain, with any management, of twelve thousand men: enough to rush Deraa, to smash all the railway lines, even to take Damascus by surprise. Any one of these things would make the position of the Beersheba army critical: and my temptation to stake our capital instantly upon the issue was very sore.

Not for the first or last time service to two masters irked me. I was one of Allenby's officers, and in his confidence: in return, he expected me to do the best I could for him. I was Feisal's adviser, and Feisal relied upon the honesty and competence of my advice so far as often to take it without argument. Yet I could not explain to Allenby the whole Arab situation, nor disclose the full British plan to Feisal.

The local people were imploring us to come. Sheikh Talal el Hareidhin, leader of the hollow country about Deraa, sent in repeated

8. *Seven Pillars*, pp. 380–381.

messages that, with a few of our riders as proof of Arab support, he would give us Deraa. Such an exploit would have done the Allenby business, but was not one which Feisal could scrupulously afford unless he had a fair hope of then establishing himself there. Deraa's sudden capture, followed by a retreat, would have involved the massacre, or the ruin of all the splendid peasantry of the district.

They could only rise once, and their effort on that occasion must be decisive. To call them out now was to risk the best asset Feisal held for eventual success, on the speculation that Allenby's first attack would sweep the enemy before it, and that the month of November would be rainless, favourable to a rapid advance.

I weighed the English army in my mind, and could not honestly assure myself of them. The men were often gallant fighters, but their generals as often gave away in stupidity what they had gained in ignorance. Allenby was quite untried, sent to us with a not-blameless record from France, and his troops had broken down in and been broken by the Murray period. Of course, we were fighting for an Allied victory, and since the English were the leading partners, the Arabs would have, in the last resort, to be sacrificed for them. But was it the last resort? The war generally was going neither well nor very ill, and it seemed as though there might be time for another try next year. So I decided to postpone the hazard for the Arabs' sake.[9]

There is no need for an elaborate explanation of Lawrence's words in the light of fact and truth. The Turkish Army was not 'hollow' as Lawrence claimed, since it was the same army that repulsed the British twice from Gaza with heavy losses in spite of their superiority in numbers and equipment. Had the Turks been as weak as Lawrence would have us believe, why were the British not able to defeat them at a time when the strength of their army amounted to ninety-two thousand against thirty-one thousand Turks? Lawrence's claim that the bedouin and the settled peoples of Hauran and Jebel Druze were ready to rebel does not square with the facts, although it does titillate Arab pride and feeling. There was just not enough enlightenment at that time to spark off such general support. This is especially true of the Druze, most of whom remained on the side of the Turks until the last days of the war, and for further proof we have only to look at the people of Ma'an, who also fought on the side of the Turks for the duration of the war. Added to all this is the fact that Talal al-Hareidhin was not the leader of the hollow country around Dera'a, since the leading Hauran Sheikhs are well known and Talal was of secondary importance in Hau-

9. *Seven Pillars*, pp. 385–386.

ran.. Furthermore, Talal had not yet sent any letters to Feisal. Apart from their exaggeration and boastfulness, Lawrence's claims reveal an astounding ignorance of the psychology of the people and the stage of their development. As for his last statement *that he decided to postpone the hazard* of occupying Dera'a and Damascus, as if the Northern Army were under his personal command, and the people of Hauran and Jebel Druze and the bedouin tribes at his beck and call—this is just a further indication of his inventiveness and conceit.

We can, however, conclude from Lawrence's statement that Allenby had asked him to attempt to cut the railway line at a strategic point at the rear of the Turkish Army. Allenby's aim was to disrupt Turkish communications during the period from 5 to 8 November.

Lawrence returned to Aqaba after having promised to blow up a bridge in the Yarmuk Valley which was the main communication artery between Syria and Palestine. Soon after his return, he wrote an article in the *Arab Bulletin* describing this attempt. Here is a summary of his description of the raid:

I left Akaba on October 24, with Capt. G. Lloyd, Lieut. Wood, R.E. and the Indian Machine Gun Company. The Indians took two Vickers, and I took two Lewis guns with me. We marched to Rum.... We crossed the railway just south of Bir el-Shedia and reached el-Jefer on October 28. Capt. Lloyd returned to Aqaba from there. Sherif Ali ibn Hussein overtook us, and the party marched to Bair, picked up Sheikh Mifleh el-Zebn and fifteen Sukhur and reached Amri on November 2. On November 5 we camped at Kseir el-Hallabat, and on the 7th failed to rush the bridge at Tell el-Shehab, and returned to Kseir. Thence the Indian M.G. Company with Lieut. Wood, returned to Azrak. I went with sixty Arabs to Minefir, blew up a train at Kil. 172 on November 11 and reached Azrak on the 12th.

My intention had been to reach Jisr el-Hemmi on November 3, but this proved impossible, since rain had made the Jaulaan plain too slippery for our camels, and the Turks had put hundreds of woodcutters in the Irbid hills. This closed both the north and south roads, and left Tell el-Shehab.... My first plan was to rush it by camel marches of fifty miles a day. This idea also failed, since by their best efforts the Indian Machine Gun Company were only able to do thirty to thirty-five miles a day, and even this pace cut up their camels very quickly....

. . . I decided, therefore, to raise an Arab force, and descend on the bridge in strength. The Abu Tayi refused to come, only fifteen

Sukhur would take it on, and I had to rely mainly on thirty Serahin recruits at Azrak. . . . For the last stage to the bridge, as hard riding was involved, I picked out six of the Indians, with their officer, and we got actually to the bridge at midnight on November 7. It is a position of some strength, but could, I think, be rushed by twenty decent men. The Indians with me were too few to attempt it, and the Serahin, as soon as the Turks opened fire, dumped their dynamite into the valley and bolted. In the circumstances I called everyone off as quickly as possible and went back to Kseir el-Hallabat. The Indians with us were very tired with the ride. . . . The Bedu and the Sherif wanted to do something more before returning to Azrak. . . .

The situation was explained to the Sherif, who said it would be enough to mine a train, without making a machine gun attack upon it. The Bedu agreed, and we went off together. The party was composed of Sherif Ali with ten servants, myself with one, twenty Sukhur and thirty Serahin. None of us had any food at all. We went to Minifir, to Kil. 172, where I mined the line in June last. As the Bedu had lost my dynamite at the bridge I was only able to put 30 lbs. into the mine, which I laid on the crown of a four meter culvert . . . and took the wires as far up the hill-side toward cover as they would reach. Owing to the shortage of cable this was only sixty yards, and we had to leave the ends buried, for fear of patrols. A train came down before dawn on the 10th, too fast for me to get to the exploder from my watching place. In the morning of the 10th a train of refugees came up at four miles an hour from the south. The exploder failed to work, and the whole train crawled past me as I lay on the flat next the wires. For some reason no one shot at me, and after it had passed I took the exploder away and overhauled it, while a Turkish patrol came up and searched the ground very carefully. That night we slept on the head of the wires, and no train appeared, till 10 a.m. on November 11. Then a troop train of twelve coaches and two locomotives came down from the north at twenty miles an hour. I touched off under the engine and the explosion was tremendous. Something must have happened to the boiler for I was knocked backwards and boiler plates flew about in all directions. One fragment smashed the exploder, which I therefore left in place, with the wires. The first engine fell into the valley on the east side of the line; the second upended into the space where the culvert had been, and toppled over on to the tender of the first. . . . Meanwhile I made quite creditable time across the open, up-hill towards the Arabs, who had a fair position, and were shooting fast over me into the coaches, which were crowded with soldiers. The Turkish losses were obviously quite heavy. Unfortunately many of the Serahin had no rifles, and could only throw unavailing stones. The Turks took cover behind the bank, and opened a fairly hot fire at us. They were about 200 strong by now. Sherif Ali brought down a party of twenty-two to meet me, but lost seven killed and more wounded and had some narrow escapes himself before getting back.

The train may have contained someone of importance, for there were a flagged saloon-car. . . . The Turks, seeing us so few, put in an attack later which cost them about twenty casualties, and then began to work up the slopes to right and left of us. So we went off, and reached Azrak next day. . . .

The march also showed the staying qualities of the Bedouins. They rode ninety miles without food or rest on the 8th, ate a small meal on the morning of the 9th and sat out hungry two nights and three days of bitterly cold wind and rain. . . .[10]

This article was about two and a half pages long, but in *Seven Pillars* he devoted sixty-seven pages, or close to thirty thousand words, to an elaborate description of every detail. We might recall at this point that the raid took thirty-fours days (24 October to 26 November) and that the raiders took a crescent-like route, to avoid contact with enemy posts and installations. That route extended over 420 miles from Aqaba to the Yarmuk river. Lawrence's account in *Seven Pillars* includes many details which have no direct connexion with the Revolt, but which none the less illustrate part of the general framework within which the Revolt was operating. The path was certainly not strewn with roses and scented herbs. During the raid in question Lawrence displayed the same fortitude and patience in the face of difficulties as on other occasions, and it is important to acknowledge the merits of his purely military efforts.

We find Lawrence showering praise on Sherif Ali ibn al-Hussein al-Harithi, saying that Ali was a physically splendid young man who could outstrip a trotting camel on his feet, keep his speed over half a mile and then leap into the saddle. According to Lawrence Ali had also distinguished himself in Feisal's early raids around Medina and later had 'out-newcombed Newcombe' about Ula; he was of proved courage, resource and energy.

There had never been any adventure, since our beginning, too dangerous for Ali to attempt, nor a disaster too deep for him to face with his high yell of a laugh. . . . He was impertinent, headstrong, conceited; as reckless in word as in deed . . . and fairly educated for a person whose native ambition was to excel the nomads of the desert in war and sport.[11]

10. *Arab Bulletin* (16 December 1917), No. 73.
11. *Seven Pillars*, p. 388.

Lawrence also says that Ali, having been Jemal's guest in Damascus, had learned something about Syria.

But Lawrence did not have one word of praise for Abdul Kader al-Jezairi. Abdul Kader, he said:

. . . had been enlarged by the Turks upon request of the Khedive Abbas Hilmi, and sent down by him on private business to Mecca. He went there, saw King Hussein, and came back with a crimson banner, and noble gifts, his crazy mind half-persuaded of our right, and glowing jerkily with excitement.

To Feisal he offered the bodies and souls of his villagers, sturdy, hard-smiting Algerian exiles living compactly along the north bank of the Yarmuk. We seized at the chance this would give us to control for a little time the middle section of the Valley railway, including two or three main bridges. . . .

While we were in this train of mind arrived a telegram from Colonel Bremond, warning us that Abd el Kader was a spy in pay of the Turks. It was disconcerting. We watched him narrowly, but found no proof of the charge. . . .

Feisal told Abd el Kader to ride with Ali and myself. . . . His pride was hurt by our companionship; for the tribes greeted Ali as greater, and treated me as better, than himself. His bullet-headed stupidity broke down Ali's self-control twice or thrice into painful scenes. . . .[12]

Lawrence goes on to say that Abdul Kader accompanied them as far as Azraq, whence he left stealthily with his seven followers to Jebel Druze. He adds that he later learned from the Emir of Salkhad that Abdul Kader unfolded the banner of the Revolt as he entered Jebel Druze and that, in reply to a Turkish protest, he threatened to behead Jemal Pasha. He went on in this defiant manner to Dera'a without being hampered by the Turks, who knew of his craziness. They did not even believe his statement that the Arabs were planning to blow up the Yarmuk bridge.

We recall here that Lawrence made no mention of Abdul Kader in his report. He stated that, because of the rain and numerous wood-cutters working for the Turks, there was no longer room for an attempt at Himma in the Yarmuk valley. Lawrence's arguments here do not hold water because the soil of Ramtha, through which the raiders passed, was no shallower than that of the Irbid area. He was forgetting the steep descent of the Yarmuk valley, which is impossible for camels. We may add that the villages owned by the family of Abdul Kader lie

12. *Seven Pillars*, pp. 389–390.

on the northern side of the Yarmuk valley and that it was very difficult to get to the Himma bridge through these villages. Surely in two days' time the Turks would have been able to cut off the raiders on their way back, inflict severe losses on them and ruthlessly punish all their supporters. There is no doubt that Lawrence was piqued by Abdul Kader's haughtiness, and he accused him of religious fanaticism and derided his refusal to march with him in the same procession. We shall see that later, after the Arabs had entered Damascus, Lawrence quarrelled with Abdul Kader and accused him of working against the interests of the Revolt.

Emir Mohammed Said al-Jezairi has informed me that his brother Abdul Kader fled from Bursa (formerly Brusa) in Anatolia, to which the Turks had exiled him and travelled to Mecca on a Pilgrimage. King Hussein welcomed him and gave him a banner of the Revolt, which Abdul Kader promised to raise in Syria. The King requested him to go to Aqaba and make the necessary arrangements with Feisal. But Abdul Kader 'was surprised at Aqaba by his introduction to Lawrence, the British spy'. Feisal asked him to help blow up the Tell Shehab Bridge. Abdul Kader objected to this but Feisal replied, 'We are obliged to go along with these people, because we are fighting with the help of their money and their arms.' So Abdul Kader accompanied them to Azraq, where he informed al-Harithi and Lawrence that his spirit was not in this operation, and that he wished to travel on to Syria and raise the banner of the Revolt there.

In the event Lawrence, George Lloyd, Lieutenant Wood and the Indians reached Rum first, where they were later joined by Ali al-Harithi and Abdul Kader. Lawrence and his companions crossed the railway line and he stated that they heard gunfire from afar and realized that Ali and Abdul Kader were being intercepted by the Turks while crossing the line. Lawrence went on until he reached Jefer where he was hospitably received by Auda Abu Tayeh. A few hours later Ali arrived with the news that he had lost two men in the skirmish with the Turks.

At Jefer Lawrence did not find the support which he had expected. He did not say whether he talked to Auda and requested his help, but he did state that Za'al neither welcomed nor encouraged the idea, saying that it involved great dangers and that he would take part in it only if Lawrence personally requested him to do so. Lawrence tells us nothing of the attitude of Ali al-Harithi, the official leader of the raid and the man whom the bedouin regarded as Feisal's representative. Lawrence rejects Za'al's argument, saying that success had changed him completely and made him a prudent man, whose new wealth made life precious to him.

Lloyd returned from Jefer to Aqaba while Lawrence, according to his own statement, spent the night with the Huweitat working to smooth over troubles between Auda and his men, who were disputing as to the method Auda should use in distributing the money he was receiving from Feisal. He claims, of course, that he succeeded in producing amity between them, without mentioning Ali or Abdul Kader.

The raiders left Jefer and moved northwards. In Bair they were received enthusiastically by Sheikh Mifleh al-Zebn. They spoke to Mifleh about their intended raid, and he agreed to accompany them with fifteen of the best warriors in his tribe, including his seventeen-year-old son Turki. At this point we find some contradiction in Lawrence's statements, since initially he had said that the purpose of the raid was to blow up a bridge in the Yarmuk valley with the help of Abdul Kader's followers, and that because of Abdul Kader's help they decided to do away with the Huweitat and Beni Sakhr. This hardly squares with his later statement that he tried in vain to enlist some Huweitat for the raid, and that he and Ali ibn al-Hussein succeeded in securing the help of Beni Sakhr, while Abdul Kader, who was still with them, had shown no signs until then of intending to break the pledge he had given.

The considerably augmented party left Bair, and as they passed through Qasr Amrah they were met by two Sakhr horsemen, Fahad and his brother Adhoub of al-Zebn clan, who had come to join the campaign. Accompanied by these two they next came across fighting men of the Serhan tribe who were on their way to swear allegiance to Feisal at Aqaba, and to offer their services to the Revolt. After exchanging greetings they returned together to the Serhan tents at Ain al-Beidha, a few miles east of Azraq. There the question of which route to take and which bridge to demolish came up again. The Serhan said that the western bridge at Himma was impossible because no party could slip through undetected by the hundreds of military wood-cutters with whom the Turks had littered the forests in the area. According to Lawrence the Serhan professed great suspicion of Abdul Kader and his villages. As for Tell Shehab, they feared lest the villagers, their traditional enemies, attack them in the rear. The Serhan agreed to take part in the raid only after considerable persuasion on the part of Ali ibn al-Hussein and the Zebn Sheikhs, Mifleh, Fahad and Adhoub.

The party then reached Azraq, where, according to Lawrence, they missed Abdul Kader, discovering a short while later that he and his followers had left them stealthily in the direction of Jebel Druze. It thus became impossible for them to reach Wadi Khaled, and the party feared that Abdul Kader would betray them to the Turks, who could easily trap them at the bridge. It seemed to them then that Tell Shehab was their only possible target. However, after taking the advice of Fahad, they decided to push on none the less, 'trusting to the usual incompetence'[13] of the enemy. On their march they passed through Wadi al-Harith and Abu Sawana, crossed the railway line and reached Ghadir al-Abyadh, north of Mafraq. On the recommendation of Mifleh they decided to spend the day at this rocky depression. During that time Ali and Lawrence made final arrangements: they must reach Tell Shehab, blow up the bridge and get back east of the railway by dawn. This was a ride of at least eighty miles; therefore they needed to pick their best camels and best riders. The Indians had been tired out by the march from Aqaba, so Lawrence picked out their six best riders armed with Vickers machine-guns. It was decided that the Beni Sakhr would be their storming party, while part of the Serahin would carry the explosives. The rest of the Serahin were to remain with the camels and the Indians. Thus the party in the last stage consisted of Ali al-Harithi and his followers, Lawrence, Lieutenant Wood and the Indians, forty Serahin and twenty Beni Sakhr. The Arabs and the Indians who were left behind were instructed to return during the night to Abu Sawana and remain there until they were joined by their raiding comrades.

A little after dusk on the evening of 6 November, the party left Ghadir al-Abyadh heading north, guided by Mifleh. They

13. *Seven Pillars*, p. 415.

rode into the plain east of Ramtha, then took a straight route
to the edge of the valley overlooking the Tell Shehab Bridge,
where the Yarmuk waters formed a great waterfall that dinned
loudly in the ears. Mifleh brought his camel to her knees and
the rest followed suit. The men then started their march towards
the bridge, fifteen of them carrying sacks of dynamite. The Beni
Sakhr men under Adhoub sank into the dark slopes before them
to scout the way. They reached the bridge and saw the guard's
tent pitched under the wall of the opposite bank. The Indians
took up their position opposite the Turkish guard, while Ali,
Lawrence, the Beni Sakhr, and the Serahin marched to the railway line just before it curved to the bridge. As their leaders
were preparing to start their work a bedouin accidentally
dropped his rifle. The sound was heard by the Turkish guard,
who challenged loudly and fired. The rest of the guards rushed
into their trenches and opened fire. The Serahin had previously
learned that gelatine would go off if hit, so they dropped the sacks
over the edge and fled. After that the rest of the men retreated,
there being no hope of success once they had lost their supply
of dynamite. Each man hurried to his camel and the retreat
started along the same road they had taken a little earlier. The
firing and clamour woke the neighbouring villagers, who gave
chase but were unable to overtake the raiders. At length the
party reached Abu Sawana, where their companions were
waiting.

4. THE MUNIFA TRAIN

They were all feeling bitter because of the failure to achieve
the object for which they had risked their lives. They started
thinking of another attempt of some sort to make up for their
failure. They still had some reserve sticks of gelatine and Ali
al-Harithi suddenly said, 'let us blow up a train'. His words
were heard with universal joy, but the raiders were faced with
another obstacle—their supply of food had run out, and although
the bedouin could have borne hunger without difficulty, the
Indians, who possessed the only effective weapons, namely the
machine-guns, could not. There was no point in risking an
attack on a train without adequate means of defence and with
no means of attacking the passengers. In answer to Lawrence's
hesitation, Ali said that it would be enough to blow up the

train, leaving the rest of the task to him and the bedouin. The Indians and Lieutenant Wood accordingly left for Azraq, while the rest—about sixty warriors—headed west towards the railway line.

The first thing they did was to hide the explosive in the arch of the culvert at km.172 at Munifa. The men tied their animals behind a hill to the north of the culvert and lay in wait for the arrival of the expected train. On the following day a short train rushed by at speed before they could attach the wire to the exploder; so they had to sit and wait. Watchmen were posted to the north and south on the hill-tops to notify them of the approach of the next train. It was a difficult and cheerless watch because of the cold, the wind, the constant drizzle and the lack of food. At noon another train passed by and Lawrence pushed down the handle of the exploder, but nothing happened. Lawrence said that he was in great danger because the coaches of the train were full of soldiers; but they ignored him thinking he was a casual bedouin.

They passed their second night at Munifa under the bare sky. In the morning a third train came and they were able to see clearly that it had two engines and twelve passenger coaches. Lawrence touched off under the first locomotive on the bridge, and there was a tremendous explosion. Lawrence says that the ground spouted blackly into his face and he was sent spinning, to sit up with the shirt torn to his shoulder and the blood dripping from his left arm. He felt a great pain in his right foot but hopped on it towards the upper valley. There the Arabs were shooting into the crowded coaches, while the enemy began to return fire. Finding himself between the two parties Lawrence lay down on the ground:

> Ali saw me fall, and thinking that I was hard hit ran out, with Turki and about twenty men of his servants and the Beni Sakhr, to help me. The Turks found their range and got seven of them in a few seconds. The others, in a rush, were about me—fit models, after their activity, for a sculptor. . . .
> We scrambled back into cover together, and there, secretly, I felt myself over, to find I had not once been really hurt; though besides the bruises and cuts of the boiler-plate and a broken toe, I had five different bullet-grazes on me (some of them uncomfortably deep) and my clothes ripped to pieces.[14]

14. *Seven Pillars*, p. 431

It became clear that the explosion had destroyed the arch of the culvert, wrecked the first engine, toppled the second locomotive, derailed the first three waggons and destroyed them. One of the coaches was a saloon decorated with flags and it was later discovered that Mehmed Jemal Pasha, commander of the Eighth Army Corps, was one of the passengers. Ali and his men soon realized that they had no chance of a fight against the four hundred officers and men on the train, and although some bedouin were able to get very close to the train and pick up about sixty rifles and odd pieces of luggage, they had to withdraw in the face of heavy fire from the Turks. Then they discovered that Sheikh Fahad was missing and some of them thought he had been hit in his first attempt to rescue Lawrence. So Adhoub raced downhill followed by Mifleh, and they soon returned with Fahad. He had been hit by a bullet which passed through his face and tongue and knocked out four teeth. He had fallen unconscious, but had revived a little later and was trying to crawl up the hill.

The Turks began to march towards the Arabs and when they came sufficiently close, the Arabs suddenly opened up on them with heavy rifle fire, killing twenty men, while the others were forced to retreat. They soon marched again from two sides in an attempt to surround the Arab position, and the latter had to withdraw in haste. Lawrence was dragging along, so Ali and Turki had to stay behind the others and protect him from the Turks. Finally they reached the place where they had left their camels, on which they made their way east as fast as they could; on the next day, 12 November, they reached Azraq.

It is worth noting here that in their attempt to rescue Lawrence after the explosion, the Arabs lost seven men while several others were seriously injured. Ali al-Harithi himself had a very narrow escape. This makes it clear that the Arabs were innocent of the accusation made by the prejudiced who said that they were fighting merely for money and booty. If they had been they would not have faced death and suffered these losses. They were fighting for their ideals. Lawrence indeed owed them his life in this engagement, as in the other adventures he underwent in their company. The fact that he came safely through all his adventures and travels in Arab countries testifies to Arab loyalty, nobility and courage. Is there a greater sacrifice a warrior can make than to risk his life for a comrade-in-arms?

It is fortunate that Sheikh Adhoub al-Zebn[15] and Sheikh Turki al-Mifleh are still alive, and I had the chance to speak to them while I was preparing this book. They both recall the events of the Arab Revolt very well after forty-four years, and can still remember Lawrence clearly. I was informed by both that the Zebn Sheikhs, Fahad, Mifleh and Adhoub had been in touch with the leaders of the Revolt since the arrival of Sherif Nassir at the Huweitat tents in June 1917. Adhoub said that he, together with sixty Beni Sakhr horsemen, had gone to meet Sherif Nassir at Bair, where they offered to join the expedition he was leading. The Sherif pointed out the dangers to which their families would be exposed if they joined him, since the Turks were sure to take their revenge on them. He advised them to return and move their tents to the desert east of the railway line, and join him afterwards. Turki said that Mifleh, his father, had gone to Bair because of a previous agreement between him and Auda Abu Tayeh. As soon as Adhoub returned to the tents of his tribe, they were attacked by a Turkish force in combination with some Balqa tribes. As a result of the engagement, the Zebn tribe had to retreat, and their encampment was plundered by the attackers. Both sides lost a few men. Adhoub informed me that he and Fahad had joined Feisal later at Aqaba. A month before the raid on Tell Shehab, Feisal had told them that he was going to entrust them with a special task, details of which would be revealed at the proper time. Adhoub and Fahad then returned to their tents and waited for Feisal's instructions, while Mifleh al-Zebn was in turn expecting the arrival of Sherif Ali. Mifleh eventually sent a messenger to Adhoub and Fahad informing them of Sherif Ali's arrival. They hurried out, with seven of their relatives, to meet him. When the party reached Ghadir al-Abyadh, Adhoub, at the Sherif's request, went out to scout the Tell Shehab route. Having reached the edge of the valley overlooking the bridge, he returned to Ghadir al-Abyadh and informed the Sherif that the road was safe. At sunset the party set out for the bridge, but the Turkish watch heard their footsteps on the rails, called out and, receiving no answer, opened fire. Adhoub criticized the plan of attack, saying that they would

15. After returning from Tell Shehab, Lawrence wrote a letter dated 13 November 1917 from Azraq to Colonel Joyce in which he said that he had found Mifleh, Fahad, and Adhoub at Bair and that they had done most splendidly. 'I think them three of the best Arab sheiks I have met . . .' (Selected Letters, p. 107).

definitely have succeeded if they had gone straight to blow up the columns of the bridge, where the sound of the falling water would have prevented the Turkish guard from hearing their movements. On their return, they were chased by another Beni Sakhr clan, but Adhoub recognized their Sheikh and went to him with the news that they were a Sherifian party, which settled the matter. Adhoub and Turki could remember the train incident clearly, and insisted that Lawrence was more than 200 metres from the culvert. Turki said that he and Sherif Ali were standing beside Lawrence when he touched off the explosives. Adhoub told me that nine people were killed and twelve wounded in the attack on the train, because the Turks were firing a machine-gun, and both stated that Jemal Pasha's aide-de-camp was among those killed on the train. Among the Arab casualties was Hmoud, a slave of Emir Feisal and a courageous horseman nick-named Emir (Prince). Turki said that after the return to Azraq Lawrence gave him four handfuls of gold.

Feisal's instructions required Ali al-Harithi to remain in Azraq and convert it into a front-line base for establishing contact with Syria, spreading Revolt propaganda, collecting information, and strengthening ties with Nuri as-Sha'alan and the Ruwalla tribes. Together with the Indians and his own men he repaired the old fort for this purpose, and despatched a caravan to Jebel Druze for provisions. When his presence at Azraq became known, delegations representing various bedouin tribes, Jebel Druze and Hauran began to arrive daily to offer their allegiance. It soon became clear that this base was becoming a shelter for all those who were dissatisfied with Turkish rule in Syria, as well as for Arab military men who wished to desert the Turkish Army. Even the Armenians began to pour in. Lawrence seized this opportunity to praise Ali once more, saying that he was Feisal's greatest asset in the north and that his imposing and delightful personality was an effective factor in attracting people and convincing them of the rightness of Arab Revolt.

No one could see him without the desire to see him again; especially when he smiled, as he did rarely, with both mouth and eyes at once. His beauty was a conscious weapon. He dressed spotlessly, all in black or all in white; and he studied gesture.

Fortune had added physical perfection and unusual grace, but these qualities were only the just expression of his powers. They made

obvious the pluck which never yielded, which would have let him be
cut to pieces, holding on.[16]

5. THE LEGEND OF DERA'A

Lawrence took up residence in one of the rooms of the fort, and
he has described the arrival of the delegations and the manner in
which Ali received them; he has also described the rain, the
storm, the visiting and love songs in the night. In Lawrence's
table of movements we note that he spent ten days in Azraq
before he left for Aqaba. It is clear from his account of the many
things he saw that he spent the whole period in Azraq, but he
claims on the other hand that in the last days of his stay he
went out on an adventure which in its pecularities and its events
surpassed all his previous and subsequent enterprises. Here is a
summary of this alleged adventure, which I give at this point,
although I am thoroughly convinced that it never happened
at all:

> ... Very painfully I drew myself again in to the present, and forced
> my mind to say that it must use this wintry weather to explore the
> country lying round about Deraa.
> As I was thinking how I would ride, there came to us, unheralded,
> one morning in the rain, Talal el Hareidhin, sheikh of Tafas. He was
> a famous outlaw with a price upon his head; but so great that he
> rode about as he pleased. In two wild years he had killed, according
> to report, some twenty-three of the Turks. His six followers were
> splendidly mounted, and himself the most dashing figure of a man
> in the height of Hauran fashion. ...
> He swaggered to our coffee-hearth, as a man sure of his welcome,
> greeting Ali boisterously. ... He was ardently ours, and we rejoiced,
> since his name was one to conjure with in Hauran. When a day had
> made me sure of him, I took him secretly to the palm-garden, and
> told him my ambition to see his neighbourhood. The idea delighted
> him, and he companioned me for the march as thoroughly and cheer-
> fully as only a Syrian on a good horse could. Halim and Faris, men
> specially engaged, rode with me as guards.
> We went past Umtaiye, looking at tracks, wells and lava-fields,
> crossed the line to Sheikh Saad, and turned south to Tafas, where
> Talal was at home. Next day we went on to Tell Arar, a splendid
> position closing the Damascus railway and commanding Deraa.
> Afterwards we rode through tricky rolling country to Mezerib on the
> Palestine railway; planning, here also, for the next time; when with
> men, money and guns we should start the general rising to win
> inevitable victory. ...

16. *Seven Pillars*, p. 437.

Properly to round off this spying of the hollow land of Hauran, it was necessary to visit Deraa, its chief town. . . . Talal, however, could not venture in with me since he was too well known in the place. So we parted from him . . . and rode southward along the line until near Deraa. There we dismounted. The boy, Halim took the ponies, and set off for Nisib, south of Deraa. My plan was to work round the railway station and town with Faris, and reach Nisib after sunset. . . .[17]

According to Lawrence's account, he exchanged clothes with Halim, and walked barefoot with Faris. He was still limping from the broken foot acquired when Jemal's train was blown up. They entered the town, surveyed the station and the aerodrome, then:

Someone called out in Turkish, we walked on deafly; but a sergeant came after, and took me roughly by the arm, saying 'the Bey wants you'. There were too many witnesses for fight or flight, so I went readily. He took no notice of Faris.[18]

After that Lawrence described in detail how he was taken to Nahi Bey, and how Nahi wanted him to fulfil his pleasure; how he refused and kicked the Turkish officer in his stomach. Nahi was enraged, and ordered three of his men to teach Lawrence a lesson, first pulling up a fold of flesh over Lawrence's ribs himself, and working the point of his bayonet through till the blood trickled down his side. Lawrence went on to describe how the three men then flogged him mercilessly until he bled all over and lost consciousness. A corporal kicked Lawrence with his nailed boot and damaged one of his ribs. They then carried him back to Nahi Bey, who rejected him in haste, 'as a thing too torn and bloody for his bed'.[19] Then they took him to the room next door, where he spent the night. Before dawn he put on a suit of shoddy clothes which he had found in the room, slipped out of the window and left the town. To the south he found a valley, which seemed to provide the hidden road by which their projected raid could attain Dera'a, and surprise the Turks. 'So, in escaping I solved, too late, the problem which had brought me to Dera'a.'[20] Further on Lawrence came across a bedouin of the Serdyeh on his way to Nisib, who had pity on him and mounted him on his camel. In the village he found his two comrades Halim and Faris, and the three went on horseback to Azraq. Although

17. *Seven Pillars*, pp. 439–441.   18. *Ibid.*, p. 442.
19. *Ibid.*, p. 445.   20. *Ibid.*, p. 446.

Lawrence veiled his statements in mystery, he claimed, in a private letter he later wrote to Charlotte Shaw, wife of Bernard Shaw, that Nahi Bey did actually violate him in Dera'a, but that he could not muster up enough courage to reveal the truth in his book.

This is the account as Lawrence gave it and it was taken by his biographers to be the truth. I find the whole story highly implausible. We must bear in mind that the period Lawrence spent at Azraq did not exceed ten days (12–22 November). Surely this was too short a time for Lawrence to recover from the wounds he suffered during the attack on the train; the five bullets that grazed different parts of his body 'some of them uncomfortably deep' and the broken toe? How could he also have spent part of this period witnessing the arrival at Azraq of the caravans of bedouin, Haurani, Druse and Armenians seeking Ali al-Harithi? No matter what we believe about Lawrence's agility, strength and wiriness, he was still flesh and blood. It would have taken at least five days to travel from Azraq to Tafas, spend some time as Talal's guest, wander in Tell Arar, Sheikh Saad and Muzeirib, and spend one night in Dera'a and one in Nisib. Are we to suppose that he recovered from his wounds, regained his complete health and saw all that he did in five short days? And after that notorious night which he claimed to have gone through in Dera'a, how could he have returned immediately to Azraq, then travelled directly to Aqaba on a four-hundred-mile trip, which would have taken four days of constant travel? One could not expect any human body to regain its strength in less than a fortnight after the torture he claimed to have suffered at Dera'a. But here we have a man who has been at the point of death during the night, beginning a strenuous journey the following morning. Besides, whereabouts was the hidden road he claimed to have discovered? Surely all the roads leading to Dera'a would have been well known to the Hauran people supporting the Revolt? In any case, Dera'a is open on all four sides on to the Hauran plain; it is certainly not situated in an inaccessible mountainous area. Last but not least, we cannot fail to wonder why Lawrence ignored Dera'a and his alleged visit to it in his report published in the *Arab Bulletin,* and why he remained silent about it during the years preceding the writing of *Seven Pillars of Wisdom*?

Nassir al-Fawaz has informed me that the Governor and O.C. of the garrison at Dera'a during the war was Hajem Muhyi al-Din Bey, who afterwards returned to his home-town Ismir and became a member of the Turkish National Assembly. He was not the kind of man who would degrade himself in the way described by Lawrence, nor would he have allowed anything of the kind to happen within his command. Faiz al-Ghussein has also assured me that he is fully convinced the episode never happened at all, but is purely imaginary. He attributes it to Lawrence's literary inclinations. It is unfortunate that Talal, the only witness, was killed during the war. As for Faris and Halim, they are two names that Lawrence must have picked up as they are very common among the Arabs. I have not found one person in Transjordan and Syria who had heard of this story or knew anything about it. Not fully satisfied with all this I visited Dera'a and Tafas and interviewed some old men, one of whom was a close companion of Talal. I was assured that Talal spent the last two years of the War in Jebel Druze to avoid being arrested by the Turks. He never came back to Hauran until September 1918 when he accompanied the Arab Expedition and was killed in the fighting.

The weather at Azraq was very bad, with storms and snow. Lawrence decided to return to Aqaba. He handed over what money he had to Sherif Ali, commended the Indians to his care and took leave of him in an emotional parting. He then took one of his followers, Raheil by name, and the two travelled south on their camels. He tells us of his great will-power, which demanded that he bear the difficulties of travel patiently. He passed through Wadi Butom, Bair and Jefer. He tells us that he was so tired that he began to feel faint, until he found himself 'Divided into two parts'. When he approached Rumm, he was swaying to the right and left on his camel, lost in a heavy drowsiness which was like the swoon of dying. Raheil collected him out of his death-sleep by jerking his head-stall and striking him, while he shouted that they had lost their direction.

Lawrence reached Aqaba on 26 November. Twelve days later he boarded a plane for General Allenby's camp, fearing all the time Allenby's wrath because of the failure of the Yarmuk Bridge raid. Allenby, however, had inflicted a series of defeats on the Turks, capturing Beersheba (31 October), Gaza (7 November) and Jerusalem (9 December); so Lawrence's failure did not really worry him. As a staff officer to General Clayton, Lawrence had the opportunity of entering Jerusalem with Allenby. He said that for him the moment of entering Jerusalem was 'the supreme moment of the war'.

Luck served Lawrence once again. General Allenby delegated Colonel Newcombe at the head of a small force, British and Arab, to assist in the attack on Gaza and Beersheba by way of engaging in military activities behind enemy lines. Newcombe conducted successful operations near Hebron and drew back part of the Turkish forces, which he continued to engage until his detachment was compelled to surrender. Consequently, Lawrence was left without a competitor of note in the field of demolition.

At this point we may pause a little to take a look at Lawrence's activities after the conquest of Aqaba on 6 July 1917:

7 July–3 August: Egypt and Jedda.

4–5 August: Aqaba and Gueira.

6–16 August: Egypt.

17 August–6 September: Aqaba and Quntilla.

7–22 September: Railway raid at Harat al-Amareh (a culvert and a train destroyed).

27 September–9 October: Railway raid at Bir Shedia (a bridge and a train destroyed).

10–14 October: Egypt.

15–23 October: Aqaba.

24 October–26 November: Tell Shehab raid (a culvert and a train destroyed).

27 November–25 December: Aqaba, Gaza, Cairo, Jerusalem.

This table shows that Lawrence spent no more than 30 days at Aqaba, Northern Army Headquarters, spread out over a period of nearly six months, and he was away from all fighting for nearly two months. He used his technical experience to participate in exploding mines in three raids, which were always led by one of the Sherifs. We have seen that the Harat al-Amareh raid got out of control because he tried to act independently. The bedouin almost rebelled against him and he had to return to

Aqaba and seek Feisal, who sent a Sherif and a number of his
own men with him, after which the raid went well.

Had Lawrence been the leader of the Revolt, or of its Northern
Army—as his admirers would have us believe—he would have
spent most of his time at his own headquarters—supervising
his ever-growing army, sending expeditions to the several fronts,
issuing orders for the movements of his military units, co-ordinating plans, equipping the army and discharging the responsibilities that are the business of an army commander.

The fact is that the command of the army was in the hands
of Feisal and his high-ranking officers, such as Ja'afar al-Askari,
Nuri as-Said and Maulud Mukhlis. In conducting Bedouin
affairs and running their raids, Feisal depended on a number
of Sherifs who, owing to their special position and their kinship
to Feisal, were especially qualified to play this role. A mere
glance at the activities of Emir Zeid and Sherifs Nassir, Ali, Ibn
Areid, Abdul Mu'in, Shakrani, Mastur and Tekheimi, would
reveal the important part they played in directing the Bedouin
and leading their raids.

During the long stretches when Lawrence was away in Egypt
and Palestine, or when, as we have seen, he was accompanying a raid, the Northern Army, with its regular and
irregular forces, was engaging the enemy in a series of hard
battles, both in front-line positions and on light raids. Lawrence,
of course, played a part, but it was a part that did not, by any
means, amount to actual leadership of the army; nor was it the
role of a chief adviser to the commander.

It remains for us to make a brief survey of the activities of the
Northern Army during this and subsequent periods, in order
to give the reader a general impression of the situation, not
forgetting that the Eastern and Southern Armies were engaged
to their maximum capacity in the Median area.

5

REGULAR AND IRREGULAR

1. THE ATTACKS BY THE BENI ATIYEH

AFTER the occupation of Aqaba, Sherif Nassir set up head-quarters there, while Auda Abu Tayeh settled at Gueira, half way between Aqaba and Ma'an.

The Turks were facing considerable physical problems, the most important being lack of water and bad roads between Ma'an and Aqaba. It was these difficulties—in addition to the lack of a sufficient regular force—that prevented them from launching an all-out attack on Aqaba. But they did not prevent the daily bombing of Arab positions at Gueira, and they also carried out a few raids on Aqaba itself. British aircraft retaliated on 28 August and next day dropped thirty-two bombs on Ma'an, followed by seventy-four bombs on Fuweilah and Abu al-Lissan.

At first the Turks had taken up position at Fuweila and Abu al-Lissan, and then they marched on Delagha, west of Abu al-Lissan, but Auda attacked them and compelled them to retreat to Wahida with losses.

The Arab front extended north to Ghrandal and Wadi Musa. A report dated 27 August stated that the regular troops at Aqaba reached a total of 2,000 under the command of Ja'afar Pasha. They consisted of 1,600 infantry divided into two regiments, 300 cavalry and camel corps, and 150 artillery. Ja'afar was busy training this force with the help of a number of Arab staff officers and Colonel Joyce of the British Military Mission.

In September, a Turkish battalion marched on Delagha, but the Arab forces succeeded in pushing it back after heavy fighting. After the arrival of Feisal at Aqaba, Syrian groups started to slip in and there began a full-scale desertion of Arab officers from the Turkish side to join their Arab brothers-in-arms. Even the bedouin of the Beersheba area changed their attitude towards the British when King Hussein sent Sherif Abdullah ibn Hamzeh to gather support for the Allies.

The *Arab Bulletin* of 8 October reports that during the three months of July, August and September, thirty raids were conducted on the railway line between Buwat station in the south and Ghadir al-Haj in the north. The total number of rails removed was 7,630, plus an undefined number assailed by purely Arab parties which did not report details of their achievements. On the basis of these reports we may conclude that the total number of rails damaged by the Arabs was close to 10,000. Reports also indicated that during this period over thirty bridges were demolished, the most important being the bridge north of Abu al-Na'am station, in Emir Abdullah's sector.

Late in September Sherif Abdul Mu'in, with some two hundred bedouin attacked the subsidiary railway line connecting Uneiza station with the Shobek Forest (Hisheh), from which the Turks were carrying lumber for use as fuel for the trains. Maulud Mukhlis also took part in this raid with thirty regulars and two machine guns. The force occupied the village of Shobak and received the surrender of its small garrison. The Arabs removed about three hundred rails then attacked the Turkish company guarding the forest and took twenty prisoners, but they failed to defeat the Turks and returned to Wadi Musa.

The *Arab Bulletin* of 21 October reports that King Hussein promised to pay Feisal a hundred thousand pounds as soon as he had definitely severed the railway between Ma'an and Medina. This money was to be a reward to the men taking part in that operation. This is clear evidence that the Arabs were working for the isolation of Medina in the hope of capturing it, and that there was no factual basis for the suggestion that there was a planned policy requiring the line to remain working.

In the meantime Merzuk al-Tekheimi and the Beni Atiyeh were making raids on the railway line close to Tebuk. The most important operation in this sector was the attack on a strong Turkish post 'Hill Post 4' about half-way between Dhat al-Haj and Bir Hirmas stations. The Arabs captured this position and retained it for four days (18–21 October). The force consisted of

400 warriors from Beni Atiyeh, Huweitat, Ruwalla and Sherarat.
The Turkish force was made up of 180 men, of whom 103 were
either killed or captured. The raiding party succeeded in derailing a train, but were unable to inflict extensive damage owing
to the lack of explosives. The activities of the Arabs in this
sector spread between the stations of Tebuk and Wadi Ithil and
between the stations of Hezm and Mahtab. The total loss of the
Turks in these operations amounted to no fewer than 250, dead
and captured. It is to be noted that no officers assisted the
bedouin in these activities. General Brémond, however, puts
the attackers at 2,000 and states that they damaged a train and
killed or captured 300 Turks, and that this victory was widely
acclaimed. In one of his reports Colonel Joyce says that the
Beni Atiyeh brought 28 prisoners-of-war to Aqaba, including
an officer, and I have found among the papers of Subhi al-
Khadra[1] a statement that the Arabs took 260 prisoners in these
operations.

Early in October, Ja'afar al-Askari, accompanied by Sherif
Ali al-Harithi and Colonel Joyce, inspected the front, which
stretched from Aqaba to Gueira, Delagha and Wadi Musa and
included Ghrandal and Wadi Araba. Joyce's report mentioned
that a party of Egyptian labourers were improving the Wadi
Itm road to make it fit for cars and that Rashid al-Madfa'i was
commanding the regulars at Gueira (400 infantry, eighty mounted troops, two guns and two machine-guns). The report gave
high praise to the loyalty of the people of Wadi Musa. The
Turkish forces were stationed at Abu al-Lissan and Ain Besta.
The report also stated that the Wadi Musa force, made up of
300 regular mounted men, two mountain guns and four machine
guns, was commanded by Maulud, and that a number of
Bedouin took part in picketing distant hills. It was very cold,
and the troops were living under miserable conditions, with only
one blanket each. The Ghrandal garrison consisted of 150
Bedouin under one of the Sherifs.

2. THE BATTLE OF WADI MUSA

Finally the Turks decided to launch a major offensive on Arab
positions in Wadi Musa, since Arab operations had spread and

1. The late Subhi al-Khadra, at that time, Intelligence Officer in the Northern
Arab Army.

their activities had increased, especially after their attack on the Shobak Forest. For this purpose the Turks had in readiness three infantry battalions, a Circassian cavalry regiment which they brought from Tebuk, a company of mounted infantry, six quick-firing mountain guns and two field guns, supported by one aeroplane. Mehmed Jemal Pasha personally commanded this force, which marched in three columns from Shobak, Ma'an and Besta. The Arab force consisted of 350 regulars under Maulud, two mountain guns and four machine-guns, in addition to Sherif Abdul Mu'in's force of 180 bedouin.

The Turkish attack started at dawn on 21 October with heavy artillery fire on Arab positions and the Turks were able to capture the Arab outer works. The bedouin retired to the hills south of the village, while the regulars held on to the northern hills and subjected the Turks, attacking from east, to a cross fire. Only one small Turkish party got down into the Wadi and it was soon expelled. Towards evening the bedouin encircled the Turkish left flank and forced a retreat, capturing twenty men. Bedouin pressure increased at dusk, when they also took fourteen men of the Medical Corps and seized some animals. The Turks retreated in haste leaving their dead and wounded behind. According to Maulud's report the total losses of the enemy amounted to four hundred men, dead, wounded and captured. According to Colonel Joyce the Arabs had about forty killed and wounded.

A Turkish officer, giving an account of this attack, said that Turkish aircraft were bombing Arab positions from an altitude of only three hundred metres and that the Turks, following heavy bombardment, carried out three attacks, the most ferocious being the last, in which the two forces engaged in hand-to-hand fighting and displayed great courage. He claimed that the Turks lost 200 men (dead and wounded) before Jemal Pasha gave the order to retreat because of the critical situation in the Tebuk area.

Nuri as-Said stated in his lectures that the Wadi Musa garrison continued to resist until dusk and inflicted heavy losses on the attackers, but had to retreat towards Petra under pressure. They threw their two mountain guns from the top of the mountain to the valley for fear that they might be seized by the Turks. Only two hours later, some Wadi Musa horsemen informed Maulud that they had defeated the Turks, and returned with his men to the positions which he had vacated in the evening. The Arabs seized a number of rifles, machine-guns and different kinds of equipment, in addition to several prisoners. According to General Brémond, 'it was a magnificent success, which does the greatest honour to the leader (Maulud) and his troops'.[2]

Following this battle, the Wadi Musa garrison was brought up to eight hundred regulars, while the Turks retreated from Besta on 22 November and increased their forces at Abu al-Lissan to four infantry battalions, four mountain guns and four machine-guns.

On 5 November, Emir Zeid arrived at Aqaba with sixteen hundred men. On 17 November, a Beni Sakhr force under Sherif Hussein al-Shakrani attacked the railway line at a point close to Hesa station. This party also engaged a Turkish detachment, destroyed a bridge and took seventeen prisoners. Around the middle of the month the regulars of Wadi Musa had moved to Gueira, having been replaced by irregular volunteers.

Towards the end of the month, the Turks marched on Gueira with two mounted infantry battalions, two guns and a machine-gun company. But the Arab command detailed Maulud to repel the attack with an infantry battalion, a machine-gun company and a cavalry detachment. The opposing forces met at Mreigha, and the Turks were compelled to retreat to Ain Wahida. Fighting was resumed and the Arabs succeeded in ousting the Turks from Wahida after having inflicted some losses on them both in men and equipment. But in the middle of December, another Turkish force of four battalions, and two artillery batteries, tried to regain Wahida, and the same Arab force pushed them 8 miles back to Semna. Arabs and Turks then resorted to an exchange of surprise attacks.

During the month of December, the headquarters of the Northern Army was transferred from Aqaba to Gueira, and early in January, 1918, Arab pressure increased and the Turks had to withdraw also from Abu al-Lissan. Thus we see that both the regulars and irregulars of the Northern Army were conducting continuous military operations and inflicting heavy losses on the enemy. We also see that it was the permanent bases which the Arabs had set up at Aqaba, Gueira and Wadi Musa that made possible the raids on the railway line and stations.

2. *Le Hedjaz dans la Guerre Mondiale*, p. 218.

3. THE CAPTURE OF TAFILEH

Following the capture of Jerusalem by the British and the subsequent British threat to Jericho, Emir Feisal determined to
push his forces northwards in an attempt to effect direct contact
with the British across the Dead Sea. General Allenby requested
Feisal to do all he could to cut the Dead Sea passage, which the
Turks were using for transporting supplies and grain to their
forces in Jericho. He also requested that pressure be mounted
on the Kerak area, whose grain was the main source of supply
to the Turks in Medina and the railway stations.

It was a severe winter that year and the British had not supplied the Arab Army with winter clothes and blankets. As a
result of this and of the lack of adequate protective measures,
a number of Arab soldiers and a large number of their animals
perished.[3] In spite of all this, however, Feisal was determined
to commence his activities, and he appointed Emir Zeid to
command the move to the north.

Towards the end of December Arab columns mounted a three-
pronged attack. The first column under Sherif Mastur headed
for Tafileh, aided by the Jazi Huweitat under Sheikh Hamad
ibn Jazi. The second column under Sherif Nassir and Nuri
as-Said, aided by the Tawaiha Huweitat and the Beni Sakhr
tribesmen, headed for the station of Jurf al-Darawish. Shobak
was the destination of the third column under Sherif Abdul
Mu'in.

Nuri as-Said described the attack on Jurf al-Darawish on
12 January 1918, as follows:

We chose this station because it had a large bridge, and its garrison amounted to only two weak battalions with one gun. Accordingly
we detailed an infantry battalion of about 300, two mountain guns,
eight machine guns and a Bedouin force of about 1,500, mostly from
Beni Sakhr. I left my post as Chief-of-Staff of the Northern Army and
took temporary command of this force with Sherif Nassir. On our
way we crossed the railway line north of Ma'an and spent two nights
in the open air. Shortly before dawn of the third day we launched a
surprise attack on the station with the result that the Turkish garrison surrendered after less than two hours of fighting.[4]

3. According to the *Arab Bulletin*, ten men died of cold in one day; Kassem
Raji, commander of the 2nd Division, resigned because of the lack of facilities
and equipment for his troops
4. Nuri as-Said, *Muhadarat 'an al-Herakat al-'Askariyyeh Lil-Jaysh al'-Arabi fi
al-Hijaz wa Suriyya* (Lectures on the Military Operations of the Arab Army in
Hejaz and Syria) *1916–1918* (1947).

The Turks had installed a mountain gun and two machine-guns on an artificial hill behind the station, but the Arabs succeeded in stationing themselves by night on a hill opposite, cutting the railway line on both sides and setting up two ambushes north and south of the station to prevent the arrival of reinforcements. Under cover of darkness Nuri as-Said marched with his regular force and took up positions close to the station. At dawn he installed his two guns on the edge of the hill, fired at the Turkish gun and silenced it. At this point the Huweitat and Beni Sakhr made a dash on their camels towards the enemy before Nuri could stop them. Fortunately this Bedouin attack created panic among the Turks on the hill and they fled towards the station building. During the ensuing exchange of fire Nuri sent a cavalry unit to reconnoitre the southern area, while he proceeded to the hill and found the Turkish gun in a serviceable condition. Thus all he needed to do was to turn it towards the station building. He fired one shell and it penetrated the wall of the building, at which the enthusiasm of the Arabs became so great that they rushed at the demoralized Turks, who immediately surrendered. Arab technicians proceeded to blow up the water well and the platform, destroy two trains after despoiling them of supplies and equipment, and dynamite the bridge nearby. Since it was impossible for the Arabs to hold the station for long, because of the distance between them and their communication centres, Nuri as-Said returned with his soldiers and the prisoners to Gueira, while Sherif Nassir headed towards Tafileh. The enemy lost eighty dead and 200 prisoners, including seven officers, and the Arabs seized twenty-five mules, a gun, two machine-guns and a quantity of mixed equipment. In the meantime Sherif Abdul Mu'in advanced from Wadi Musa to Shobek and its adjoining forest (Hisheh), which after some resistance, the Turks had to evacuate for Uneiza station. The Arabs also cut the subsidiary railway line running from Uneiza to the forest. On the other hand, Sherif Mastur with some regulars and a number of Jazi horsemen, headed towards Tafileh by way of Wadi Araba, Mastur reached Tafileh from the west, while Nassir was approaching it from the east, accompanied by Auda Abu Tayeh with about one hundred Bedouin and a regular detachment under Rasim Sardast.

The Tafileh garrison was made up of 150 officers and men,

but their strength or weakness depended on the attitude of the local population. When Nassir approached the suburbs of the town he sent a message to the paramount sheikh of Tafileh, Dhiab al-Auran, informing him of his arrival with Auda. And although Dhiab had been in touch with Emir Feisal and was Auda's friend, the inhabitants of Tafileh at first intended to oppose the Sherif because of the traditional enmity between village and tribe. They had gone out to Ais, a hilly position on the eastern outskirts of the town, and exchanged fire with Nassir and Auda. Dhiab, however, immediately contacted his followers and informed them that he had decided to side with the leaders of the Arab Revolt. A cease-fire was arranged and the whole population of Tafileh joined the Sherif.

At the beginning of this operation the men of the Tafileh garrison and the Tafileh employees had met in Government House and prepared to meet any eventuality. When the people of Tafileh joined the Revolt, the Sherif sent them two messengers with the demand that they should surrender. But they refused for fear the bedouin might murder them and declared that they would surrender only to a regular force. When Nassir received their answer he sent Captain Rasim to Government House, and the Turks surrendered to him. Thus Tafileh fell to Nassir and Auda on 15 January 1918. In the evening Sherif Mastur and Hamad ibn Jazi entered the town from the south, while Emir Zeid and Ja'afar al-Askari, at the head of a small regular force, arrived on the following day. Because of the feeling of ill-will between Auda and Hamad, Zeid asked Auda to return to his tents in Jefer. The prisoners were sent to Aqaba, except for the Arabs among them, who chose to join the forces of the Revolt. One of these, Captain Zeki al-Halabi, was appointed by Zeid to be District Officer at Tafileh.

We thus see that the Revolt extended to Tafileh by way of its own people and their desire to join the revolt.[5] Had the people of Tafileh insisted on resisting and co-operated with the Turkish garrison, the task of the leaders of the Revolt would have been extremely difficult. Lawrence's statements about the dispute betwen the Auran and Mheisin families do not square with the

5. 'Sheikh Diab el Auran, the chief sheikh of Tafileh, had written to Sherif Feisal informing him that on the arrival of a Sherif, Tafileh would be handed over.' *Arab Bulletin* (27 January 1918), No. 77.

facts, because traditional differences were forgotten in these circumstances. There is no truth in Lawrence's claim that Auda threatened and cursed the inhabitants of Tafileh. Auda came to Tafileh as Dhiab's friend and the area was not within his sphere of influence. Besides, the force that he and the Sherif commanded was not in a position to fight its way into the town. General Muhammad Ali al-Ajluni, who was at the time a regular officer in Sherif Mastur's force, has stated that Captain Zeki al-Halabi, commander of the Turkish garrison, had been in touch with Feisal and had actually helped the forces of the Revolt to enter the town.

4. TELL AL-SHAHM

We left Lawrence travelling between Egypt, Jerusalem and General Headquarters. On 25 December 1917, we find him back in Aqaba. He said that Joyce informed him that things were going well, and that the situation had improved since Maulud's victory. Joyce also said that the raids which the Arabs were launching on the railway line had forced the Turks to withdraw some of their forces from Abu al-Lissan in order to strengthen their weakened watchposts along the line.

Maulud boldly threw out posts to places on the plateau, and began to harry the supply caravans from Maan. . . . At last they were too weak to hold the wide position, and, early in January, Maulud was able to force them out towards Mreigha. The Beduin caught the Turks moving, and cut up the hindmost battalion. This threw the Turks back precipitately, to Uheida, only six miles from Maan, and when we pressed after menacingly, they withdrew to Semna, the outpost line of Maan three miles out. So by January the seventh Maulud was containing Maan directly.[6]

Joyce and Lawrence decided to reconnoitre the line near Mudowwara station by means of the armoured cars and a section of ten-pounder mountain-guns mounted on Talbot cars. Since Joyce held higher rank than Lawrence, he was responsible for the raid. The following is a summary extract from his report:

The cars left Gueira at 9 a.m. on December 30 and arrived at a point about twelve miles west of Mudowara by sundown. . . . On the morning of January 1 a reconnaissance was again made, on foot, which showed that the line between Tel el-Shahim and Wadi Rethm station was defended by three small entrenched posts, two on

6. *Seven Pillars*, p. 457.

hill tops and one dug in near a large seven-arch culvert due east of our point of observation. Owing to the nature of the country it would have been impossible to approach the line in order to lay a mine without being observed, and as there were no Arabs co-operating, the idea of laying a mine had to be abandoned. It was accordingly decided to attack the entrenched post near the culvert above referred to....

The ten-pounder gun came into action at 1,500 yards from the position, having somewhat misjudged the distance. It came under a very hot rifle fire and had to be withdrawn after firing a few rounds. The armoured cars approached the post and fired several belts from their maxims into it at close range, but the number of casualties inflicted were not ascertainable. There was no way of enfilading the fort, and as no definite result could be obtained by maxim gun fire the cars were eventually withdrawn....

Two armoured cars escorting the ten-pounder mountain-gun then proceeded to Tel el Shahim station, and the mountain-gun fired about thirty rounds high explosive with good results. Station buildings were hit, and trucks standing in the station were destroyed. The armoured cars approached the station and fired on the windows, doors, etc., of the building and completely silenced all enemy resistance from this point. The cars contain such small crews that it was impracticable for them to leave the cars and endeavour to capture the station....

The arrival of armoured cars on the railway line was undoubtedly a surprise to the Turks; although the cars have been for nine months in the Hejaz, this was the first occasion on which they got within effective range of the line.[7]

This report gives a clear picture of the detached military spirit in which Colonel Joyce wrote. He mentions neither himself nor Lawrence. Lawrence mentions that for the first time in his life, he was at a fight as a spectator and that he was happy to be with his countrymen and talk to them in English, 'For me it was a holiday, with not an Arab near, before whom I must play out my tedious part.'[8]

On 2 January, Joyce and Lawrence returned to Aqaba at the same time as Sa'ad al-Sikeini, an Ageyl volunteer trained in the use of explosives. Sa'ad reported that he had destroyed a train which carried Suleiman Pasha ibn Rafadeh, Sheikh of Billi and a friend to the Turks. Sa'ad added that he had waited with a small number of men for five whole days until the train they were expecting had arrived. The train had ten carriages full of

7. *Arab Bulletin*, 27 January 1918, No. 77
8. *Seven Pillars*, p. 458.

REGULAR AND IRREGULAR 131

flour and food-stuffs. The engine was completely wrecked, but reinforcements from a nearby Turkish position forced the bedouin to withdraw before plundering the train. None the less they succeeded in capturing twenty-four thousand pounds in gold and five horses. Five Turkish officers were killed and several other ranks. Sa'ad's severe features appear in a portrait in *Seven Pillars*. Lawrence described him elsewhere as:

> ... a dour puritan, who saw his men dragging chests of gold and rich merchandise from the train which he had blown up by a mine. He left them plundering while he carefully rolled up and carried away the wire and electrical gear with which he had fired this mine, and with which he meant to fire the next.[9]

At the same time Sherif Muhammad Ali Beidawi, with some Beni Atiyeh and a French detachment under Captain Pizani, was launching repeated attacks on the line near Mudowwara station. Lawrence stated that after his return to Aqaba he was mainly concerned with the body-guard which he formed for his private protection. He claimed that the Turks began by offering a reward of a hundred pounds for a British officer alive or dead, and that they increased the general figure as time went on, with a special bid for him. He and Ali al-Harithi were at the head of their list, with a reward of twenty thousand pounds alive or ten thousand pounds dead. He mentions that he appointed Abdullah al-Nahabi and Abdullah al-Za'agi to lead his body-guard of approaching ninety men.[10] He paid twice the salary they would normally get in the army; this made the service enviable, and put the eager spirits in the area at his disposal. They dressed like 'a bed of tulips, in every colour but white...and they travel day and night at my whim, and make it a point of honour never to mention fatigue'. As a result sixty of them died in his service. Undoubtedly, Lawrence greatly exaggerated the merits of his body-guard whom he enlisted to vie with the leaders of the Revolt. How could he—the lover of flashy appearances—let an opportunity like this go by, when he had enough money to indulge his tastes? Al-Ajluni has described his men as 'servants, followers and bedouin mercenaries,' Lawrence endowed them with heroic characteristics like Alexandre Dumas's Three Mus-

9. *Oriental Assembly*, p. 155.
10. In a letter which he wrote on 15 July 1918, he mentioned that his body-guard consisted of fifty tribesmen.

keteers. Evidence of Lawrence's lack of precision is to be found in the photograph published by Robert Graves in *Lawrence and the Arabs*, with the caption 'Lawrence and his bodyguard at Aqaba—Summer, 1918', which included only fourteen men all wearing different clothes. In a memorandum which appeared in the *Arab Bulletin* of 24 May 1919, Lawrence said:

An Arab party of 20 men (my servants), marched once with all their kit from Abu el Lissan to Aqaba (60 miles) in just over five hours.

In a letter to Robert Graves he mentioned that he learned Arabic from his *servants*. There has been unanimous agreement among all those I have talked to who knew him, that his followers were in fact servants and mercenaries and that their number never exceeded 15 from various tribes. Their main task was to work with him as guides and informers. Also, their being with him conferred on him the right of *Khuwa* (brotherhood), which meant that, in accordance with accepted bedouin convention, nobody would do anything to harm him.

It appears from Lawrence's records and writings that he did nothing during the twenty days between his return to Aqaba and his arrival at Tafileh on 20 January, five days after it was captured.

5. THE BATTLE OF TAFILEH

Zeid and Ja'afar entered Tafileh immediately after Sherif Nassir. Zeid was accompanied by a detachment of regular troops but had to leave them in Petra because of the lack of food and transport. He began to distribute rewards among the sheikhs and men of the area on the grounds that they were volunteers in the service of the Revolt. Then he despatched Sherif Mastur together with some horsemen to Wadi Hesa to set up a front-line position between Kerak and Tafileh. Zeid also sent several letters to the shiekhs of Kerak urging them to support the Revolt.

The Turkish High Command was deeply concerned at the fall of Tafileh and decided to retake it in an effort to prevent the forces of the Revolt from entering Kerak, which was the seat of the District Mutasarref and an important supply centre. To attain this, Brigadier Hamid Fakhri gathered together a force made up of three infantry battalions (900 officers and men) and a cavalry company, which he strengthened with two Austrian Howitzer mountain guns and 23 machine-guns. On 19 January the force reached Kerak, where it was joined by the commander of the Kerak garrison and a number of Kerak horsemen.. From there Fakhri headed south to the great Hesa Valley which separates Kerak from Tafileh. Over-confident in the efficiency of his force, he fired his guns intermittently in the direction of Tafileh hoping to terrify the local population.

On the morning of 24 January, the Arabs at Wadi Hesa were faced by the Turkish force approaching from the other side of the valley. Soon Tafileh heard the news that Hamid Fakhri had solemnly vowed to destroy the town and wreak vengeance on it with the sword, because its inhabitants had helped the Revolt and forced the Turkish garrison to surrender. What happened, however, was the exact opposite of what Hamid Fakhri had expected. Sherif Mastur's horsemen put up a stiff resistance against the Turkish vanguard in the heart of the valley, thus forcing it to stay close to the main body. Mastur had been joined by a large number of Tafileh villagers and Bedouin, who were spending the winter in the valley, in addition to several Kerak horsemen. The local population, old and young, were armed with rifles which were easy to obtain in the area.

The Turks had to slow down their march considerably at Wadi Hesa, which extended from north to south over a distance of 40 kms. The Wadi, barren, rugged and dangerous, was too much for the Turkish force which was mostly made up of infantry with supplies, equipment and fodder for their animals. Some mules were laboriously dragging the two heavy guns while others carried the machine-guns and equipment.. This forced the Turks to take the long Sultani pathway. In consequence they had to spend the first half of that night in the heart of the valley. Shortly after midnight they started climbing the southern ascent in the hope of reaching the plateau by morning. In fact, the Tafileh battle started that very night because the Bedouin and local population, who usually sought the valley in winter for warmth, started launching surprise attacks on the flanks of the marching force. These attacks struck panic into the Turks and caused losses in both men and animals.

Early in the morning the Turkish vanguard climbed the shoulder of the valley, reached the Hadd al-Dakik knoll, then

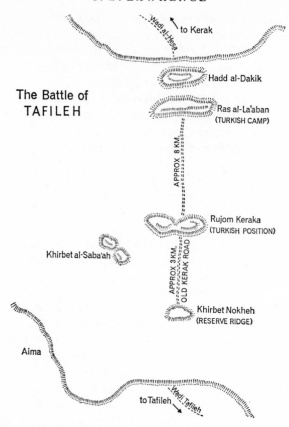

The Battle of
TAFILEH

to Kerak

Wadi al-Hesa

Hadd al-Dakik

Ras al-La'aban
(TURKISH CAMP)

APPROX 8 KM

Rujom Keraka
(TURKISH POSITION)

Khirbet al-Saba'ah

APPROX 3 KM

OLD KERAK ROAD

Khirbet Nokheh
(RESERVE RIDGE)

Aima

to Tafileh

Wadi Tafileh

advanced to the Ras al-La'aban knoll on the edge of the plateau, where it encamped. Its fighting elements then marched with the two guns and machine-guns to Rujom Keraka ridge. Simultaneously, however, the people of Tafileh, Sanfaha and Aima, accompanied by several bedouin, started arriving at the position and firing on the Turks.

Emir Zeid's force at Tafileh was not large enough to meet the Turks face to face in the field under the existing uneven conditions. Zeid's regulars did not exceed sixty men, made up of the four Vickers machine-gun units under Lieutenant Subhi al-Umari,[11] the two mountain-gun crews (with only eight rounds

11. I have greatly benefited from the memoirs of Subhi al-Umari in manuscript, which he has kindly put at my disposal in addition to explaining several points in his numerous letters to me. Subhi al-Umari had deserted from the

for each) and twelve cavalry. In addition there were fifty volunteers under Captain Ismail Namek (who later became Chief of Staff of the Iraqi Army). There were also two hundred Hejazi bedouin, who were Zeid's personal retinue, plus five of Lawrence's followers. The regulars were commanded by Captain Abdullah al-Dleimi, who had arrived the day before to replace Captain Rasim Sardast. Thus they were both able to take part in the battle. No wonder Zeid hesitated to march with this small force and meet the heavily armed regular Turkish force in a decisive battle. It was clear that the bedouin could not hold their ground in the face of Turkish artillery and could not employ their technique of hit-and-run against a regular force that operated on a unified plan. And what could sixty Arab regulars do against a thousand Turkish regulars?

Zeid had received greatly exaggerated reports about the strength of the Turks. He therefore set up his entrenchments in the hills south of Tafileh and telegraphed to Emir Feisal informing him of the Turkish advance, requesting reinforcements. His plan was to withdraw to Wadi Musa in case he could not repulse the Turks. But the battle was forced upon him by the civilians, who were lying in ambush along knolls and ravines with which they were thoroughly familiar. From there they went out against the Turks, killed, plundered and returned feeling secure in their swiftness. The battle was also forced because the Turkish commander and his staff officers did not fully realize the danger they were in and did not see that they were risking the lives of their men in a rough and difficult country, surrounded as they were by a hostile population.

Sheikh Dhiab played an important part in this battle and co-operated with Zeid in encouraging the civilians to go out and meet the Turks and in sending messengers to the neighbouring villagers, alerting them, and urging them to join the battle. It was bitter cold and the heavy fog made visibility extremely poor.

Early on the morning of 25 January, Zeid had sent one of his mountain guns, two of his machine-guns and his twelve cavalry-

---

Turkish army, joined Feisal in the autumn of 1917 and took part in most of the subsequent battles, displaying great courage in the last battle with the Turks north of Aleppo. As a result the British decorated him with the Military Cross. This Arab officer fought in battles of liberation against the Turks, the British and the French and on several occasions was condemned to death. For a while he was a member of the Syrian parliament. (See *Arab Bulletin,* 30 October 1917.)

men under Captain Abdullah to meet the enemy. The local bedouin and villagers were encouraged at the sight of this small force. Abdullah engaged the Turkish cavalry and was able to drive them back. He persisted stubbornly in his fight in the face of heavy enemy fire until five of his men were killed, one gun put out of action and all ammunition was finished. Then he retired to report to Zeid and ask him to advance to the battlefield with all his available forces.

The Turks, however, were able to advance very slowly against the sniping of local men and bedouin. They occupied Rujom Keraka just before noon, while the Jazi horsemen and the villagers retreated to 'Khirbet Nokheh',[12] three kms. away. This stretch ran across furrowed ground through which the Kerak road passed. Here the Turks posted their guns and machine-guns and started firing, some of the shells falling on the eastern outskirts of Tafileh.

But the slow movement of the Turks, their hesitation and confusion, gave the initiative to the Arabs whose effective resistance enhanced Zeid's hopes for success. He marched with the rest of his force to the battlefield, reached Khirbet Nokheh at noon and hurriedly despatched Rasim at the head of the mounted men to support the men who were engaging the left flank of the enemy.

Meanwhile hundreds of nearby villagers and Bedouins had flocked to the battlefield. Some advanced to take part in the fighting, while others waited and bided their time. About 150 men from the villages of Aima, Rihab and Dabba, only one-third of whom had rifles, gathered opposite the right flank of the enemy. They spread on a rugged hill called Khirbet al-Saba'ah and watched developments.

Shortly after noon the battle took a decisive turn which ultimately caused the defeat of the Turks. We may summarize what happened from the memoirs of Subhi al-Umari, who was then commanding the machine-gun unit:

I fixed the two machine-guns then sat down and waited and looked at the hill occupied by the enemy; I saw no point in opening fire because of the distance between us. Shortly after the arrival of Emir Zeid and Lawrence I spotted a gradually growing party of peasants on a small hill about one kilometre from the right flank of the enemy.

12. 'Reserve Ridge' according to *Seven Pillars*

Suddenly an idea struck me and I said to myself, 'Why don't I go to them with my machine-guns and urge them to advance on the enemy flank?' I knew the effect of machine-guns on the morale of the peasants. So I decided to put my idea to the test without asking the Emir's permission because I knew that he would not have approved my plan. My men and I carried the machine-guns, knowing that we had to cross very quickly a dangerous expanse of land that fell within the range of enemy fire. We made a dash for it and reached our destination without any of us being hit. Later on I heard that the Emir was shocked at my move and had decided to punish me. We crawled sideways until we reached the foot of the hill occupied by the enemy, while the armed peasants sneaked in after us. We then climbed the hill, approached the enemy position unnoticed and opened fire suddenly.

At the same time the peasants advanced and started firing on the Turks, who turned their machine-guns and fired on them, but with no success because there was little use in their firing from an elevated position. The Turkish unit nearest to us suffered several casualties so its commander ordered his soldiers to change their line and face the peasants who had got dangerously close to them. At this point an unexpected thing happened, which I believe was one of the most important reasons for the defeat of the Turks: as soon as the Turkish soldiers got up to change their direction, the peasants thought they were preparing to flee. They cheered loudly and attacked. The unit fell into disorder which, strangely, spread to other units. The machine-guns were left lying on the ground and clamour arose on both sides. I was later informed by a Turkish officer who had been captured that the Turkish commander had in the afternoon decided to keep his troops where they were until the following morning, because he had estimated that he could not attack the Arab position and reach Tafileh before sunset. He therefore called his officers to the rear to inform them of his decision. By sheer coincidence, our flank attack took place at a time when the Turkish units had no officers, a fact which led to their defeat in this strange fashion. The Turkish commander acted in this way out of conceit and reckless-ness.[13]

Faced with this unexpected turn, Hamid Fakhri mounted his horse and ordered his staff officers to carry their rifles and join the lines. But he was soon hit and fell to the ground. There was confusion among the Turks and they retreated in disorder. At this the Arabs in Khirbet Nokheh advanced across the plain with their banner, firing their rifles and machine-guns. Similarly, the first sign of disarray among the Turks encouraged the rest of Zeid's forces to close in from three sides on the retreating

13. Subhi al-Umari.

enemy, who began to get rid of their heavy equipment piece-meal. Because of the great pressure on them, however, the retreat speedily turned into a humiliating defeat. The Turks had carried their wounded commander with them but he died on the edge of the slope and was hurriedly buried there. Thus by the time the battle ended so unexpectedly for both sides the Arabs had gained a considerable victory. They seized the two guns, twenty-three machine-guns, two hundred and fifty horses and mules and captured two hundred and eighteen Turkish soldiers including twelve officers. The dead were at least four hundred.[14] The bedouin gave chase to the beaten Turks in the valley, and I was told that the number of Turks who returned to Kerak was less than fifty. Doubtless, it was the sudden attack of Subhi and the villagers of Aima that tipped the balance in favour of the Arabs; it is thus safe to say that the villagers and the bedouin were the actual victors. No doubt, the presence of Emir Zeid at the head of his regulars and irregulars, in addition to their heavy weapons, encouraged and enabled the local population to fight. Had Zeid withdrawn his troops, the villagers could have done nothing but disperse and take refuge in the valleys west of Tafileh.

The above is based on information which I have personally obtained from a number of officers and from several old men of Tafileh and Aimeh who took part in the battle. I actually in-spected the site of the battle. Most of the people I have talked to recall that they had seen Lawrence but that he was not an outstanding figure in the Revolt and therefore did not draw their special attention. One of them said to me that he remembered Lawrence sitting in the presence of Emir Zeid, silent most of the time, with his head between his hands. He heard him once answer a question by saying, 'I am from the Dumaniyeh' (a Huweitat tribe). This indicates that Lawrence had attached himself to a tribe, as was customary for foreigners in the

14. Emir Zeid himself has kindly supplied me with these figures. Turkish sources however state that Hamid Fakhri's force was 600 strong and that 21 officers and 420 soldiers returned to Kerak, which puts their losses at 159 dead and captured. There is no doubt that the Turkish figures are not precise because the inhabitants of Tafileh have informed me that the men of one of their clans alone returned with 75 prisoners. Emir Zeid used to pay one gold pound for each prisoner, in accordance with Feisal's instructions. Dr. Ahmed Qadri says that Zeid threatened to execute five Turkish officers for each Arab executed by the Turks, with the result that afterwards the Turks did not dare to execute any of their Arab political prisoners.

desert. As regards Lawrence's statement that he used to walk bare-footed and that thorns made his feet bleed, it gave rise to much laughter from those I talked to because they themselves did not walk bare-footed nor could they have done so on the rugged ground in the cold month of January. They recall that Lawrence wore the uniform of an Arab officer, plus the traditional Arab head-dress and an ordinary pair of shoes. They also said that when Lawrence spoke Arabic he could not conceal the fact that he was a foreigner. They were unanimous in agreeing that the battle was a haphazard affair, very much like partisan battles, and that Zeid and his officers ran the battle after the peasants and Bedouin had succeeded in hampering the Turkish advance. None of the people I spoke to recalled seeing Lawrence give an order or direct anybody to do anything. None of them believed that Lawrence was in any position of power, nor did they think any of the people of Tafileh were prepared to be influenced by him. The developments of the battle were not the result of predetermined planning, but grew out of natural impromptu circumstances. The people of Aima, for instance, attacked the right flank of the Turks because the route from their village led them naturally to that flank; the Jazi horsemen (the Matalga) fought against the Turks because they considered themselves part of the Arab Army and not because Lawrence had asked them to do so.

Subhi al-Umari has informed me that after the battle Zeid embraced and congratulated him and Feisal promoted him to the rank of First Lieutenant and rewarded him with £2,000 in gold, which he distributed among his men. He also mentioned that Lawrence came on the following day and took a photograph of the Arab officers with the captured machine-guns. Subhi had met Lawrence for the first time at Tafileh while the latter was engaged in removing lice from his inner garment.

We must, however, look at Lawrence's version of the battle of Tafileh, for his biographers consider that this was the only regular battle he supervised and conducted, and they take it as evidence of his rare military genius and superior leadership. This is to be expected, for these writers have based their views on Lawrence's own statements.

Lawrence managed to catch up with the leaders of the Revolt who had preceded him to Tafileh. The easy entry of the Arabs had led him into thinking that it was still possible to go forward. (He was in the habit of giving Allenby the impression that every Arab advance was a result of his own leadership and guidance.) Lawrence never explained his reason for not participating in the advance to the north, but he did say that 'Feisal has delegated command of this push towards the Dead Sea to his young half-brother Zeid',[15] a statement which indicates clearly enough that Lawrence was not always consulted.

We might say, therefore, that it was sheer coincidence that enabled Lawrence to witness the battle of Tafileh, the death of Hamid Fakhri and the defeat of the Turks. It was reasonable, however, that Lawrence should write a report about this important battle in which the Arabs were so successful, but it was not at all reasonable that he should claim for himself credit which he did not merit, secure in the knowledge that he was writing in English to his own English Command.

Lawrence wrote his report on the second day of the battle, and it appeared in the *Arab Bulletin* in two and a half pages which we might summarize as follows:

A Turkish temporary regiment, commanded by Hamid Fakhri Bey . . . was railed to Kalaat el Hasa station January 19 and left Kerak on January 23 to retake Tafila. . . . On January 24, they came in contact in the afternoon with our patrols in Seil el Hasa, and by night had driven them back into Tafila. The Sherifian officers had laid out a defensive position on the south bank of the great valley in which Tafila stands, and Sherif Zeid left for this about midnight, taking with him the sixty regulars and 400 irregulars . . . who had come with him from Akaba. . . .

Tafila of course panicked, and as Diab el-Auran had given us ominous reports of the disaffection and treachery of the villagers, I went down from my house before dawn into the crowded streets, to listen to what was being said. . . . Everyone was screaming with terror, goods were being bundled out of the houses into the streets, which were packed with women and men. Mounted Arabs were galloping up and down, firing wildly into the air. . . . Just at dawn the enemy bullets began to fall in the olive gardens, and I went out to Sherif Zeid and persuaded him to send Abdullah Effendi . . . with two *fusils mitrailleurs* to support the peasants who were still holding the northern crest. His arrival stimulated them to a counter-attack in which they drove the Turkish cavalry back over the near ridge, across a small plain to the first of the low ridges falling into Wadi el-Hasa. He took this ridge also, and was there held up, as the

15. *Seven Pillars*, p. 473.

Turkish main body was posted just behind it. The fighting became
very hot, with huge bursts of Turkish machine-gun fire and a good
deal of shelling.

Zeid hesitated to send forward reinforcements, so I went up to
Abdullah's position (about seven miles north of Tafila) to report. On
my way I met him returning, having had five men killed and one
gun put out of action, and having finished his ammunition. We sent
back urgent messages to Zeid to send forward a mountain gun, any
available machine-guns, and what men he could collect, to a reserve
position, which was the southern end of the little plain between the
Hasa valley and the Tafila valley. . . .

After Abdullah had gone I went up to the front, and found things
rather difficult. It was being held by thirty Ibn Jazi Howeitat,
mounted, and about thirty villagers. The Turks were working
through the pass . . . and concentrating the fire of about fifteen
machine-guns on the face and flank of the mound we were holding.
. . . Our people were short of ammunition, and the loss of the position was obviously only a matter of minutes. . . .

The Motalga horsemen were given all the cartridges we could
collect, and the footmen ran back over the plain. I was among them,
since I had come straight up the cliffs from Tafila, and my animals
had not caught me up. The mounted men held out for fifteen
minutes more, and then galloped back to us unhurt. We collected
in the reserve position, a ridge about sixty feet high, commanding
an excellent view of the plain. It was now noon, we had lost about
fifteen men and had about eighty left, but a few minutes later about
120 Ageyl came up, and my men with a Hotchkiss automatic, and
Lutfi el-Aseli with two. We then held our own easily till 3 p.m. when
Sherifs Zeid and Mastur came up with Rasim and Abdullah, one
Egyptian army 2·95 mountain gun, two Vickers, two large Hotchkiss,
and five *fusils mitrailleurs,* with twenty mule M.I., thirty Motalga
horse, and about 200 villagers. The Turks were trying to shell and
machine-gun our ridge, but found difficulty in ranging. They had
occupied our old front line, and we had its range (3,100 yards) exactly
as I had paced it on my way back. . . . We mounted all our materials
on our ridge, and Rasim took all the mounted men (now about
eighty) to the right, to work up beyond the eastern boundary ridge.
He was able to get forward unseen, till he had turned the Turkish
flank at 2,000 yards. He then made a dismounted attack of ten men
and five *fusils mitrailleurs,* keeping his horse in reserve. . . . A reinforcement of 100 men from Aima now reached us . . . and we sent
them, with three Hotchkiss automatics, to our left flank. They crept
down behind the western ridge of the plain till within 200 yards
of the Turkish Maxims, without being seen, as we opened across the
plain a frontal attack of eighteen men, two Vickers, and two large
Hotchkiss. . . . Our left flank were finally able by a sudden burst
of fire to wipe out the Turkish machine-gunners and rush the guns.
The mounted men then charged the retreating Turks from our right

flank, while we sent forward the infantry and the banners in the
centre. They occupied the Turkish line at sunset, and chased the
enemy back past their guns into the bed of Wadi Hasa. . . . Our
people mostly gave up the pursuit at this point . . . but the Bedouins
of Kerak took it up and harried the flying mob all night.

Our losses were about twenty-five killed and forty wounded. The
Ibn Jazi Howeitat, under Hamad el Arar, did splendidly, and the
villagers were very steady and good.[16]

We note from this report that the job Lawrence claimed to
have done did not go beyond 'persuading' Zeid to send Abdullah
al-Dleimi to support the men who were fighting the enemy. We
also note that he did not claim to have directed the battle or
given any orders. Even so he was rewarded with the D.S.O., one
of the highest military decorations in the British Army, and was
given an exceptional promotion to the rank of Colonel.

Turning to *Seven Pillars* we note that his account of this battle
came to about three thousand words. We know that in 1921 he
spent more than three months in Transjordan and made a tour
of the battlefields from Azraq in the north to Aqaba in the south,
while working at the same time on his book. His account received wide publicity through *Seven Pillars* and through being
reproduced later by his biographers. A quick glance at it reveals
several contradictions:

Lawrence claimed that the Turkish advance created panic in
the town of Tafileh, but this is untrue because, as Lawrence
himself admitted, the inhabitants of Tafileh had been putting
up a stiff resistance ever since the Turks reached Wadi Hesa
and all through the night, and they had succeeded in delaying
the Turks' march. How can his description of panic on the one
hand be reconciled with a reference to daring and resistance on
the other? Lawrence also stated that Sheikh Dhiab had been
telling harrowing tales of the disaffection of the townspeople,
which is also untrue, for Dhiab was actually leading the people's
resistance. I have spoken to several people of the Auran and
Mheisin, but none of them has referred to any 'disaffection' at
the time. In his memoirs, Al Ajluni says: 'We entered Tafileh
. . . and did not notice any disagreement among the population,
who received us with a uniformly warm welcome. Perhaps Lawrence has based this verdict on his own method of noticing
peculiar phenomena, no matter how trivial.' As for Lawrence's

16. *Op. cit.* (18 February 1918), No. 79.

statement that the Mheisin Sheikhs went to Aqaba as Feisal's reluctant guests, it represents only half the truth. In *Seven Pillars* he said that it was he who sent Hamad ibn Jazi and the Jazi horsemen to the field, yet he did not mention anything of the sort in his report. He described Zeid as a cool and gallant fighter with the temperament of a professional officer, but he soon accused him of being excessively cautious. He also said that he walked from Tafileh to the edge of Wadi Hesa, a distance of ten kilometres (with no shoes), but it is hard to understand how a commander could allow himself to walk such a long distance in order to present his report. He admitted that he met Abdullah going back to Tafileh, having used up all his ammunition, in order to get up Zeid with all his men for a battle with the enemy; 'so nothing remained for me to add to his message'. Then comes an admission that he was unarmed which made Metaab al-Jazi furious. He added that he ran all the way from Rujom Keraka to Khirbet Nokheh and that when Metaab caught up with him he lent Lawrence his stirrup to hurry him along. Lawrence then slept 'a blessed hour'. But what kind of commander would hold on to one of his men's stirrups while the horse galloped at top speed? All he did after his sleep was to wake up to welcome Zeid and his force when they arrived, after which the battle took its natural course. When the battle was over, Lawrence was exhausted while 'Zeid beside me clapped his hands with joy at the beautiful order of our plan . . .'.[17] He added that because of the angers and exertions of the battle his mind was so tired that he was unable to go down and save the Turks, which was something he could have done anyway. Then he rather modestly adds 'By my decision to fight, I had killed twenty or thirty of our six hundred men . . .'.[18]

There is no doubt of Lawrence's sense of humour. He was at pains to admit his own pranks, but his biographers were prone to take them seriously. Note for instance the comment he makes on his own report of the battle:

. . . nothing came of all the loss and effort, except a report which I sent over to the British headquarters in Palestine for the staff's consumption. It was meanly written for effect, full of quaint smiles and mock simplicities; and made them think me a modest amateur, doing his best after the great models; not a clown, leering after them.

17. *Op. cit.*, p. 482.   18. *Ibid.*, p. 482.

... Like the battle, it was a nearly-proof parody of regulation use. Headquarters loved it, and innocently, to crown the jest, offered me a decoration on the strength of it. We should have more bright breasts in the Army if each man was able without witnesses, to write out his own despatch.[19]

Lawrence says that when Arab pressure on the Turks increased, Hamid Fakhri 'collected his Staff and Headquarters, and told each man to take a rifle. "I have been forty years a soldier, but never saw I rebels fight like these. Enter the ranks . . .".'[20] Moreover Al-Ajluni says that a captured Turkish Colonel informed him that 'they were surprised by what they met in this battle; they had not expected the Arabs to conduct military activities with such great skill'.

Thus we see that in his first report, although he placed himself in the limelight, Lawrence did not claim that he conducted the battle. In *Seven Pillars*, however, he claimed that the Turkish march had angered him so that 'bad temper and conceit united for this time to make me not content to know my power, but determined to give public advertisement of it to the enemy and to everyone'.[21] In spite of this, Lawrence did not clarify sufficiently the way he commanded the battle, and we have been unable to find any convincing material proof that he could have commanded it under the prevailing conditions.

6. AL-MAZRA'A AND MUDOWWARA

Arab victories did not cease at this point. Sherif Abdullah Ibn Hamzeh was co-operating in Wadi Araba with the Terabin, a Beersheba tribe. According to prearranged plans to cut the Turkish communication line and supply centres, he marched with seventy horsemen in the direction of the little lake port at Mazra'a, where a Turkish force was supplying the army in Jericho using boats across the Dead Sea. At dawn on 28 January the Arabs attacked the Turkish positions, and the Turks, taken by surprise, surrendered without putting up any resistance. The Arabs scuttled the seven boats which the Turks were using. Then they burned the Turkish huts and installations, seized their stock of grain and sent their sixty prisoners to Aqaba. This Arab victory was a fulfilment of their promise to Allenby who was preparing to march on Jericho.

19. *Seven Pillars*, p. 483.   20. *Ibid.*, p. 481.   21. *Ibid.*, p. 476.

The Northern Army did not restrict its activities during this period to Tafileh and Ghor al-Mazra'a. Around the middle of January Emir Feisal had prepared an attack which he led himself with the purpose of taking Mudawwara station. The operation was organized on the basis of full co-operation between the Arab regulars, armoured cars and the ten-pounder battery of the British mission as well as a French contingent with a mountain gun. In addition to the Emir, Colonel Joyce, Major Maynard and Nuri as-Said held positions of command, and the force consisted of one hundred regulars, two guns and two British aircraft. The irregular force was made up of Beni Atiyeh under Sherif Muhammad Ali Beidawi, the Imran under Sherif Hazza and the Huweitat under Sherif Hashem. The attack started on 23 January. Meanwhile the Turks had securely fortified this important station and were defending it with 300 infantry, two guns and four machine-guns. Artillery led the attack at dawn with a heavy volley of fire; one detached post held by twenty Turks was rushed and captured, five Turks were killed and fifteen were taken prisoner. But the attack failed to attain its ultimate objective because the number of regulars was insufficient to take such a fortified position and because the bedouin did not dare assault entrenchments. The guns alone were not able to force the garrison to surrender. The aircraft dropped over three-quarters of a ton of explosive on the station and put the enemy aeroplane, which had arrived that day, out of action. The Arabs were operating under several disadvantages, not least of which was the lack of water. The Emir had to give permission to the bedouin to retreat to the position of Abu Suwaneh. Colonel Joyce has stated that the Beni Atiyeh had refused at the very beginning to march with Feisal unless they were paid their allocations, which they believed they fully deserved, and that Feisal had to send to Gueira for money which he distributed among them before they agreed to set out. On the second day strong Turkish reinforcements arrived from the north, so the Arabs returned to Aqaba. Joyce complained that the Arabs did not attack Turkish entrenchments; his complaint indicates, however, that he did not fully understand the bedouin temperament in spite of the fact that he had been working with them, for bedouin by instinct will not attack under unequal circumstances. But, he did say, at the end of his report, that 'The Arabs were in no way disconcerted by their failure to take the station, and are now concentrating for a fresh offensive.' [22]

An official report stated that Feisal's regular army increased during that month—January 1918—to three thousand regulars, thirteen guns and twenty-five machine-guns.

7. THE STORM

After the battle, Lawrence spent ten days in Tafileh during which, he says, the situation was beginning to improve in and around the town after Feisal had sent a quantity of food and supplies. The Kerak tribes had established daily contact with Emir Zeid and had promised to co-operate with him and to fight on his side if he should decide to advance. But a very severe winter had already set in and Lawrence recalled that he lived in a two-room house with twenty-eight men including some of his followers—Za'agi, Abdullah, Awad al-Sherari, and his camel driver Mahmas. (This house is still standing.) Lawrence says that the days were long and heavy, the nights were bitterly cold and the wind swept into them in hindering blizzards outside, while they suffered from smoke, leakage and the stench of filth inside. He therefore decided to travel south to Feisal and obtain a sum of money to spend on the next stage of activity as soon as the weather improved. By that time Zeid had spent all he had on the local inhabitants who had helped him in the Tafileh, Ghor at-Mazra'a and Shobek operations.

On 4 March, Lawrence left Tafileh with four bedouin. They passed through Rashadieh and spent the night near Odroh close to a shelter which they hoped would provide some protection from the icy cold of the night. In the morning they travelled south to Abu al-Lissan and Gueira, where Lawrence stayed—'Lazy nights, three of them, in the armoured car tent at Gueira were pleasant, with Alan Dawnay, Joyce, and others talking, and Tafileh to boast about.' [23]

Then thirty thousand pounds in gold and his cream camel Wodheiha came up from Aqaba. Feisal lent him two Ateiba men, Serj and Rameid; and, to help carry the gold, added to the party Sheik Motlog al-Awar, and twenty Huweitat. The gold was in bags, a thousand pounds each, of which Lawrence gave two each to fourteen of the Huweitat and took the last two himself.

22. *Arab Bulletin* (18 February 1918), No. 79, p. 54.   23. *Seven Pillars*, p. 490.

Lawrence and his companions left Gueira at noon for the north and in the afternoon they passed by Sherif Fahad's tent, where Motlog decided to spend the night because it had started to rain; but Lawrence rode on with Serj and Rameid together with six Shobek-bound Huweitat, who had joined their party. In the evening they came upon Kaabar al-Abid where Saleh ibn Shefia and a hundred Yanbo' warriors were encamped.[24] They spent the night with Saleh, who gave Lawrence a new garment.

In the morning Lawrence passed through a point close to Abu al-Lissan where Maulud and his regular troops were camped. On this occasion Lawrence pays tribute to Maulud and his men.

These men of Maulud's had been camped in this place, four thousand feet above the sea, for two months without relief. They had to live in shallow dug-outs on the hill-side. They had no fuel except the sparse, wet wormwood, over which they were just able to bake their necessary bread every other day. They had no clothes but khaki drill uniform of the British summer sort. They slept in their rain-sodden verminous pits on empty or half-empty flour-sacks, six or eight of them together in a knotted bunch, that enough of the worn blankets might be pooled for warmth.

Rather more than half of them died or were injured by the cold and wet; yet the others maintained their watch, exchanging shots daily with the Turkish outposts, and protected only by the inclement weather from crushing counter-attack. We owed much to them, and more to Maulud, whose fortitude stiffened them in their duty.

The old scarred warrior's history in the Turkish army was a catalogue of affairs provoked by his sturdy sense of Arab honour and nationality, a creed for which three or four times he had sacrificed his prospects. It must have been a strong creed which enabled him to endure cheerfully three winter months in front of Maan and to share out enough spirit among five hundred ordinary men to keep them stout-heartedly about him.[25]

Lawrence rode on to Besta over the high ground where the wind buffeted him so much that he could not cover more than one mile in a whole hour. When night came he and his party were so tired that they decided to spend the night in the open. They built up the nine camels in a phalanx, and lay between them for warmth.

On the third day they reached the desolate ruins of Odroh, where the six Huweitat parted from them ten miles from Shobek

24. Saleh was the man who led the attack on Wejh.
25. *Seven Pillars,* p. 492.

to spend some time with the bedouin there, Serj and Rameid, in their turn, insisted on spending the night there on the plea of exhaustion. Lawrence decided to go on alone to Shobek and took the four thousand pounds from Serj and Rameid. He went on until after sunset, when he reached the old fort of Shobek and sought the hospitality of Sherif Abdul Mu'in who was living there with 200 men. In the morning he continued his journey till he reached Tafileh in the evening, where he 'gave Zeid his letters and some money, and went gladly to bed . . .'.[26]

Ghweileb al-Sheibani, a Hejazi who took part in the Revolt and who still lives in Amman, claims that Feisal detailed him and two others to accompany Lawrence from Gueira to Tafileh. He bears witness to Lawrence's iron will and to his great powers of endurance, but he does not agree with everything Lawrence said about this journey. On the other hand Sheikh Mirri and Mohammed al-Asbali,[27] who were serving with Zeid in Tafileh, insist that Feisal and Zeid were continuously in touch through messengers.

8. CLAIMS AND CONTRADICTIONS

Lawrence has given a detailed account of his trip from Tafileh to Gueira and back. From this account we can visualize the hardships he went through and appreciate his endurance, strength and toughness. Although he speaks about the sluggishness of his companions he also excuses them on the grounds that he himself was a product of a cold climate, and therefore naturally better equipped to weather the cold. Also, his camel was stronger than theirs. We must not forget that the whole of Feisal's army operated under the same severe conditions with the result that many men perished of cold and the lack of adequate protection from it. Of course, many members of the Arab Army had to make journeys during the snowstorm Lawrence described, but, not having Lawrence's literary talent, none of them could describe the hardship and suffering endured.

Another Englishman, Lieutenant Kirkbride, recalls the storm, for he was ordered to travel from Beersheba to Tafileh to inves-

26. *Seven Pillars*, p. 498.
27. Mohammed al-Asbali al-Sheheri, whose portrait appears in *Seven Pillars*, knew Lawrence during the Revolt and during the period which Lawrence spent in Amman in 1921 when Kennington arrived to draw his portraits for *Seven Pillars*.

tigate the possibilities of making a motor-track to supply the Arab Army from Palestine instead of from Egypt, and of improving the collection of intelligence. The journey he made with his companions coincided with the storm, and they suffered severely from its effects. Reaching Tafileh on the same day as Lawrence, Kirkbride saw him, 'dressed in wet and bedraggled Arab clothes and shaking with cold and fatigue'.[28]

Lawrence reached Tafileh on 11 February, where, according to him, he spent two days, during which the weather improved and he decided to make a reconnaissance north in preparation for fresh activities. Before setting out he asked Zeid to collect the remaining twenty-four thousand pounds from Motlog as soon as the latter arrived at Tafileh and to spend what he deemed necessary until his return. His trip took one week, during which he crossed Wadi Hesa, and rode as far as the edge of the Jordan Valley where he discovered that the Turks were in Jericho. He claimed to have passed through Buseira, Ghor al-Safi, Wadi Dhahl, Seil al-Hesa and Hesban; and stated that his trip was very reassuring and that there was a good possibility of effecting contact with the British. He noted that the weather had improved to the point where activities could be instantly resumed.

Here is a summary of Lawrence's account of what happened next:

Zeid heard me coldly . . . then I began to repeat my programme of what we might fairly do. Zeid stopped me: 'But that will need a lot of money'. I said, 'Not at all': our funds in hand would cover it, and more. Zeid replied that he had nothing; and when I gaped at him, muttered rather shamefacedly that he had spent all I brought, I thought he was joking: but he went on to say that so much had been due to Dhiab, Sheikh of Tafileh; so much to the villagers; so much to the Jazi Howeitat; so much to the Beni Sakhr. . . .

I was aghast; for this meant the complete ruin of my plans and hopes, the collapse of our effort to keep faith with Allenby. Zeid stuck to his word that the money was all gone. Afterwards I went off to learn the truth from Nasir, who was in bed with fever. He despondently said that everything was wrong—Zeid too young and shy to counter his dishonest, cowardly counsellors.

All night I thought over what could be done, but found a blank; and when morning came could only send word to Zeid that, if he would not return the money, I must go away. He sent me back his

28. Sir Alec Kirkbride, *A Crackle Of Thorns* (1956), p. 6.

supposed account of the spent money. While we were packing, Joyce and Marshall arrived. They had ridden from Guweira to give me a pleasant surprise. I told them why it had happened that I was going back to Allenby to put my further employment in his hands. Joyce made a vain appeal to Zeid, and promised to explain to Feisal.

. . . So I was able, with only four men, to set off, late that very afternoon, for Beersheba, the quickest way to British Head-quarters. . . .[29]

We know that Zeid was the responsible commander of the Tafileh front, and Lawrence himself has pointed this out: 'Feisal had delegated command of this push towards the Dead Sea to . . . Zeid. It was Zeid's first office in the north, and he set out eager with hope.' [30]

It has become clear to us that Lawrence went to Tafileh after its capture exactly as did Ja'afar al-Askari: as a visitor, and not a commander. From what quarter did his new powers come then? With regard to the money, Emir Zeid has informed me that Lawrence's special allotment was only ten thousand pounds. In any case, the money was legitimately spent. The people of Tafileh tell me that the Sheikhs in the area, and their followers who were treated as enlisted men in the Revolt, were entitled to regular wages. And at any rate thirty thousand pounds is not too great a sum, considering the extent of Zeid's responsibilities and the rewards he had to give to those who took part in the battle of 25 January, plus the compensation he had to pay to the families of those who were killed that day. Lawrence has told us that he lent Sherif Abdul Mu'in the sum of five hundred pounds in Shobek because the Sherif had run out of money and had informed Lawrence that he and his men would starve or rob unless money came along in time. Sherif Hussein al-Shakrani, who was with Zeid at the time, has said, in answer to a question I put to him, that he had no knowledge of this and that he had not heard of what Lawrence claimed to have happened. He did say, however, that Zeid was brave and generous and that Feisal loved and respected him. He added that Zeid was reticent by nature and that Sherif Nassir was not in Tafileh at the time. At this point it is necessary for us to compare Lawrence's claim that he left Tafileh determined to break off completely with the Arab Revolt, with the statement made by Sir Alec Kirkbride that he

29. *Seven Pillars*, pp. 499–500.
30. *Ibid.*, p. 473.

accompanied Lawrence for two days on his way back to Beer-sheba:

> When saying good-bye, Lawrence asked me if I would like to be attached to the Arab Army; I accepted the offer with gratitude, and in due course he made the necessary arrangements with General Headquarters.[31]

This leads us to seek an explanation of the discrepancy between Lawrence's statement that he was breaking off with the Revolt and his offer to Kirkbride before arriving at General Headquarters. As a comment upon a question I put to him about Lawrence's claim that he intended to resign from the Arab Army, Emir Zeid replied with the laconic 'And why didn't he?' This rhetorical question, added to all the other evidence, leads me to doubt the truth of Lawrence's statement.

31. *A Crackle Of Thorns*, p. 7.

6

ADVANCE AND RETREAT

1. LAWRENCE AT BRITISH HEADQUARTERS

WE must now trace the movements of the Arab Revolt and particularly of the Northern Army, which had become the effective force because of the relative attention which the British had given it. The exceptionally severe winter was over, and spring, which is usually more favourable to military operations, was beginning. In this chapter we shall deal with the second Turkish attack on Tafileh and with the great Arab offensive against Ma'an and the railway stations. We shall also describe the two British attacks on Salt and Amman and study Lawrence's movements during this period.

On 19 February, Lawrence left Tafileh for Beersheba and did not return to Aqaba until 4 March. Two days later he returned to Egypt, where he spent the next ten days.

But first let us trace Lawrence's activities during this period as described in *Seven Pillars*. When he reached Beersheba he went through to Allenby's Headquarters and met Dr. Hogarth to whom he explained his business, claiming that because Zeid had spent all the money he had, his plan for advancing to the mouth of the Jordan River had been frustrated. He complained that he was tired of the part he was playing and of not being given any definite orders. Diplomatically, Hogarth made no reply but took him to Clayton, who explained that preparations were on foot for a major offensive against the Turks, with a view to putting Turkey out of the war for good in the spring. Clayton also explained that the British Army was to co-operate fully with the Arabs in launching this attack. He added that in the new circumstances there could be no question of letting Lawrence off. Lawrence met Allenby later on, and was told that the British Army intended to advance north as soon as possible, with Damascus, or even Aleppo, as the objective. Allenby wanted to know if the Arabs could relieve him of the burden of securing his eastern flank to forestall any Turkish counter-attack on that sector. At this point, Lawrence has said, he again had to put on his 'mantle of fraud in the East', and therefore did not even mention the reasons which had brought him across, but offered his suggestions with regard to the new objectives: the first thing to do was to take Ma'an, and, to secure this, 700 baggage camels were needed. Lawrence also requested more guns and machine-guns, plus assurance against a Turkish counter-attack from Amman, while the Arabs dealt with Ma'an.

On this basis a scheme was worked out. Allenby ordered down to Gueira from Beersheba two units of the Camel Transport Corps, and promised to send the requested guns soon. He also said that he intended to occupy Salt shortly and hold on to it— a step which would prevent the Turks from attacking the Arabs.

On 28 February, Lawrence attended a Corps Conference, at which it was decided that the Arab Army should move instantly to take Ma'an,[1] and that the British should cross the Jordan River, occupy Salt and destroy as much of the railway south of Amman as possible, especially the great tunnel. Lawrence mentioned that he wore Arab clothes for this conference. With these arrangements completed, Lawrence went on to Cairo, then returned to Aqaba 'to make my new terms with Feisal'.[2] He told Feisal that they had treated him badly, in diverting without his knowledge, money of the special account which he had drawn solely for the Dead Sea Campaign, and that unless his advice was respected it would be impossible for him to carry on. This would imply that he had returned to dictate his terms to Feisal, but there are indications that he never behaved towards Feisal in this manner but always showed unbounded loyalty. Doubtless, he did not conceal his self-satisfaction when he declared that Allenby 'as thanks for the Dead Sea and Aba el Lissan, had put three hundred thousand pounds into my inde-

1. The attack was not actually launched until forty days later.
2. *Seven Pillars*, p. 504.

pendent credit, and given us a train of seven hundred pack-camels complete with personnel and equipment'.[3]

Lawrence's personal gains, especially his promotion to the rank of Colonel and the award of the D.S.O., indicate that he was not in fact the scapegoat that he was trying to make himself out to be in *Seven Pillars*.

2. THE RAID ON FASSUA'

Two events took place at about this time: an attempted attack on Fassua',[4] and fierce engagements with the second Turkish expedition to regain Tafileh.

The Fassua' raid was one link in a chain of attacks that the Arabs were conducting on the railway line.. Previous to this raid there was unusual activity on the part of Arab Army officers, who were deeply worried by news of secret agreements among the Allies for the division of Arab countries and by the pro-Zionist Balfour Declaration. In this connexion the *Arab Bulletin* complained that certain Syrian officers in the Eastern Army were meddling with politics and attributed their inactivity to suspicions about secret agreements among the Allies. It even went on to say that Emir Abdullah, influenced by these officers, had shown 'some reluctance to undertake any serious operations against the railway'. It is not surprising, therefore, that a new movement took place among the officers of the Northern Army, which almost amounted to mutiny, for they had started to suspect British intentions and behaviour and in particular those of Joyce and Lawrence. They began to press for an immediate attack on Ma'an and went so far as to present a petition to this effect to Feisal.

Orders went out for immediate preparations to attack Fassua'. Maulud, Commander of the First Division, was to lead this raid, but he refused because of the political considerations we have mentioned and because he and his companions feared that the British were deliberately directing Arab efforts to useless and indecisive activity. As a result of Maulud's disposition, he was removed from his position of command and taken into custody. Ja'afar Pasha was then entrusted with the task of commanding the raiding force.

The force, which was made up of an infantry battalion and

3. *Seven Pillars*, p. 505.
4. A small fortress to the west of Akabat al-Hejazieh station (south of Ma'an).

a number of machine-guns, set out from Abu al-Lissan but was hindered by a severe storm accompanied by heavy rain and intense cold. The men had to spend the night in the open, the storm having separated them from the camels that carried their tents, luggage and provisions, with the result that several soldiers perished from the cold. The force had no option but to make its way back on the following day, where it was met by Feisal coming to their relief with a party of medical men. Al-Ajluni, who was one of the officers of that force, states that he and his companions spent the whole night cutting down shrubs to make a fire for warmth so that they might escape freezing to death. As a result of this failure and of increased discontent among the officers, Maulud was reinstated in his previous position.

General Headquarters had meanwhile sent down Colonel Dawnay, a competent Staff Officer, to join Feisal and to co-operate with the Arab command in devising suitable plans for the attack on Ma'an.

Lawrence claimed that he was the first to propose the plan of attacking Ma'an and that he and his British colleagues were of the opinion that the Arab Army should first attack the stations north and south of Ma'an, in an attempt to demolish enemy installations thoroughly. He argued that this would isolate Ma'an and force the Turkish garrison to leave its entrenchments for a battle in the open. This would make it easier for the Arabs to capture Ma'an. According to Lawrence, however, the Arab officers turned down this plan and insisted on a direct onslaught, which led to their ultimate failure. But information available to us from Arab sources indicates that the disagreement between Arab and British officers revolved not around the details of the plan of attack but around whether to attack Ma'an at all. Lawrence's account suggests that he was being wise after the event, for the *Arab Bulletin* made no mention of the situation he described and after his report on the battle of Tafileh, Lawrence did not publish any reports on military activities for some months. Arab sources are unanimously agreed that it was Allenby who asked the Arabs to attack Ma'an in order to secure his positions at Salt and Amman.

Official British sources confirm the fact that Allenby had requested the Arabs to attack Ma'an, so that the Turks would be too occupied to attack his army in Palestine, which had been seriously jeopardized by the withdrawal in March 1918, of a number of its most effective divisions to assist in the European front. In so far as the Arab attack fulfilled this purpose, it can be regarded in no other way than as successful.

3. THE TURKS REGAIN TAFILEH

The second battle for Tafileh began late in February. The weather had improved and the Turks feared that the Arabs would make a further advance towards Kerak. At Amman they therefore prepared for a fresh expedition, which consisted of three infantry battalions, two mule-mounted companies and a number of German detachments, supported by eight guns, two machine-gun companies and two aeroplanes. The Turks followed a plan radically different from the one they had used earlier. This force left Amman by train: one column detrained at Hesa station, the other at Jurf al-Darawish. Skirmishes began to take place as soon as the two columns advanced towards Tafileh. On 25 February there was an engagement between a small Arab force and a German cavalry patrol, in which the enemy was eventually forced to withdraw with some losses.

When news of the Turkish march reached Zeid, he instantly set out to resist it. The ensuing battles lasted for a week; Zeid's regular force participating in addition to volunteers from Tafileh and neighbouring villages, the Jazi Huweitat, and tribesmen of Beni Sakhr, Menain and Hejaya. A number of Sherifs assisted Zeid in leading the men in the engagements. Since the ground all along the route of the Turkish march was almost level, and since the enemy force marched only during the day at short stages and camped during the night close together, the Arabs were not able to engage the enemy in a critical position. They thus could not make use of their mobility nor could they benefit from the enemy's mistakes. The engagements were therefore mostly brief but fierce. When the Hejaya and Menain bedouin tried to intercept the Turkish vanguard, they were overwhelmed and a number of their men were killed including some sheikhs.

The first major battle took place at Khirbet al-Tuwaneh, halfway between Tafileh and Jurf al-Darawish. Powerful Turkish artillery forced Zeid into evacuating the position and retreating to Khirbet al-Harir, then to Jebel al-Musalla and Khirbet Abur.

During his retreat Zeid set up defensive entrenchments in each of these positions. He made his last stand at Khirbet al-Ais, over-looking Tafileh, and resisted for a whole day, thus giving the inhabitants of Tafileh time to evacuate their town. This was done when it became clear to Zeid that his forces stood no chance of repelling the enemy. On 6 March after the inhabitants of the town had sought shelter in Wadi Araba, the Turks entered Tafileh and plundered it. Zeid withdrew south, carrying all his guns and equipment after burning all provisions that he could not transport. The Turks followed Zeid to Rashadieh, but soon retreated again. In fact the Turkish occupation of Tafileh did not exceed ten days, after which they started retreating to Amman. On 18 March Sherif Nassir led his followers back to Tafileh, while Zeid camped at Shobek for a few days, then marched to Abu al-Lissan to take part in the impending attack on Ma'an. Commenting on this battle, the Emir said, 'The Turks attacked with overwhelming force which compelled us to retreat. Decision for evacuation of Tafileh was made by H.Q., not at my wish.'

The head of the Turkish Intelligence branch has said that the Turkish High Command issued orders to Mehmed Jemal Pasha to move to Jurf al-Darawish station and command the Turkish forces, which were massed secretly, to regain Tafileh. Called 'punitive forces', they were under a German officer named Meyer. When Jemal Pasha arrived he had a dispute with the German officers as to who was to lead the operation. The Arabs had ambushed a company of German cavalry, killing twenty-five Germans. For this reason Jemal insisted on commanding the forces himself on the grounds that he was more familiar with the country. Liman von Sanders described this attack as 'violent but successful'.

General Brémond has stated that the Turkish force was made up of nearly three thousand men, aided by Austro-German elements, artillery and three planes, which had been withdrawn from the Nablus front. He also stated that a French lieutenant was with Zeid all the while, and that this lieutenant mentions in a report that Zeid sent him with a detachment of regulars and 300 bedouin. On 3 March they engaged the Turkish force. He added that at the first explosion the bedouin took to their heels, but the French lieutenant and his men resisted until they ran out of equipment in the evening, when they had to retreat. On the following day Zeid advanced with four thousand men to meet the enemy, but at night enemy flash-lights created panic among the bedouin, who fled and plundered Tafileh. On 5 March, according to Brémond, Zeid burnt Tafileh and retreated. The least that can be said about Brémond's claims is that they are complete fabrications.

It is important to note that Jericho fell into the hands of the British on 21 February. This date coincided with the period during which the Turks assembled their forces for the second assault on Tafileh. Thus we see that the Turks retreated from the town in order to reinforce their defences in the Jordan Valley against the British onslaught. Furthermore, the Turks were in no position to leave such a large force and its equipment inactive in a remote position like Tafileh, from which it would be almost impossible for them to call it to the defence of any other endangered positions. It is well known that the Turkish forces were not as numerous as the opposing British Army pressing on them from the west. General Liman von Sanders, who had taken over the supreme command of the Turkish armies in Palestine in February, has recorded that von Falkenhausen, Chief of Staff of the Turkish Seventh Army, informed him on his arrival that 'the British were so superior along the entire front, that they could pierce the front at any time and place they might select'.[5] The retreat of the Turks was, therefore, natural enough and in line with their military capabilities. It seems that they considered this retreat to be only temporary, because their scouting patrols stationed at Hesa and Jurf al-Darawish carried on in the Tafileh area without interruption. In fact, one of their patrols returned in late March to Khirbet al-Ais overlooking Tafileh and captured a number of the inhabitants. The Turkish officers then tried to bully Sheikh Dhiab al-Auran into working with them against the Revolt. When Feisal found out that the Tafileh sheikhs were in correspondence with the Turks, he ordered the arrest of about thirty of their men who were with him at Gueira and Abu al-Lissan. Most of them were from the Auran and Mheisen clans. The prisoners were sent by sea to Jedda, thence to Mecca. After a while King Hussein released most of them, but he held on to five men who remained as

5. Liddell Hart, '*T. E. Lawrence' in Arabia and After* (1945), p. 284.

his guests until the end of the war. The primary purpose behind their arrest was to prevent their relatives from co-operating with the Turks.

4. THE BRITISH AT SALT AND AMMAN

What was Lawrence doing during these bitter battles? He spent two days at Aqaba (4–5 March) to brief Feisal on Allenby's future plans. He then went to Egypt and Palestine and did not return until the middle of March. He says that Allenby's plan aimed at reaching Salt around 30 March. Feisal, therefore, delegated Sheikh Merzuk al-Tekheimi to man the Beni Sakhr area in order to effect contact with the British forces and co-operate with them in case they succeeded in establishing themselves at Salt and Amman. Lawrence, on the other hand, spent more than two weeks doing nothing in particular. Part of this period he spent at Shobek with Zeid and Nassir. But he did not record anything about what he heard from Zeid with regard to the second battle of Tafileh. He merely presented his own point of view and that of his British colleagues regarding the ideal method of defeating the Turks in Ma'an. He also tells us of the insistence of the Arab officers, Maulud in particular, on taking Ma'an by direct and immediate assault. He complains that the Arab plan had to be adopted because of their insistence.

Meanwhile, the British Army had engaged the Turks in a fierce battle west of Jericho. The Turks had to evacuate the town on 21 February, and they settled down on the eastern bank of the River Jordan, but they held on to a bridge-head on the west bank, at Ghoraniyeh. On 9 March the British attacked this bridge and fighting continued for four days. As a result, the British succeeded in occupying some important positions. Undoubtedly, this British attack was instrumental in bringing about the withdrawal of the Turks from Tafileh, since they needed reinforcements for their western front. According to Wavell:

> The activities of Feisal's Arabs were of great value to the E.E.F. They safeguarded its flank south of the Dead Sea from Turkish raids towards Beersheba or Hebron, deprived the Turks of the supplies they had been drawing from the areas about Kerak and Ma'an, and caused a constant drain of men and material on their scanty reserves.[6]

6. A. P. Wavell, *The Palestine Campaigns* (1936), pp. 179–180.

The British started their first offensive against the east bank
of the Jordan on 21 March. Heavy rains had swollen the river
and two days were lost in forcing a crossing. They captured
Shunet Nimrin in the valley, then advanced uphill and were
able to enter Salt on the evening of 25 March and started attacking Amman. The Turks, making use of the British delay, had
brought over hurried reinforcements and posted their heavy
guns on strongly fortified positions. After four days of fighting
the British had to withdraw on the night of 31 March without
succeeding in destroying the tunnel south of Amman.

Lawrence claimed that he left Army Headquarters at Abu al-
Lissan with Merzuk al-Tekheimi on 2 April. They headed north
with two thousand Serahin camels carrying ammunition and
food. Merzuk was at the head of the Ageyl volunteers. Lawrence had his bodyguard with him. On the next day they crossed
the railway line at a point close to Uneiza station. On 7 April
they reached Atara, a valley to the east of Zizia, a dwelling-place
of the Beni Sakhr in winter and spring. There they were received
by Mifleh, Fahad and Adhoub. Shortly, news reached them that
the British had entered Salt, so they started making preparations
with the Beni Sakhr for a march west to Madaba. But further
news was received that the British had just evacuated Salt and
that they had failed to storm the tunnel south of Amman.
Adhoub was despatched to Amman to find out how things really
stood, and he returned after a few hours with the news that the
British had indeed made a retreat. Lawrence went on to say that
he saw a group of gipsy families camped near the Beni Sakhr
tents, and he wished to make use of them. So he and Farraj hired
three of the gipsy women, wrapped themselves up in similar
attire and strolled disguised through the town. Then they hurriedly returned to their party at Wadi Atara. They later made
their way to the suburbs of Ma'an, where the Arabs had been
attacking Turkish entrenchments for two days. We should
notice at this point that the British had withdrawn from Amman
and Salt before Lawrence left Abu al-Lissan.

I have no idea where Lawrence's figure of two thousand
camels came from. The Serahin usually had their tents to the
north of Azraq. Besides, how did the Serahin come by this huge
number of camels? The bedouin's camels in March are usually
weak and exhausted from the bitterness of the winter, and they

are generally unfit for use until May or later. Adhoub has informed me that the camels accompanying Lawrence and Merzuk did not exceed one hundred. As for Lawrence's alleged visit to Amman in the disguise of a gipsy woman, Adhoub and Turki do not give it much credence, claiming that Lawrence never wandered out of their encampment. Adhoub says that Lawrence could not have been absent for long without being missed. Besides, neither Adhoub nor Turki recall that any gipsies were there; they insist that had the event actually taken place they could not have failed to notice it. When I related Lawrence's story they threw up their hands and laughed.

Nuri as-Said has stated that the Turks made a counter-attack on the British forces attacking Amman. He adds that the British had to withdraw after suffering a considerable number of casualties, in addition to losing many prisoners.

The British High Command requested us to mount our offensive on the Turkish forces in an effort to relieve the pressure on them in the Jordan valley. As a result of long talks that took several days, we decided to attack the Ma'an garrison.[7]

This statement is at variance with what Lawrence has said. But it is perfectly reasonable, for the Turks continued with their counter-attack after 2 April, making heavy attacks from the bridge-head which they had held on the River Jordan since well before the British attack. There is nothing strange, therefore, in the British asking their allies for support.

As Lawrence claimed to have previous knowledge of Allenby's plans it is impossible to comprehend why he did not arrive in the Amman area before the end of March, while the British were attacking Amman and occupying Salt. It is clear that his coming was not for purely military purposes. He did not write of a military force, but of two thousand camels carrying ammunition and food. Where, then, did the ammunition and food come from? And for whom was it destined? The fact is that Feisal had sent Merzuk al-Tekheimi to stay for a while in the Beni Sakhr area, to try to win the rest of their clans to the side of the Revolt. Having heard of the British attack, Lawrence followed Merzuk there, but on hearing that the attack had failed, he returned to the Ma'an area.

7. Nuri as-Said, *op. cit.*, p. 43.

5. THE BATTLES OF MA'AN

Be that as it may, the Arab Army launched a general offensive against the Turkish lines. This offensive may be considered the greatest battle that the Arabs fought in the Revolt. The regular force engaged exceeded four thousand, in addition to several thousand bedouin volunteers under the Sherifs.

On 8 April 1918 Feisal, Ja'afar, Nuri and Dawnay held a military conference to agree on the final details of the projected attack. It was arranged that the attack should be launched by three columns, from the centre, south and north. Nuri, who was Chief of Staff, opened the attack by storming Ghadir al-Haj, the next station south of Ma'an, at dawn on 11 April. He had an infantry brigade, the French battery and the armoured cars. At the same time the Commander-in-Chief, Ja'afar al-Askari, with an infantry brigade and battery of mountain-guns attacked and captured Jerdun Station, immediately to the north of Ma'an. The two columns were supported by bedouin and volunteer forces. They succeeded in occupying the two stations after heavy fighting and took seven hundred prisoners.

Early on 13 April, the centre column under Maulud Mukhlis succeeded in capturing Jebel Semna, five kilometres from Ma'an. This he did with the help of the French battery and some bedouin forces under Auda Abu Tayeh. On seeing the Turks withdraw in a leisurely fashion, Maulud was enraged and led a number of irregular horsemen into the attack upon the retreating Turkish unit. A Turkish soldier, seeing that the attackers were few, made a halt and fired on their leader, who was hit in the thigh. Maulud fell from his horse and was carried back.

It was on this day that Lawrence returned from the north. He says that he met Maulud as he was being carried on a stretcher. When he asked what had happened to him, Maulud answered, 'Yes, indeed, Lurens Bey, I am hurt: but, thanks be to God, it is nothing. We have taken Semna.' [8]

On 16 April, following this initial success, the Arab Army launched an attack on the Ma'an entrenchments. Fighting continued for the whole day and the Arabs occupied the outer entrenchments. On the following day the Arabs resumed the attack with renewed vigour, and some Arab units actually

8. *Seven Pillars*, p. 518.

reached the railway station. Resistance was expected to collapse at any moment. But the French artillery, which was covering the attackers, ceased fire and the attackers were left with no cover. Seizing this opportunity, the Turks rushed at them with machine-gun fire from an adjoining hill and forced them to retreat. Added to this, the bedouin did not attack from the eastern flank as was expected. At night Emir Feisal gave the order for retreat to a safe distance, to avoid further losses. Captain Pisani has claimed that the French guns had run out of ammunition, adding that he had given warning beforehand to Nuri as-Said that he had only a limited number of shells. Nuri on the other hand, has expressed great surprise at the behaviour of the French commander:

I still remember quite vividly that this battery did not do its job and that it fired a few shells only, to determine distance and direction. This did not involve more than 20 shells.

He also said that when Lawrence arrived at the station

I expressed to him my pain and anger at the French guns ceasing fire and at the failure of the bedouin to attack as agreed. He returned: and in the afternoon I received a note from him explaining that the battery commander had returned to camp because his ammunition had run out and he saw no reason why he should remain in the battlefield. As for the planned attack of the tribesmen, he informed me that he had no idea why they failed to carry out their part of the plan.[9]

The Arabs captured about seventy Turks in their attack on Ma'an itself.[10] Their own losses amounted to about two hundred and fifty killed and wounded. Nuri as-Said says that the casualties were almost thirty per cent of the whole force. It appears from information published after the war that the Turks were about to surrender and that had the French artillery continued its barrage of fire the Arabs would definitely have captured this fortified position. However, in spite of the fact that the Arabs finally retreated, this battle gave evidence of the excellent standard which the regulars had attained both in training and in morale.

Lawrence says that he returned to Wahida and met Feisal

9. Nuri as-Said, op. cit., pp. 45–6.
10. The inhabitants of Ma'an supported the Turks in this battle and contributed to the Arab failure in so far as there was a lack of confidence between the townspeople and the bedouin at the time.

there. He adds that Auda Abu Tayeh asserted that he did all he could on that day but that conditions were not suitable for bedouin attacks. Lawrence goes on to say that he spent the next few days watching military operations, adding that the Tawaiha tribes captured two outposts to the east of Ma'an station. Saleh ibn Shafia succeeded in capturing a breastwork with a machine-gun and twenty Turkish prisoners.

On 19 April, the Arabs attacked the railway near Tell al-Shahm with the help of the British Military Mission. They captured all Turkish positions around the station, then attacked Tell al-Shahm itself with the help of British armoured cars and bedouin forces under Sherif Hazzaa, and were able to capture the station and take fifty-four prisoners. On the following day the Turks evacuated Ramleh station, which the Arabs then occupied and destroyed. The Arabs succeeded in doing extensive damage to the railway line betwen Ma'an and Mudowwara, including seven railway stations. The Turks were unable to repair the line because rail reserves had run out.[11]

On 18 April, when Emir Feisal halted the attack on Ma'an, Lawrence went south, where Colonel Dawnay and Sherif Hazzaa were preparing to attack the Tell al-Shahm station. Lawrence wrote:

So I . . . offered myself, delicately, as an interpreter. . . . Fortunately he [Dawnay] received me well, and took me round his lines. . . .[12]

Dawnay had the Egyptian Camel company under Captain Peake (who later became commander of the Arab Legion). Hazzaa was leading the Imran bedouin. Four British aeroplanes, three armoured cars with machine-guns and two ten-pounder guns were assisting in the attack. With his usual attention to detail, Lawrence described the capture of the station and the direct bedouin attack. He paused, however, to say that the bedouin indulged in 'the maddest looting of their history' calling them 'wolves, not yet sated'.[13] At the same time he admits that he

11. Before the war there had been in Medina the equivalent of 100 kms. of rails, since the Ottoman Government was intending to extend the railway to Mecca. Medina also had an eight-hundred-man battalion trained in railway construction and repair. That was why work on the railway line had continued, since the Turks could easily repair the parts damaged by the Arabs. These conditions prevailed until the Turks ran out of rails. The line between Damascus and Medina covers 1,307 kms.

12. *Seven Pillars*, p. 521.   13. *Ibid.*, p. 523.

'gained the station bell' (which he later took to Oxford).[14] On the following day, they occupied Ramleh station, following its evacuation by the Turks. After a day's rest, the Arab force marched north to Wadi al-Rutm station, which they captured with little difficulty. Lawrence then set off with two armoured cars to explore Mudowwara, but he soon returned with the advice that they delay their attack on this station because of the strong Turkish defences there. They persevered in destroying line and bridges and in removing rails at leisure. At the same time Feisal dispatched Muhammed al-Dheilan at the head of a number of Tawaiha men; they destroyed the railway line from Ma'an to Ghadir al-Haj, Shedia, Aqaba, Batn al-Ghul and Wadi al-Rutm stations. They removed the remaining rails. Thus about 100 kms. of line were destroyed, and the line remained unserviceable until the end of the war.

At this time a new officer, Captain Young, came from Iraq to assist Lawrence. He was a professional officer and spoke Arabic fluently. His task was to double Lawrence's role with the tribes. Lawrence was not happy with this appointment and he did not trust Young. He suspected that his new colleague was there to spy on him, and he was therefore anxious to get rid of him as soon as possible.[15] He wrote, however, that he handed over to Young the possible project of combining Zeid, Nassir and Merzuk for an attempt to make an eighty-mile-long interruption of the railway from Ma'an northward.

The Turks had brought over strong reinforcements from Syria when the British began their attack on Salt and Amman. The Amman garrison was increased to five thousand. After the retreat of the British the Turks sent large reinforcements to Ma'an by train and on beasts of burden. These reinforcements enabled the Turks to recapture Jerdun station and to strengthen the Ma'an garrison after it had come so close to surrender.

The Beni Sakhr, together with Merzuk al-Tekheimi, had carried out several raids on the railway line north of Hesa station, at the time when the main attack on Ma'an was in progress. But these raids had not been sufficiently effective to alter the course of the battle.

14. Colonel Peake says that he removed the bell of Dera'a station after the Arabs captured it, and that on Lawrence's request he gave it to him.
15. Anthony Nutting, *Lawrence of Arabia* (1961), p. 136.

Following the failure of the Arab attack on Ma'an, the British army launched a second offensive on Salt. On 29 April, Shunet Nimrin on the east bank of the Jordan was attacked, while other British forces made a dash for Salt, which they entered on 30 April. The Turks, however, counter-attacked at Salt and the Jordan Valley, and on 3 May pushed the British back to the west bank.

After Lawrence had viewed the damage operations on the railway line between Ma'an and Mudowwara he 'went down to Akaba, and took ship for Suez, to discuss futures with Allenby'.[16] He informs us that he was surprised upon arrival with the news of the second march on Amman and Salt. According to him, this march was based on a promise from the sheikhs of Beni Sakhr, who had gone to Jerusalem and Jericho and declared their readiness to assist the British forces by cutting the Wadi Seer road if the attack were renewed, asserting that twenty thousand of their men at Thamad wells stood in perfect readiness. Of these sheikhs, Lawrence singled out Fahad al-Zebn for special mention. He did not hide his contempt for the British for believing the sheikhs and marching on Salt and Amman only to find out that there was not a single Beni Sakhr warrior there. As a result the Turks succeeded in pushing them back after inflicting considerable losses. Allenby's timely order for retreat saved the British from being trapped. Lawrence's satisfaction at the outcome was the result of his indignation because the British commanders had co-operated with the bedouin without consulting him. He regarded bedouin affairs as his own province, and believed that he could have saved the British this disastrous experience with the bedouin.

In fact, the *Arab Bulletin* of 30 April states that delegates from Beni Sakhr arrived at Jerusalem, expressed their hatred of the Turks and offered their services should they at any time be required. The delegates included also representatives of the Ghanamat, Isa, and Hejaya tribes, and were headed by Sheikh Fahad al-Zebn of the Beni Sakhr. They said that the tribesmen had buried all their feuds at the Sherif's desire.

It is interesting to note that the Official History of these campaigns states that it was the Arab successes at Tafileh and Ghor al-Mazraa which in fact encouraged Allenby to launch his

16. *Seven Pillars*, p. 524.

first attack on Salt, particularly as the Turkish attack on Tafileh
had weakened their Amman garrison. It also states that the
failure of the British to keep Salt enabled the Turks to hold on
to Ma'an and repulse Arab attacks on the town. The failure of
the second expedition is attributed to 'the inability of the 60th
Division to capture the enemy's position at Shunet Nimrin' . . .[17]
It is evident that this failure is not to be attributed to bedouin
deceit, as Lawrence would have us believe. Wavell insists, however, that 'Though the raid ended in a distinct tactical defeat,
the strategical effect was favourable in that from now onward
one-third of the total Turkish forces was stationed east of the
Jordan'. . . for fear that Allenby's next attack might come
against his left.[18]

What had actually happened was that Merzuk al-Tekheimi had
sent a letter to British headquarters in Jerusalem with some
bedouin chieftains who were ignorant of its contents. Merzuk
offered to co-operate with the British in a second attack on
Amman, because he had heard of the difficulties the British had
faced in their first attack as a result of the apathy of the inhabitants. He realized that with a measure of co-operation between the British and the Arabs on the first attack, it would have
been possible to blow up the railway tunnel south of Amman.
It is certain that Merzuk's letter did not contain promises he
was incapable of fulfilling. It is also certain that the British did
not give Merzuk previous warning of their second attack. This
indicates that they did not believe in the efficacy of Arab co-
operation until they had safely established themselves at Salt.
Furthermore, the Beni Sakhr could not possibly have assembled
at Wadi al-Seer because of hostilities with the Belqa tribes.
In any case, the failure of the British to occupy Salt was useful
to Lawrence in that it much strengthened his personal position.
The British staff 'agreed to let me know if any thing of the sort
[moving irregulars] was ever required' . . .[19]

Lawrence believed that the withdrawal in March of some
strong divisions from Allenby's army might give the Turks
a chance to sweep the Arabs off Abu al-Lissan. He therefore
asked for repeated air raids on the Hejaz Railway, and on

17. *Military Operations*, Part I, p. 367.
18. *The Palestine Campaigns*, pp. 188–189.
19. *T. E. Lawrence to his Biographers*, Part II, p. 110.

orders from Allenby these were later carried out by the Air Force.

Lawrence then learned that Allenby was planning to disband the Imperial Camel Brigade in Sinai. He therefore requested two thousand camels to reinforce divisional transport and movement in the Northern Army. Lawrence surrounded his efforts to get the camels with a certain bravado. After dwelling on the Quartermaster-General's strong opposition to the scheme, he informs us that Allenby asked him at dinner what he wanted the camels for. Then came Lawrence's enthusiastic reply, 'To put a thousand men into Dera'a any day you please.' [20] This magic answer held sway, and the camels were regally granted.

On the following day, 4 May, Lawrence was off to break the news to Feisal. He discussed various subjects with Feisal, then sprang the good news.

Finally, I remarked that Allenby had given us two thousand camels. Feisal gasped and caught my knees, saying. 'How?' I told him all the story. He leaped up and kissed me; then he clapped his hands loudly. Hejris' black shape appeared at the tent-door. 'Hurry', cried Feisal, 'call them'. Hejris asked whom. 'Oh, Fahad, Abdulla el Feir, Auda, Motlog, Zaal. . . .' 'And not Mirzuk?' queried Hejris mildly. Feisal shouted at him for a fool, and the black ran off; while I said, 'It is nearly finished. Soon you can let me go'. He protested, saying that I must remain with them always, and not just till Damascus, as I had promised in Um Lejj. I, who wanted so to get away.[21]

No wonder Feisal was pleased; no wonder every Arab was delighted. Two thousand camels were no small matter: with them the Arab Army could move much more freely and expand its operations. It is not strange that Lawrence was thanked, admired, and regarded as a loyal friend to the Arabs with their interests at heart. This incident is an example of Lawrence's dealings with the Arabs and should be a reminder of Feisal's critical need for any kind of help he could get in the relentless battle.

As a result of Lawrence's success in this matter, Captain Young was put in charge of equipment and transport. This squared with Lawrence's desires, for Young was no longer a rival. Contact with the bedouin remained firmly in Lawrence's hands.

20. *Seven Pillars*, p. 527.   21. *Ibid.*, p. 527.

6. ATTACKS ON THE STATIONS

The Arab attack in April attained one of the primary aims of the Hejaz operations, in that the railway line south of Ma'an was damaged for a considerable distance. Turkish communications between Medina and the northern stations were cut off. The Arab Army therefore moved in force to the railway line north of Ma'an. Its purpose was to destroy the line to the point of preventing the Turks from setting up a large force at Ma'an, which could, if allowed to assemble, attack Arab positions in the Semna hills. These operations were placed under Emir Zeid and were to be carried out by regular forces. The Arab Army established a base at Fejeij, four miles south of Odroh, as a spring-board for impending operations. Nuri as-Said commanded the regular force, which consisted of about 1,200 regular troops, two eighteen-pounder field guns, two mountain guns and two companies of machine-guns. The French contingent also operated with this force. Their regulars were led by Sherif Nassir, comprising two Ageyl companies and Huweitat, Beni Sakhr, Darausha, Juwabra, Menain and Naimat elements, in addition to a regular contingent under Rasim and the Egyptian Camel company under Captain Peake. Captain Hornby, expert in demolitions, was also attached to this force. During the second half of April and the first half of May all efforts were directed towards damaging the railway line between Ma'an and Mudowwara station. Consequently operations to the north of Ma'an did not get started until after 10 May.

At dawn on 11 May the regular forces, consisting of two infantry battalions and a cavalry battalion under Nuri as-Said, attacked Jerdun station, with the help of artillery and three British aeroplanes. The Turks were taken by surprise and, after putting up a brief resistance, surrendered. They lost thirty men, a hundred and fifty prisoners, one mountain gun, a number of machine-guns and a large quantity of equipment. The Arabs also demolished Turkish installations, seven trucks in the station and a water tank. They destroyed a considerable section of the line and three masonry bridges. This battle is known as the Second Jerdun Battle. On 14 May, the Arabs had to withdraw because their water supply had run out. So the Turks reoccupied the station, repaired and reinforced it.

On 17 May, Arab regular troops again attacked Jerdun. An infantry battalion reached the outer entrenchments around the station, but the Turks, who were fully prepared, launched a concentrated counter-attack and forced the Arabs to withdraw. In this engagement the Turks resorted to a trick used by the Germans on the western front. A number of Turks in the front line held up their hands as a gesture of surrender, but when Arab troops approached to receive their surrender, they were met by heavy machine-gun fire and by hand grenades from a trench in the rear. Most of those who advanced were killed or wounded. The battalion Commander, six officers, and twenty-three men were killed, and a hundred and one were wounded. The Turkish losses were estimated at forty killed and eighteen captured. On the arrival of enemy reinforcements from Uneiza station, the Arabs retreated.

Early in May, Sherif Nassir had conducted several raids on the railway line. On 8 May, he attacked Kutrani station and took some prisoners. The raid was repeated on the following day with no marked success. On 12 May, Nassir attacked again. Failing to capture the station, he damaged a section of line. On 18 May he set out from the base at Fejeij, supported by a regular Arab contingent and the Egyptian Camel company. This mixed force rushed Hesa station on 23 May and took sixty-five prisoners. The Arabs seized two machine-guns and a quantity of weapons and equipment, and destroyed the station installations, including two water tanks. They then destroyed a section of the line north and south of the station and some bridges. On the following day Fareifra station was captured; sixty prisoners and one machine-gun were taken; station installations, including a number of wagons, were demolished. They also raided Manzil (Sultani) and Jurf al-Darawish stations and carried out extensive demolitions on the section of line between Jurf al-Darawish and Hesa.

Arab raids then extended to Kutrani station in the north, where some bridges were destroyed, and rails were removed in several places. In fact the railway line in that area was in the hands of the Arabs for almost two weeks, and demolition was carried out between Kutrani and Jurf al-Darawish. In all, about 14 kms. of line were destroyed. On 26 May, an attack by a force of regular troops was made on the line between Ma'an and Jerdun. A considerable section of line was cut and two bridges were destroyed. The Turks launched an unsuccessful counter-attack, while other Arab detachments were removing more rails south of Ma'an.

As a result of these continuous attacks the Turks brought over three thousand regulars in late May and reinforced their station garrisons. Command was turned over to German and Austrian officers. These reinforcements, which came from the Nablus front, were supported by heavy artillery. At the same time German aeroplanes attacked Arab camps at Wadi al-Hesa, inflicting considerable losses and blunting the edge of their attacks on the line. In June, British aeroplanes began to assist the Arabs in their attack on the stations and on enemy dispositions.

The reports of Colonel Joyce make clear that the Northern Army was facing considerable technical difficulties with respect to provisions, reinforcements and equipment. He even admits that equipment available was not enough. Further, the regulars suffered from an outbreak of fever during the summer as they had suffered from severe cold in winter. All this was a result of the lack of essential services, particularly in the field of medical facilities.

As a result of supply shortages, Peake returned with his company to Abu al-Lissan. In this connexion he has reported that he was almost taken by the Turks while operating between al-Hesa and Fareifra. He adds that he owed his life to an Arab travelling from Tafileh to Feisal's camp. As a result he rewarded his Arab rescuer with some gold pounds he was carrying in a bag for incidental expenses.

However, in spite of all the difficulties and obstacles, the Arabs continued their attacks during June and July, though in the former month the *Arab Bulletin* reports that intermittent fever among Feisal's regular troops and shortage of munitions limited operations. On 12 June an Arab force comprising two regular companies and two French guns, together with some Ruwalla, rushed Turkish posts between Jurf al-Darawish and Uneiza, capturing fifty-one prisoners and a machine-gun. Arab demolition of the line north of Uneiza was so extensive that it took the Turks some weeks to repair it, despite the fact that they worked night and day.

We can realize the difficulties Feisal was facing from a telegram he sent to Allenby during May 1918:

In the event of fresh Turkish offensive operations I do not consider that the Arab Army in its present condition can successfully
deal with them. In that case I foresee considerable danger of Arabs
being compelled by the enemy to retire from the positions captured
by them in the recent fighting, and communications with Ma'an re-
opened in consequence. It is vitally necessary that our army should
be reinforced and I trust General Allenby will assist us and send all
volunteers from Egypt and Palestine as quickly as possible. I also
ask that no effort should be spared to enlist volunteers from prisoner-
of-war camps in India and Mesopotamia. I have great fears that a
check to our Army at this time would preclude our taking offensive
later on, and I feel I must report that if I am to fulfil my duty to
you.

Allenby sent him a reassuring reply, realizing to the full

... the added strain that is imposed upon your Army at the present
time by the special effort which enemy is making to recover in part
at least the losses he sustained at your hands, but remembering the
great achievements of your gallant troops I await with confidence the
sure overthrow of his designs and the final victory of your arms which
the Arabs' steadfast valour must inevitably ensure.

On 22 June Sherif Nassir was attacked at Wadi Hesa by an
enemy column of two battalions with a field battery and two
machine-gun companies. After a sharp fight Nassir drove the
Turks back, killing twenty and taking fifteen prisoners, including an officer.

On 24 June the Arabs attacked and captured a Turkish
convoy between Uneiza and Jerdun and seized its supplies and
munitions. On 30 June they heavily bombarded Ma'an, while
on 28 June bedouin of Beni Atiyeh had attacked Haret al-
Amareh station, south of Mudowwara, captured it and removed
a number of rails. They also destroyed some culverts. The Arab
force took sixty prisoners, including four officers, in addition to
a machine-gun. The bedouin were supported by a machine-gun
detachment and two ten-pounder guns. The *Arab Bulletin* states
that the bedouin carried out the attacks with great dash, without
waiting for the ten-pounders to come into action. Their loss
amounted to seven killed and eighteen wounded.

On 3 July the Huweitat attacked a Turkish detachment south
of Ma'an and took about fifty prisoners. British aeroplanes had

bombed Ma'an on 2 July and on 5 July they raided Kutrani station and dropped several bombs. On 4 July the Arabs had rushed a post between Uneiza and Jerdun and taken fifteen prisoners; they demolished the track over a distance of five kilometres, and wrecked a bridge. Meanwhile, the Turks had set up a series of strong-posts on the railway line, each within range of the other. Each post had fifteen to twenty men. This system curtailed Arab raids on reinforcements and convoys.

On 4 July Sherif Nassir's force attacked a Turkish scouting detachment, pushing it back and killing six of its men. Three Arabs were wounded. On 15 July British aeroplanes bombed Kutrani station, where an enemy force of two thousand officers and men with heavy artillery was assembled. On 29 July the Arabs captured a detachment of twenty-one Turks who were trying to repair the telegraph line between Uneiza and Jerdun.

Two demonstrations by the Turks against Semna, during July, were easily repulsed. On 18 July a Turkish force set forth from Kutrani station to Wadi al-Hesa and opened fire on the sleeping Arabs, who lost about ten men killed and wounded; Sheikh Merzuk al-Tekheimi was among the wounded. The Arabs made good their escape owing to the mobility of a regular detachment and its smart handling of two small mountain-guns. They even took eleven Turks prisoner and inflicted considerable casualties on the enemy.

On 20 July a section of the Sherifian Camel Corps attacked and occupied Tabiat al-Hamra between Ma'an and Jerdun. The Turks lost seven soldiers and twenty-three others were taken prisoner. During the night the Arabs carried out extensive demolition on the railway line between Ma'an and Jerdun. The Imran bedouin, however, evacuated the station in defiance of Feisal's orders. Turks from Ma'an immediately re-occupied the post. A demonstration against the place was made on 26 July by two companies of the Arab Army, supported by two armoured cars. Six Turks were killed, and although the Arabs lost only three men, they did not succeed in capturing the station.

On 21 July the Arabs attacked Jerdun station for the fourth time. The reason for this attack was the arrival of strong Turkish reinforcements estimated at one division, with several Howitzers. The Arabs were afraid that the Turks might assemble sufficient forces to march against their camps in Wahida and Abu al-

Lissan. The Northern Army therefore prepared an expedition comprising three infantry battalions, a cavalry battalion, with artillery and a bedouin force to attack the station from the east. The attack started at dawn. A sharp battle was fought between the assailants, who were advancing on level ground, and the defenders in their entrenchments. The situation became more critical when one of the Arab battalions advanced on the station defences one hour before the scheduled time. The enemy opened up with all available fire and inflicted heavy casualties on the advancing troops including the battalion commander himself. Furthermore, the bedouin made absolutely no effort, because bedouin irregulars do not always dare to attack entrenched positions. In spite of the courage displayed by Arab troops, their heavy losses led Emir Feisal to halt the attack and retreat to Waheida. Military operations were directed by Nuri as-Said and Rashid al-Madfai. Nuri states that the casualties amounted to more than half the strength of a battalion and a quarter of another. Casualties among officers have been estimated at sixty per cent, including two battalion commanders. Nuri provides no figures, but the *Arab Bulletin* stated that the Arabs lost seventy men, while casualties among the Turks were put at seventeen killed and twenty-seven wounded.

Colonel Joyce, writing from Abu al-Lissan on 13 August explains the causes of the failure of this attack. The bedouin, he says, attended only as spectators. Two of the guns broke down after firing a few rounds, and, though aeroplanes and an armoured car co-operated, enemy guns were not silenced and continued to fire all day. The Sherifian infantry advanced with great dash to within three hundred yards of the enemy position, where they were held up by the fire of four machine-guns. Despite the lack of support and reserves, they held their position for six hours, and finally withdrew in good order, bringing their wounded with them. Arab losses were somewhat heavier than those of the Turks, but against this Joyce sets the considerable demolitions carried out, under cover of this attack, north and south of the station.

According to the records of the German general Staff:

The destruction of twenty-five Railway Bridges on the Hejaz Railway line from May 1–19 shows how difficult it was to maintain the Hejaz Railway in operation.

In their counter-attack on Fareifra the Turks used a mixed force of cavalry and mounted infantry. While Nassir was engaging them with his machine-guns, Auda attacked their camels and captured them. But in spite of that the Turks succeeded in commanding the line, because their aeroplanes lent them cover and harassed the Arabs with constant air-raids.

7. THE DESTRUCTION OF MUDOWWARA

Mudowwara station had held out all through this period. Assaults on it were consistently repulsed because it was strongly fortified. The forces that had previously attacked it did not have sufficient strength to occupy it. Extensive Arab demolitions in April had isolated this station from Ma'an and from the main field of operations. However, while in Egypt, Colonel Dawnay conjectured that a British attack on Mudowwara might distract the attention of the Turks from Allenby's impending attack on Palestine. Consequently he and Lawrence obtained from General Headquarters a loan of two Camel Corps companies under Major Buxton. Young informs us that he and Colonel Joyce had opposed this idea when Lawrence came down to Aqaba to propose it. They feared that the presence of these troops might give rise to friction with Arab regulars. They also feared general Arab reaction to the arrival of the two companies. Besides, they could hardly conceal their surprise at Lawrence's change of opinion, since he had always opposed the idea of bringing British forces to the Arab army's area of operation. His argument had always been that this was an Arab war, which the Arabs alone were entitled to handle. Now Lawrence was arguing that British troops would have no contact with Arab regulars and that he had obtained Feisal's approval, adding that the companies were to accomplish a limited military operation in as short a time as possible, and then return to their base.

The two companies, comprising three hundred men, arrived in Aqaba from Suez on 30 July. Lawrence went down to Aqaba to meet them. To minimize possible friction, he assembled the men and delivered a precautionary address, saying that if any were offended or insulted they might do well to turn the other cheek. Nuri as-Said said that the force was made up of Australian camelry, fully equipped, adding: 'They had light machine-guns, called Hotchkiss, which we were seeing for the first time, and which cooled in the air.'

On 2 August the force set out from Aqaba by Wadi Itm for Rumm. Lawrence guided the men over this first stage. The Huweitat showed themselves most resentful at the appearance of the force, but Lawrence and Sherif Hazzaa did much to allay trouble with the Sheikhs, although this did not prevent odd tribesmen from sniping the party during hours of darkness. On the following day Lawrence felt that it was safe for him to go back, while Major Sterling was left with Buxton and his men. Sterling had arrived from Egypt with a car for Feisal's use and had stayed on with the Arab army as a member of the British Military Mission.

The Camel Corps companies set forth towards Mudowwara. At dawn on 8 August, they converged on the station in three parties. The British plan was based on the idea of an indirect approach to come between the station and its guardian redoubts, and attack both from the inner side. The bombing parties stole in and caught two of the redoubts and the station itself unawares. The northern redoubt, however, offered a hot resistance for an hour until it was battered into surrender by shells from the motor guns. They then destroyed the station, with its water-tower, steam pumps and wells. One hundred and fifty Turkish prisoners were taken for a British loss of seven killed and ten wounded. The *Arab Bulletin* stated that the Turks' losses were thirty-five killed and a hundred and fifty-two officers and men captured, adding that a considerable quantity of military stores, including two guns and three machine-guns, was seized.

In a report written after the battle, Buxton says that he removed two thousand yards of rail south of the station, getting the prisoners to work on this project. He was supported in his attack by a Talbot car and aeroplanes, which bombed Turkish entrenchments and redoubts.

After completing its task, Buxton's force marched north to Jefer. There Lawrence and Joyce, who had arrived by car, greeted them on 12 August. Lawrence then went on to Azraq by car to find out if the road was serviceable to vehicles. On his return from Azraq he joined the Camel Corps companies at Bair and escorted them west to Muaggar, fifteen miles south-east of Amman. Their object was to destroy the tunnel south of

Amman, but a Turkish reconnaisance plane spotted the party, robbing it of the all-important element of surprise. For fear that an engagement with the Turks would be too expensive. Lawrence and Major Buxton decided to abandon the attempt. On the evening of 20 August they returned to Azraq, and from there went on to Bair and Aqaba. On 6 September the two companies reached Beersheba..

8. WAR AND POLITICS

Lawrence's itinerary indicates that he spent the month of May moving between British Headquarters and Aqaba. He does not seem to have been engaged on a definite assignment, except that he did mention a trip at the end of the month to visit Nassir, Auda, Hornby and Peake at Wadi al-Hesa. He did not mention taking part in any military activity.

He returned to Abu al-Lissan on 8 June and assured Feisal that Nassir's demolitions on the railway line would require a whole month for the Turks to repair. He added that this communication problem would delay Turkish preparations for an attack on Abu al-Lissan for a further two months. After this long period, he argued, the camels of the Arab army would be in good shape, so that fresh Arab operations might then begin.

Lawrence informs us that at this point he suggested to Feisal that he should ask King Hussein to transfer to him the regular units of Ali and Abdullah. This reinforcement would raise Feisal's force to ten thousand strong, in uniformed men. Lawrence says that Feisal fell in with the proposal, and gave him letters to his father advising it.

Here is an abridgement of Lawrence's account of what happened:

For dealing with the King I relied on joint-action by Wingate and Allenby, his paymasters. I decided to go up to Egypt personally, to press them to write him letters of the necessary stiffness. In Cairo, Dawnay agreed both to the transfer of the southern regulars, and to the independent offensive. We went to Wingate, argued it, and convinced him that the ideas were good. He wrote letters to King Hussein, strongly advising the reinforcement of Feisal. I pressed him to make clear to the King that the continuance of a war-subsidy would depend on his giving effect to our advice: but he refused to be stringent, and couched the letter in terms of politeness, which would be lost on the hard and suspicious old man in Mecca.

Yet the effort promised so much for us that we went up to Allenby, to beg his help with the King. . . .

We unrolled before him our scheme. . . . He listened smiling, and said that we were three days too late. . . . On June the fifteenth it had been the considered opinion of a private conference that the army would be capable of a general and sustained offensive in September. . . .

Our role would be as laid down in the spring; we must make the Deraa raid on the 2,000 new camels. . . .

Our hopes of victory had been too often dashed for me to take this as assured. So, for second string, I got Allenby's blessing upon the transfer of Ali's and Abdulla's khaki-clad contingents; and set off, fortified, to Jeddah, where I had no more success than I expected. The King had got wind of my purpose and took refuge, on the pretext of Ramadhan, in Mecca, his inaccessible capital. We talked over the telephone, King Hussein sheltering himself behind the incompetence of the operators in the Mecca exchange, whenever the subject turned dangerous. My thronged mind was not in the mood for farce, so I rang off, put Feisal's, Wingate's and Allenby's letters back unopened into my bag and returned to Cairo in the next ship.[22]

On 11 July, after Lawrence had returned from Jedda to Egypt and Palestine, he and Dawnay reviewed British plans for the impending campaign. These plans were primarily aimed at making the Turks believe that attack was going to come from the Jordan Valley eastwards, while the real intention was to strike close to the coast. While in Egypt, Dawnay and Lawrence had found out that the Turks intended to attack Arab positions at Abu al-Lissan. They had already brought over large forces and defeated Nassir's men at Wadi al-Hesa. Dawnay and Lawrence then requested General Headquarters to lend them the two Imperial Camel Corps companies for the attack on Mudowwara.

Thus after an absence of fifty days in Egypt, Palestine and Jedda, Lawrence returned to Aqaba on 28 July. This shows that he could not have been directing the Arabs, particularly since he was absent from the Arab army's field of activity for three of the first nine months of 1918. It is regrettable that English writers have exploited every means to emphasize the importance of Lawrence's work with the Arabs. Captain Liddell Hart, for instance, says that there was a lull during the time Lawrence spent away from the Northern Army; this is not true. He adds that, because of Lawrence's absence, the Arab army

22. *Seven Pillars*, pp. 533–534.

suffered a series of setbacks, the most important being their defeat at Jerdun. He attributes the failure of the Arabs to occupy Ma'an to their acting contrary to Lawrence's advice. (The same reason, incidentally, is advanced for the British failure to keep Salt.)

Lawrence accompanied Buxton's Corps as guide, then returned to Aqaba and Gueira. Hearing that Feisal was at Jefer, he left by plane to join him. Feisal had gone to Jefer to meet Nuri as-Sha'alan, who later arrived at Feisal's camp on 7 August and wrote from there to King Hussein, expressing his desire to take part in the fighting against the Turks. Feisal met Nuri and his Ruwalla companions to draw up a plan for the impending operation. Lawrence gives us a vivid description of Feisal's meeting with the Ruwalla sheikhs, in which he 'brought nationality to their minds in a phrase, which set them thinking of Arab history and language'.[23] The sheikhs were won over to a man.

On this occasion Lawrence considered the ambiguous role that he had played with the Arabs and his deceit in assuring them that England would keep her plighted word. He went on to say that he exploited their highest ideals and made their love of freedom one more tool to help England win. He admitted that in so doing he forfeited his honour. He added that his part was worked out so flippantly that none but Joyce, Naseeb al-Bekri and Muhammed al-Dheilan seemed to know that he was acting. He continued:

Yet I cannot put down my acquiescence in the Arab fraud to weakness of character or native hypocrisy: though of course I must have had some tendency, some aptitude, for deceit, or I would not have deceived men so well, and persisted two years in bringing to success a deceit which others had framed and set afoot.[24]

9. THE TURKS OFFER PEACE

Lawrence flew back from Jefer to Gueira, then on to Aqaba, where he met Colonel Dawnay. On the following day Dawnay went up to Abu al-Lissan to beg Feisal to do nothing rash, as the British push was a chance and if it failed the Arabs would find themselves in a critical position, in which the British might not be able to help.

23. *Seven Pillars*, p. 547.   24. *Ibid.*, p. 552.

Allenby begged Feisal particularly not to rush upon Damascus, but to hold his hand till events were surely favourable. Lawrence added that this caution had come on his account. One night at General Headquarters he had blurted out that to the Arabs 1918 seemed the last chance and that they would take Damascus anyhow, whatever happened at Dera'a or Ramle. According to Lawrence, Feisal smiled wisely at Dawnay's homily and replied that he would try that autumn for Damascus 'though the heavens fell', and that, if the British were not able to carry their share of the attack, he would save his own people by making a separate peace with Turkey.

I do not believe Lawrence's story about a 'separate peace with Turkey' because Feisal was known to be level-headed and prudent. In any case his position would not have allowed him to make such a dangerous and important declaration. The explanation of this is that in *Seven Pillars* Lawrence was pretending that he had previous knowledge of the Turkish peace overtures to the Arabs at the time.

The fact is that the Communist Party, which took over in Russia in November 1917, published some secret documents of treaties and agreements which had been contracted between the Allies. One of these published documents was the Sykes-Picot agreement, signed in the spring of 1916, by which Britain and France agreed to divide and rule Greater Syria and Iraq. When the documents were published, Ahmed Jemal Pasha sent two letters to Feisal and Ja'afar al-Askari informing them of the treacherous intentions of the Allies towards the Arabs and suggesting that the Arabs come to terms with Turkey, Feisal sent these two letters to King Hussein, who, in turn, sent them on to the British High Commissioner in Egypt, requesting a clarification. He also instructed Feisal to reject the Turkish proposal. The British Government officially denied the existence of this treaty and accused Jemal Pasha of ignorance and malice. The Turks made another bid for peace when Emir Mohammed Said al-Jezairi came to Feisal with a letter dated 5 August 1918, from Jemal Pasha the Lesser. On 20 August the two men held a meeting, which was kept secret from all except Nuri as-Said, Ahmad Qadri and Faiz al-Ghussein. Feisal's reply was that the Arabs demanded that their status with the Ottoman Government should be similar to that of Bavaria with Prussia. Al-Jezairi returned to Salt, where he reported to Jemal and handed him Feisal's letter. With his Staff Officers Jemal decided to telegraph Constantinople, requesting their government to make a formal acknowledgement of Arab independence. This done, the Government prepared a draft law and submitted it to the Sultan, who put his seal to it. All this, however, came too late, for by that time Turkey had already been compelled to sign a truce after its overwhelming defeat in Palestine and Syria.

In his memoirs, Ahmad Qadri states that the publication of the Sykes-Picot agreement and the resultant unrest among the army officers prompted Feisal to negotiate with the Turks when their peace offer came. Feisal went on for a while with the negotiations so as to forestall criticism from those who wanted a break with the Allies for disregarding their own pledges and laying plans in advance for dissecting and ruling the Arab countries.

Lawrence gave a somewhat garbled account in *Seven Pillars*. He confused Ahmed Jemal with Jemal the Lesser,[25] and said that the Ottoman Government at first agreed on a form of autonomy for Hejaz and later for Syria and Iraq. Jemal's deputy, according to Lawrence, offered a crown to Hussein as King of these three countries. Finally the Turks offered to appoint Hussein Caliph over the Muslims. Lawrence's mis-statements are obvious. He was seizing this opportunity to claim that he had betrayed the existence of the Sykes-Picot agreement to Feisal at an early stage. But this could not possibly have been true because the treaty was secret: even the High Commissioner in Egypt knew nothing about it. Where could Lawrence have come by this information? Let us pause for a moment over Lawrence's statement: 'I begged him to trust not in our promises, like his father, but in his own strong performance.'[26] Apart from contradicting his own previous claim of having deceived the Arabs, he was indulging here in an act that was damaging to his own country. It is strange that Lawrence considers himself to be an Arab at this point:

25. There were three Turkish Jemals: Ahmed Jemal Pasha, nicknamed 'the Butcher', who left Syria in the Autumn of 1917; his successor in the Fourth Army command, Jemal Pasha the Lesser, to whose integrity and good character many have borne witness; and Mehmed Jemal Pasha III, who for a while led the Ma'an Corps.
26. *Seven Pillars*, p. 555.

At first *we* were offered autonomy. . . . After Allenby's defeat at Salt, he sent down to *us* the Emir Mohammed Said. . . . He was very modest as he stood before Feisal and offered him Jemal's peace.[27]

This last statement is particularly interesting since on 20 August Lawrence was at Muaggar with Major Buxton's Camel Corps, and did not return to Abu al-Lissan until six days later. Lawrence went on to say that Mustafa Kemal begged Feisal not to play into Jemal's hands. He also claimed that he did not disclose the Turko-Arab talks, because he feared that the British might be shaken at Feisal's entertaining the idea of separate negotiations.

These statements are complete nonsense, for Mustafa Kemal was never in communication with Feisal, nor could we possibly imagine his being so on the basis outlined by Lawrence. Had the latter known of the talks, failure to inform his superiors would have been considered gross dereliction of duty, if not worse. There is further proof of Lawrence's ignorance of the negotiations at the time they were taking place. He gives us to understand that they were held during his stay at Abu al-Lissan and Aqaba, when Major Buxton's Camel Corps was engaged in attacking Mudowwara (5–11 August). Chapter CII of *Seven Pillars* opens with the following remark:

After the peace-talk we could set again to clean work. . . . Therefore [Joyce and myself] ran out to Jefer to meet the victorious Camel Corps . . . delighted at their Mudowwara success.[28]

On 11 August he went to Jefer and accompanied the Camel Corps to Bair and Muaggar with the object of rushing the tunnel south of Amman. He did not return to Abu al-Lissan until 26 August, while Emir Said was in Ma'an and Feisal's camp from 17 to 22 August.

On 10 August, at a military ceremony at General Headquarters in Palestine, General Allenby decorated Ja'afar Pasha al-Askari with a distinguished British medal. On the following day the *Gibla* gazette of the Hejazi Government, published a royal proclamation from King Hussein saying that fools were calling Ja'afar the General Officer Commanding the Arab Northern Army, whereas there was no such rank in the Arab army, wherein Sheikh Ja'afar, like any other, was doing his duty.

27. *Seven Pillars*, pp. 554–556 (my italics).   28. *Ibid.*, p. 557.

Naturally, this proclamation had an effect on the morale of Ja'afar and his colleagues in the Northern Army. Ja'afar proffered his resignation to Feisal, who refused to accept it and exchanged a series of telegrams with King Hussein. Lawrence claimed that in one of these telegrams Feisal himself offered to resign his command of the Northern Army. The *Arab Bulletin* of 24 September 1918, stated that the situation was the result of a misunderstanding, augmented by intriguers in Aqaba and Mecca, adding that the intervention of the High Commissioner and General Allenby brought King Hussein to 'reason', and that his last messages showed that he appreciated their action and that, so far as he was concerned, the matter was satisfactorily ended.

The King's viewpoint is perfectly clear. He was in fact the supreme Commander of the armies of the Revolt and the ultimate source from which his sons derived their authority. He therefore reserved for himself the right to confer ranks and titles on the officers. The King must have been greatly annoyed to know that the British had, without his knowledge, conferred a medal on Ja'afar. For in spite of his repeated avowals of confidence in the British, he was in fact wary of their designs on Arab countries. He was particularly careful not to allow any of their actions to smack of interference in matters that he considered purely internal or completely dependent on his sole judgement.

Lawrence, however, exploited this unfortunate incident to the full, for the sake both of attacking the King and of enhancing his own stature. His desire to belittle the King had a clear motive: he was driven to it by the old grudge that he had harboured since the King had refused to meet him at Jedda, while he was in Hejaz to transfer all regular Arab forces in the south to Feisal's command. In his book, exaggeration hammers in the impression that the Revolt was on the verge of collapse. He would have us believe that he himself was the only one capable of overcoming all obstacles and patching up all differences. From it we understand that Lawrence mutilated undesirable passages in Hussein's telegrams to Feisal to make them more palatable for him and his officers. We are informed that the men of the Arab army became mutinous and this, were it not for Lawrence's sagacity and tact, could have led to a pitiable state of schism. Lawrence also declared that he entertained the possibility

of promising Feisal the direct support of the British Government
and driving him into Damascus as sovereign prince. But Feisal
was not the type that Lawrence imagined him to be. Perhaps the
strangest item in Lawrence's imaginary account is his claim that
Feisal offered to serve under him, but that he—Lawrence—
declined on the grounds that this would not fit in with Feisal's
position and prestige. He would have us believe that this was a
great personal sacrifice on his part for the sake of Feisal and the
Arabs.

7

THE FINAL CAMPAIGN

1. THE FINAL CAMPAIGN

THE months of September and October, 1918, saw the final phase of the First World War in Syria. The British army in Southern Palestine had completed its preparations for the great offensive, which was to be launched on 19 September. It was decided that the Arab Army was to play an extensive role in the impending military operations.

It would be as well, before proceeding to describe this campaign, to provide the reader with a general picture of the positions and conditions of the enemy armies in Palestine and Transjordan.[1]

1. The Turkish forces were organized into three armies. The Commander-in-Chief, General Liman von Sanders, had his headquarters at Nazareth. The Eighth Army, consisting of ten thousand men and a hundred and fifty-seven guns, was under Jewad Pasha, with headquarters at Tulkarm. The Seventh Army, consisting of seven thousand men and a hundred and eleven guns, was under Mustapha Kemal Pasha, with headquarters at Nablus. The Fourth Army, consisting of eight thousand men and seventy-four guns, was under Jemal Pasha the Lesser. It lay to the east of the Jordan river with headquarters at Amman. The Ma'an and Amman-Ma'an Line of Communications Corps, plus General Reserve amounted to nine thousand men and sixty guns. The sum total came to thirty-four thousand men and four hundred and two guns.

2. General Allenby had sixty-nine thousand men and five hundred and forty guns.

---

1. The account that follows is taken from A. P. Wavell, the *Palestine Campaigns* (1936), pp. 94–95.

3. Emir Feisal had eight thousand Arab regulars of all ranks (in addition to volunteers and partisans).

These figures, both for the Turks and the British, include only sabres and rifles. The ration strength of the Turkish Army south of Damascus was over a hundred thousand, while the ration strength of Allenby's army was approximately three hundred and forty thousand. The approximate number of animals in Allenby's army was sixty-two thousand horses, forty-four thousand mules, thirty-six thousand camels and twelve thousand five hundred donkeys, while the number of animals in the Turkish army amounted to a mere fraction of this.

When Allenby completed his preparations, he massed the main body of his forces on the western front, facing the Turkish Eighth Army. In the Jordan Valley a Mounted Division and eight battalions of infantry under Major-General Chaytor were to give demonstrations in order to induce the enemy to believe that an attack from this front was intended.

The official British publication *Military Operations in Egypt and Palestine* furnishes information about the Turkish forces which the Arabs were to engage:

A few figures will assist to show the value of the Arab operations to the E.E.F. after the call had come to it to send to France most of its best troops. The ration strength of the Hejaz Expeditionary Force . . . was about 12,000. . . . This force should have been invaluable to Liman either at the moment of Sir Edmund Allenby's greatest embarrassment or that of the final offensive. Turkey's German advisers and the most enlightened Turkish officers had again and again urged the evacuation of Medina, but the authorities in Constantinople had always wavered. Strategically the city was worthless at this moment, but politically and from the religious point of view it had yet the value of its traditions and dignity. . . . It is possible, however, that the enemy would actually have done so . . . if his communications had not been severed by the operations of April. After that the hazard was too great. There was only a trifling amount of rolling stock left south of Mudauwara, so that the whole evacuation would have had to be carried out by route march at least as far as Ma'an. In the Ma'an area, north of the breach in the railway, there were over 4,000 men. Another 6,000 from the whole area, between Tafila and Medina, were evacuated as prisoners of war to Egypt up to the end of August 1918. Deaths of sickness accounted for many more. The casualties in killed and wounded were, according to Arab claims, 5,500. . . . The fact remains that prior to the final offensive with its thousands of prisoners, the Arab campaign killed, wounded, captured or contained well over 25,000 troops. . . . The Arabs gave the British invaluable aid while largely dependent upon them for their opportunities.[2]

The Arab Army was given an important role to play. A mobile force was to make a surprise attack on Dera'a, which was the corner-stone of Turkish communications. The object was to destroy the three railway lines around Dera'a and cut off Turkish armies in Palestine and Transjordan from their source of reinforcement and supply in Damascus. The Arab attacks on the line were to begin three days earlier than Allenby's intended offensive of 19 September.

The two thousand riding camels given by Allenby to the Arab Army enabled Feisal to carry out this task, because the raiding force had to take its route along the edge of the desert, where food and fodder was scarce. Water, however, was available at Azraq and at some pools along the route to Dera'a.

When it was finally decided to form this mobile force, Feisal presided over a military conference attended by high-ranking Arab and British officers. The items on the agenda were: necessary supplies for the expedition, and the route it was to take. As a result of the talks, it was decided that the expedition was to consist of five hundred regulars, apart from the troops needed for transport, supplies and equipment. It was found that three thousand were sufficient for the transport of troops and provisions. Feisal detailed Brigadier Nuri as-Said to lead the regulars and put at his disposal the best infantrymen in the Arab Army. The Arab command requested a number of modern machine-guns, and British Headquarters sent twenty-eight Hotchkiss and four heavy Vickers. It was decided that the expedition should be accompanied by Captain Pisani's French battery and Captain Peake's Camel Corps Company (a detachment of Egyptians and a handful of Indians). Also to go were three armoured cars, five lorries and two aeroplanes.

On 30 August, the first provisions caravan left Aqaba for Azraq. It consisted of six hundred camels, guarded by sixty-five Egyptians and Indians armed with machine-guns. The second caravan, consisting of eight hundred camels, followed on 3 September. Captain Young was the officer in charge of transport and equipment.

2. *Military Operations*, II, pp. 408–409.

Emir Feisal decided to command the expedition personally. Officers of the regular force included Tahsin Ali, Jemil al-Medfai, Ali Jawdet al-Ayyubi and Abdul Hamid al-Shaliji. British officers were Joyce, Lawrence, Lord Winterton, Young, Peake, and Kirkbride. Sherif Nassir ibn Ali led the bedouin horsemen, who started assembling at Azraq.

The main body of the Northern Army remained at Abu al-Lissan and Semna under Emir Zeid and Ja'afar al-Askari. Their task was to continue applying pressure on the Turks at Ma'an and along the railway line. A number of irregular volunteer parties led by some Sherifs together with a few Indians under Major Hornby stayed close to Hesa station.

But Feisal did not concentrate solely on military matters. He engaged politically in rousing the inhabitants of the districts in which the battles were to be waged. When Sherif Nassir left for Azraq, Feisal furnished him with a general manifesto, announcing that Nassir and Naseeb al-Bekri were Feisal's deputies, with whom the people should co-operate in liberating their country from the Turkish yoke. 'Get to Work!' was the Emir's call to the fighters. 'The liberation of Syria is at hand. We shall launch the major offensive in a few days. So, tomorrow, march with the Bedouin force and the mass of rebels to Azraq: the regular army will follow. I will be with you in a matter of days; so go ahead and declare the Revolt in all parts of Syria.'

The regular force left Abu al-Lissan for Azraq on 31 August. It crossed the railway line south of Ma'an, passed through Jefer and Bair and reached Azraq on 6 September. Emir Feisal, Nuri as-Said, Joyce and Lawrence left Abu al-Lissan by car on 4 September. When he reached Azraq, Feisal decided to make it his headquarters, where heavy equipment was to be deposited. The force prepared a landing strip, which received two of the four aeroplanes operating with the Northern Army. Just before the Emir arrived, bedouin forces under Nuri as-Sha'alan and Auda started arriving at Azraq.

2. DEMOLITION AROUND DERA'A

By 12 September the expedition was ready at Azraq. The previous day a British aeroplane carrying a staff officer with the latest news of Allenby's plans had arrived. With all preparations complete, operations started on 13 September. As a first step of the over-all Arab plan, Peake's camel company, supported by two armoured cars, went off to demolish a railway bridge near Mafraq, with the object of cutting reinforcements from Dera'a to Amman. Peake, however, failed to accomplish this task, because he lost his way and found himself in Zerqa and not at Mafraq. Having ascertained that there were signs of strong resistance at Zerqa, he decided to turn back.

At dawn on 14 September the main body, about one thousand three hundred regulars and irregulars, marched forth from Azraq. The following evening, they reached Umtaiye, with its Roman remains and its pool full of water.

On the same day, a British aeroplane brought down a Turkish fighter. Slightly damaged, it had to return to Palestine for repairs.

Peake was ordered once again to attempt cutting the line. He set out with his force from Umtaiye westward, and reached an unguarded spot, between Mafraq and Nisib, at midnight of 14/15 September. There he demolished a three-column bridge,[3] with the result that communications were cut between Dera'a and Amman.

Lawrence also participated in the task of cutting the line. On the morning of 16 September, while the main body continued its march towards Dera'a, he moved westward to the railway (km. 149) near Jabir station, together with Joyce, Lord Winterton and a small party of men. Two armoured cars carried the party and their explosives, while the other two went along as escort. On reaching the appointed place, the armoured cars moved to engage the defending redoubt, while Lawrence and his companions drove to the bridge. The Turks surrendered after a brief resistance. Lawrence and his companions then proceeded to insert charges in the spandrils and arches of the bridge. They ignited, and the bridge toppled over. As they finished, enemy patrols were seen approaching. The vehicles hurried east, then moved north to catch up with the main body near the outskirts of Dera'a.

Nuri as-Said led the regulars. On the morning of 17 September he reached the railway line at Tell Arar, some five miles north of Dera'a. The regular force was supported by about a thousand warriors—bedouin horsemen, villagers and Hejazi

3. Lawrence gives us to understand that Peake demolished this bridge on the night of 19/20 September. The date shown above is the correct one.

volunteers. Nuri started firing his guns at the Turkish redoubt near Tell Arar, from which the Turks were firing at the assailants. After a few shells from Nuri's guns, enemy fire ceased. The bedouin horsemen attacked the garrison and finished it off. In this way, the Arabs gained control of a section of line between Damascus and Dera'a, which was the main means of transport to Palestine and Transjordan. Nuri then posted his guns on Tell Arar, to resist possible enemy attacks, while the demolition party began its work of destroying the line and removing rails. Shortly afterwards, eight enemy aeroplanes approached from Dera'a, and bombed the Arab party. The bedouin dispersed in the plain, but the regulars fired their guns and machine-guns in the direction of the aircraft. These made a steep rise and started firing indiscriminately. Only two Arabs were killed, half an hour after the attack had started.

Meanwhile the other British plane had arrived and engaged the Turkish force in a short battle. It was soon shot down, but the pilot emerged unhurt from the wreckage. Nuri by then had decided to move to the second target. Collecting three hundred and fifty regulars and two French guns, he set off for Muzeirib station, to cut the railway line south of Dera'a, where it branched off to Palestine. Nuri was accompanied by Sherif Nassir, who led a party of bedouin. Lawrence soon caught up with them, while the others remained at Tell Arar to continue demolishing the line: the Camel Company did the actual demolition, and the other regulars, with two guns and the armoured cars, guarded the company from enemy raids. Over three kilometres of line were damaged. The Turks were unable to repair this section until the evening of 24 September, just before their withdrawal from Dera'a.[4]

The inhabitants of neighbouring villages came out in force to participate in the Revolt. On their way to catch up with the regulars, the bedouin were attacked by enemy aeroplanes, and Lawrence was hit in the arm by a splinter from a bomb, but the wound was slight.

The Arab force drew near Muzeirib in the afternoon. After

4. Captain Peake returned from Tell Arar to Azraq on the morning of 18 September, to fetch a supply of explosives. He then returned to Umtaiye at noon on 20 September. He did 140 miles in forty-one hours on camel-back. His average speed approximately equals Lawrence's average from Aqaba to Suez: 170 miles in forty-nine hours.

a few point-blank shells, they attacked the station under machine-gun cover. After a short battle, during which a number of defenders were killed, the station garrison surrendered. The Arabs took forty prisoners. Lawrence and Young cut the telegraph, while the soldiers dynamited the rails, blew the points and wrecked the station. They then set fire to a number of station trucks, while the villagers plundered everything.

When the sun had set, hundreds of villagers, attracted by the blaze, came pouring down. Among them was the Sheikh of Tell al-Shehab, together with an Armenian officer, commanding the garrison of the neighbouring bridge. The two offered to help the Arab force to subdue the garrison of the bridge, so that it might be the more easily destroyed. At night, the force set out with Nassir, Nuri and Lawrence. But they discovered that a train carrying a German–Turkish contingent sent up by Liman von Sanders to relieve Dera'a had just arrived. This forced a change of plan. Nuri as-Said offered to take the place by a direct assault but Lawrence voted against this, on the grounds that the Arabs had that day twice cut the Damascus–Palestine railway and that their activities had brought German reserves from the front. This went beyond what Allenby expected from the Arabs. Nuri, after a moment's thought agreed, and the Arab force returned to Muzeirib that same night. Lawrence's statement that they 'felt that something must be done to avenge the forfeited bridge' and that accordingly 'two parties . . . , with guides of Tallal's men, went beyond Shehab and cut the line twice behind it on deserted gradients' is untrue.

Before dawn, the rest of the regulars arrived at Muzeirib from Tell Arar, with the other two French guns. Joyce and the Camel Company returned immediately from Tell Arar to Umtaiye, where it was arranged that all Arab contingents should assemble after completing their task. They were to await developments contingent upon the progress of the British offensive in Palestine.

Early on 18 September, Nuri, Nassir and Lawrence left Muzeirib for the south, and arrived at Nisib in the evening, having passed east of Ramtha. Here the regulars posted their guns on an elevated crest and fired on the station, which was hit by several shells. Infantry, supported by the machine-gun contingent, attacked enemy entrenchments and engaged the Turks in heavy fighting. The real objective of the Arabs, however, was not Nisib

station itself but the important and strongly garrisoned bridge
north of the village. Nuri as-Said turned some of his guns and
machine-guns on the bridge-post, while other machine-guns
directed their fire on the village. Soon, the village elders came
out and protested that they had done no wrong. Nuri insisted
that he would go on firing on the village until the enemy evacuated it. The elders promised to eject the Turks from the houses.
So station and bridge were divided. The battle between the
Arabs and the Turks then gathered force and the bridge garrison had to leave their ditches and entrenchments and join the
station garrison. At this point, Lawrence made for the bridge,
piled gun-cotton against the piers and ignited the fuses. The
three-arched bridge collapsed in ruins.

Nuri meanwhile was hurrying his forces down east in the
failing light. After a three-mile march, the commanders of the
expedition called a halt. Their two days of dangerous activity
had wearied them, and they decided to sleep in the open.

Lawrence claimed that Nisib bridge was the seventy-ninth
he had demolished. The following is a list of those bridges and
culverts in whose demolition Lawrence participated:

>Wadi Ais, 2 April 1917
>Munifa, 2 June 1917
>Haret al-Amareh, 17 September 1917
>Shedia, 6 October 1917
>Munifa, 11 November 1917
>Jabir Station, 16 September 1918
>Nisib Station, 18 September 1918

Total: 7 bridges, some of them culverts.

His claim to a small bridge at Baalbek and ten bridges near
Ghadir al-Haj station has a purely fictitious basis, whilst the rest
of the total must be attributed to exaggeration.

The Arabs accomplished all that Allenby had requested of
them. Their military operations, carried out in difficult conditions hundreds of miles away from their bases, were an outstanding example of courage and determination. Had the Turks possessed a good intelligence service and some sort of motor transport, they could have easily attacked Azraq and cut off the Arab
expedition in the rear. Indeed, the Arab raid on the railway

line at Dera'a was an act of great daring, for the town was the nerve centre of the Turkish communication system and the main link between three strong armies and their reinforcement base at Damascus. The Arab expedition could very possibly have met a strong enemy force during its operations in the vicinity of Dera'a; it could have been ambushed or severely depleted. The fact that it attained its objectives without suffering heavy loss is a tribute to its military capacities and achievement.

At dawn on 19 September, Allenby began his main offensive against the lines of the Seventh and Eighth Armies, while Liman von Sanders was engaged in dispatching his reserve contingents to ward off the Arab threat to Dera'a. The British attack was overwhelmingly successful. Most of the Eighth Army units were completely submerged, and their line of retreat blocked. British aeroplanes bombed the Faria road in the Nablus mountains, to block the Seventh Army's line of retreat.

The Arabs could do nothing but await developments in Palestine. Their force was not sufficiently strong to occupy Dera'a and face those Turkish units of the Seventh and Eighth Armies which might succeed in reaching the town. Nor could it have confronted the Fourth Army, which was preparing to retreat *en masse* at an opportune moment. In addition, the Arabs had no air cover, at a time when the Turks in Dera'a had nine aeroplanes and the British Army had a considerable number, while their dispositions were more critical and more hazardous than the others. Their forces suffered much from Turkish air raids but were unable to strike back, in spite of casualties and in spite of the resultant demoralization of bedouin and irregulars.

3. ATTACK AND DEFENCE

Arab military activity aroused deep concern among the Turks, who assembled their forces and sent some aeroplanes to bomb Arab positions. In the early hours of 19 September, the expedition was rudely awakened by a volley of shells falling on their camp. The Turks had sent an armoured train from Amman, mounting a field gun to shell Arab positions. They seemed to have had precise information of the whereabouts of the force. In addition, a Turkish aeroplane was guiding the gun-crew. Regulars were immediately ordered to head east as fast as conditions allowed. After they were safely out of range, the Turkish gun bombarded the small village of Taibeh, as a punishment for allowing the Camel Company to pass through unmolested.

The force reached Umtaiye, where Joyce, the Camel Company and many partisans were waiting. Lawrence had heard of the landing close by of an enemy aeroplane; so he and the pilot of the aeroplane which had crashed at Tell Arar took two armoured cars to scout the landing position. On arrival they saw not one but three aeroplanes: two were taking off; but the engine of the third failed to start. Lawrence and his companion put several hundred bullets in the fuselage 'till it danced under the rain'. The Turks burned it in the afternoon.

At night, some Arab units under Nuri as-Said set out with one armoured car for the railway line. They destroyed some culverts, and, at km. 154, removed a number of rails to delay repairs on the bridge near Jabir station. Lawrence accompanied this raid but lost his way in the darkness.

The expedition spent the day at Umtaiye. But when the Turks found out their whereabouts, they harrassed them with continuous air-raids, killing a number of regulars and French gunners. Late the following night, Nuri as-Said conferred with the other officers, and it was agreed to move the force south to Um al-Surab. Early on 20 September, the move was completed.

From Um al-Surab Lawrence and Joyce returned to Azraq, which they reached in the evening. Joyce was on his way to Abu al-Lissan. He had made up his mind that it was his duty to remain with Zeid and Ja'afar, awaiting developments. At Azraq, Lawrence met with Feisal and Nuri as-Sha'alan. Soon the promised aeroplane arrived with news of Allenby's victory and Lawrence returned in it to Palestine, to request from Allenby sufficient air-cover for the Arab expedition in its critical situation.

At General Headquarters, Lawrence found Allenby pleased at the success of his plans. He sketched out his intentions to Lawrence, declaring that there would be no slackening in the pursuit of the Turks. The next step was to consist of three more thrusts: one by Chaytor's New Zealanders across Jordan to Amman; one by Barrow and the Indians across Jordan to Dera'a; and the third by Chauvel's Australians across Jordan to Kuneitra. Barrow and Chauvel on attaining the first objectives would converge on Damascus. The Arabs were to assist the three columns, and they were not to take Damascus before the arrival of the British Army. Lawrence then asked for aeroplanes to fight off the Turkish planes; Allenby arranged for two Bristol fighters and a D.H.9 to give air-cover and support to the Arab Army.

Lawrence returned with the three planes to Um al-Surab on 22 September. On the same day, some Turkish planes tried to bomb the Arab camp and the British planes were put to immediate use. Two enemy machines were brought down in flames. The same day, Lawrence went to Azraq by plane. When Feisal got the details of Allenby's victories, he set out by car to Um al-Surab, taking Nuri as-Sha'alan and Lawrence with him.

When it became clear that the Fourth Army was beginning to withdraw from Amman, Feisal decided to call upon the rest of the Ruwalla horse to take part in the final battle. They numbered over two thousand. Thus the expedition grew to four thousand regulars and irregulars. On the morning of 23 September, Lawrence, Jemil al-Madfai and Winterton proceeded by car to the railway line south of Mafraq. Attempting to blow up a bridge as usual, they were met with strong resistance, which compelled them to return to camp empty-handed. Lawrence says that on their return to Um al-Surab, they found that Nassir intended to pitch camp once more at Umtaiye. So they moved on the same day. At night the Handley-Page bombed Mafraq station. After several hundred-pound bombs had crashed into the sidings, the latter caught fire, and the Turks' shooting stopped.

The Fourth Army was slow in retreating from Salt and Amman, because the Turkish Command either underestimated or failed to grasp the extent of the defeat suffered by the Seventh and Eighth Armies, and therefore thought it possible to wait for the column retreating from Ma'an, to help it make its way to Dera'a as well. British forces had tried to push the Turks up the Jordan Valley, but without success. Realizing how dangerous the Arab Army between Amman and Dera'a was becoming, the Fourth Army began to retreat, leaving a battalion behind in Amman to try to hold it until the arrival of the column from Ma'an. This battalion offered a brave resistance and the British could not enter Amman until 25 September, after the last Turkish trains had left. The Ma'an corps was delayed because of Arab harrassment and attacks during retreat. The British failed in their attempt to cut the Fourth Army line of retreat, but

bridges damaged by the Arabs in the north brought Turkish
trains to a halt. The men came streaming out in a loose mob,
and the Beni Hassan began cutting off stragglers and weak
detachments.

4. THE CAPTURE OF DERA'A

Feisal held a conference with the expedition commanders, to
discuss future plans. Lawrence said that he proposed that they
march north into Sheikh Sa'ad village, north-west of Dera'a, to
cut the Fourth Army's line of retreat at this important strategic
position. He adds that Talal, Nuri as-Sha'alan, Nassir and Nuri
as-Said agreed; so they prepared to strike camp. Nuri as-Said,
however, says that he proposed that the expedition march behind
the Dera'a line, because that position was expected to be on the
route of the withdrawing Turkish army;

but some saw the need for raids behind the Fourth Army, in the
direction of Mafraq Station. The majority of opinions favoured this
latter course. In order to sort out the differences of opinion between
us and the British officers, we went to Emir Feisal, and Lawrence
came along with us. We surveyed both suggestions with his Highness,
who commanded that we raid Mafraq Station for one day, then go
to Sheikh Sa'ad village to carry out raids on the lines of communication of the Turkish Army.

Nuri's remarks give us to understand that the conference was
held before the attack on Mafraq station on 23 September, as
mentioned above. But the important thing here is the obvious
contradiction between the claims of Lawrence and Nuri, each
trying to take credit for what happened, and Nuri's unequivocal
statement that the British officers opposed the move towards
Dera'a and preferred to stay in the vicinity of Mafraq. Major
Young, on the other hand, has clarified his position in the conference, which rested on the assumption that the Arabs had done
enough and that common sense would require them to move east
to Jebel Druze and await the occupation of Dera'a by the British.
His argument was that the retreating Turks, numbering several
thousand, could easily wipe out the regular Arab force, which
consisted of under a thousand men.

When this plan was agreed upon, Feisal returned to Azraq.
It is important to note here that Sherif Nassir was Feisal's deputy
in commanding irregular forces, while Nuri as-Said commanded

the whole regular body. Young records that whereas he and others had always thought of Lawrence as Feisal's liaison officer with Allenby, Lawrence himself had the impression that Young and his colleagues were under his orders.

Among the decisions taken in the conference was one requiring all armoured cars to return to Azraq, and the aeroplanes to Palestine. Lawrence's point was that the Hauran country was not suitable for armoured car activity, besides the fact that fuel was running short.

The planes flew west. Shortly afterwards one returned to report that a large force of enemy cavalry was on its way from the railway line east towards the Arab positions. Accordingly, Nassir led the Ruwalla and Hauran horse to repel them, while the regulars and other fighters continued their march to the north. This manoeuvre succeeded and the Arabs captured several hundred men, while the rest of the Turkish force retreated along the railway line, heading for Dera'a.

The expedition set forth from Umtaiye at noon on 25 September and spent the first night at Nuweimeh. Lawrence records that Sabin (meaning Young) came to him near midnight, and suggested that the Arabs fall back to Bosra, where the Druzes were collecting under Naseeb al-Bekri as Feisal's deputy. Commenting on this suggestion, Lawrence wrote:

This attitude passed me by, since, if we withdrew to Jebel Druse, we ended our active service before the game was won, leaving the last brunt on Allenby. I was very jealous for the Arab honour, in whose service I would go forward at all costs. They had joined the war to win freedom, and the recovery of their old capital by force of their own arms was the sign they would best understand.[5]

Bedouin and villagers joined the marching force and at night Nassir and Nuri as-Sha'alan returned to join the regulars. Early in the morning, the expedition resumed its march, reaching the railway line near Tell Arar, which the Turks had repaired only a day earlier. The Arabs damaged the line again and removed its rails so that the Turks were not able to use it in their retreat to Damascus. As a consequence, six trains, unable to withdraw from Dera'a, were seized by the Arabs.

On the same day—26 September—groups of irregulars separated from the main body to widen the scope of activities.

5. *Seven Pillars*, pp. 623–624.

In company with the Hauran horse, Telal occupied Ezraa, while Auda made for Khirbet al-Ghazala station. Nuri as-Sha'alan swept his men down the Dera'a road on the chance of cutting off Turkish parties. The main party under Nassir and Nuri as-Said, together with Lawrence, took a route past the village of Sheikh Miskin and reached the village of Sheikh Sa'ad at dawn on 27 September.

The parties that had gone out on their own soon came back to join the main force: Talal returned, after having stormed Ezraa and put its garrison to flight; Auda returned with two hundred prisoners from Khirbet al-Ghazala, announcing that he had captured a derelict train; Nuri as-Sha'alan returned with four hundred prisoners and a number of mules and machine-guns. The Arabs were unable to attack the main retreating forces, but they dealt severe blows on small parties. At noon on 27 September, only twenty-four hours after the operation was launched, the Arabs had taken over two thousand prisoners.

Meanwhile, there arrived at Sheikh Sa'ad a detachment of Turks, Austrians and Germans, with eight machine-guns. The Arabs surrounded this detachment, capturing all who were not killed in the fighting. Word came in that the Turks at Dera'a had set fire to their own aeroplanes and store-houses and stood ready to evacuate the town. A British plane dropped word that British troops were near Ramtha and that two strong Turkish columns one of four thousand, one of two thousand, were retiring from Dera'a and Muzeirib respectively towards the Arabs at Sheikh Sa'ad. Faced with this serious danger, the expedition began to make preparations for engaging the enemy forces by surprise attacks.

On the morning of the 27th, messengers from Tafas arrived with a request for help from the expedition in repulsing an attack from the Turkish column whose way of retreat had come by their village. This request, however, was greeted with little enthusiasm by the Arab commanders, who had spent the night in vigorous activity, and whose men were exhausted. Furthermore, they had no idea of the enemy strength. With Talal al-Hreidhin listening, Nuri as-Sha'alan openly criticized the Haurani attitude, saying, 'The Hauran sheikhs must defend your honour and protect your property. They must do what we are doing.' Deeply affected by this remark, Talal returned to his

village with some bedouin volunteers and engaged the Turks
with brave determination, giving his life in the encounter. Soon
afterwards a large section of the Arab force made for Tafas, preceded by volunteers under Nassir, Auda and Lawrence. They
engaged the Turks and kept them busy until Nuri as-Said arrived
on the scene with his regulars, and started firing on the Turks
with two guns and machine-guns. This attack of the regulars
came as a complete surprise to the Turks, who made a hurried
retreat towards Dera'a. In this connexion, Nuri as-Said said:

> Word reached us that the retreating Turkish cavalry division had
> massacred the inhabitants of Tafas, murdering women and chil-
> dren. We sent a force to protect the people of the village and attack
> the Turkish division. While the enemy troops were taking a rest at
> Tafas, our force attacked them. There was sharp fighting between
> the two parties, in which the Turks used hand grenades, killing
> Talal, Sheikh of Tafas, and a number of Tafas inhabitants and some
> bedouin. We opened fire with our mountain guns, which surprised
> the enemy, and led to their dispersal. Many wounded men and
> prisoners fell into our hands.

Another source[6] reports that the force which passed through
Tafas was the remnant of Mustapha Kemal Pasha's army. It had
watered on the previous day at Ain Shallaleh, then camped at
sunset near the village of Turra, where it spent the night unmolested. But during its retreat at dawn the following day, it
was attacked in the rear by some villagers. The troops retaliated,
killing some of the villagers, including Talal. With regard to
the murder of women and children, this source says that there is
no truth in this report; nothing of the sort happened, either at
Turra or at Tafas.

Nuri as-Said's statements give us to understand that credit for
dispersing the Turks goes to the mountain-guns, and that a considerable number of prisoners and wounded men were taken by
the Arabs. This goes counter to Lawrence's statement, 'By my
order we took no prisoners, for the only time in our war.'[7]

Clamour arose in the Hauran villages that day. Thousands of
inhabitants rose to meet the retreating enemy, who had weighed

6. Sayyid Nassir al-Fawwaz, whose father was chief of Remtha and surrounding villages. Nassir himself served as officer in the Ottoman army during
the war. As for Talal, he was not the sheikh of Tafas and chief of Hauran as
Lawrence and Nuri reported; he was sheikh of the Hreidhin, a Tafas clan. His
distinction rests on the fact that he joined the Arab Revolt.

7. *Seven Pillars*, p. 632 (my italics).

down with oppression both them and their ancestors. The wide plains became a theatre for a huge, unorganized battle, with two peoples playing a part: the one seeking liberty and emancipation from the other. Old and new feuds were crying to be settled.

At sunset on 27 September, the Arabs entered Dera'a. The Ruwalla horse had divided into two groups: the first, under Khalid al-Sha'alan, pursued the main Turkish column, while the second under Terad, Khalid's brother, attacked Dera'a and captured it, taking five hundred prisoners.[8] When news of this reached Sherif Nassir, after the battle with the other Turkish column around Tafas, he set out at night for Dera'a. Early in the morning, he made for Government House, on which he raised the Arab flag. Then, in the name of the independent Arab Government, he appointed a military Governor, set up a police force to keep the peace and started to organize a system of local administration. As for Nuri as-Said with his regular force, he entered Dera'a on the evening of 28 September. Dr. Ahmad Qadri and Lawrence had entered Dera'a with Nassir, but Lawrence reported that he entered it alone.[9]

5. THE LIBERATION OF DAMASCUS

In the meantime the Indian division under General Barrow was advancing from Ramtha to Dera'a. When word of this advance reached the Arab commanders at Dera'a, Lawrence volunteered to go west and meet Barrow, to forestall a possible attack by his division on Dera'a itself. The British, in fact, had not heard of the developments at Dera'a and Hauran—their aeroplanes had even bombed the regular Arab force as it made its way into the town that morning. So Lawrence and Kirkbride went along to contact the vanguard of the advancing division. On meeting General Barrow, Lawrence informed him that Dera'a was already in the hands of the Arabs, Britain's allies. At first General Barrow tried to ignore the Arabs there—he even asked that Nuri as-Said should remove himself and his men from the town. But, with some persistence, Lawrence succeeded in winning him over, especially after presenting him with the text of Britain's

8. A boy was born to Terad al-Sha'alan that year, whom he named Lawrence. We might also mention that Newcombe called his son Lawrence as well.

9. Lawrence always avoided mixing with educated Arabs. Several examples attest to this. Dr. Ahmad Qadri was a founder of the Fetat Arab Society. He accompanied the Damascus expedition with Nuri as-Said.

declaration that the Arabs could retain any position they captured by force of their own arms. Lawrence was carrying a recommendation from Clayton to this effect. The General finally had to recognize the right of the Arab forces. He requested that they secure forage and food-stuff for his division, then made for Government House, where he saluted the Arab flag.

Arab gains were mounting by the hour. With several thousand prisoners already in hand, Arab regular forces had to accept the surrender of other Turkish troops, who gave themselves up for fear of perishing at civilian hands. Villagers and bedouin brought in prisoners in flocks. The Arabs also seized a large number of animals and a huge quantity of light weapons.

On 29 September, Feisal entered Dera'a by car, and started making preparations for the march on Damascus and rallying local leaders with a view to having them take part in the liberation of Damascus and the rest of Syrian territory.

General Barrow, as well as Nuri as-Said and his regular force, remained in Dera'a for one night and a day. The irregulars, numbering about three thousand, headed north in the direction of Damascus, on horses and camels, and gave chase to the retreating Turks, dealing heavy blows as they went. They were led by Sherif Nassir, Nuri as-Sha'alan, Auda Abu Tayeh and other tribal chiefs, in addition to desert horse and Hauran sheikhs.

On the morning of 29 September, the Indian division set forth from Dera'a in the direction of Damascus, while Arab regulars, at the request of General Barrow, covered their right flank. Lawrence, however, stayed behind to see Feisal, and spent the night at Dera'a. Early next day, he left Dera'a by car with Major Stirling.

Battle with the retreating Turks continued to rage for two days. When they reached the village of Kiswe, ten miles south of Damascus, their original number of six thousand had decreased to four thousand. At Kiswe, the Turks set up new defensive entrenchments. Arab regulars and irregulars had reached Masmieh and decided to storm the Turks' position during the night. A sharp battle ensued, which resulted in the defeat of the Turks, who left behind three gun batteries and eighteen machine-guns. The Arabs entered the village in the small hours of 30 September.

Lawrence records that he caught up with the forces of Nassir and Nuri as-Sha'alan, who had kept up an uninterrupted battle with the Turks until they killed most of them. He was told that Auda had preceded them to Jebel Mani', to rally his friends of the Walad Ali tribe and await the retreating Turks. Lawrence tells us that he asked Nassir and Nuri as-Sha'alan to engage the Turks for an hour or so, while he went by car to seek help from the Indian division marching to their left. But his attempt was only partially successful, because a surly colonel, who had at first agreed to launch a mounted attack on the Turks, soon ordered a retirement after the Turks had fired one or two shells from their little guns. Seeking the General, Lawrence requested a renewal of the attack. A brigade, supported by artillery, was set in motion. Night fell, and the Turks broke up and went streaming up towards the Mani' peaks, where Auda and his supporters were lying in ambush. There Auda killed, plundered and captured till dawn. The last of the Turkish Fourth Army, which for two years had been the stumbling-block in the way of the liberation of Syria, met its end.

On the evening of 30 September, Sherif Nassir sent messengers to the Arab leaders at Damascus, requesting them to organize the city's administration and notifying them of his intended arrival on the following day. While Turkish and German units were leaving the city, Damascus leaders raised the Arab flag on Government House and at night bedouin and Druzes started to file into the city. In the morning, Sherif Nassir, at the head of his forces, entered the city in the name of its Arab Government. Lawrence remarked that Nassir fully deserved this distinction, as 'a privilege of his fifty battles'.[10]

Damascus was thus liberated from the yoke of Ottoman rule, by which it and other Arab countries had been oppressed for four centuries. The city gave the Arab Army an unparalleled welcome and public celebrations continued for some days, reaching their peak on 3 October, when Feisal ibn al-Hussein entered the city from Dera'a—from Medina, in fact, at the culmination of a long twenty-eight month march.

Lawrence's report on this expedition appeared in the *Arab Bulletin* of 22 October 1918. This report differs in several particulars from his account in *Seven Pillars*. For instance, it gives the numbers of the two Turkish columns advancing from the

10. *Seven Pillars*, p. 644.

west on Sheikh Sa'ad as six thousand and two thousand respectively, while in *Seven Pillars* the first column is put at four thousand only. The report states that the Turks raped 'all the women they could catch' at Turra and Tafas and that Sherif Bey, the Turkish Commander of the Lance rear-guard, angered at the Arab attack, ordered the inhabitants of Tafas to be killed. 'These included some twenty small children (killed with lances and rifles), and about forty women.' In *Seven Pillars*, he says that those killed were 'perhaps twenty in all',[11] and that the Turks committed their atrocities before the arrival of the Arab Army. He does not mention Turra at all. In the report he uses the plural form *we*: 'We ordered "no prisoners"', meaning the expedition commanders and himself. While in *Seven Pillars* he says, 'By my order we took no prisoners . . .',[12] with the implication that he was the Commander-in-Chief. Speaking of Turkish atrocities in his report, he represents the Turks as ferocious beasts, forcing down pregnant women on bayonets. He speaks of watching the Turks 'swing their wounded by the hands and feet into a burning railway truck, as had been the lot of the Arab Army at Jerdun'. But this statement has not been confirmed by any of the Arab Army officers I have approached on the subject. The report also states that, between Dera'a and Damascus, the Arabs killed nearly five thousand Turks, captured about eight thousand and counted spoils of about a hundred and fifty machine-guns and from twenty-five to thirty guns. Pointing out discrepancies in figures or narration is not our main concern, however. What interests us is the fact that, in the report, Lawrence does not stand out too conspicuously, while *Seven Pillars* clearly gives the impression that Lawrence was the prime mover in the Arab operations, that his orders were obeyed without question, and that he was the man who did all the planning, anticipating, thinking and accomplishing. Finally, the report makes no mention whatsoever of the theatrical role which, in *Seven Pillars*, he claimed to have played with General Barrow.

Lowell Thomas tells us that one of Lawrence's first moves on entering Damascus was to visit the tomb of Saladin and remove a satin flag and a bronze laurel wreath, which Kaiser Wilhelm II had placed there during a visit to Damascus in 1898. Thomas says, 'The bronze wreath now adorns the office of the curator of

11. *Op. cit.*, p. 631. 12. *Ibid.*, p. 632.

the British War Museum, while the Kaiser's flag returned with
me to America.' [13] Emir Said al-Jezairi reports that Lawrence
also took away the Arab flag which his brother Abdul Kader
had brought from Mecca, and which he himself had raised on
Government House.

We should return at this point to developments at Ma'an.
Ignorant of British and Arab plans, the Turks had prepared an
expedition in the middle of September, which marched south
from Amman to recapture Tafileh. The expedition reached the
outskirts of the town without meeting much resistance because
Emir Zeid had assembled all the regular forces around Ma'an.
At the same time, the Turks at Ma'an attacked Arab positions
on the Semna hills, but failed to make any progress and retired.
On 22 September, the Turkish forces were surprised by an order
to make a hurried retreat, which they nevertheless carried out
by way of the railway line, under gun protection. Joined on the
way by the garrisons of the stations and other outposts, they
reached Zizia station on 28 September, after the Eighth Corps of
the Fourth Army had left Amman. As soon as the Turkish forces
retreated from Ma'an, Emir Zeid entered the town and sent some
light detachments to engage the Turkish rear. Bedouin detachments along the railway line also took part in engaging the
Turks, retarding their delay and inflicting losses upon them.
Consequently the Turks, after reaching Zizia, could make no
further progress, but were surrounded by bedouin forces numbering several thousand. When the British dispatched a brigade
from Amman to meet the Turkish force, the Turkish commander Ali Wahbi Bey declared his readiness to surrender, on
condition that his men were permitted to keep their weapons
in order to protect themselves from bedouin attacks. Permission granted, the Turks, numbering some four thousand, were
led to Amman, where they surrendered their arms.

6. FIRST DAYS IN DAMASCUS

After the withdrawal of the Turks from Damascus, a temporary
government was set up there under Emir Said al-Jezairi until
Feisal entered the city, when a military government, headed by
General Ali Rida al-Rikabi, was established. Beirut notables
had sent a cable addressed to the Arab Command, reporting

13. Lowell Thomas, *With Lawrence in Arabia* (1924), p. 291.

that Turkish authorities had evacuated the city and requesting that a representative of the Sherif should be sent down to organize the new administration. Nuri as-Said replied that an Arab Army force would reach Beirut before long, and requested that they raise the Arab flag on Government House. Nuri as-Said said that he showed Feisal

... the cable from the Beirut notables and my reply. His Highness ordered that a token force under General Shukri al-Ayyubi be sent immediately to occupy Beirut. His Highness sent for al-Ayyubi Pasha, and notified him of this.

Al-Ayyubi left for Beirut with a hundred men, arriving there on 6 October.

Unfortunately, some Druzes and bedouin who had entered Damascus after the Turkish withdrawal carried out extensive looting of Turkish munition stores on the night of 1 October. Nuri as-Said, who was in charge of order and security, feared that the looting might extend to the commercial market and shops and ordered the newly-appointed Arab Commander of Damascus to block the way against the bedouin and fire on anyone carrying stolen goods. The bedouin were to be immediately ejected from the city. The Damascus Commander promptly carried out this order, killing more than twenty recalcitrant bedouin.

On 3 October, Feisal entered Damascus, at the same time as Allenby. Here is Lawrence's account of Feisal's arrival:

Then we were told that Feisal's special train had just arrived from Deraa. A message was hurriedly sent him by Young's mouth, and we waited till he came, upon a tide of cheering which beat up against our windows. It was fitting the two chiefs should meet for the first time in the heart of their victory; with myself still acting as the interpreter between them.

Allenby gave me a telegram from the Foreign Office, recognizing to the Arabs the status of belligerents; and told me to translate it to the Emir: but none of us knew what it meant in English, let alone in Arabic: and Feisal, smiling through the tears which the welcome of his people had forced from him, put it aside....[14]

7. ALEPPO AND MEDINA

The Allies continued their north-bound march, with the object of forcing the Turks to keep up their retreat. The Turkish

14. *Seven Pillars*, pp. 659–660.

forces were given no chance to reassemble or to set up new defence positions. Western sources are almost unanimously agreed that Allenby had sent a request to Feisal that the Arabs should participate in this final march. But we are indebted to Nuri as-Said for clarifying the Arab viewpoint. In the third section of his lectures, we are told that Feisal and Allenby discussed future moves. The British Command favoured a plan requiring the army to wait along the Damascus–Riak–Beirut road, while British forces reassembled, organized their communication lines and repaired the railway. (There were no British forces near Damascus at the time except the cavalry, while infantry divisions were still south of the Tiberias–Haifa line.) Feisal's opinion, however, was radically different. He pointed out that Arab forces—regulars as well as irregulars—could march with all speed to the north and obtain foodstuffs from the places through which they would pass. Allenby fell in with Feisal's plan and announced his willingness to send part of the British cavalry behind the Arab forces, if the Arabs would guarantee forage and food, which Feisal promised to ensure. Feisal sent letters to Arab leaders in the north requesting them to help the British and see to their needs.

On this basis, the Arab expedition set forth from Damascus on 11 October. Regulars were led by Ali Jawdat al-Ayyubi, volunteers by Sherif Nassir. The French battery remained behind in Damascus, just as the British detachment had done earlier at Dera'a. The expedition reached Homs and Hama without meeting any resistance. There Nuri as-Said caught up with it and took command. Nuri has said that the distance between the Arab rear and British van exceeded fifty kilometres.

On 22 October the Arabs and the British engaged the Turks, under Mustapha Kemal, at Aleppo. With the help of large forces from the Aneza tribe, the Arabs compelled the Turks, who had been taken by surprise, to retreat. The British clashed with the Turks at Muslimmieh station—a railway junction between Syria and Iraq; a British battalion was repulsed with heavy losses and had to make a retreat. But the Arabs stormed and captured the station on 26 October. Truce between Turkey and the Allies was contracted on 1 November 1918.

To return to Medina: Emirs Ali and Abdullah kept up the siege and continued to engage its garrison and the other station garrisons up to Medain Saleh and Tebuk in the north. The British had neglected the armies of Ali and Abdullah, sending neither sufficient artillery nor effective military equipment. The dispatch of regulars from Egyptian prison camps was restricted to Emir Feisal's Army. Added to this, it was not until after the battles of the Northern Army around Ma'an in April 1918, and the blowing up of the Mudowwara station by the British in August that the railway line was completely cut. Besides, the Arabs were prevented from bombarding Medina by their regard for its sanctity to the Muslim world, and in any case they had no heavy guns. These reasons combined to enable the Turkish Army at Medina, under Fakhri Pasha, to hold out for thirty-one months (June 1916–January 1919).

When truce was contracted between the Ottoman Government and the Allies, Emir Ali sent Fakhri Pasha the text of the truce agreement and urged him to surrender. But Fakhri refused, saying that the Holy City would not surrender except over his dead body. The Allies then procured an official order to this effect from the Ottoman Minister for War to Fakhri Pasha. Nevertheless, Fakhri still insisted on keeping Medina.

Consequently, the Arab Army tightened the siege. The Turks were in a sorry position, and as soon as their officers got wind of the truce, they started surrendering with their units to the Arabs *en masse*. This wholesale surrender compelled Fakhri Pasha to withdraw from the Ula district early in December. Desertion of units continued, and the Turks had to withdraw from Awali and Bir Mashi as well. When desertion was followed by insubordination, Fakhri Pasha had to give in and send a delegation on 4 January 1919, to Bir Derwish, Ali's headquarters, to negotiate peace. Soon after, he gave himself up and the Arabs entered Medina. The number of those who surrendered exceeded twelve thousand, in addition to another four thousand dead, wounded or captured while the siege was on. That is to say, Fakhri Pasha's force comprised no fewer than sixteen thousand men, operating between Medina and Tebuk. Turkish prisoners were transported to Yanbo', then by sea to prison camps in Egypt.

The Arab siege of Medina is no less important than the operations of the Northern Army in Transjordan and Syria. But it would be out of place here to give a detailed exposition of the siege, during which fighting was carried on as it was in the north, by attacks on railway stations, the removal of rails, the demolition of bridges and surprise attacks on Turkish garrisons. Arab forces in Hejaz were able to engage a strong Turkish Army, no less powerful than the Fourth Army in Transjordan. Had this army been transferred to the Palestine front, the British would not have found it so easy to defeat the Turks in September.

Reliable sources indicate that, during the critical weeks preceding Allenby's attack, Emir Feisal's army had engaged nearly half of the Turkish forces south of Damascus. These Turkish forces comprised the Second and Eighth Army Corps as well as the garrisons along the Hejaz railway between Ma'an and Amman; these together totalled some fourteen thousand officers and men. The fighting strength of Turkish armies south of Damascus was thirty-four thousand. The ration strength of the regular forces in the Arab Army was eight thousand. Chaytor's force at Jericho was the only British assistance the Arabs had in engaging the Turkish Fourth Army. Adding the army cut off in Hejaz to that in Jordan, we see that the total force facing the Arabs was not smaller than that facing the British.

As a consequence, Allenby was able to concentrate three army corps, totalling sixty-nine thousand fighting men, as against twenty thousand Turks. The full significance of this can be grasped only when we bring to mind the incomparable difference between the superior numbers, equipment and resources of the British and the limitations of the Arabs in all these fields.

Nor should we forget that the Arab Revolt had caused communications to be severed between the three Turkish divisions in Yemen and southern Arabia on the one hand and their bases of supply and reinforcement in Syria on the other. As a result, these three divisions remained inactive for the whole duration of the war.

A glance at these figures would suffice to impress upon us the value of the Arab contribution to Allenby's successes. This contribution becomes all the more impressive when we realize that the whole Fourth Army could have made an orderly retreat, had it not been for the Arab stand in its rear and their repeated attacks, which dispersed the enemy, most of whose men were killed or captured.

Commanders of the enemy forces subsequently made statements recognizing the importance of the Arab Revolt. Ahmed Jemal Pasha, for instance, says that without the Arab Revolt the British could not have won their victories in Palestine. Liman von Sanders states that the Arab Revolt so influenced the Arabs that the British forces advancing towards Jerusalem found themselves fighting in a friendly country, while the Turks who were defending their own territory found themselves fighting in the midst of a decidedly hostile population. We know that Liman von Sanders had thought of frustrating Allenby's attack by effecting a withdrawal to a rear line.

I gave up the idea, because we would have had to relinquish the Hejaz railway . . . and because we could no longer have stopped the progress of the Arab insurrection in the rear of our army.[15]

Lawrence claimed to have governed Damascus for three days (1–3 October), adding that he decided to leave the city on the fourth day, for fear that his new powers might tempt him to stay. This was the period immediately following the withdrawal of the Turks and preceding the entry of Feisal into Damascus. But there seems to be no confirmation of this claim from any quarter. For on the morning of 1 October, Sherif Nassir and Nuri as-Said entered Damascus at the head of the irregular and regular forces respectively. Nuri as-Said's statements give us to understand that he was the military governor of Damascus during this period. Sherif Nassir was the ultimate authority, representing Emir Feisal.

What actually took place was that Brigadier General Behjet Bey, deputy *vali* of Syria, was the last Turkish official to leave Damascus on 30 September. Before his departure he had met Shukri Pasha al-Ayyubi and handed the city over to him. Al-Ayyubi immediately made for the citadel prison, flung its doors wide open and, in the name of King Hussein, freed its four thousand prisoners. At the same time Emir Said al-Jezairi got in touch with Jemal Pasha the Lesser, and, obtaining five hundred rifles from him, with which he armed his followers, proceeded to take over the responsibility of government. On the same day he telegraphed the mayors of Syrian cities, including Beirut, to inform them of the establishment of a Hashemite Arab Government, on behalf of King Hussein.

15. Cited by Liddell Hart in *T. E. Lawrence,* p. 341.

The Al-Jazairis, a family of Algerians, were a notable Damascus family with considerable prestige; as feudal lords, they had armed followers. This family had been persecuted by the Turks, who had condemned some of its members to death and banished others. But as the Arab Revolt grew more formidable, the Turks tried to be friendly with the remaining notables, among whom were Said al-Jezairi and his brother Abdul Kader. It is on record that Abdul Kader interceded with Jemal Pasha the Lesser on behalf of some prisoners, and succeeded in securing their release.

In response to inquiries, Emir Said wrote to me saying that on 30 September he raised the Arab flag on Government House. This was the flag which King Hussein had given to Abdul Kader, Said's brother. Said then declared the independence of the Arab nation, and handed over the reins of government to Sherif Nassir as soon as the latter arrived.

But Nassir evinced surprise at my action and informed me that Feisal had sent me a letter delegating it to me to run the administration until his arrival. But men greedy for power plotted with Lawrence to murder me and my brother. Lawrence's claim that he deposed me is a lie. I addressed Sherif Nassir, saying 'We have raised this flag and now we leave it to you to protect.'

Faiz al-Ghussein informed me that Feisal had asked him to enter Damascus secretly and work with the nationalists on raising the flag in Emir Said's possession, before the actual entry of the forces. But he was prevented by the retreat of the Turks from arriving on time. He also said that Lawrence's hatred for Abdul Kader lay behind his opposition to the Algerians, adding that Abdul Kader attacked Lawrence in Government House with a dagger, but that Auda Abu Tayeh intervened and rescued him.

Dr. Ahmad Qadri has this to say:

We asked Ali Rida Pasha al-Rikabi and Shukri al-Ayyubi to form a national government, without waiting for us to enter the city. Since Rida Pasha was not in Damascus at the time, the task fell to Shukri al-Ayyubi, who raised the flag on Government House. A good-hearted man, he joined up with Emir Said and his brother Abdul Kader, and accepted their precedence over him. When I reached Government House, I found that Lawrence had already arrived there. We were surprised to see him there because the afore-mentioned were not nationalists working with Feisal; on the contrary they were working with the Ottoman Government, and were in touch with France. We could not bear this after the spectacular victory we had just won. When Lawrence expressed a desire to depose them, I agreed and we entered the grand hall at Government House to discuss this with Sherif Nassir. But we were surprised by shouting and clamour in the next room between Auda Abu Tayeh and Sultan al-Atrash; so we went out to mediate. . . . Emir Said seized the opportunity and persuaded Sherif Nassir to take some rest in his house. So the Sherif left Government House. This went according to a predetermined plan aimed at averting the storm. It was not wise for Sherif Nassir to leave Government House in the critical situation at Damascus during these crucial hours, when one would have expected him to be engaged in running the affairs of his government. Arab forces had taken over the official buildings, and the British vanguard had arrived. So Sherif Nassir was requested by the notables to return immediately to Government House. Accordingly he returned with Emir Said and his brother. We came to an understanding with Sherif Nassir, who then asked Emir Said to keep to his house. But the Emir was not easily intimidated. So Lawrence grew angry at him and said, 'This is the decision of those concerned. If you don't behave, Sherif Nassir will order his forces to arrest you. You should know that the British forces are also ready to help the Arabs in enforcing order and quiet in the city.' Said left in a huff. Ali Rida al-Rikabi arrived in due course and took control. When Feisal entered Damascus, Lawrence asked leave to depart, then left for his country.

It was only natural that there should be some confusion in a city like Damascus in these circumstances. The Turks had left before a new administration could be set up to fill the gap. In fact, things settled down neither quickly nor easily. Al-Rikabi was driven into fixing a scaffold in the yard outside Government House, announcing that he would hang all who disregarded Government authority. It was obvious that Emir Said had wanted to head the Government by force; and in the absence of a group that could withstand his followers, he was able to go on for two days, during which he obtained the support of Sherif Nassir. But Emir Feisal and his close associates had already decided on Al-Rikabi because of his previous contact with the independence movement, quite apart from the fact that he was fully qualified for the task. Had he not been delayed, he would have taken over immediately after the withdrawal of the Turks.

I sought out information on this episode from the well-known Syrian statesman, the late Faris al-Khouri. Strongly denying that Lawrence interfered in the affairs of Government, he informed me that he and seven other leaders took control after the Turkish withdrawal, and elected Shukri al-Ayyubi to head the provisional government. Al-Rikabi then arrived and, at Feisal's command, took over the Government. With regard to the administration, Akram al-Rikabi says 'It was headed by whoever arrived at Government House first.'

Abdul Kader al-Jezairi was shot by the police for refusing to abide by orders to keep the peace. We thus see that the first days of Arab occupation in Damascus bordered on chaos. It is certain that Lawrence's authority did not exceed that of Sherif Nassir, Said al-Jezairi or Nuri as-Said. He must have enjoyed a measure of influence and respect as a representative of Britain and a close friend of Feisal's, but I have found no evidence supporting his claim that he wielded actual authority at Damascus. This claim should be lumped together with those many others which have been proved untrue.

8

WAR AND PEACE

1. LAWRENCE LEAVES DAMASCUS

In the last chapter of *Seven Pillars*, Lawrence gives an account of his last days at Damascus. He described Feisal's meeting with Allenby and his own role as interpreter. He concludes with the following words:

> When Feisal had gone, I made to Allenby the last (and also I think the first) request I ever made him for myself—leave to go away. For a while he would not have it; but I reasoned, reminding him of his year-old promise, and pointing out how much easier the New Law would be if my spur were absent from the people. In the end he agreed; and then at once I knew how much I was sorry.[1]

Many have wondered at the motives which led Lawrence to leave Damascus after the final victory, at a time when conditions were favourable for his remaining close to Feisal and playing the part of which he had perhaps been dreaming: to become the moving force behind the throne. The following is an account by Colonel Peake:

> I asked him why he was leaving us and he said: 'I am going because the entry into Damascus was the climax.' Then he added after a pause: 'Never wait for the anti-climax. Come out on the crest of the wave, and don't wallow out in its trough.'[2]

There are some who believe that after entering Damascus Allenby wished to appoint two liaison officers, one British and another French. When news of this reached Lawrence he told Allenby that he could not consent to work with a French officer and asked for leave. The leave was granted and he left Damascus.

Anthony Nutting believes that Feisal was not as fond of Law-

1. *Seven Pillars*, p. 660.   2. C. E. Jarvis, *Arab Command* (1946), p. 52.

rence as people imagined and that he did not invite him to stay with him in Damascus. Nutting, however, quotes a friend of Lawrence as saying that Lawrence felt that the next round would be fought at the conference table in Europe and that he would be more useful to the Arabs if he hastened to London.

In a letter to Major R. H. Scott from Cairo dated 14 October 1918, Lawrence says:

> As we hoped we got to Damascus, and there I had to leave the Arabs—it is a pity to go, and it would have been unwise to stay. I feel like a man who has suddenly dropped a heavy load. . . .[3]

Lawrence left Damascus on 4 October, and went to Cairo. After spending a few days there, he left for England. On 4 November he submitted a secret report to the Foreign Office, saying that the war in Hejaz had really come to an end with the occupation of Aqaba, and that, thereafter, Emir Feisal had undertaken the liberation of Syria with a regular army of Syrians and Iraqis. The opinion Lawrence expressed in this report was that Syria governed by Syrians was far better than Syria under the French. His report was followed by some suggestions with regard to the future of Arab countries: Hejaz should have full independence; Iraq should become a British mandated territory, and Feisal should be given virtually the whole of Syria save for a strip of coast including Beirut, which should be conceded to France. As for the Balfour Declaration (see p. 221), he asserted that the Arabs were agreeable provided that the arrangement was under British control and did not involve the creation of a Jewish national state. Another version has it that Lawrence suggested the creation of three Arab states outside Hejaz: Syria under Emir Feisal, Lower Mesopotamia under Emir Abdullah and Upper Mesopotamia under Emir Zeid.

It is hard to understand why Lawrence expressed these views, since he knew full well that the Arabs had declared their Revolt for the sole purpose of obtaining their independence and unity. Had they known the real intentions of the States to which they allied themselves, they would never have given them full confidence and they would have rejected this alliance. Lawrence's suggestions, based as they were on the Sykes-Picot agreement and fully in accord with the views of imperialistically-minded

3. *Selected Letters*, p. 112.

politicians in London and Paris, indicated quite clearly that he had no very profound understanding of the realities of Arab aspirations.

The partition of greater Syria was the worst blow that befell the Arabs. From it have grown the Palestine catastrophe and all the other misfortunes resulting from the dismemberment of an organic whole. Our present generation has suffered immeasurably from it. For centuries greater Syria has been the moving spirit of the Arab countries, their centre of leadership and their source of development and progress. Greater Syria stands in relationship to the rest of Arab territory as the head does to the body.

2. ARABS INVITED TO PEACE CONFERENCE

The Arabs attached great hopes to their alliance with Britain. King Hussein had unlimited confidence in her plighted word, particularly because he believed that an alliance between the Arabs and the British would be beneficial to both. The Arabs did in fact obtain several promises and pledges from Britain. McMahon's letters supported the Arab right to independence and unity. Britain's Declaration to the Seven Arabs, dated 16 June 1918, the Anglo-French declaration of 7 November 1918, and President Wilson's Fourteen Points—all emphasized the right of nations to determine their own fate, and opposed the imposition on any people of a rule which they did not want or a ruler they would not accept.

For this reason King Hussein and his sons, in addition to Arab commanders and leaders, anxiously awaited the end of the war, which would bring about the withdrawal of foreign troops and enable them to form the government or governments most suited to their needs. General Allenby's stock reply to Syrian protests against measures which they considered unacceptable was that they were all temporary, forced upon them by the conditions and limitations of war. Final solutions, he asserted, would be reached in a special conference attended by responsible statesmen. Military measures, he emphasized, would in no way affect the nature of political solutions.

But when the time for the projected allied conference came, there was an obvious reluctance to invite the Arabs. Britain was taking into account France's opposition to such an invitation.

British officials in the Middle East, headed by Wingate and Allenby, supported Arab representation, with the recommendation that Feisal should be the Arab delegate. They urged their Government to take a positive stand towards this question. Thus, on 4 November 1918, Allenby wired the War Office in the following terms:

My chief Political Officer has received a telegram from the Foreign Office asking whether the present moment is propitious for inviting King Hussein to nominate a representative to represent his views at any Inter-Allied Conference regarding a settlement of Asiatic Turkey. I consider it very important that the King of the Hejaz should be told immediately that he will have the right and will be invited to send an Arab representative to any Inter-Allied Conference regarding a settlement of the liberated areas where Arab interests are concerned, and that his representative will attend the Peace Conference. The assurance that I have given with the approval of the War Office will not be fulfilled unless this is done. The Arabs trust implicitly in Great Britain. All confidence in the good faith of the Allies will be destroyed if our pledges are not kept.[4]

On 8 November Lawrence sent the following telegram from the Foreign Office to King Hussein:

I believe there will be conversations in Paris in fifteen days' time between the Allies about the question of the Arabs. General Allenby has telegraphed that you will want to have a representative there. If this is so, I hope you will send Feisal since his splendid victories have given him a personal reputation in Europe. . . . If you agree please telegraph him to get ready to leave Syria at once for about a month, and ask General Allenby for a ship to take him to France. You should meanwhile telegraph to the Governments of Great Britain, France, the United States and Italy telling them that your son is proceeding at once to Paris as your representative.[5]

The British Government finally issued an official invitation to King Hussein, advising him to appoint Feisal to represent him at the conference.

On 12 November King Hussein sent a telegram to Feisal appointing him his personal representative. Among other things the King said:

Our faithful ally, Great Britain, desires your presence as a representative of Arab interests and of all that may be basic to their life, whether it concerns boundaries or administration, within the bounds of the facts known to you. In accordance with Great Britain's view,

4. Lord Birdwood, *Nuri as-Said* (1959), p. 102.   5. *Ibid.*

make for Paris with all possible speed. Since our only connection is with Great Britain, and since we have no relationship or any occasion for one with any other country in the bases of our policy, restrict your observations and whatever else you see fit, to its leaders and esteemed representatives, whether they be your conference colleagues or Britain's political representatives. Act in accordance with what they request from you by word or deed, whether it be inside the conference or outside it, and avoid all else. This is the extent of your authority with reference to the conference and the good of the people.[6]

This telegram gives a clear picture of the extent of King Hussein's confidence in his ally, and of the hopes which he attached to her co-operation. He still believed that Britain would fulfil all her promises and pledges, rather than turn her back upon her Arab friends. It is for this reason that we find him urging Feisal not to deal with France: French ambitions in Syria were apparent, while Britain was still declaring its best intentions towards the Arabs on all occasions.

On 16 November, the Foreign Office transmitted a telegram from Lawrence to Feisal advising him to be prepared for a six weeks' stay in Europe and to come in Arab clothes.

Bring with you one Iraqi officer, if possible Nuri as-Said, and two of your leading Syrian supporters....

There followed details of Foreign Office administrative arrangements. Lawrence informed Feisal that he would be attached to him throughout his stay.[7]

3. FEISAL IN FRANCE AND ENGLAND

Feisal sailed from Beirut on 22 November. Travelling on the British cruiser *Gloucester,* he reached Marseilles four days later. He was accompanied by Nuri as-Said, Rustum Heidar, Dr. Ahmad Qadri, Tahsin Qadri and Faiz al-Ghussein.

The French Government was irritated that Feisal had not consulted them on the question of his departure, and that the invitation to King Hussein had been extended by Britain alone. The French did not conceal their irritation, but told King Hussein, through their representative at Jedda, that while Emir Feisal would be received in France with the honour due to the son of a sovereign who was a friend and an ally of France,

6. Hafeth Wahba, *Jazairet al-Arab fi al-Qarn al-'Ishrin.*   7. Birdwood, p. 103.

it would be impossible to regard the Emir as being in charge of any official mission, since the French Government had not been informed in any way of his visit. In his book *Le Hedjaz dans la Guerre Mondiale,* Colonel Brémond reports that he was called to the French Ministry of Foreign Affairs, where he was instructed by M. Jean Gout, Under-Secretary for Asia, to receive Emir Feisal at Marseilles. According to Brémond the following were among the instructions issued:

> Treat the Emir Feisal as if he were a General and a distinguished person but without any diplomatic standing. Tell him that he has been badly advised. He should have talked to M. Georges Picot before coming here. Tell him that the British Government does not do everything and should not have advised him to come here without consulting the French Government. Arrange matters in such a way as not to bring him to Paris without further instructions. . . . Take him round to see anything you like. Take him to General Gouraud who is with the IVth Army in Strasburg and who will decorate the Emir with the Insignia of the Order of 'Grand Officer'. . . . With Lawrence, one must make things very clear and show him that he is on the wrong path. If he comes here as a British Colonel, in British uniform, we shall welcome him. But we shall not accept him if he comes as an Arab and remains disguised as such.[8]

The British Foreign Office delegated Lawrence to meet Feisal at Marseilles, where M. Bertrand also met him on behalf of the French. Lawrence had arrived in Arab clothes, and Bertrand seized the first opportunity to acquaint Feisal with the instructions of the French Government in this regard. According to Brémond, Feisal replied without hesitation that Lawrence would leave France immediately and that he had already asked Lawrence to leave for England. After receiving Feisal's instructions, Lawrence went to M. Bertrand and said to him, 'You are expelling me. I shall leave this evening.' Refusing to part with his Arab clothes, he returned home. Later, it is said, he returned his Croix de Guerre to the French Government.

Behind this treatment of Lawrence by the French was the belief that he was working against French interests and urging Feisal to oppose their ambitions. The French also believed that the British Government's invitation to Hussein to take part in the Peace Conference was Lawrence's doing. Lawrence had declared that his wearing Arab clothes was the best method of

8. Cited in Zeine N. Zeine, *The Struggle for Arab Independence,* p. 53.

publicizing his sympathy for the Arabs and adding his voice to theirs. Anthony Nutting believes that Feisal ordered Lawrence to return to London and keep away from him, which he takes as a sign that contrary to popular belief Feisal had no affection for Lawrence and did not care for Lawrence's presence at his side. I disagree with Nutting's interpretation, because Feisal was attaching great hopes to Great Britain's word and believed that Lawrence could be a helpful and useful element. Feisal was too wise and cautious to behave erratically for no reason. It is clear that he disclosed France's attitude to Lawrence, who preferred to depart rather than parade as the victim in front of Brémond with whom his relations had been strained since their days in Hejaz. It is likely that in *Le Hedjaz dans la Guerre Mondiale* Brémond falsified Feisal's position for the sake of belittling Lawrence.

After visiting Alsace, Feisal expressed his wish to go on to Paris and begin the political efforts for which he had come to France. Brémond's instructions were to keep the Emir away from Paris, but at Feisal's insistence, he wired his government and obtained permission for Feisal to visit the capital. A meeting with the French President was arranged for 7 December. The Arab historian Amin Said reports that a Feisal A.D.C. told him that the British Government had interceded with the French on Feisal's behalf, and that this intercession came as a result of Lawrence's insistence. We should remember, however, that Feisal was not an idle onlooker. According to Brémond, the Emir took him aside and said, 'We have fought side by side, hence we are brethren-in-arms. I have confidence in your loyalty and integrity. Tell me frankly how things stand. Also inform me without equivocation whether or no the French Government wishes me to go to Paris. I have left my brother Zeid in Damascus to act for me, and he is young. Since conditions are not settled there, it is better for me to return if I am going to waste my time here.' This frank talk may have produced the desired effect, since it would have been unreasonable for France to be hostile to her guest Feisal at a time when the situation in Syria had not crystallized in her favour, when negotiations had not yet started and when Britain's attitude had not been clearly defined.

The French President received Feisal in Paris. Then on 10 December, the Emir sailed to Britain from Calais. There he was met by Lawrence on behalf of the British Government. Lawrence invited Brémond to visit Britain, assuring him that he would be cordially received. Thanking him for this invitation, Brémond replied that he considered his task completed at that point. It has been reported that Lawrence said to Brémond at Calais, 'You kicked me out and here I am back again.'

The Emir had a warm welcome in London. On 12 December 1918, he was received by the King. Lawrence, in Arab clothes, accompanied Feisal to Buckingham Palace. His appearance shocked a certain person, who rebuked him for coming to the Palace in foreign uniform. Lawrence replied, 'When a man serves two masters and has to offend one of these, it is better to offend the more powerful. I've come here as interpreter to the Emir Feisal, whose uniform this is.'

The Emir stayed twenty-five days in England, and met a number of British officials. It was clear that the British Government wanted him to come to some sort of understanding with France. On 6 January 1919, he returned to Paris for the Peace Conference. In his memoirs Dr. Ahmad Qadri says,

Lawrence never parted from the Emir in London, and looked to all his needs. When Feisal met King George, he accompanied him as interpreter.

While Feisal was in France, the French Prime Minister, Clemenceau, visited London on 1 December 1918. Lloyd George has this to say of the visit:

When Clemenceau came to London after the War I drove with him to the French Embassy. After we reached the Embassy he asked me what it was that I specially wanted from the French. I instantly replied that I wanted Mosul attached to Irak, and Palestine from Dan to Beersheba under British Control. Without any hesitation he agreed.[9]

It was natural enough for Clemenceau to agree 'without any hesitation', for in return he wanted Britain to agree to French demands, especially for a mandate over the whole of Greater Syria.

At this point we must return to the Anglo-Franco-Russian agreement of April–May 1916. Under its provisions Russia was to take Constantinople and a stretch of territory in Anatolia

9. David Lloyd George, *The Truth About the Peace Treaties* (1938), Vol. II, p. 1038.

adjacent to the Caucasus border. France was to govern directly the Syrian coast from Acre in the south to Alexandretta in the north. Iraq, from Basra in the south to Baghdad and Baaquba in the north, was to be under Britain's direct rule. There were to be two Arab states, with some sort of independence, under foreign tutelage. The first would comprise inner Syria and Mosul, attached to France. The other would extend from Kirkuk in the north to Transjordan and Negev in the south, attached to Britain. Because of its religious importance, Palestine was to be an international zone. The Anglo-French section of the agreement is known as the Sykes-Picot agreement, after the names of the British and French delegates respectively who signed it on behalf of their governments. Palestine's international status was altered after the fall of the Tsarist regime in Russia, for, on 2 November 1917, the British Government issued the notorious Balfour Declaration, which stated that the British Government viewed with favour the establishment in Palestine of a national home for the Jewish people. In making this declaration the British Government was moved mainly by two considerations: to win over the support of World Jewry, particularly in the United States, where Jewish influence was greatest; and to secure Palestine as a bulwark to the British position in Egypt and the Suez Canal. After the War Britain began to seek the inclusion of Mosul in its portion of the spoils, to secure its oil. In this they were encouraged by the fact that France wanted Syria at any cost. France of course had to have Britain's concurrence to this, both because Britain was all-important in international politics and because the armies of Britain and its Arab allies were still occupying Syria.

It is apparent that Britain was trying to effect a compromise between the ambitions of France and the demands of the Arabs, to whom, after all, these countries belonged. And although Britain was convinced that such a compromise was possible, she was determined at the same time to keep Iraq and Palestine for herself. Britain made it abundantly clear that the fate of Iraq and Palestine was not negotiable, and therefore employed every possible means to place France and the Arabs at opposite ends of the pole. The short-sighted political outlook of France on the one hand and the military weakness of the Arabs on the other were instrumental in producing the result Britain wanted. Feisal found himself in a political quandary: his father was refusing to deviate even slightly from the principle of independence and unity for all the Arab countries; France was refusing to acknowledge the independence of inner Syria or to assist the Arabs in their demands for the independence of Iraq and Palestine; and Britain was saying to each, 'There is your adversary. We agree to your demands, but that adversary will not budge.'

The view of the French was that, with the loss of a million men in the War, they could not be expected to take British promises to the Arabs too seriously. Besides, there was a surge of imperialistic feeling among Frenchmen generally, who saw no logical reason for desisting from their ambitious course. Frenchmen everywhere were wondering whether Britain would really give up Iraq and its oil, merely to keep her plighted word with the Arabs. Britain in her turn confirmed these suspicions, on the grounds that, since Iraq did not figure much in the Arab Revolt, it fell outside the pale of post-war settlements.

4. THE PEACE CONFERENCE AND THE ARABS

Feisal returned to Paris for the Peace Conference, for which preparations were on foot. Lawrence came in January as a member of a delegation from the Foreign Office, whose business was to handle Eastern affairs. In this capacity he was safe from French opposition. He spent the time alternately with the Arab and British delegations, wearing Arab clothes while in Feisal's company and his military uniform while engaged on business related to his work as a member of the British delegation. He basked in reflected glory in Paris because of the popularity of Feisal, a famous, personally impressive and exotically clad Arab prince. Lawrence later stayed in the Emir's private wing at the hotel, and generally worked in the capacity of liaison-officer between Feisal and the British delegation.

Feisal's position at this time should be realistically assessed. This was his first visit to Europe, and it was the first time he had ever been entrusted with a political task of such magnitude, requiring wisdom, subtlety and experience. He was in a completely new environment, which must have seemed rather impressive to him after Constantinople, Syria and Hejaz. He had had no experience in political manoeuvring, nor did he realize that politics were completely divorced from morality. It is scarcely surprising that he should have depended on Lawrence, an educated European of tact and subtlety, who spoke fluent French. Lawrence had shared with the Arabs two years of experience in the Revolt, in which they had found little for which to blame him, and during which he had constantly declared his friendship for them, claiming to care for their interests and to be prepared to die in their cause. As usual, Lawrence took pains to make himself useful to the Emir, with his opinions, his abundance of information, his experience and education. He also took pains to be the first to carry to the Emir news of developments in the political situation, particularly that aspect of it which most concerned the Arab countries. He tried to advise the Emir on what was and what was not to be done, on what was and what was not possible. At the same time he managed to strengthen his position with the British delegation, from Lloyd George, the Prime Minister, downwards, on the grounds that he was not only Feisal's spokesman but also an expert on Arab affairs and Arab history who knew what the Arabs would and would not accept. He thus succeeded in becoming the major channel of contact between Feisal and the British delegation, just as he had previously succeeded in playing the same role between Feisal and Allenby.

When he first arrived in Paris, Feisal had added Awni Abdul Hadi to his retinue and made him a member of the Arab delegation, in order to have the benefit of his experience.[10] Awni Abdul Hadi reports that on the second day of Feisal's arrival he was visited by M. Gout, who welcomed him on behalf of the French Government. Gout then informed him that the French Government regretted that it could not reserve any seats in the Versailles Conference for the Arab delegation, on the grounds that the Great Powers had not yet recognized the Hejaz Government. This was a shock to Feisal, who had come from his country in response to an official invitation from Britain, to state his people's case and their desire for unity and independence. He felt that his presence in France was futile, and that he would now be powerless to do anything in the service of his people. When

10. Awni Abdul Hadi was born in 1889 and graduated in law from Paris. He was a founder of the 'Fetat' secret party. Feisal's private secretary and an Arab representative at Versailles, he was later condemned to death by the French. He is well known in the Arab movement, and an outstanding Palestinian leader. He held several important positions, and in 1955 was Jordan's Foreign Minister.

on the following day Lawrence heard of what had happened, he made no comment, but quietly left Feisal (this was his habit on such occasions). In the evening, however, he returned and said to Feisal in his slight Arabic: '*Sidi,* Lloyd George sends you his greetings and informs you that you will have not one, but two, seats at the Peace Conference at Versailles.'

Feisal's happiness and his gratitude to this useful friend who could intercede with the British Government can readily be imagined. Awni comments on this: 'Lawrence's subtlety is apparent here. For first he made Feisal feel that the British were his real friends, and secondly he made him realize—more than ever before—that he—Lawrence—had great influence with the British Prime Minister. The Emir was convinced that Lawrence could help the Arabs in persuading British politicians to view Arab demands with favour.'

Brémond wrote:

'Clemenceau agreed to accept Feisal at the Peace Conference in deference to Lord Curzon's intercession, although he had at the beginning refused.'

Clemenceau had met serious opposition from his cabinet to Arab representation at the conference, and was able to persuade them only after a heated debate. Brémond comments on this by saying that this incident confirmed Feisal's belief in the value of British support.

The Peace Conference opened on 18 January 1919. The Arabs were represented by two delegates—Feisal himself and Rustom Heidar, Chief of his Diwan.

The Arabs found a new champion for their cause in the person of President Wilson of the United States, on whom they built great hopes. Through his influence the delegates of the five Great Powers at the conference (the United States, Britain, France, Italy, Japan) approved a decision to separate Armenia and the Arab countries from Turkey and conduct a plebiscite to decide their fate—this despite the fact that British and French statesmen wished to keep the Arab question pending until final peace with the Turkish Government.

On 6 March the Emir submitted the Arab case to the Council of Ten and spoke for twenty minutes.[11] Among other things the

11. The Council of Ten consisted of two delegates representing each of the five Great Powers.

Emir declared that his father was asking for the right of self-determination for the Arabs, in addition to recognition for the Arab countries as an independent geographical entity. In reply to a question by President Wilson as to whether the Arab countries would prefer to be united, to divide into two or more states, or to submit to a mandate of one or more nations, he said, 'It would be better for them to be independent and united.'

Feisal had spent the whole of the previous night working on his speech in Arabic, assisted by Rustom Heidar and Awni Abdul Hadi. Lawrence translated the speech into English, again with the help of Rustom and Awni. When Feisal had finished reading it to the Council, Lawrence rose, resplendent in complete Arab dress, and read the translation. Apart from Feisal, this session was attended by Rustom, Awni and Nuri as-Said.

Other opinions were heard by the Conference with regard to the future of Syria. Then on 21 March, in response to President Wilson's insistence, it was decided to send out a commission of inquiry representing the Allies to determine the wishes of the people in Greater Syria.

While Feisal was busy approaching statesmen of the Great Powers to argue the justice of Arab demands, he was visited by M. Jean Gout of the French delegation, whose mission inspired the Emir with feelings of alarm and suspicion. Gout told him that the attempt to omit him from participation in the Peace Conference had been deliberate, that the English were only playing with him, and that the sooner Feisal ceased to listen to the mischief-makers who were working against France, the better it would be for him. France, he said, recognized no Arab army in Syria, and Allenby lied if he said they did. Lawrence reports that he found Feisal pacing the floor in the hotel in the small hours of the morning, looking extremely worried.

Feisal soon discovered that the British were, in fact, giving way to the wishes of the French. The French delegation to the Peace Conference had been bitterly criticized in French influential circles for agreeing to take part in the commission of inquiry, on the pretext that the Syrian people were in no position to answer the questions put to them, and the French Government had subsequently resorted to various excuses, making it clear to Feisal that the French were not serious and might not

take part in the commission of inquiry after all. He therefore
went to President Wilson, who gave him his solemn word that the
American delegation would be sent out, regardless of the attitude
of France or Britain.[12] Feisal's suspicions proved well-founded,
for France laid down a condition that a previous agreement
should be reached among the governments concerned on the
manner of conducting the inquiry. But President Wilson refused
to be tied down to any conditions. Consequently, France refused
to send out its delegation, and Britain followed suit. It should
be remembered that this happened after Britain had already
announced the appointment of Sir Henry McMahon and Dr.
Hogarth to their delegation and after France had declared that
its own delegation would be led by M. Henry Lange.

The Emir then decided to return home and prepare public
opinion to receive the commission. He therefore left France for
Syria, reaching Beirut on 30 April. Before leaving, however, the
Emir had paid M. Clemenceau a long visit, during which he was
told that France would recognize the independence of Syria in
return for Syrian recognition of French interests. Feisal promised
to work for peace and amity.

What was Lawrence doing at this time? Awni Abdul Hadi,
who had got to know him rather well in Paris, gives us a clear
picture of the part he played. The following are excerpts (in
translation) from a private letter written by Awni:

> The part that Lawrence played during the War brought him nearer
> to Feisal. . . . When Feisal went to Europe he did not hesitate to
> draw Lawrence closer to him because he was in need of his services
> once again. Also there is no doubt that Lawrence wished to make
> use of Feisal in attaining British objectives. Here Lawrence played
> an important part and displayed great subtlety in fulfilling the role
> of liaison-officer between Feisal and British officials. He also played
> an important part in helping the Zionists, since he viewed Zionism
> with unmistakable favour, in spite of all that has been said about his
> attachment to the Arabs. He was an Englishman, first and foremost,
> and always worked for British interests. In this connection, he pur-
> sued two contradictory courses of action: the first prompted by an

12. 'Mrs. Wilson was in Paris when Emir Feisal arrived for the first time. She
met him there and admired him in her own American way, and later wrote him
several letters. She used to say that his face reflected the picture of Christ. I
believe that she was largely instrumental in bringing about the decision to
send out the King-Crane commission to Syria.' (Translated from the Arabic of
M'uarrokh al-Thawret al-Arabiyyeh (Historian of the Arab Revolt) *Al-Malik
Feisal al-Awwal* (King Feisal I).)

inclination towards the Arabs (whenever he felt that the British were in need of the Arabs), and the other, without doubt, manifested by a liking for the Jews and Zionism. I believe that deep in his heart he was more inclined towards Zionism, out of a belief that Zionism best served the interests of Britain. But first I will try to elucidate the political circumstances which compelled Feisal to rely, during his stay in Europe, more and more heavily on Lawrence.

Lawrence was extremely sly. . . . He pretended that he was more Arab than English and that he knew Arabic as well as any Arab. But the fact is that he did not know Arabic all that well, but spoke it with an obvious accent. He worked for the good of his own country, and it was in this spirit that he worked with Feisal in London and Paris. An indication of his slyness appears in the fact that he pretended to have great respect for Feisal and the Arabs. He always addressed Feisal in traditional Arab fashion as *Sidi*.

Lawrence tried on several occasions to prove to Feisal that he—Lawrence—enjoyed the respect and confidence of the British Government, and in this way he made Feisal stick to him all the more tenaciously. And in spite of that, he would follow Feisal like a shadow, never allowing him out of his sight (Britain's sight, that is). His prime object was to make Feisal cling to the British and come to believe that they were his only real friends. He stayed with the Arab delegation at the Hotel Continental and later at the chateau reserved by the French Government for this delegation, thus making it possible for himself to follow Feisal's every move. One day when Feisal visited M. Clemenceau in his office (I was with Feisal), Clemenceau asked Feisal, 'Why don't you trust me, when I consider myself an enemy to imperialism and have written a number of books and articles against imperialism? Why don't you then place your hand in mine so that we may become friends, since I have fought imperialism for fifty years?' Feisal, who was always quick-witted, answered, 'Sir, if I were sure that you would always be Prime Minister of France, I would not hesitate to offer you my hand. But I am afraid that one day the Premiership would fall upon another person who might well follow an imperialistic policy.' When Feisal rose to leave Clemenceau's office, Clemenceau got up and walked with him to the outer terrace. Looking around him, Feisal, to his surprise, saw Lawrence sitting there. Lawrence rose to his feet and Feisal felt that he should, out of courtesy, introduce him to Clemenceau, who shook hands and exchanged with him some commonplace remarks. It was strange that Lawrence should be wearing the uniform of a British officer, instead of the Arab clothes which he usually wore in Feisal's company.

Is this not strange indeed? What was Lawrence doing there, and why did he follow Feisal when Feisal never mentioned his visit nor asked him to follow him? It is clear that Lawrence wanted to be noticed by Clemenceau. Imagine a man like him of a relatively humble station and simple rank meeting a great man like Clemenceau. Perhaps he also wanted to add this incident to the record of his adventures in order to be able to say later that he met Clemenceau. For there was in fact no possibility for one of Lawrence's station at the time to meet a great man like Clemenceau.

The fact is that Feisal was gradually convinced that he could not dispense with Lawrence in the task of cementing Anglo-Arab friendship. He was also convinced that Lawrence was the only Englishman who could intercede with the British Government in a way that would make Britain accede to Arab demands. It was strange that the British Government should in turn have believed that Lawrence was the only man through whom Britain could get out of Feisal all she wanted.

5. ZIONIST ENDEAVOURS

We must now turn to the Zionist claim that Feisal signed an agreement with Chaim Weizmann relating to Jewish ambitions in Palestine. Much has been published on this subject, either supporting or denying the existence of such an agreement. We are, however, inclined to disbelieve this claim because the Zionists did not make it public until after the death of King Feisal in 1936. Awni Abdul Hadi promptly issued a strong denial of Zionist allegations. He said that he was secretary to Feisal at London and Paris, but had no knowledge of this. News of such an agreement was especially surprising, since Feisal never concealed anything from members of his delegation. Similarly, Faiz al-Ghussein has assured me personally that he never heard of this agreement. Feisal could not possibly have put his signature to anything that would have harmed the Arab cause, because of his zealous nationalistic spirit, which was above suspicion. Besides, the Zionists' claim that this agreement was signed in London on 3 January 1919, while Feisal's reservation refers to a memorandum dated 4 January. The following is a translation of the reservation which Feisal is said to have added in his own hand to the Agreement:

Provided the Arabs obtain their independence as demanded in my Memorandum dated the 4th of January, 1919, to the Foreign Office of the Government of Great Britain, I shall concur in the above articles. But if the slightest modification or departure were to be made (*sc.* in relation to the demands in the Memorandum) I shall not then be bound by a single word of the present Agreement which shall be deemed void and of no account or validity, and I shall not be answerable in any way whatsoever.[13]

13. George Antonius, *The Arab Awakening* (1938), p. 439.

Doubting the existence of this agreement does not in any way lessen our conviction of the great pressure that the British Government was applying on Feisal to come to terms with the Zionists. Lawrence was the instrument of this pressure, because the British Government knew very well that he enjoyed Feisal's confidence and that Feisal believed he aimed at nothing but good for the Arabs. Lawrence showed great enthusiasm for the Arab good, under the pretext that coming to terms with Zionism could bring no harm to the Arabs as long as all the Arab demands for independence were met. Furthermore, Zionism had not, by that time, fully revealed its intentions. We might do well to recall Hogarth's assurances to King Hussein that the Balfour Declaration would not prejudice the political, economic, civil or religious rights of the Arabs in Palestine. In a speech delivered in Jerusalem on 27 April 1918, Weizmann insisted that the fears of the Arabs in Palestine that they might be compelled to leave their country or change their status were completely unfounded. He added that those who spread such rumours were common enemies to the Arabs and the Jews, whose purpose was to create confusion.

In his book *Trial and Error* Weizmann admits that Lawrence was of great help to the Zionists and that he was the author of the agreement presented to Feisal. He also says:

I would like at this point to pay tribute to the services which T. E. Lawrence rendered our cause, and to add something regarding his remarkable personality. I had met Lawrence fleetingly in Egypt, with Allenby, and later in Palestine. I was to meet him quite often later, and he was an occasional visitor to our house in London. His relationship to the Zionist movement was a very positive one, in spite of the fact that he was strongly pro-Arab, and he has mistakenly been represented as anti-Zionist. It was his view . . . that the Jews would be of great help to the Arabs, and that the Arab world stood to gain much from a Jewish Homeland in Palestine.[14]

The letter that the Zionists claimed Feisal had written on 3 March 1919, to Mr. Felix Frankfurter, then a member of the American Zionist Delegation, is certainly a forgery. Anybody who reads the letter cannot escape this conclusion because of its deliberateness and affectation. Awni Abdul Hadi has this to say:

I can make assurances that Feisal never wrote such a letter. If the letter was real why have the Zionists failed to produce its

14. Chaim Weizmann, *Trial and Error* (1950), pp. 294–295.

original text with Feisal's signature? All they did produce was a second typewritten carbon copy, with the word 'Feisal' in one corner. The first time the Jews produced this alleged letter was before the Shaw Committee in Palestine in 1929. When I looked at the letter it immediately struck me as being a forgery. Nevertheless, I cabled Feisal, who was then King of Iraq, and received a reply from the Chief of protocol at the Royal Iraqi Court, saying, 'His Majesty does not recall writing anything of the sort with his knowledge'. It is probable that Lawrence had sent this letter without Feisal's knowledge.

It might be useful to quote more fully from Awni Abdul Hadi, to clarify this important point and define Feisal's attitude to Lawrence:

Feisal was an extremely intelligent man, but in 1919 he had not become expert at political manoeuvring, and his political experience was still limited. Although he was a sane thinker and a staunch nationalist, he was fully cognizant of his great need for British help to the Arab military effort during the Revolt. He, therefore, cultivated Lawrence and began to use him for achieving his aims. But there is no doubt that Lawrence himself knew how to exploit Arab needs in order to benefit from Feisal and influence him. As regards Lawrence's Zionist propensities, I recall that, during Feisal's visit to London in 1919, an English lady (Mrs. Brook wife of a maritime-line director) invited a number of Arabs and Britishers to her home to protest against the pro-Zionist policy of Great Britain. I was with Feisal at the time and was invited to that meeting. Lawrence had also been invited but had declined. When I arrived at Mrs. Brook's house, she received me with tears in her eyes, looking terribly upset. Surprised at her receiving me in this manner, I asked the cause of her annoyance, at which she produced a letter of protest from Lawrence saying that he would not attend an anti-Zionist meeting, because anti-Zionism did not serve Britain's interests.
What in fact facilitated Lawrence's efforts in getting close to Feisal and posing as his friend and adviser was the fact that Lawrence was an extremely intelligent and educated man, in addition to being industrious and active. Lawrence offered Feisal many services in conducting the operations of the Revolt. No wonder then that Feisal's confidence in him grew when he came to Europe. An additional factor in strengthening their relationship was the many difficulties that Feisal faced during his stay in Paris and London, particularly because he was still relatively inexperienced in political matters and had not as yet become acquainted with many western political leaders.
I believe that Feisal began to discover Lawrence's true nature in London, particularly after the incident at Mrs. Brook's. Although Feisal did not attend that meeting, I nevertheless informed him of

what had happened. Needless to say he was annoyed at Lawrence's behaviour. But what could he do, when he needed him so badly?

Doubtless, Feisal was under much British pressure, primarily because he had the impression that France was an avowed imperialist country with wide ambitions in Syria. Feisal knew very well that among the member countries in the Peace Conference at Versailles, Britain was the only power concerned for the future of Syria, by virtue of the pledges which it had previously given to King Hussein. As an illustration of Feisal's attitude to the British Government I would like to relate the following incident:

During the Peace Conference at Versailles Feisal visited M. Pichon, the French Foreign Minister, in his office. I was in attendance. Pichon seized this opportunity to ask Feisal the following question with a view to embarrassing him, 'I see, your Highness, that you are constantly demanding the independence of Syria, while I have never heard you demand that Palestine be independent. Is Palestine then not Arab?'

Feisal replied, 'Your Excellency, every time I have demanded the independence of Syria, I have felt that there was on the British side —from Lloyd George down to the most junior British official—a favourable response. Promise me, in your capacity as Foreign Minister of France, to respond favourably to my demand for the independence of Palestine, and I will promise you not to leave your office before demanding at the top of my voice that Palestine be independent. But you have completely neglected me for demanding Syrian independence, and, if I demanded the same for Palestine, the British Government would act in similar fashion, particularly since all the member countries at the Versailles Conference are not the least bit interested in our affairs. Where would we stand then?'

Pichon replied that previous commitments between France and Britain would not allow him to make such a pledge.

6. THE KING-CRANE COMMISSION

When Feisal returned to Damascus in early May 1919 he was enthusiastically received. Addressing Syrian delegations which were at hand from all parts of Greater Syria, he said that he had demanded full rights for the Arab countries, adding, 'I have defended the right of Syria and its natural borders. I have said that the Syrians are asking for the independence of their natural territory and refuse to share it with any partner whatsoever.' This indicates that Feisal had insisted on independence for the whole of Syria, not excluding Palestine.

Feisal had pinned great hopes on the King-Crane Commission, because he believed that President Wilson could use his country's influence to persuade France and Britain to accept the principle of self-determination and to respect the right of nations to choose their own form of government. If a mandate were inevitable, then Feisal hoped the nations concerned would, at least, have the right to choose the mandatory power that was to run their affairs. The Emir therefore began to prepare the minds of his countrymen for taking a unified attitude to the Commission. France, through M. Picot, its High Commissioner at Beirut, had submitted to Emir Feisal's specific suggestions aimed at settling their differences. But, hoping to achieve full independence for Arab countries through the work of the King-Crane Commission, he turned down their proposals.

Meanwhile, the people of Greater Syria had elected their representatives who also met at Damascus on 7 June. Delegates from Damascus and Aleppo worked side by side with those from the Lebanon, Palestine and Transjordan.

The King-Crane Commission arrived in Palestine on 10 June, then visited Damascus, Beirut and most cities in Greater Syria. In all, it spent forty-two days in Syria, where most people were unanimous in their demand for independence. Syrians favoured a plan whereby Syria would obtain technical aid from the United States, or, if such aid was not forthcoming, from Britain. They refused the idea of a French mandate and Jewish immigration. The Commission returned to Paris in August, only to find that the situation had changed. Its members gave up and returned to Washington, where their report was put on the shelf, not to be published until 1922. Arab hopes were shattered because President Wilson had failed to curb the imperialistic spirit of Britain and France. Their aspirations were further damaged after his defeat in his own country and the subsequent withdrawal of the United States from the League of Nations to pursue a policy of isolation.

In September 1919, Lloyd George invited Emir Feisal to visit Europe once again. The Governments of Great Britain and France had come to an agreement concerning Syria, and this invitation was sent out with the purpose of ensuring Arab approval of what was really a *fait accompli*.

7. THE PETROLEUM POLICY

Feisal arrived in London on 19 September. He was met by General Allenby, who took him to meet the Prime Minister.

When Lloyd George informed him of the agreement between Britain and France, the Emir protested strongly, whereupon the British advised him to go to Paris and come to terms with the French. After some hesitation he yielded to the British Government's pressure and went to Paris. On 27 November he had a long interview with Clemenceau during which the conditions of a provisional Franco-Arab arrangement were agreed upon, Feisal having been let down so badly by Britain and the United States. The agreement stipulated that the occupation by France of the Lebanon and the rest of the coastal regions of Syria be respected by the Arab Government. It also stipulated that the Arab Government should henceforth turn to France for any assistance it might require. The arrangement was to be regarded as provisional pending final settlement by the Peace Conference. Feisal agreed to this because it was the only alternative to a military confrontation with the French Army.

King Hussein had sent his personal physician, Dr. Thabet Numan, to Paris with a written order to Feisal warning him against signing any agreement contrary to previous pledges. Dr. Numan arrived before the signing of the agreement and consequently Feisal merely initialled it and informed Clemenceau that final ratification was to await consultation with his countrymen.

The agreement contracted between Britain and France on 15 September 1919, gave Britain the following concessions:

1. The inclusion of Mosul in the Iraqi borders.
2. The recognition of Palestine as British-mandated territory.
3. The recognition of Iraq as British-mandated territory.
4. The preservation of Transjordan under British Mandate.

In November General Gouraud arrived in Beirut. At about the same time the British evacuated Northern Syria and the Lebanon, with the result that hostilities broke out between the Arabs and the French. Emotions were aroused in Syria and Feisal returned in January 1920 to try to obtain a specific mandate from the National Congress for the implementation of his peaceful policy. He found the majority of the leaders in dismay at the prospect of dividing the country. Extremists had the upper hand; on 8 March Feisal was proclaimed King, in the hope that accomplished fact might speak louder than words.

Britain and France retaliated by taking steps to convene an early conference of the Supreme Council. They also invited Feisal to return to Europe. The Supreme Council met at San Remo and took its decisions on 25 April. Iraq and Greater Syria were to be placed under mandatory rule. Syria was to be broken up into three, and the mandate for Palestine was to carry with it an obligation to apply the Balfour Declaration. At the same time Lloyd George and the French Prime Minister Millerand came to an agreement concerning their respective shares of oil, by which France was to obtain twenty-five per cent of the proceeds of Iraq's oil. The French Army marched on Damascus in July 1920 and put an end by force of arms to Syrian independence.[15]

Britain thus turned against the Arabs for the sake of Mosul's oil. Mr. Crane of the King-Crane Commission has said that, when they left Paris for the Middle East in the summer of 1919, they had high hopes of liberating Syria. He ruefully adds that upon their return they discovered that Syria had been sold by the British for Mosul's oil, which the French had let go as a price for obtaining a free hand in Syria.[16]

To return to our main theme. Lawrence left Paris for Cairo in April 1919 to collect some personal papers and his reports published in the *Arab Bulletin,* which he was to use in writing his book on the Arab Revolt and the part he had played in it. But his plane crashed in Rome and his injuries included three ribs and a collar-bone broken. After three months in Rome he continued his journey to Cairo. He then returned to Paris to join the members of the Arab delegation, who had stayed behind in the French capital. Liddell Hart reports that Lawrence informed him that he had survived seven plane crashes, each of which could have been fatal.

Towards the end of August he returned to London with some chapters of his book. That same month the American journalist and propagandist Lowell Thomas had begun his series of lectures on the Palestine battles and the Arab Revolt, documented by cinematograph pictures. Lawrence was the main attraction

15. When the French marched on Damascus, Lawrence wrote a letter to the Editor of *The Times,* in which he said that the Arabs rebelled against the Turks 'because they wanted independence', not 'to change masters'. (*Selected Letters,* p. 121.)

16. Amin Said, *The Great Arab Revolt,* Vol. II, pp. 90–1.

of these publicity stunts, which made his name a byword in the West.

After he was demobilized from military service in September, Lawrence spent some time in London. He was then elected to a seven years' research fellowship at All Souls College, Oxford, to enable him to devote his time to writing on Middle East history. He spent some months at Oxford working on his book on the Revolt. There are no indications that he played any part in politics during Feisal's second visit to Europe. He does not seem even to have accompanied Feisal during his second short stay in London.

Nutting states that Lawrence had been excluded from discussions with the Emir on the personal instructions of the British Prime Minister. However, his relationship with the British Government was not severed, for in May 1920 he co-operated with Hogarth and Gertrude Bell in writing a draft mandate for Iraq in accordance with the San Remo agreements.

Feisal left Damascus for Haifa, where Mr. Stanton, Governor of Haifa, tried to persuade him to go to Hejaz instead of Europe. But he refused and left Palestine in late August after having received twenty-five thousand pounds from his father in allowances for himself and his retinue (he had left Damascus with no money). In Italy he prepared a detailed memorandum about the various stages of the Arab case and its development, which General Haddad Pasha carried to London and handed to Lloyd George. The British Government then invited Feisal to visit London, where he met King George V and Lord Curzon, the British Foreign Minister.

In February 1921, the League of Nations announced the mandate for Syria, Palestine and Iraq. Feisal sent a protest in his father's name stating that King Hussein had refused to concur with the Versailles Treaty because it had included a stipulation for mandate by the Great Powers over some Arab countries, and that it was for this reason that Hejaz had not joined the League of Nations. He demanded that the Great Powers reconsider their position and respect the people's wishes in choosing their own form of Government.

In March, an international conference was held in London to look into the problems of the Middle East. The Emir sent Haddad Pasha to represent him at the conference, where Haddad

read a statement explaining the Arab case and pointing out that
the Arabs had joined the war because they wanted independence, but that the Great Powers had then proceeded to divide
their countries in spite of agreements, promises and assurances.
'I stand here on behalf of the Arabs and demand independence
and unity for which we fought and for which Arab blood was
shed.' The statement went on to say that the population of Iraq
did not exceed two and a half million and yet there was a British
garrison of two hundred and twenty thousand; that Palestine
had fifty thousand British troops for six hundred thousand inhabitants; and that the regions of Syria occupied by the French
had a hundred and sixty thousand Frenchmen for two million
inhabitants.

It should be noted at this point that Feisal concentrated on
demanding that Great Britain should accede to Arab demands
in the regions under her own control, as she had declared her
inability to persuade or exert pressure on the French. The revolt
in Iraq, which had started in July 1920, had done much to bring
home to the British Government the justice of Arab demands
and the realization that rule by force was unacceptable to aspir-
ing nations. Britain had assembled a strong army to quell the
rebellion, while politicians sought a solution acceptable to
the people of Iraq, without jeopardizing British interests in the
area. It cost the British Exchequer over forty million pounds
to suppress the revolt—four times the sum Britain had spent on
the whole of the Arab Revolt, in cash, weapons and supplies.
A particular consequence of this revolt was that public opinion
in Britain began to voice complaints against excessive expenditure abroad and exorbitant taxation at home. This was an additional factor in prompting the British Government to seek a
peaceful solution to the problem.

8. NATIONAL RULE IN IRAQ AND TRANSJORDAN

Feisal engaged in extensive diplomatic activity in London. He
was in constant touch with British politicians, notables and men
of influence. Doubtless, Lawrence was in frequent contact with
him during this period.

As a consequence of the new British outlook on Middle East
politics, the British Prime Minister took Middle East problems
out of the hands of the Foreign Minister Lord Curzon, who was

known for his old-fashioned imperialistic policies, and put them under the Colonial Office, with Winston Churchill at its head. Churchill, who held up-to-date imperialistic views, was faced with a many-sided task. At one and the same time, he was aiming at sorting things out in the Middle East, cutting down expenditure, preserving British interests and carrying out British commitments to the Arabs.

Churchill wrote that in the spring of 1921 he was sent to the Colonial Office to take over British business in the Middle East and reduce matters to some kind of order.

At that time we had recently suppressed a most dangerous and bloody rebellion in Iraq, and upwards of 40,000 troops, at a cost of £30,000,000 a year, were required to preserve order. This could not go on. In Palestine the strife between the Arabs and the Jews threatened at any moment to take the form of actual violence. The Arab chieftains, driven out of Syria with many of their followers —all of them our late allies—lurked furious in the deserts beyond the Jordon. Egypt was in ferment. . . .[17]

In February Churchill formed a Middle East Department in the Colonial Office. A number of experts in Middle Eastern affairs, who had served in the area during the war formed the nucleus. Among them were Young, Meinertzhagen, Bullard and Cornwallis. Churchill said that he resolved to add Lawrence to their number. But when he broached this project to them, 'they were frankly aghast—"What! Wilt thou bridle the wild ass of the desert?" '[18] Their attitude was dictated by a sincere conviction that Lawrence could never work at the routine of public office. However, Churchill persisted and the post of Adviser on Arab affairs to the Department was offered to Lawrence, who accepted at once. This post carried a salary of one thousand two hundred pounds a year. It appears from a letter by Lawrence to Robert Graves that he took up his new position in December 1920.

In London Churchill looked into all possible solutions, meeting Feisal more than once. Since the idea of self-rule for Iraq was favoured by most, it was agreed, in consultation with Feisal, to meet the Iraqis half-way and recognize their independence. Following a national plebiscite, Feisal was to be named King of Iraq, upon which the mandate would be annulled and a treaty

17. *T. E. Lawrence by his Friends*, p. 159.   18. *Ibid.*, p. 160.

would be signed between the two countries. Sir Reader Bullard says, 'All present were of the opinion that the best solution was that the Amir Faisal should become ruler of Iraq . . .'.[19]

In this connexion Bullard tells the following story to illustrate a facet of Lawrence's mind and the methods he used to attract attention:

It was Young who was responsible for a proposal that was made to the Palestine Arabs in 1921. The Arabs objected strongly to the Jewish Agency, as a government in the Government, and it occurred to Young that it might be possible to create an Arab Agency with certain rights and obligations. The Arabs rejected the proposal. . . . The morning after Young had produced this idea he put it to Lawrence at the Colonial Office and Lawrence thought it hopeful. The two of them were soon summoned by Mr. Churchill to discuss the current crisis in Palestine. Presently Young came down, much amused. At a suitable moment in the discussion, Lawrence, with a deprecating look at Young, had produced the Arab Agency suggestion as though it was his own. This is the most striking instance I know of Lawrence's love of the limelight—a weakness which he despised but nevertheless indulged.[20]

Churchill then decided to go to the Middle East, to carry out his new policies and conclude agreements on final details with responsible leaders and officials in the area. On 12 March 1921 he convened a conference at Cairo, to which practically all the high ranking British officials in the Middle East were summoned. Leading representatives from the War Office and the Air Ministry also attended. Those present included Sir Percy Cox, High Commissioner in Iraq, Sir Herbert Samuel, High Commissioner in Palestine, General Haldein, Miss Gertrude Bell, Lawrence, Young and Trenchard. Ja'afar Pasha al-Askari was also invited to Cairo for consultations.

His biographers represent Lawrence at this period as the man who produced all the solutions and formed the soundest opinions on all problems, to an extent where the others had nothing to do but agree. Liddell Hart goes so far as to say that Lawrence was the one to suggest to Lloyd George the transfer of Middle Eastern affairs from Curzon at the Foreign Office to Churchill at the Colonial Office.

Iraqi leaders had announced at Damascus, on 8 March 1920

19. Sir Reader Bullard, *The Camels Must Go* (1961), p. 117.
20. *Ibid.*, p. 121.

that they had proclaimed Emir Abdullah King of Iraq. They had approached King Hussein on this issue during their revolt. It is no secret that King Hussein had made substantial financial contributions to the revolt in Iraq. Feisal had been approached by the British on the subject of the Iraqi throne, but he declined at first on the plea that his brother Abdullah had a better claim to it. Lawrence reported that he and a number of friends spent a whole night at the house of Lord Winterton persuading Feisal to nominate himself, until he reluctantly agreed. In any case it was imperative that such nomination should first come from King Hussein, for the Iraqi leaders and chieftains had been addressing him, in writing and through their delegations, as King of the Arabs. When the Cairo Conference was over, Feisal sailed from England in April. After spending some time in Cairo he went to Hejaz, where he met his father, who, on 10 June 1921, handed him a letter addressed to the people of Iraq, saying that he was sending Feisal to them 'in fulfilment of your wishes and in accordance with your will'. Feisal's subsequent arrival in Iraq and his nomination by national plebiscite for the Iraqi throne is familiar history.

While in Cairo, Churchill had been faced with another problem. Early in November 1920, Emir Abdullah had arrived at Ma'an from Hejaz, in response to several telegrams to King Hussein from Syrian leaders in Transjordan requesting the King to send one of his sons to lead national forces against the French. Transjordan had been left alone after the French attack: the French had made no effort to occupy it as part of Feisal's kingdom, and the British, who had a mandate to run its affairs, had not bothered to set up a civil administration. King Hussein, on the other hand, had always considered the Ma'an–Aqaba area as part of Hejaz, and accordingly had continued to send administrative officers to it since the end of the war.

Emir Abdullah arrived at Ma'an at the head of a military force, declaring that his purpose was to liberate Syria. He asked the Syrians, and in particular the military, to come to his support. The French, who were becoming deeply worried at Abdullah's activity, assembled their forces at Hauran, while urging the British Government to turn the Emir out. Britain requested Feisal to approach his father and his brother and ask them to refrain from any activity inimical to France; and also to dissuade Abdullah from inciting the people of Transjordan. The High Commissioner at Jerusalem sent a delegate to the Emir requesting him to leave Ma'an or at least to refrain from engaging in hostile activities. But the enthusiasm of the inhabitants of Transjordan for the Emir and their loyalty encouraged him to ignore British advice and actually to advance on Amman, which he reached on 2 March 1921.

From Cairo, Churchill sent word to the Emir that he was planning to come to Jerusalem and conduct talks with him. It was agreed that a meeting would be held on 28 March. At Salt, on his way to Jerusalem, the Emir was met by Air-Marshal Salmond and Colonel Lawrence, who had come to meet him and accompany him to Jerusalem. The Emir and his companions spent that night at Salt, where Lawrence informed him of what Churchill was going to say. In his book *Political Dictates* (p. 24) the Emir gives the following account of his conversation with Lawrence:

> At night Lawrence informed me of the subject of the impending meeting, whose purpose was to urge the necessity of helping Britain to install Feisal on the throne of Iraq, because France objected to his return to Syria. France also objected to the return of Zeid, whom she considered more of an enemy than Feisal himself. He asked me to stay in Transjordan and set up a civil administration, free from any violence with respect to its political objectives. He said to me, 'You are well-known for sacrificing your personal ambitions for your country, so stay here. If you succeed you will achieve the unity of Syria in six months. God willing, we will visit you in Damascus to offer our congratulations.'

Next day the Emir went to Jerusalem, accompanied by a number of Syrian national leaders. They had a British military car driven by a sergeant, and Lawrence accompanied the Emir. As they neared Jerusalem, they were met by a motor-cyclist, who turned round and told their driver not to stop for the crowds who had come to greet them at Bethany. The Emir protested against this, because the people of Jerusalem had come out to greet him and courtesy demanded that he should stop and greet them in return. Lawrence, however, apologized to the Emir, saying that he could not order the driver to act against instructions. The car passed the crowds at full speed, and they were disappointed. But the Emir could do nothing to make up for the unseemly behaviour of the Palestine Government.

The Emir and Churchill met on 29 March. Their meeting
was attended by Herbert Samuel, Wyndham Deedes, Lawrence
and Awni Abdul Hadi. Churchill repeated to the Emir what he
—the Emir—had already heard from Lawrence at Salt. Consequently, he agreed to stay on in Transjordan, after he had
obtained the approval of the Syrian leaders who were with him
in Jerusalem.

When the Palestine case came up in the meeting, the Emir
protested against the Balfour Declaration, saying, 'We shall not
agree to the annihilation of the Arabs for the sake of the Jews.
The Arabs are not like trees, which, when cut, grow again.' Commenting on this meeting, Awni Abdul Hadi has said, 'Zionist
plans and ambitions for Palestine were discussed at this meeting. The Emir protested against these plans, but Lawrence
displayed great enthusiasm for them and endorsed the position
of Churchill and Samuel. I remember this very clearly.'

Churchill returned to London, while Lawrence stayed behind
in Palestine and Transjordan for a period of six weeks, most
of which he spent at Amman.

9. LAWRENCE NEGOTIATES WITH KING HUSSEIN

In May Lawrence returned to England. Pursuing his work at
the Colonial Office, he worked with his colleagues in the Middle
East Department on a draft treaty which the British Government was intending to propose to King Hussein. In a letter to
C. M. Doughty, dated 13 June 1921, he wrote:

> Abdulla is in Transjordan, carrying on a government there with
> our help, but without any formal appointment. Indeed he refused
> one, until his father had been consulted, and had approved. . . .[21]

The patent of his appointment, dated 30 June, to negotiate
the treaty with Hussein, referred to Lawrence as 'Companion
of Our Most Honourable Order of the Bath, Companion of Our
Distinguished Service Order'. This means that he had not denuded himself of his honours, as he would have us believe. On
8 July, he sailed to the Middle East, where he spent some time
at Aden before reaching Jedda late in August 1921. He was
accompanied on this trip by General Haddad.

King Hussein came to Jedda with his two sons Emirs Ali and

21. *Selected Letters*, p. 127.

Zeid to meet Lawrence. Sheikh Faud al-Khatib, the Hejazi Foreign Minister, also came to the meeting.

Opening the discussion, Lawrence said to the King, 'There is a debt which we would like to pay, but which could not be discharged in its entirety at once. A considerable instalment will be paid now pending complete settlement in the future.' The King replied, 'You have come; hence we should talk and negotiate; you are welcome.'

The meeting was resumed on the following day. Lawrence presented the draft treaty to the King who proceeded to debate its contents, requesting that a clause should be included to the effect that Palestine would be independent and become part of the Arab union. The King then debated other articles, and insisted at the end that all pledges to the Arabs should be scrupulously observed. When Lawrence made it clear that this could not be done at present, the King refused to accept the draft treaty. During this discussion, Lawrence said to the King, 'Palestine does not want you', upon which the King replied, 'This does not affect us, for I am not asking this for myself or for my sons; all we are asking is that Britain keep her plighted word to the Arabs, and if it does, my sons and I would leave the land of the Arabs if necessary.'

After lengthy discussions Lawrence agreed to add a new article, stipulating that this treaty would not run contrary to any pledge or promise made to the Arabs during the war. The King still did not accept this, making it a condition that Britain fulfil its promises in their entirety, with the concession that the fate of Syria would be taken up separately with France. He added, 'The Arabs have placed the cause of their countries in my hands; hence it is not within my power to deviate from their demands for freedom.'

The King's retinue were unanimous in urging the King to accept the proposed treaty; the King's own family, including the Queen herself, were also urging him to accept. But he insisted on refusing it. Annoyed by their insistence, he made his way to the roof of his house and, looking in the direction of Al-Ka'aba in Mecca, swore by its God that he would not sign any treaty that would not fulfil all previous promises. He then secluded himself, refusing to see anybody. When his sons saw this they refrained from further discussion with him and arranged with Lawrence to have him visit Emir Abdullah at Amman and come to an agreement with him regarding the treaty, which he would sign in the name of his father and send on to him for final ratification.

Behind the insistence of the King's family was Lawrence's threat that a refusal of the draft treaty would have unpleasant consequences. In fact he was echoing the threat which Churchill had made to Emir Abdullah in Jerusalem six months earlier: 'If you do not do so, you may lose everything, as it is possible that Ibn Saud may reach Mecca in three days, and England has done what she can.' Briefly the British proposals were that Hussein should wash his hands of Arab affairs and direct all his attention to Hejaz, content that Feisal had ascended the throne of Iraq and Abdullah had become Emir of Transjordan. The King was further urged that he might do well to be content with an alliance with Great Britain, in the hope that she would curb his ambitious neighbours, who were thirsty for expansion and conquest. Furthermore, Britain would continue paying the monthly subsidy into the Hejaz treasury. Hussein had no eye for personal gain. He looked on himself rather as a keeper of a sacred trust and a representative of the spirit of the Arab nation, who could not possibly condone imperialistic designs on Arab countries. The seventy-year-old King held obstinately to his convictions for the safeguarding of his nation's destiny, and he did not hide his contempt for Lawrence and the offers he brought.

Lawrence on his part acted on the suggestions of the King's family. On 12 October, he reached Amman, where he discussed with Emir Abdullah the articles of the draft treaty in the light of the amendments made at Jedda. Making further amendments, the Emir signed the draft treaty and sent it on to his father with a letter asking for permission to sign the treaty in the King's name. But Hussein refused to receive the letter, which he returned sealed to his son. Thus the negotiations came to nothing and Lawrence failed to accomplish his task. His resentment against the King was boundless.

Here is the text of what Graves wrote and Lawrence approved:

Lawrence went to Jiddah in June 1921 and tried to make the treaty with Hussein to which he refers above. Hussein kept him arguing for two months in the heat (hoping to break down British opposition to his paramount position above other Arab princes) and finally put him off altogether, suggesting that he should continue the negotiations with his son Abdulla in Amman. Lawrence sent a cipher cable to Lord Curzon, the Foreign Minister. 'Can do nothing with Hussein. Are you fed up or shall I carry on with Abdulla?' [22]

Curzon gave his consent to continued negotiations with Abdullah.

We gather from Philby that, during his stay in Amman, Lawrence had received a telegram from the Foreign Office, authorizing him to conclude the Anglo-Hejazi treaty with Emir Abdullah on the lines proposed by him in an earlier cable. On 8 December 1921, the treaty was signed and required only ratification by King Hussein and King George, before it came into force for the prescribed period of seven years. Philby says,

Neither bribes nor threats had any power to move the old man, who was thoroughly disgruntled with our attitude towards the whole problem. Eventually Lawrence gave it up as a bad job and left Jidda recommending that the Hejaz subsidy be discontinued and Hussein be left to stew in his own juice.[23]

According to Philby, Lawrence's job was to try to induce King Hussein 'to give his approval to the general lines of British policy in the Middle East, and in particular to that part of it which related to the Zionist dispensation in Palestine'.[24] King Abdullah on the other hand says,

Lawrence and Haddad came and the Anglo-Hejazi treaty was concluded, after my father had authorised me to enter into fruitful discussions. However, Palestinian Arab circles influenced my father, who refused to ratify it unless the Balfour Declaration was declared void.[25]

It is obvious that King Abdullah was following a policy of obtaining what he could, then moving on to further demands. He was convinced that a negative policy would be harmful to the Arab cause. It is also obvious that Hussein had despaired of the Allies and had no further doubts about their evil intentions towards the Arabs. It was in this spirit that he insisted on the annulment of the Balfour Declaration, apart from his almost clairvoyant insight into the Zionist threat to the Arab nation.

A study of the draft treaty shows that in Article 2 the British

22. *T. E. Lawrence to his Biographers*, Part I, p. 115.
23. H. St. John Philby, *Arabian Days* (1948), p. 288.   24. *Ibid.*
25. Abdullah ibn al-Hussein, *al-'Amali al-Siyasyyah* (Political Dictates), p. 26.

Government was prepared to undertake to prevent any aggression on Hejaz from neighbouring territory by all possible means, including the withholding of all subsidies. According to Article 17, King Hussein was expected to recognize Britain's special position in Iraq and Palestine, and to help Great Britain in upholding her position in these two countries.

There can be no doubt that Article 17 was the major obstacle in the way of the signing of the treaty. This article was Britain's main concern at that moment, mainly because she wanted to invest her Zionist policy with some form of legality, by making it a subject of agreement between her and Hussein. Once the King of the Arabs, the guardian of Arab interests and protector of their cause, approved it, what argument would there be for the rest of the Arabs? The more closely one views this episode the more amazing Lawrence's behaviour seems. Even Philby himself has called the draft treaty 'somehow insulting'.

Hussein's viewpoint, which was shared by the Arab nationalists, was perfectly clear. At the end of the war he had taken it for granted that the obstacles or difficulties which confronted the Arabs had arisen not through the activities of Britain, but through those of the other western countries. Hussein's viewpoint comes out clearly in a note which he sent in October 1918 to the British High Commissioner in Egypt, in reply to the British invitation to the Peace Conference. He said:

> With regard to our case and discussions concerning it at the Peace Conference, I stipulate and say it now that we have no connection with the Conference or any other body. I believe it is better that the decisions of the Conference be not transmitted to us through the Conference, because I would be a renegade from God's mercy if I accepted them.

By this the King meant that Britain was the only country in alliance with him and that she, as friend and ally, was answerable to him in carrying out Arab demands.

When Lawrence came to him with the request 'to recognise the special position of Great Britain in Iraq and Palestine', Hussein's psychological shock was proportionate to the degree of confidence he had had in the British. He was plainly being asked to acknowledge the mandate of Britain over Palestine, which carried with it an obligation to create a home for the Jews in a country which was not only Arab but also holy to Islam.

And yet he had received the pledges of McMahon and the assurances of Commander Hogarth. He inquired about these, about the Anglo-French declaration and the letter which Sir Reginald Wingate had sent him from Egypt on 19 April 1917, expressing the hope that King Hussein would not forget the profound respect with which Great Britain viewed its obligations, and assuring him that Britain was the defender of all that was right and just, being as it was the faithful ally that would never go back on its word. No wonder then that Hussein departed from his usual courtesy and was somewhat curt with Lawrence for coming on this mission and contemptuous of the British Government's attempt to buy him with a subsidy and with the promise to curb Ibn Saud's ambitions in Hejaz, which he considered morally indefensible. Hussein must have also wondered if Britain's new promise really carried weight in view of the failure of the British Government to respect weightier and more binding pledges.

Hussein was not the narrow-minded bigot portrayed by Lawrence for the sake of his western audience. He might have been prepared to agree, on humane principles, to the immigration of a few thousand Jews, provided that this did not jeopardize Arab political, economic, religious and civil rights. Indeed, in his counter-draft of Article 17, he proposed that Palestine be constituted into an independent state with a national government representing all the inhabitants, including the Jews, and that it be expressly allowed the faculty of joining a federation of Arab states. Hussein had been in close touch with the Arabs of Palestine and was fully cognizant of the dangers to which they and their country were exposed.

We must remember that after first meeting King Hussein at Jedda in late July 1917, Lawrence had expressed an opinion of him that was completely different from the later view which he expressed after their second meeting, during which Lawrence had failed to persuade him to accept British policies. After the first meeting he had said in the *Arab Bulletin* of 12 August 1917:

I do not think that all the temptations of the world would persuade Sherif Hussein to run counter to his principles. His transparent honesty and strength of conviction . . . will at all costs ensure his shaping his conduct exactly in accordance with his promised word.

On the other hand, Liddell Hart reports that Lawrence once told him:

> King Hussein used to threaten to abdicate. I wished he would, but was never funny about it. The old man was a tragic figure in his way: brave, obstinate, hopelessly out of date: exasperating.[26]

Just as Lawrence claimed to have reduced Lord Curzon to tears with harsh language,[27] so he claimed to have done the same with Hussein himself. In a telegram which Lawrence sent from Jedda concerning the state of deadlock to which the talks had come, he said, 'The occasion was unique in my experience in that not only the Foreign Secretary but the King also burst into tears.' [28] Those who knew the King's strength of spirit would easily realize how silly and unfair Lawrence was in inventing this story. How apt they must have thought Gertrude Bell's remark to Lawrence at the Cairo Conference: 'You little imp.' [29]

In his *Memoirs,* King Abdullah states that Lawrence intimated through a messenger that he could be King of Hejaz:

> . . . on the grounds that my father was obstinate in clinging to his own opinion. I said to his messenger, 'Tell your friend that my father is my lord and King. As for him (your friend), he has done me and the Arabs a great service by saying that my father is obstinate in clinging to his opinion, for it seems that they (the British) want somebody with no opinions of his own, so that Lawrence could do what he pleases.[30]

In a letter that Lawrence sent to Robert Graves on 28 June 1927, we find the following remarks about King Hussein:

> My object with the Arabs: to make them stand on their own feet. To do this it was necessary to check the centralising policy of King Hussein, who envisaged a united Arab world under himself at Mecca. Mecca was a hotbed of religion, quite impossible as the capital of any sort of state. . . . Yet for the war we had to pretend that he led, since unity is necessary in a movement. So we put up with Hussein till the Armistice, and then tried to put him quietly into his place.[31]

26. Liddell Hart, *T. E. Lawrence,* p. 413.
27. 'Curzon burst into tears, great drops running down his cheeks, to an accompaniment of slow sobs.' (Robert Graves, *Lawrence and the Arabs* (1928), p. 402.)
28. *The Camels Must Go,* p. 122.   29. *Ibid.,* p. 121.
30. *Memoirs of King Abdullah,* p. 40.
31. *T. E. Lawrence to his Biographers,* Part I, p. 51.

Philby gives us a clear picture of Lawrence's feelings towards King Hussein. Speaking about his first meeting with Lawrence in Crete he says:

He had had no news of recent Arabian developments and listened with rapt interest to my detailed account of them, punctuating it with chuckles—he did not like King Hussein—and such exclamations as 'Good, good' and 'Excellent'.[32]

Philby says elsewhere that

. . . the shock of the ignominious defeat of the Sharifian army by Ibn Saud in May 1919 was light-heartedly absorbed by him [Lawrence] in a sense of almost personal triumph over the obstinate old King Hussein, who had always, and quite openly, opposed his plans. . . .[33]

A further indication of the extent of Lawrence's grudge against the King is revealed by a letter he wrote from Karachi in 1928 in which he said, 'I was glad beyond words when he went.'[34] (i.e. left Hejaz as a result of the Saudi attack.)

Philby reports that Lawrence left Amman for Jedda on 8 December 1921, the day the treaty was signed. He adds:

Lawrence's mission to Jidda was a failure, as King Hussein resolutely refused to accord any kind of recognition to the Jewish National Home policy in Palestine, which was apparently the required *sine-qua-non quid-pro-quo* for the treaty of Amman. . . . All he handed over to me on his departure was a few confidential documents, including the printed record of the McMahon correspondence with Sharif Husain before the Arab Revolt, and a small sheet of paper containing his accounts of the expenditure of about £100,000 during his short term of office. One item of £10,000 was simply written off as 'lost or mislaid'.[35]

Lawrence's stay in Transjordan extended to about two and a half months during which he acted as British Representative. Winston Churchill has recorded that he sent him out to Transjordan as a last attempt to keep him in Government service after Lawrence had tried to resign his position. Sudden difficulties had arisen in Transjordan, and Lawrence was given plenary powers.

32. *Arabian Days*, p. 181.
33. H. St. John Philby, *Forty Years in the Wilderness* (1957), p. 86.
34. *Selected Letters*, p. 266.
35. *Forty Years in the Wilderness*, pp. 107–108.

He used them with his old vigour. He removed officers. He used force. He restored complete tranquillity. Everyone was delighted with the success of his mission, but nothing would persuade him to continue.[36]

Churchill's memory seems to have failed him here, because Lawrence's return to the Middle East this time was to negotiate with King Hussein, whom he actually met at Jedda. His return to Amman was merely to complete negotiations. Lawrence does not seem to have done anything exceptionally outstanding in Transjordan, nor are there any indications that he used force or removed any officers.

In a letter from Cairo to Eric Kennington, dated 1 October 1921, Lawrence wrote:

Tomorrow I go to Trans-jordan, to end that farce. It makes me feel like a baby-killer. The last two months I've been in the Red Sea, and things are not ended there.[37]

In his report on Transjordan, dated 24 October, Lawrence says that he went over to Amman on 12 October 'to enquire into the present position there'.[38] He then speaks about the Air Force in Transjordan and the armoured cars attached to it.

From *Arab Command,* the biography of Colonel Peake Pasha, commander of the Arab Legion (1921–1939), we see that Lawrence was not a desk man.

He insisted upon seeing things for himself, and so he and Peake toured all over the country on camels or by car, deciding on the various police posts....[39]

Lawrence and Peake also visited together 'their old haunts' along the Hejaz railway, as Lawrence was revising *Seven Pillars* at the time. We are told that Lawrence hated office work so much that one day,

collecting a number of files which he considered unnecessary, he shoved them into the waste-paper basket . . . among the papers destroyed were several passports awaiting endorsement, and there was considerable trouble when the owners came to collect them.[40]

Peake informs us that

Lawrence was an amusing guest to entertain, but he was a man of moods; on some evenings he would be the best of company with most

36. *T. E. Lawrence by his Friends,* p. 162.   37. *Selected Letters,* p. 129.
38. *Ibid.,* p. 130.   39. *Arab Command,* p. 83.   40. *Ibid.,* p. 84.

entertaining stories . . . ; on others, he would be depressed, uncommunicative. . . .

The Lawrence of the Arab Revolt and the Lawrence of the Colonial Office were not quite the same man, for the first was essentially one of great personality, ready to make lightning decisions and to act on them . . . ; whilst the second, in his new rôle as a civil servant, felt stultified and unable to use effectually the qualities that had made him great.[41]

Peake says that he and Lawrence shared the same house, where Lawrence had a bedouin tent pitched in the yard to receive the groups of bedouin who invariably came with him whenever he returned from his trips.

Lawrence had suggested Philby as a suitable replacement in Amman as British Representative, 'in view of my intimate connection with Ibn Sa'ud'.[42] It seems more likely to us that his real motive in doing this was his hatred for King Hussein. Philby further states that Herbert Samuel informed him that he had to call Lawrence in temporarily to straighten things out in Transjordan, which was giving Samuel a great deal of trouble. By trouble he meant the difficulties between the national government in Transjordan and the French. In a private letter Lawrence himself also referred to French obstinacy.

Philby says that Churchill sent Lawrence to Transjordan after hearing of the rising at Kura in May 1921. This rising, however, was not quelled until May 1922, well after Lawrence had left Transjordan for good. Philby adds that on 28 November 1921, he was present at a conference held by Herbert Samuel and attended by Lawrence, Deedes, Storrs and Abramson, in which Lawrence did most of the talking, dealing point by point as he read through certain proposals recently forwarded to the Secretary of State for the Colonies by the High Commissioner.

As he talked on I noticed signs of uneasiness and perturbation in Samuel's face. At last, unable to bear it longer, he interrupted: 'But all that is surely entirely different from what you told me when you were last here?' 'Oh yes,' said Lawrence impishly, 'but, you see, I have entirely changed my mind since then.'[43]

Lawrence's earlier position had been that the situation in Transjordan should be altered, while now he was pleading that the existing regime should have another chance. He was now of

41. *Arab Command*, p. 85.   42. *Forty Years*, p. 92.   43. *Arabian Days*, p. 209.

the opinion that the Transjordan Government would have to agree in the end to have a British officer command the Reserve Force and Public Security, with the additional concession that this officer would have a seat in the Cabinet. Describing his early days in Transjordan, Philby says,

> I leave all business to Lawrence who, in spite of his repeated assertions that he has handed over the reins of office to me, finds that he cannot divest himself of its functions. He must carry on while he remains here, and I am well content to let him do so.[44]

After failing to persuade King Hussein to ratify the treaty, Lawrence returned to England, and in July 1922 resigned from his post at the Colonial Office. From that date his relationship with the Arabs was completely and finally severed.

10. LAWRENCE LATER ON

We are concerned with Lawrence's life after that only for the sake of giving the reader a brief account of his later activities to complete the picture. Winston Churchill stated that he tried very hard to keep Lawrence in the Civil Service, requesting him to choose virtually any position he liked. But Lawrence insisted on resigning. Two months later he enlisted in the ranks of the Air Force, under the name Ross. Some have conjectured that he did so in protest against Britain's breach of faith with the Arabs. But surely this cannot be true, because he had declared quite candidly his conviction that Britain had in fact fulfilled all her obligations and that the Arabs had nothing more to demand.

He had considerable difficulty in joining the Air Force, but someone influential arranged it for him. We are told that when doctors on the medical board saw the scars on his back, they declared him unfit for military service. However, responsible officials insisted that he be accepted, and procured a health certificate from a civilian doctor, testifying to his fitness. Four months later the tightly-kept secret of his identity leaked out and found its way into the pages of a newspaper, whereupon Lawrence was discharged from the Air Force.

In March 1923, through the influence of his friends, he joined the Royal Tank Corps as a recruit, with the name of T. E. Shaw. It has been said that he chose this name because of his

44. *Forty Years*, p. 97.

friendship with George Bernard Shaw and his wife. Lawrence, however, hated his life in the Corps, and tried more than once to get a transfer to the Air Force, but with no success. When he finally threatened to commit suicide, Bernard Shaw wrote a letter to Mr. Baldwin, the British Prime Minister, saying that Lawrence's suicide would be a scandal, particularly since Lowell Thomas had made him a national hero. Baldwin intervened and had him returned to the Air Force in 1925, after he had spent twenty-eight months in the Tank Corps.

Early in 1927 he was transferred to Karachi in India, from where he wrote that he despised the Indians and was revolted that his organs were similar to theirs. While in India he translated Homer's *Odyssey* from Greek for a fee of six hundred pounds. He was then transferred to Miranshah, on the borders of Afghanistan, in 1929, where he was accused by some newspapers of being a spy. His name had, in fact, been mentioned in a Russian military Court, where some officers of whom Stalin was trying to rid himself were accused of having made contact with British Intelligence, through Lawrence. Perhaps because of this Lawrence was recalled to England.

In February 1935 he left the Air Force and declared that he was going to seek peace and rest in a secluded house he had bought and furnished. But he did not live long enough to enjoy it, for on 13 May 1935, while riding his motor-cycle at his usual full speed, he came upon two boys on bicycles just as he was making a rather sharp turn. Swerving violently to avoid them, he lost control and was hurled to the ground. Seriously injured and unconscious, he was removed to a hospital, where, six days later, he died.

11. FRIEND OF THE ARABS?

Much has been said about Lawrence's sympathy for the Arabs and his zeal for their interests. This impression might very well have remained unaltered indefinitely had Lawrence refrained from taking part in the Cairo Conference and in the subsequent manoeuvres engineered by Winston Churchill. But this, and his open assertion that the solutions proposed by Churchill and himself constituted a complete discharge of British responsibilities to the Arabs, have permanently discredited Lawrence's claims to have been wholeheartedly pro-Arab.

In the draft preface, written on 18 November 1922, to the unpublished Oxford text of *Seven Pillars of Wisdom,* Lawrence said:

That stage ended in March 1921, when Mr. Winston Churchill took charge of the Middle East. He set honesty before expediency in order to fulfil our promises in the letter and in the spirit. He executed the whole McMahon undertaking (called a treaty by some who have not seen it) for Palestine, for Trans-jordania, and for Arabia. In Mesopotamia he went far beyond its provisions, giving to the Arabs more, and reserving for us much less, than Sir Henry McMahon had thought fit.

In the affairs of French Syria he was not able to interfere, and the Sherif of Mecca can fairly complain that the settlement there is not yet in accordance with the Anglo-French agreement of 1916, or with our word to him. . . .

I do not wish to publish secret documents, nor to make long explanations: but must put on record my conviction that England is out of the Arab affair with clean hands. Some Arab advocates . . . have rejected my judgment on this point. Like a tedious Pensioner I showed them my wounds (over sixty I have, each scar evidence of a pain incurred in Arab service) as proof I had worked sincerely on their side.[45]

In a footnote to p. 276 of the published edition of *Seven Pillars* Lawrence says,

. . . Mr. Winston Churchill was entrusted by our harassed Cabinet with the settlement of the Middle East; and in a few weeks, at his conference in Cairo, he made straight all the tangle, finding solu· tions fulfilling (I think) our promises in letter and spirit (where humanly possible) without sacrificing any interest of our Empire or any interest of the peoples concerned. So we were quit of the war-time Eastern adventure, with clean hands, but three years too late to earn the gratitude which peoples, if not states, can pay.

In 1929 he was to write to Professor Yale that the Sykes-Picot agreement was the Arab 'sheet-anchor', but that 'by the mandate swindle England and France got the lot',[46] concluding:

It is my deliberate opinion that the Winston Churchill settlement of 1921–2 (in which I shared) honourably fulfils the whole of the promise we made to the Arabs, in so far as the so-called British spheres are concerned.[47]

Lawrence had envisaged self-rule for Arab countries, under British tutelage. In a letter to Lord Curzon, dated 25 September

45. *Selected Letters,* pp. 136–137.
46. *Selected Letters,* p. 397.   47. *Selected Letters,* p. 346.

1919, Lawrence wrote that his own ambition was that 'the Arabs should be Britain's first brown Dominion and not our last brown colony'.[48] Lawrence's admirers might, if they please, feel some gratification at his desire to raise Arab status from 'colony' to 'dominion'. In this, at any rate, lies the secret of his hatred for France, since he was afraid France might succeed in enveloping one or more Arab countries, thus depriving Britain of complete hegemony over the whole Arab area.

The western observer may find satisfaction in these statements. He may shrug his shoulders in unconcern. But for an Arab, Lawrence's words cut to the quick. The partition of Greater Syria was the greatest blow inflicted on the Arab nation in modern times. The Arabs who took up arms against the Turks were aiming at nothing less than a united Arab state, or at least a confederation of Arab states. The partition of the one homeland into four parts was the last thing the Arabs wanted or expected. The evils of this partition, engineered by Britain and France, are still being felt in the Arab world today. As time passed, the separate governments that were set up as a result of this partition have become bound up in the preservation of their independent status, a state of affairs that is tearing up the whole concept of Arab unity. Partition and mandate, however, are nothing compared to the catastrophe that has befallen the Arab nation as a result of the Jewish National Home policy, which Britain has carried out by force of arms, and which had been approved by the Cairo Conference and regarded by Lawrence as an honourable settlement. Had Lawrence lived to see a million Arabs thrown out of their homes and dispersed in all parts of the world, he would have witnessed the consequences of that settlement—and the scars of pledges kept and friendship honoured.

Had Lawrence been a real friend of the Arabs, humanely sensitive to the reality of their hopes and aims, he would have refused to take part in the Conference, or at least he would have declared his opposition to the unjust policies of his Government in Palestine—policies that aimed at seizing a country from the people who inhabited it and bestowing it on an alien people. There is no doubt that the settlement with regard to Iraq and Transjordan was far more acceptable than direct British rule,

48. *Selected Leters*, p. 291.

but this should not lead us to lose sight of the fact that Britain agreed to this settlement in an attempt to preserve her own interests, to cut down expenditure and to prevent the shedding of British blood.

Dr. Abdul Rahman Shahbender, one of the seven Syrian leaders to whom Britain made its famous Declaration, makes the following comment:

> When the Cairo Conference was convened in 1921, I met Lawrence, who was in a civilian suit, his eyes shining. In the course of conversation I asked him if he was happy with the goings-on at the Conference, upon which he showed great repugnance at the proceedings, saying, among other things, 'I wish I had never come to this place, never met these people, never seen these faces; how nice it would be for me to return home.' These remarks indicated to me at the time that his desires, to which we had grown accustomed during the Revolt, were falling on deaf ears. I remained with this impression until I saw a letter from his own pen expressing frank acceptance of Mr. Churchill's settlement of Arab Affairs. I was amazed at this strange contradiction.

Just as people believed that Lawrence denuded himself of his honours in protest against Britain's treatment of the Arabs, they have also accepted the theory that he joined the army as a private for the same reason, to punish himself for taking part in the fraud. The statements we have already quoted from Lawrence indicate quite decisively that his conscience was clear with regard to Churchill's settlement, and that he considered the debt to the Arabs to have been satisfactorily discharged. Commenting on this subject, Sir Lewis Namier has made nonsense of the story that Lawrence joined the army because the British Government had let down the Arabs:

> He never felt that way, and as adviser for Arab affairs to Mr. Churchill had full scope for working further on their behalf.[49]

Namier adds that Lawrence had told him that it was decided at the Cairo Conference

> to include Transjordan in Palestine, to make it indistinguishable from Palestine, and to open it to Jewish immigration. . . .[50]

According to Namier, Lawrence added that the arrival of Emir Abdullah led the British Government to grant self-rule to Transjordan, because

49. *T. E. Lawrence by his Friends*, p. 189.   50. *Ibid.*, p. 190.

'To stop him would have required troops and money.' It was decided to negotiate with him.[51]

Reporting a conversation between him and Lawrence, Alec Dixon says that Lawrence's

visit to the Hejaz in 1921 had been almost too much for him and that the mental strain to which he was subjected during the negotions had been worse than anything he had known during the campaign.[52]

Lawrence's brother Arnold, who published Lawrence's books after his death, has said:

His conscience was satisfied by the creation of autonomous Arab states with provision for their ultimate independence in connection with the British Empire; he wished this connection to endure, envisaging Egypt and 'Iraq as virtual Dominions. . . . When he left the Colonial Office he anticipated a long-protracted British administration of Palestine, ending in a comparatively amicable solution of the problem, in favour, I think, of a Jewish majority in the distant future.[53]

There was reason, then, for some of those who knew him best to mistrust Lawrence's intentions. King Abdullah openly declared that Lawrence was working against the Arabs and the Hashemite family, whilst his close friend Sir Ronald Storrs wrote:

I myself incline to doubt whether King Hussein ever loved Lawrence. There were moments when he and his sons suspected him of working against them, and more than once let fall hints to confidants that he should not be allowed to mingle too much with the Arab tribesmen. Feisal spoke of him to me with a good-humoured tolerance which I should have resented more if I had ever imagined that kings could like king-makers.[54]

Needless to say, it could not have been expected that King Feisal, with his usual tact, would have said much against Lawrence after all the years he had spent with him. Mrs. Steuart Erskine recalls that when she asked Feisal for his opinion on Lawrence, he replied in French:

Lawrence? He has said many things about me which are not a bit true and I should probably say things about him which would not be true either. He was a genius, of course, but not for this age.[55]

51. *T. E. Lawrence by his Friends*, p. 191.   52. *Ibid.*, pp. 279–280.
53. *Ibid.*, p. 317.   54. *Orientations*, pp. 519–520.
55. Beatrice Caroline Erskine, *King Faisal of Iraq* (1933), p. 51.

9

SUMMING UP

1. THE EXPENSES OF THE REVOLT

WITHOUT the Arab Revolt Lawrence and the Lawrence legend would not have seen the light of day. The Arab Revolt, therefore, ought to be regarded as the root, and Lawrence as the offshoot, whereas the imagination of western writers has reversed the picture, portraying the Revolt as of Lawrence's making.

Some western writers have unrestrainedly criticized the Arabs and their Revolt, wondering if what it achieved was really worth the expense incurred by the British Government to sustain it. It is necessary therefore to consider the question of the cost first, before proceeding to an assessment of what was achieved by the Revolt, as compared with the total military effort on the field of battle.

Sir Ronald Storrs has given adequate information on the total cost of the Revolt.

The gold dispatched (by Britain) was less than 10 per cent of the total cost to the British taxpayer of the Revolt in the Desert, which amounted to £11,000,000. In addition to the initial sums I took, Hussain received from 8 August 1916, £125,000 a month: in all less than one million sterling. The remaining ten millions represent military operations and supplies from Great Britain.[1]

Out of this amount, Lawrence expended five hundred thousand pounds.

How important does this sum appear when we realize that Great Britain assigned one million, four hundred thousand troops to the eastern front, and spent seven hundred and fifty million pounds on that front alone;[2] and does it not pale by com-

1. *Orientations*, p. 177.
2. *Lord Curzon's Memorandum to Emir Feisal*, 9 October 1919.

parison with the sixty million pounds spent by Great Britain to preserve order in Iraq in 1921–1922—six times the amount it spent on the Revolt in a similar period of time?

All the money received by the Arabs was spent on the military effort. The Sherif and his sons were constantly urging Great Britain to send more, because what they were given did not cover their needs. We are told in the *Arab Bulletin* of 3 January 1918, that

> About a half of the subsidy for the present month (January 1918) was sent to Sherifs Abdullah and Ali; most of the remainder was allotted to Sherif Feisal for himself and Sherif Zeid, the King retaining only one-tenth for expenses at Mecca and Jeddah.

I have been told by many participants in the Revolt that Emirs Ali, Abdullah, Feisal and Zeid never actually handled any money. It was distributed among the tribes and regulars by officials especially employed for this purpose.

Some writers have drawn a dazzling picture of the flow of gold into Arab countries. But the truth is rather different, for we have it on the authority of British writings that the wages allotted to bedouin tribes were not paid on time, and sometimes never reached them at all. The tribes were often driven to a refusal to fight until their allocations were paid. The *Arab Bulletin* bears sufficient witness to this. The regular troops fared still worse, for their meagre wages were not paid with any regularity. Colonel Peake informs us that although the regulars demanded arrears in their wages before setting out from Ma'an to Dera'a in the final expedition, these wages were not paid until the expedition reached Azraq, and then only after much insistence, bordering on a refusal to go on. Recalling, further, that these troops were deprived of the most elementary means of protection from the bitterness of the elements, with many perishing from the cold and the lack of proper clothing, we realize that the Revolt was functioning on much less than bare necessity.

Could we not also say that the aid given by Great Britain to the Revolt was in lieu of keeping the Turks fenced within the battle-field? Lawrence himself states that it would have cost the British more to keep the Turkish prisoners in camps than it did to secure the needs of the Arab forces.

We should also remember that the allies were assisting one

another. How long could Turkey have held out without German aid? It is clear that British help came short by a considerable degree of the military and political benefits Britain reaped from the Arab effort. King Hussein himself regarded the money and supplies he received as a form of payment for the retention of Basra. It was on this basis that he later gave financial backing to the revolt in Iraq. A report published by Commander Hogarth in the *Arab Bulletin* of 11 January 1919, said:

... he (King Hussein) still vaguely forecasts a demand for about a hundred and twenty thousand pounds *per mensem*. It is not known why he estimates his future needs at so large a sum: but he gave some indication that his total is not, in fact, so much an estimate of probable deficit, as a claim for compensation. As he has revealed more than once, he means to keep to the fore the general suggestion conveyed to him in Sir H. MacMahon's verbal message of December 17, 1915, that H.M.G. might be willing to consider monetary compensation to the Arabs, if it eventually retained Basra.... The King now states that he has always written off that figure from his subsidy as representing our just debt to himself.

In spite of this, Sir Ronald Storrs says:

Nevertheless, this partial sacrifice of his name before Islam, vital to our cause though also greatly to his interest, imposed upon us the real obligation of raising and maintaining his prestige to the limit of the possible. So that for this and other reasons we were in the end committed far more deeply in bullion, in munitions of war and in promises very hard to fulfil, than most of us had dreamed of in September, 1914.[3]

The leaders of the Revolt benefited least from British money. Hussein spent his last years at Cyprus in want. Feisal left Damascus with less than seven thousand pounds which he distributed at Dera'a among Ageyl volunteers.

After they had done very well in resisting the French army, preventing it from entering Wadi Barada to effect a junction with the French forces that took the main road. They lost several men, before they were compelled to retreat.[4]

Emir Abdullah left Hejaz almost penniless, and had to borrow three thousand pounds from Auda Abu Tayeh at Ma'an.

It might be easy for a foreigner to speak of the Revolt in terms

3. *Orientations*, p. 178.
4. Dr. Ahmad Qadri, *My Memoirs Of The Great Arab Revolt.*

of money. But to the Arabs, the Revolt was something far more; it represented an ideal for which men were happy to give their lives. The Arabs certainly did not rebel for the sake of British gold, which, in any case, soon found its way out again. And can the eleven million pounds be compared in any way with the Arab effort and Arab sacrifice? At the Peace Conference, Feisal declared that the Arabs had put a hundred thousand troops into the battlefield, of whom ten thousand died for the cause they cherished.

Allenby's action in giving Lawrence five hundred thousand pounds as an independent fund to spend on the operations he directed or took part in, was indeed strange and unprecedented. It was instrumental in enhancing Lawrence's prestige in Arab eyes. This amount of money in his hands gave him a special position with Feisal, because Feisal's allocations were not sufficient to cover the expenses of his army—a fact which left him in constant need of money with which to carry out his commitments to the bedouin tribes on the one hand, and to pay the wages of his regulars and furnish their expenses on the other. He was therefore obliged to ask Lawrence for help from the money in his hands, in order to surmount the financial difficulties he had sometimes to face. Lawrence himself says,

> Allenby, as thanks for the Dead Sea and Aba el Lissan, had put three hundred thousand pounds into my independent credit. . . .[5]

The total amount at his disposal was five hundred thousand pounds. This, of course, was regarded as part of the expenditure of the Revolt, but it was spent through Lawrence, just as he saw fit. I have no doubt that most of it was spent on the operations of the Northern Army as a whole, and not restricted to the operations in which Lawrence took part (for instance, the Tell Shehab raid), because these raids were infrequent, and did not require more than a few thousand pounds. The fact that this money was allotted by Allenby to Lawrence as 'thanks for the Dead Sea and Aba el Lissan' would seem to indicate that Allenby hoped the money would enable Lawrence to win other victories. But Lawrence did nothing of real value with the money; he used it rather to enhance his own prestige with the Arabs, who, understandably enough, came to view him as a very influential man in Great

5. *Seven Pillars*, p. 505.

Britain. Allenby's action was reprehensible, especially where Feisal was concerned. The latter, however, was in no position to object or criticize, for his sole aim was to make his way to Damascus by any means and regardless of difficulties and irritations.

The worst aspect of this situation was that Lawrence and other British officers occasionally gave money directly to the bedouin. According to Major Jarvis, Colonel Peake received at Aqaba a bag containing a thousand pounds in gold, which he was to distribute among the sheikhs who were to assist him in his activities. 'The order was that not less than one thousand pounds was to be carried by every British officer in command of a column. . . .'[6] It is clear that the procedure tended to demoralize the Arabs and sow the seeds of difference among them.

2. THE ARAB MILITARY EFFORT

I have endeavoured to make a fair assessment of the Arab military effort. Not wishing to exaggerate its value and its effect on the final outcome of the war, I would only say that it should receive the appreciation it deserves, particularly when we include the political side, acknowledged by the Allies to be more important than the military aspect, and view the whole Revolt as part of the campaigns in the East.

In an account of the Arab Revolt delivered before the House of Lords, Lord Cecil once stated that at the time it was declared, the Turkish forces in Hejaz numbered twenty thousand troops and that the Arabs, after clearing the Hejaz coast from enemy forces, advanced eight hundred miles from Mecca to Tafileh. He added that the Arab forces besieged, captured or engaged forty thousand Turkish men, besides seizing more than a hundred guns.

The official British history states that the Arabs engaged twenty-five thousand enemy troops. Summarizing the Arab effort Lawrence wrote:

When peace came, we had taken thirty-five thousand prisoners, killed and wounded and worn out about as many, and occupied a hundred thousand square miles of the enemy's territory. . . .[7]

According to General Glubb, the Turkish garrison in Hejaz at the inception of the Revolt numbered fifteen thousand men,

6. *Arab Command*, p. 32   7. *Oriental Assembly*, p. 108.

of whom the Arabs captured six thousand. The garrison was then reinforced with another eight thousand men. Glubb Pasha puts the number of enemy forces engaged by the Arabs at thirty thousand. All those who have written on the Revolt admit that the Turkish Fourth Army, operating in Ma'an, Salt and Amman, could easily have retreated to Dera'a and Damascus, had it not been for the Arab expedition, which cut its line of retreat and led to its dismemberment.

Dr. Shahbender, on the other hands, says:

The Ottoman army between Ma'an and Medina exceeded 30,000 men. It had the most lethal of weapons, especially long-range artillery. At its head was an obstinate imperturbable man, Fakhri Pasha, who, together with his Unionist colleagues, was too occupied with political aspects to devote his whole-hearted attention to military considerations. He and his colleagues turned a deaf ear to the important report submitted by the Staff Officer mission which inspected Medina in 1917. The report favoured the evacuation of Medina up to Ma'an, so that the large army there could be used to meet the British marching from Egypt.

It is important that we take into consideration the divergence between the Arab and British viewpoints. The Arabs considered the Revolt a basic and vital factor, regarding the British in Egypt and Palestine and the British fleet as a catalyst which would help them win their war and earn their freedom. The British, on the other hand, regarded the Arabs as a contributory element in bringing about the defeat of Germany's junior ally, Turkey. Allenby, therefore, thought of Feisal's army as his own right flank, while Feisal looked at the British Army as the left flank of the Arab liberation movement.

Anybody attempting to assess with fairness Lawrence's role on the battle-fields of the Revolt ranging from Mecca in the south to Aleppo in the north, cannot escape the conclusion that it was a modest one. What raids could Lawrence or anybody else have carried out without the permanent base at Aqaba, Gueira and Wadi Musa, which was the centre of gravity, and maintained by the Arabs? Putting aside Lawrence's eloquence and descriptive powers, and comparing the operations in which he took part with those led by Maulud Mukhlis at Wadi Musa, Gueira, and Shobek, we are immediately struck by the absurdity of the claim that Lawrence was the hero of the Revolt. But Lawrence had the advantage of his pen, while the bedouin and Arab regulars enjoyed no such gift. And here lies the secret of his magnified stature, which he earned at the expense of others.

3. THE HERO IN THE EAST

There is, however, a more than military aspect to Lawrence in relation to the morale of the Allies. At a time when the Western Front was a picture of sordid horror, Lawrence could be presented to the British and American public as a romantic hero in the East. Most of the people who knew him intimately are unanimous in their opinion that Lawrence was a successful actor. How apt is Bernard Shaw's remark:

> When he was in the middle of the stage with ten limelights blazing on him, everybody pointed to him and said: 'See! He is in hiding. He hates publicity.' He was so conspicuous that he was bothered by it and really did make some half-hearted efforts to hide himself; but it was no use: he was the most impish of comedians. . . .[8]

and:

> Though he has been described as a shy man I never saw any sign of it. . . . He was a very strange fellow, a born actor and up to all sorts of tricks: you never knew where to have him.[9]

His wearing of Arab clothes while among the Arabs can be explained, and accepted. But what explanation is there for his parading in Arab apparel in the streets of Cairo and Jerusalem during the war and in the streets of Paris and London after it? In itself it testifies to his innate theatricality. His wearing of Arab clothes was one of his stepping-stones to fame—at the hands of the shrewd American journalist Lowell Thomas.

It is strange but true that this propagandist gave rise to the Lawrence legend in the west, even to the point of conferring on him the title Prince of Mecca. Before the United States entered the war, the Allies had numerous American supporters who were naturally interested in campaigning for Britain and France with a view to encouraging their Government to join the war on the side of the Allies. In 1917, these interested parties sent Lowell Thomas abroad as a war correspondent. Finding nothing in the western front but mud, trench-warfare, heavy

8. *T. E. Lawrence by his Friends*, p. 198.
9. *Ibid.*, p. 200. Private Meek in Shaw's *Too True to be Good* is supposed to be based on Lawrence.

artillery fire and mass annihilation of troops, Thomas was advised by his friends to make for the Middle East. He accordingly arrived in Jerusalem, where he met Lawrence in colourful Arab apparel at the residence of Ronald Storrs. Seeing this as an opportunity to present his readers with stories suggestive of the *Arabian Nights,* Thomas went to Aqaba in April 1918, whence he made his way to Gueira, where he stayed for three days. Lawrence posed before Thomas's camera, and captured his imagination with tales of his adventures and raids. The reporter returned to America to write articles on his unique experience. In New York he showed scenes of the war, and huge crowds flocked to see pictures of the Arabian and Palestine campaigns. Thomas played on the imagination of his audience, telling them strange stories about countries they had only heard about through the *Arabian Nights.* His titles are indicative: 'With Allenby in Palestine and with Lawrence in Arabia', and 'The Liberation of Holy Arabia'. One night a famous English impressario, Percy Burton, came to the show and expressed his astonishment that he, an Englishman, had had to come to New York to hear about a great British hero, whom he hitherto had not even known to exist. He invited Thomas to go to London under his aegis. Thomas says:

Now I never even had dreamed of such a thing. Moreover, I couldn't take Burton seriously and thought he was pulling my leg. By way of retaliation I tried to pull his at luncheon on the following day, pretending I would go to London IF he would procure me an invitation from the King or from the British Government. I also stipulated that he should put me at either Drury Lane or Covent Garden, supposing that such a famous sanctum sanctorum of drama and opera would be out of the question. Burton grinned, said: 'You don't want much, do you?'; we parted and I forgot all about it. One month later came a cable from London, Burton had complied with both my impossible conditions, or close enough. So I sailed for England expecting to stay a couple of weeks and return home. . . . Nevertheless, the success that awaited my show in London simply amazed me and actually upset my plans. . . . Instead of staying in London for a bare two weeks my engagement was prolonged for months and months. . . . Still the crowds came, including the Prime Minister and the Cabinet, M.P.s and their lordships from the House of Peers. . . . More than a million people in London alone came to hear me tell about Lawrence. . . .[10]

10. *T. E. Lawrence by his Friends,* pp. 172–175.

Following his success in London, Thomas travelled around the British Empire exhibiting his pictures for four years. Lawrence's story spread like wildfire and suddenly he found himself emerging from his obscure position as one of thousands of officers in the war, to become the talk of newspapers and high society, celebrated as a national hero, admired by millions.

Thomas admitted that he coloured his lectures on Lawrence with all that might help to portray him as a hero. He described him as very modest, saying that many of the pictures were taken without Lawrence's knowledge, while Lawrence had in fact interceded with Allenby for him and his cameraman Chase to visit the battlefields of the Revolt and Thomas had little difficulty in persuading Lawrence to pose for photographs. According to Thomas, Lawrence loved to show off in his 'royal Sharifian' clothes and enjoyed standing in front of the camera. He loved personal fame because he believed he fully deserved it. He went to the show in London several times. When it occurred to Thomas to write a book about him, Lawrence offered no objection, adding that he himself did not intend to write a book on the Arab Revolt (in fact he had already started *Seven Pillars*). Thomas says that Lawrence worked with him on the book.

In the course of these consultations I frequently asked him whether certain anecdotes I had gathered were true, anecdotes concerning his experiences before the War. He would laugh with glee and reply. 'History isn't made up of truth anyhow, so why worry?'[11]

4. LAWRENCE'S VIEWS AND HIS ROLE

Many of those who have written on Lawrence have ignored the fact that he was, before anything else, a British citizen with a great regard for his own country's interest. I believe that he had a real desire to see the Arabs win, simply because they were Britain's allies, whose victory would facilitate the task of the British Army marching from Egypt. With regard to his desire for the Arabs to be first at Damascus, it is obvious that he was afraid France would gain a foothold in Syria. Trusting that the Arabs would prefer connexions with Britain, he zealously strove to have their demands granted—not for their own sake but for the preservation of British interests. By virtue of his having worked with the Intelligence Service, he was fully aware of

11. *T. E. Lawrence by his Friends*, pp. 175–176.

French ambitions. This is attested to by a letter he wrote from Cairo to Hogarth on 18 March 1915, in which he said, 'The French insist upon Syria—which we are conceding to them. . . .' In the same letter he said that Alexandretta had a 'petrol spring on the beach' and 'huge iron deposits', adding that 'it is a splendid natural naval base (which *we* don't want but which no one else can have without detriment to us)'.[12] He said in another letter, 'So far as Syria is concerned it is France and not Turkey that is the enemy.' Lawrence must have thought that if the Arabs reached Syria first, they would be likely to keep it by force and arouse world opinion against France. His behaviour during negotiations with King Hussein indicates that the independence he wanted for the Arabs was of a kind that would be subject to British desires and would serve British interests. He declared publicly that such was his hope. At the close of *Seven Pillars* he says,

The strongest motive throughout had been a personal one. . . . Next in force had been a pugnacious wish to win the war: yoked to the conviction that without Arab help England could not pay the price of winning its Turkish sector.[13]

In a letter to Robert Graves, he wrote:

I want you to make it quite clear . . . how from 1916 onwards and especially in Paris I worked against the idea of an Arab Confederation being formed politically before it had become a reality commercially, economically and geographically by the slow pressure of many generations; how I worked to give the Arabs a chance to set up their provincial governments whether in Syria or in Iraq; and how in my opinion Winston Churchill's settlement has honourably fulfilled our war-obligations and my hopes.[14]

In another letter to Graves, dated 28 June 1927, he reiterates, 'The Winston solution passed my hopes: I'd have retired with less.'

Lawrence's intelligence did not serve to give him an understanding of the real motives of the Arabs. Take for example his remark in *Seven Pillars*,

In history, Syria . . . had been a prize-ring, a vassal, of Anatolia, of Greece, of Rome, of Egypt, of Arabia, of Persia, of Mesopotamia . . . Syria was by nature a vassal country.[15]

12. *Selected Letters of T. E. Lawrence*, pp. 85–86.   13. *Seven Pillars*, p. 661.
14. Robert Graves, *Lawrence and the Arabs*, p. 398.   15. *Op. cit.*, p. 336.

In a letter to his parents dated 12 February 1917, he wrote:

. . . the Arab Movement is shallow, not because the Arabs do not care, but because they are few—and in their smallness of number (which is imposed by their poverty of country) lies a good deal of their strength, for they are perhaps the most elusive enemy an army ever had, and inhabit one of the most trying countries in the world for civilized warfare. . . . Talk about Palestine or Syria or Mesopotamia is not opportune, when these three countries—with every chance—have made no effort towards freedom for themselves.[16]

The following remarks of Hubert Young are most illuminating:

An instance of the lengths to which he was prepared to go . . . was his creation of the phrase 'the first brown Dominion' for the Arab countries, and his fathering it upon Feisal himself. I was asked once by the authority concerned whether Feisal was loyal to the British Empire, and expressed the opinion that he was and would no doubt remain grateful to us for helping him to the throne of 'Iraq, but that his first and only aim was the re-establishment of an Arab Empire. 'But Lawrence says that his idea of the Arab countries is that they should form the first brown Dominion,' I was told.[17]

According to Lowell Thomas, it is not true that Lawrence declined the honours that were offered to him because of his chagrin at the treatment meted out to the Arabs after the War.

He told me in the desert that, no matter whether they were given what they wanted or not, they were incapable of pulling together and creating a great Arab state.[18]

In *Seven Pillars*, Lawrence described the Arabs as

. . . a limited, narrow-minded people, whose inert intellects lay fallow in incurious resignation. Their imaginations were vivid, but not creative. There was so little Arab art in Asia that they could almost be said to have had no art . . . they had no organizations of mind or body. They invented no systems of philosophy, no complex mythologies. . . .[19]
Arab civilizations had been of an abstract nature, moral and intellectual rather than applied; and their lack of public spirit made their excellent private qualities futile. They were fortunate in their epoch: Europe had fallen barbarous; and the memory of Greek and Latin learning was fading from men's minds.[20]

16. *The Home Letters of T. E. Lawrence and his Brothers* (ed. M. R. Lawrence), p. 335.
17. *T. E. Lawrence by his Friends*, p. 107.
18. *Ibid.*, p. 176.   19. *Seven Pillars*, p. 38.   20. *Ibid.*, p. 44.

He called the Syrians

> . . . an ape-like people having much of the Japanese quickness,
> but shallow. . . . They looked outside for help, and expected freedom
> to come by entreaty, not by sacrifice.[21]

Elsewhere he said that there was a 'hedonistic streak among
the Arabs which made them helpless slaves of carnal indulgence'.[22] At Azraq when the final expedition was ready to set
out, he said that everyone was stout and in health except himself,
'I was tired to death of these Arabs; petty incarnate Semites . . .
and for two years I had profitably shammed to be their companion!'[23]

Lawrence claimed that he knew twelve thousand Arabic words,
but this is clear exaggeration. The fact of the matter is that his
Arabic served to convey his thoughts in a limited way. All those I
have spoken with or written to have unanimously agreed that as
soon as Lawrence spoke one sentence of Arabic, it was clear to all
concerned that he was a foreigner. (Glubb had spent thirty years,
and Philby forty, among the Arabs, but neither could pass in
conversation for an Arab.) Lawrence himself said,

> I've never heard an Englishman speak Arabic well enough to be
> taken for a native of any part of the Arabic-speaking world, for
> five minutes.[24]

He commented to Captain Liddell Hart, 'No easterner would
ever have taken me for an Arab for a moment.'[25] Philby has
scotched the illusion that Lawrence knew most of the Arabic
dialects:

> That is not true. Actually his Arabic was rather poor stuff of a
> very mixed breed, and his accent was not good, though of course he
> spoke fluently enough.[26]

Subhi al-Umari assured me that Philby and Young spoke
Arabic much better than Lawrence.

5. LAWRENCE'S ZIONIST LEANINGS

Much has been said about Lawrence's Zionist leanings and his
viewing with favour their ambitions for Arab Palestine. It seems
to me that his attitude sprang from his interest in his own

---

21. *Seven Pillars*, p. 47.   22. *Ibid.*, p. 490.   23. *Ibid.*, p. 586.
24. *Lawrence and the Arabs*, p. 166.
25. Liddell Hart, *T. E. Lawrence*, f.n. p. 367.   26. *Arabian Days*, p. 210.

country's welfare, since the general impression held by some
British imperialists was that the Zionists in Palestine would
form an important bridge-head for the Empire in this sensitive
geographical position.

It appears that Lawrence had formed his first impressions on
the subject during his visit to Syria in the summer of 1909. In
a letter to his mother he describes the country in general and says
that all he saw around the lake of Tiberias were

> . . . dirty, dilapidated Bedouin tents, with the people calling to
> [passers-by] to come in and talk, while miserable curs came snapping
> at their heels: Palestine was a decent country then, and could so
> easily be made so again. The sooner the Jews farm it all the better:
> their colonies are bright spots in a desert.[27]

But Lawrence was forgetting all about the money the Jews
were spending on their colonies, while the Arabs had none. He
was also forgetting that it was not so much the faults of the Arabs
as the corrupt Ottoman administration which had brought them
to the state of affairs he so much abhorred.

In *Oriental Assembly* there is a chapter on 'The Changing
East' which gives a neat summary of Lawrence's views:

> The success of [the Zionist] scheme will involve inevitably the
> raising of the present Arab population to their own material level . . .
> and the consequences might be of the highest importance for the
> future of the Arab world. . . . However, such a contingency will not
> be for the first or even for the second generation. . . .[28]

Weizmann once claimed that Lawrence told him that the
Anglican Bishop in Jerusalem was organizing anti-Jewish propaganda. On 15 December 1921, the Bishop wrote to Lawrence
demanding a denial of this. Lawrence replied:

> I will do nothing of the sort. . . . Dr. Weizmann [is] a great man
> whose boots neither you, nor I, my dear Bishop, are fit to black.[29]

Speaking about Lawrence's feelings towards Zionism, Weizmann says:

> Lawrence readily gave not only his advice, but his personal help
> in furthering both the Zionist aspirations and an understanding
> with the Arabs. . . . In the winter of 1921 I had a long talk with him,
> our conversation turning mainly on Jewish-Arab co-operation. He

27. *Selected Letters*, p. 27.   28. *Oriental Assembly*, p. 93.
29. *Ibid.*, pp. 134–135.

regarded such co-operation as of the utmost importance, from the Jewish point of view, but equally in the interests of the Arabs. He thought that the Jews acted as a ferment and were likely to be instrumental in bringing out the latent energies of the Arab people. He thought that Arab redemption was likely to come about through Jewish redemption.[30]

The Zionist leader, Sir Lewis Namier, wrote that, in a conversation on the Cairo Conference, Lawrence told him that 'it was decided to include Transjordan in Palestine . . . and to open it to Jewish immigration'.[31] But the arrival of Abdullah in Transjordan frustrated this plan.

We should be a little reserved, however, in judging Lawrence in this connexion, because the Zionists exaggerated Lawrence's support for their projects, thereby making publicity for their own case. It was an added asset to be able to say that none other than Lawrence of Arabia was numbered among their supporters.

6. LAWRENCE'S PERSONALITY

The Arabs had no knowledge of the unusual aspects of Lawrence's character to which western biographers attached so much importance. To them he was a British officer of extraordinary mental and physical powers, but distinguished from his fellow countrymen in his modesty and simplicity and his love for the Arabs and interest in their affairs. Today, however, we know much more about Lawrence's life, his views and actions than did those who knew him at the time of the Revolt. In the light of this new knowledge we wish to take a final comprehensive look at the personality of this controversial man whose name has become permanently linked with that of the Arabs.

Lawrence suffered greatly as a result of the contradictions inherent in his nature, of his sudden and inexplicable changes of mood, of his dormant selfishness and of the sway which illusions held over him. He craved fame, while at the same time fearing it and fearing also that others should know of his craving. His love of fame was undoubtedly behind the lies he made up and the credit he claimed for deeds he had never accomplished. It is also clear that he was by nature inclined to exaggeration, as witness his statement in a letter he had written from Carchemish, 'All Syria had heard of me'. But occasionally his

30. *T. E. Lawrence by his Friends*, pp. 183–184.   31. *Ibid.*, p. 190.

conscience was worried, 'I began to wonder if all established reputations were founded, like mine, on fraud.'[32] Those who knew him well saw the depth of his love of intrigue and deceit. There is no doubt that Hogarth was right in saying that Lawrence had no morality about the means to any end on which he had determined.[33] Young confirms this by saying:

> As a statesman, T. E. possessed all the qualifications for success including, it must be admitted, the faculty of calculated unscrupulousness in the interest of his main object.[34]

In plain English he was a Machiavellian, who believed that the end justified the means.

Lawrence had a natural passion for surrounding himself with an air of mystery and a cluster of question-marks, as shown by his wearing of Arab clothes in Europe, Jerusalem and Cairo, with no obvious justification except his desire to make himself conspicuous, by the little stories he liked to weave about himself, and by the halo with which he tried to surround his name. His friend Vyvyan Richards comments:

> Few men have gathered after them so great a train of stories as he, serious and comic, and the greater proportion could only have come from his own lips; . . . his supremacy must never seem to suffer.[35]

Lawrence had great powers of endurance. In spite of his small stature he had an exceptionally strong build. These characteristics are amply borne out by the trip he took to Syria alone in 1909, on which he tramped hundreds of miles on foot, and by the way he kept up with the bedouin during the Revolt, in long-range raids, camel-riding, and in enduring hunger and thirst and surviving the severity of winter cold and the scorching summer heat. For these qualities he is to be praised and admired. He once described this aspect of his life in a letter he wrote in 1927:

> In 1914 I was a pocket Hercules, as muscularly strong as people twice my size, and more enduring than most. I saw all the other British officers' boots off in Arabia: they went to base, or to hospital, while I did two years in the fighting areas, and was nine times

32. *Seven Pillars*, p. 562.
33. *T. E. Lawrence to his Biographer* Liddell Hart, p. 188.
34. *T. E. Lawrence by his Friends*, p. 106.
35. *T. E. Lawrence*, by Vyvyan Richards, p. 14.

wounded, and five times crashed from the air, and had two goes of dysentery, and suffered enough hunger and thirst and heat and cold and exposure, not to mention deliberate maltreatment, to wreck the average constitution.[36]

According to Philby, 'he was as hard as steel'.[37]

He was equally remarkable for his indomitable spirit, which competed in powers of endurance with his body, amidst the hardships of bedouin companionship under difficult and extraordinary circumstances, for which he volunteered with little outside pressure. Although his superiors expected him to do something of value, they never thought of asking him to go to the extent to which he actually did. A good example of this is his voluntary decision to accompany Sherif Nassir and Auda Abu Tayeh on their expedition to the north. These aspects of his courage are highly creditable, even though he was by nature inclined to this kind of adventurous living, far from the restraints of officialdom.

Everyone likes his own efforts to be appreciated and sufficiently rewarded. But Lawrence was not the kind of person to expect reward through normal channels: his modesty was not deeply rooted enough. That was why he demanded to take personal command after Aqaba had fallen at the hand of Auda Abu Tayeh, why in *Seven Pillars* he voiced his determination to become a general before he was thirty, and why in general he made such an effort to impress others with the importance of what he was doing.

He once stated that he declined the position of British High Commissioner in Egypt. On another occasion he claimed to have gone to Mecca. Writing to Mr. H. R. Hadley (who later became a Muslim), he said:

So if anyone asks me if I've been there I have to say 'no' in public: but in private you can guess about it! It mustn't get into the papers because it would do the old King's reputation harm.[38]

In 1932 he wrote a letter to Wavell, in which he said:

36. *Selected Letters*, p. 239. See also his draft Preface to *Seven Pillars*, which we have quoted in Chapter 8, 11, where Lawrence said that he suffered 'sixty wounds'. He had fallen sick more than once, but succeeded in making a rapid recovery. Nevertheless, his travels were no more exhausting than those of Gertrude Bell in Arab countries before World War I, nor those of Philby or Glubb Pasha.
37. *Arabian Days*, p. 210.
38. *Selected Letters*, pp. 123–124.

Yes, I've promised not to admit the Mecca jest. I did it because I wanted to choose my own gold dagger, and it was not serious for me. Hussein will never forgive it me.[39]

I have traced Lawrence's movements and I am convinced that he never set foot in Mecca, quite apart from the consideration that King Hussein could not possibly have permitted him to do so, and it was impossible for Lawrence to reach Mecca without Hussein's knowledge.

To return to Lawrence's gold dagger (which he later sold), I might mention that Faiz al-Ghussein has assured me personally that it was a gift from Feisal, and that he—Faiz—was given a similar dagger by Feisal, which he gave to his brother after the war. His brother gave it in his turn to Major Somerset (Lord Raglan), who was political agent at Irbid and Dera'a from 1920 to 1921. In *Seven Pillars* Lawrence described how Emir Abdullah had sent Eshref Bey's dagger to his brother Feisal, who gave it as a gift to Colonel Wilson. I have been told by Mohammed al-Asbali that Lawrence had told him in private that he had travelled in Yemen, Nejd and Hejaz before the war, and that in Yemen he had made the acquaintance of Imam Yehya and visited Mecca as a Turk! Al-Asbali described Lawrence as a 'monkey, devil and trickster', adding that he kept himself down on the same level as his followers, never issuing an order but always starting things himself. He added that Lawrence never paid attention to his own comfort or asserted superiority over his servants: he always lit the fire himself.

In July 1918 he wrote to his friend Richards about his unsettled nature and his love for constant variety. His letter is packed with fulsome exaggeration:

> This is an idiot letter, and amounts to nothing except cry for a further change which is idiocy, for I change my abode every day, and my job every two days, and my language every three days, and still remain always unsatisfied. I hate being in front, and hate being back and I don't like responsibility, and I don't obey orders.[40]

I think it is wrong to believe that Lawrence adhered to a fixed principle in life. There are ample indications that he used to change his behaviour according to circumstances. He was not religious in the accepted sense of the word, and we gather from the remarks of the commander of the Air Force base at Karachi

---

39. *Selected Letters*, p. 189.   40. *Ibid.*, p. 110.

that Lawrence asked to be excused from prayers because he did not believe in the content of them.

Nobody as yet has come out with a convincing explanation of Lawrence's insistence on enlisting as a private when he could have obtained suitable work either within the Civil Service or outside it. Barring that, he could have lived quite comfortably on the proceeds of his books on the Arab Revolt; but he preferred poverty and refused to touch a single penny. Although in 1922 he declared that Great Britain had made an honourable and complete fulfilment of her pledges to the Arabs, we find him writing to Ralph H. Isham in 1927:

Did I tell you . . . that I consider what I did in Arabia morally indefensible? So I refused pay and decorations while it lasted, and will not take any personal profit out of it. . . .[41]

Lawrence's behaviour must be puzzling to anyone who tries to find a reasonable explanation of it. But Lawrence was an extremely eccentric and unusual person, and in the interests of honesty, we cannot, except with reserve and caution, apply to his works and statements a yardstick applicable to ordinary people. I regard Lawrence as a sadist, in an intellectual sense at least. One example is his execution of Hamed the Moor (supposing the story is true), one of his companions from Wejh to Wadi Ais, on the pretext that he did so to prevent a feud, while he could have easily arrested the man and handed him over to Emir Abdullah at Wadi Ais to be dealt with as he saw fit. Other examples are his account of the Turks killed at Abu al-Lissan and the manner in which he lined up the corpses by moonlight, his description of those killed in the Tafileh battle and of the dead at the Turkish hospital in Damascus, and his story of putting away Farraj after he was injured. One feels that Lawrence experienced pleasure at describing these hideous incidents.

Some writers have attributed his actions to a lack of sexual potency and Lawrence himself admitted that he was free of the sexual urge. He had grown up in a house with no women (except his mother), for he had had no sisters. He was never known to have had an intimate relationship with any woman. He was never engaged, never married and was known to shun the company of women. The circumstances of his life, moreover, required him

41. *T. E. Lawrence by his Friends*, p. 253.

to be forever in male company. He once said that there were no females in the Arab Revolt except she-camels. We also know that he could not bear anybody to touch him because of his extraordinary physical sensitivity. We might conjecture that his lack of sexual feeling had deprived him of natural sympathies and of the ordinary feelings of mercy and pity, leading him to experience pleasure—or at least not to feel repelled—at the sight of suffering. He once admitted to Robert Graves that he was incapable of falling in love or feeling love. His brother has stated that Lawrence felt profound repugnance at the very idea of sexual relationships. I have found no evidence in the Arab world, however, of Lawrence's alleged homosexuality.

7. LAWRENCE'S COMPLEX

Lawrence's biographers have left two important questions unanswered:

1. Why did Lawrence insist on keeping *Seven Pillars of Wisdom* from the public by refraining from publishing it during his lifetime?
2. Why did Lawrence co-operate with Lowell Thomas and Robert Graves in preparing their books on his life, and at the same time make it a condition that they announce that he was not their source and that he was in no way responsible for the contents of their books?

One aspect of the answer to these questions is to be found in his own book *Revolt in the Desert*. This book was neither a summary nor a systematic abridgement of *Seven Pillars of Wisdom*, for Lawrence made no major changes except to cut out chapters and certain passages and remarks here and there for undivulged reasons. We are not greatly concerned with all the chapters which Lawrence did away with. Some comprised general remarks on the Arabs and their Revolt and on his own military views and theories about guerrilla warfare. Apart from showing evidence of his conceit and love of pretence, they are relatively harmless. What does particularly concern us, however, are the suppressed chapters and remarks concerning certain definite and concrete happenings which in the original version he claimed had actually taken place. We can find no convincing justification for his deletions except the deliberate intention of keeping some alleged facts from the public.

As far as I have been able to ascertain, the most important omissions are:

1. His alleged secret trip in June 1917 to Palmyra (Tadmor), Baalbeck, Jebel Druze, and Lejah. This is altogether ignored in *Revolt in the Desert,* where he is content to say that he spent that period at Wadi Sirhan.

2. The side raid from Bair to Um Keis and the Yarmuk river, with Sheikh Za'al ibn Motleg, in the period between 20 and 27 June 1917. In *Revolt in the Desert* says only that he remained with the others at Bair.

3. His visit to the Beni Sakhr encampment in June 1917, and the claim that Fawwaz al-Faiz tried to murder him.

4. The story of Aishe Jelal al-Leil, whom he claimed to have protected after destroying the train at Haret al-Amareh station on 18 September 1917, and who later sent him a carpet from Damascus as a token of her gratitude. All he said in *Revolt in the Desert* was that Ahmed came up to him and shouted that an old woman in the last wagon but one wished to see him.[42]

5. His trip to Dera'a in November 1917. According to *Revolt in the Desert* he spent some days at Azraq, then returned south to Aqaba.

6. His trip to Palestine, with the alleged purpose of resigning from the Arab Army, after his supposed quarrel with Zeid in February 1918. In *Revolt in the Desert* he merely said that he had to return to Palestine 'for urgent consultation with Allenby'.[43]

7. His alleged visit to Amman, disguised as a gipsy woman in April 1918.

Lawrence's motive in doing this is perfectly clear. He knew very well that these stories were mere fabrications, which, if published, would prompt replies and denials from those familiar with the facts. He therefore chose to keep them secret until after his death, when, he hoped, many of those in a position to deny them would have died as well. He also hoped that the passage of time would in any case have blunted memories and made it difficult to refute his claims.

42. T. E. Lawrence, *Revolt in the Desert* (1927), p. 147.   43. *Ibid.*, p. 223.

While Lawrence himself claimed that *Revolt in the Desert* 'was abridged from *Seven Pillars of Wisdom,* and contained all that I wanted the public to know', some of his biographers were of the opinion that he did not publish the whole book to avoid hurting the feelings of people concerned who were still alive, and to avoid shocking others. But if this were true, surely he would have suppressed Chapter XXIX of *Revolt in the Desert,* which contains grave insults to King Hussein, Feisal, Ja'afar al-Askari and many others!

On the other hand we might argue that the suppressed stories do not contain scandalous allusions to anybody. They do not reveal any secrets, nor are they in any way insulting. What harm would there have been in divulging the details of his alleged visit to Ba'albak, Palmyra, Damascus, and Dera'a, or of his visit to Amman dressed as a gipsy woman, or indeed of the Aisha story? Even in *Seven Pillars,* Lawrence speaks of his secret trip to Ba'albek, Palmyra and Damascus in a mysterious language that takes us nowhere. Why was he so secretive at this point, when his biographers were unanimous in considering this his most daring and risky adventure, covering as he would have us believe over a thousand miles in completely hostile territory?

Lawrence's biographers are agreed that several aspects of his life are shrouded in mystery. Any mystery there may be stems from the lies he was in the habit of inventing, without being clear how to proceed with the elucidation of detail. Faced with this problem, he would take refuge in silence, which created a sense of elusiveness puzzling to others. His biographers accepted many of his claims as established fact, simply because he, being the only source of information about his own movements and actions, was necessarily unchallenged.

Behind the stipulation that Thomas and Graves should declare that Lawrence was not responsible for the contents of their books, there was a desire to keep the door open for retreat in the face of possible reaction to his fabrications. We know that he himself attempted to renounce Lowell Thomas, after pressure had grown for a clarification of the issues raised in the book. He was fortunate that no Arab took the time to refute the statements of Thomas and Graves when they were published. But who would take the trouble of refuting statements with whose contents

Lawrence, according to their authors, had no connexion whatsoever?

What then is the logical explanation for the motive which drove Lawrence to fabricate, then suppress these stories, to turn down offers of high positions and to insist on enlisting as a recruit in the Air Force?

On the one hand Lawrence was an imaginative adventurer, driven by his historical studies to achieve something of note, which would be the subject of people's conversation and material fit to be perpetuated in books. On the other hand he was a sensitive, educated man, who feared history's severe verdict on forgery and deceit, His 'first' nature led him to brave the elements and to take troubles and difficulties in his stride, without fully satisfying his excessive ambition. Hence his supplementary bragging, falsification and fabrication, which helped to give a picture pleasing to his imagination, satisfying to his ambition and gratifying to his yearnings. At the same time, his 'second' nature aroused the conscience of the educated man in him, who would act as auditor and judge. Lawrence found himself shaken by his own puzzling contradictions.

Deep within himself, Lawrence knew that the greater part of his fame was based on fraud. He realized fully that if he had followed the more honest path of his colleagues, he would not have enjoyed the limelight or the patronage of the great after the war. It was his sense of guilt, therefore, that drove him to the Air Force and the Tank Corps, in the hope of atoning for earlier mistakes, which haunted him in secret. If he had a perverted nature, devoid of conscience, he would have continued to exploit his unearned fame until the very end. But his conscience, coupled with his romantic imagination, drove him into a semi-hermitage of atonement. It was as if his Inner Voice had said to him: if History, which knows no mercy, stands witness to the claims through which you ascended the steps of fame, the same History will find itself forced to admit that you renounced everything and did not permit yourself to benefit from your fame in any way. It was no mean decision.

COMMENT

by A. W. LAWRENCE

In spite of the apparent indications to the contrary which I shall detail, I think this book was written with honest conviction. It represents, the Preface says, 'the Arab viewpoint' and undeniably does express the feelings of many Arabs (though not of all those I have met).

The reader may notice that nothing is said on my brother's struggle (in England) to terminate the military occupation of Iraq, and very little on the sequel, his part in setting that country on its way to independence.

A patriotic Arab may justifiably resent foolish exaggerations of the degree to which Europeans, and particularly T. E. Lawrence, helped his people towards independence. This resentment extends to *Seven Pillars*, a book avowedly so written 'that everyone may see how natural the success was and how inevitable, how little dependent on direction or brain, how much less on the outside assistance of the few British. It was an Arab war waged and led by Arabs for an Arab aim in Arabia.'[1] In fact, Allenby was the only European recognized as holding authority over any Arab forces, and he exercised it solely through their commander, Feisal. The European officers who served with them could give orders to no Arab except for the few in their employment. That being so, the extreme lengths to which Mr. Mousa goes to point out that T. E. Lawrence was not in command may seem a waste of effort; no doubt, though, the book is consciously addressed to the ignorant, who fancy that he held a clearly defined position of dominance. Actually the question should be, on which occasions and to what extent did he inspire or control activities by

---

1. *Seven Pillars*, Introductory Chapter (omitted from early editions, first published in *Oriental Assembly*, 1939).

persuasion, whether as a dispenser of British materials and gold to men ill-equipped and unpaid, or through his personal influence? The evidence of participants in the campaign is affected by each informant's nationality, rank, and political bias; naturally, too, more Europeans than Arabs published their own recollections or communicated them to authors. Even at the time, however, the question can seldom have admitted of an absolute answer, owing to the informal manner of procedure. This is clearly depicted by Colonel Joyce, the senior British military representative throughout, with reference to the first Arab War-Cabinet he himself attended.

At this, as at dozens of other conferences we attended together, Lawrence rarely spoke. He merely studied the men around him and when the argument ended, as they usually did, in smoke, he then dictated his plan of action which was usually adopted and everyone went away satisfied. It was not, as is often supposed, by his individual leadership of hordes of Bedouin that he achieved success in daring ventures, but by the wise selection of tribal leaders and by providing the essential grist to the mill in the shape of golden rewards for work well done.[2]

It should be noted that Joyce's knowledge and wisdom are beyond dispute, and British officers and Arab leaders alike have recognized the greatness of his share in the victory achieved.

M. has minimized European services to the war-effort of his countrymen. An instance can be found on page 54, where a new section opens with a truncated quotation, which, if completed, would have fitted badly with his first and third paragraphs. The sentence in *Seven Pillars* does not, unlike the quotation, limit the purpose in visiting Abdulla's camp to mere investigation of why nothing had been done for two months – incidentally a matter within the compass of an Intelligence Officer's duty; there follow the words, 'and to persuade him, if the Turks came out, to go straight at them' using means (described at some length) to block the railway along which the Turks hoped to withdraw. A second quotation on p. 55 reveals that the task of so persuading Abdulla was attempted, presumably in amplification of the documents that Feisal had provided. Yet M. sums up with the *non sequitur*, 'Here Lawrence admits that he had gone to Wadi

2. B.B.C. script, 14 July 1941; quoted by permission of Mrs. P. C. Joyce.

Ais to deliver Feisal's documents not to "find out why [Abdulla] had done nothing for two months." '

When Arab and British sources conflict in apportioning credit for some action, investigation long afterwards can rarely be definitive (to unprejudiced minds), unless the evidence of a third party can be brought to bear. It is, therefore, most unfortunate that M. has disregarded (placing no confidence in it) the book by the head of the French Mission, General Brémond,[3] which is critical of both sets of allies. Brémond may be thought to demolish the contention (pp. 66, 67) that Auda both devised and carried out the plan of capturing Aqaba from the land. For Brémond records a discussion he had with Feisal and Newcombe on 31 January 1917, showing that they had the project fully in mind two months before Auda joined them (p. 64), and does not even mention Auda in connexion with the operation; he gives the credit for that to Nassir *toujours poussé par Lawrence*. Newcombe, who was in an even better position to know the facts, had no doubt but that the scheme was 'entirely conceived by Lawrence who was its real leader and animating spirit'.[4] That opinion was held also by Bray,[5] who disapproved of attacking Aqaba by land, and by a more responsible officer who came later on the scene but could readily have ascertained the truth since he knew Arabic better than any of his colleagues – Sir Hubert Young.[6] There was, of course, nothing to stop Auda from thinking out the scheme independently and he may well have been convinced that he originated it.

A crucial point to M. (pp. 74-76) is his contention that the journey into Syria was fictitious. But Antonius, in *The Arab Awakening* (1938)),[7] describes it in a manner obviously independent of T.E.L.'s then unpublished report; two minor discrepancies can be disregarded but he includes additional matter: an account of how the meeting with Rikabi was arranged, and the several terms of a message from Feisal communicated at the meeting. Antonius must have obtained this information from one or both of those present, either directly or through one or more intermediaries (and he habitually took care to check the oral evidence he collected). On the Arab side, he could have been told

3. *Le Hedjaz dans la guerre mondiale*, pp. 133, 162.
4. J. Beraud Villars, *T. E. Lawrence*, p. 151.   5. *Shifting Sands*, p. 138.
6. *The Independent Arab*, p. 140.   7. p. 221.

by Rikabi, by Feisal (who constantly helped him), or possibly
by some member of Feisal's entourage, but apparently by no one
else. Alternatively or in addition, T.E.L. might have given the
information on an occasion mentioned by Antonius, and certainly supplied a good deal of it to two biographers of himself,
and they published some of what they learnt. Yet M. is convinced that he had wished to suppress his incautious story of a
journey which he never even started; on that argument (p. 276),
he should have said nothing about it, least of all to writers who
would irrevocably commit him in books intended for the widest
circulation. As for the deduction made by Rikabi's son (p. 77),
a general in the Turkish army would not speak openly, before
the war ended, of his own past treasonable activity. It may have
been to avoid subsequent embarrassment to Rikabi and others
that no account of these doings was included in *Seven Pillars* and
that biographers were asked to write discreetly.

The only real evidence brought against this journey is Naseeb's
recollection, forty-odd years later (p. 75), that he himself left
the base at Nebk only once, on or about 18 June 1917, whereas
S.P. and Antonius assert that he was absent early in the month.
If as *S.P.* declares,[8] his ambition was to foment and lead a rebellion on his own, a private expedition to sound local feeling would
seem a likely preliminary to his official mission of the 18th, when
he was charged to hold discussions on Feisal's behalf. A fruitless
and unexacting venture, undertaken in times full of incident,
is not, perhaps, an item that will certainly be remembered in
one's old age.

No authority is cited for the assertion (p. 74), in contradiction
to *S.P.*, 'the real facts are that when the Arabs crossed the railway
line in the direction of Aqaba they had no time to blow up a
single bridge'. And a startling lack of comprehension appears
from the next sentence, 'Had they actually damaged as many as
ten bridges, Lawrence's report could not have ignored such an
important fact.' What importance could be attached to blowing
up these little bridges at kilometere 479, within hearing of a
Turkish base a dozen miles away from which they would quickly
be repaired? M. ignores the evidence of *S.P.*[9] that the purpose
of the operation was simply to draw off Turkish troops who might
otherwise have gone to reinforce the real objective, Aqaba. The

8. pp. 274-275.   9. p. 298.

bridges rated space in *S.P.* for graphic interest but there was no occasion to mention them specifically in documents for official reading. M. is therefore wrong in alleging inconsistency between the eight sentences of *S.P.*[10] and the corresponding few words of the report (written in a state of exhaustion), 'km, 479, which we destroyed on a large scale', and he does not refer to the third account, in the *Arab Bulletin*: 'The same afternoon we descended on the line at kilometre 479, near Ghadir el Haj, and carried out extensive demolition till sunset.'[11]

M. sees further evidence of deceit in the omission, from one account or another, of diversionary side-shows obviously meant for the same purpose, of drawing off Turkish forces, and even less significant in any other respect. He builds up his case by exaggerating the aims of these detached parties; he misrepresents the attack 'near Aneyza' (p. 73, quotation) as an 'attack on Uneiza station' (p. 74), and seems to imply that a flying column which entered several places in turn, and had since moved elsewhere (p. 73), was alleged to be still occupying them (p. 74).

On p. 75 M. denies the truth of yet another part of the report, referring to an excursion to the Yarmuk valley. One of his grounds is 'Lawrence's claim that he attacked Sultani (Manzil) station', though the source (quoted on p. 73) merely says 'we also carried out demolitions against the railway at Atwi, Sultani, Minifir, and elsewhere'; it does not say that the same man went to every stretch of railway, or that any station was attacked. Another attempt at refutation depends on a non-existent contradiction between the report and *S.P.*; men escaping from suspected treachery tried to baffle pursuit by starting off in the wrong direction, but M. mistakes their 'supposed' destination for the real one (p. 76).

M. seems unable (p. 79, para 4) to appreciate the desperate urgency of sending food to a starving garrison, cumbered with many prisoners, at a place the enemy would try to recapture. I am aware of no source substantiating the 'gesticulating' and 'shuffling' described at the top of p. 80; nor, incidentally, do I know the basis for allegations in the footnote on p. 47.

On p. 85 M. alleges that T.E.L. fabricated a story, and during the following five pages confirms it himself. Likewise, on p. 106

10. *Seven Pillars*, p. 298.
11. *Secret Despatches*, p. 120. Brémond's mention of these demolitions (p. 162) cannot be from first-hand knowledge.

he complains of finding in *S.P.* no word of praise for Abdul Kader, but in the light of his own pages 210-212 one might be inclined to doubt whether any would have been justified.

It was absurd to expect two accounts of the same complex events to incorporate the identical details (p. 100). Only by jumping to an unjustified conclusion can M. assert that 'the two Darawsheh Sheikhs who returned to look for Lawrence have become in *S.P.* three persons, who do not seem to be sheikhs at all' – and actually are not said to have to come to look for him but to have helped load the camel. The formidable list of inconsistencies dwindles if closely examined; *S.P.* merely adds to the contemporary story two thefts and a divorce.

A fine character is attributed (p. 118) to Hajem, the Governor at Deraa – whose name is written 'Hajim' in the MS of *S.P.* but was disguised for publication. In an Arabic document of 1918 (preserved in King's College, London) a refugee, formerly the director of a semi-religious institution, associates him with barbarities 'in the manner of Tamberlane' including the slaughter of seven hundred men, women, and children at El-Salt.

M. should have realized (p. 155) that the controversy over attacking Ma'an is not the sort of thing normally printed in the *Arab Bulletin;* it is, however, recorded by Young, whose account[12] agrees with *S.P.*

Young's own book[13] disproves a myth (p. 165) borrowed from Nutting, that Lawrence 'was not happy with this [Young's] appointment and he did not trust Young. He suspected that his new colleague was here to spy on him, and he was therefore anxious to get rid of him as soon as possible.' Having, in fact, himself arranged for Young to come.

The secrecy attached to the Sykes-Picot agreement is exaggerated on p. 181. Far from it being the case that 'even the High Commissioner in Egypt knew nothing about it' till its publication by the Russians in November 1917, Brémond[14] heard of the agreement on a visit to Khartum, i.e. to the High Commissioner, some time before 14 January 1917, when the official summary was sent to both him and the British representative at Jedda. Nor is there any likelihood that members of the Arab Bureau were kept in ignorance.

M. cannot believe that telegrams from King Hussein, trans-

12. p. 267.   13. pp. 141—142, etc.   14. pp. 130, 131.

mitted through the British, were toned down before delivery (p. 183). Among the military archives at King's College, London, is an evident translation of one, and had the original been delivered unaltered the consequences would have been serious.

Recent testimony is cited (p. 199) that no massacres occurred at Tafas, either of villagers or, in retaliation, of Turkish soldiers. Brémond learnt of both from a French eye-witness.[15] Young was told of both, that very evening, by Arab eye-witnesses, and goes on to say, 'Ali Jaudat told me that he and Lawrence tried vainly to save a batch of prisoners from being massacred by the Bedouin, whose latent savagery had been aroused by the sight of butchered women and children.' [16] Colonel Peake authorizes me to affirm that he himself saw the bodies of men, women, and children lying in and around the village; that Turks were being chased out and killed without mercy when he came on the scene with his Camel Corps, but 'Lawrence came running to me and ordered me to restore order as soon as possible. This I was able to do'. Furthermore 'I was ordered by Lawrence to collect and guard all Turks as they arrived from the battle-field in Palestine'.[17] These hordes of stragglers were captured after the fighting at Tafas had ceased; hence the fact that many Turkish lives were saved does not, as M. claims, suggest that there had been no previous massacre of an intact column there.

A long article by Nuri as-Said in the *Baghdad Times*, part of which is quoted on p. 33, contains also a passage which states flatly that *Revolt in the Desert* (an abridgement of *S.P* issued to the public instead of the complete book) 'is throughout accurate' and merely in need of supplement as regards affairs of which the author was ignorant. Nuri wrote on the basis of personal experience as extensive and profound as anyone's, not only of the military but also of the political side of the campaign. Unfortunately no reference to his pronouncement is made in the present text, though I understand that there was mention in the Arabic original, in a chapter omitted from the translation. Deference to Nuri's authority may account for the fact that M. has tried to discredit relatively few of the incidents described in the abridgement. In contrast (pp. 275, 276), he distinguishes the pieces of

15. pp. 299, 301.　　　16. p. 251.
17. From long and detailed statements sent by Colonel F. G. Peake (Peake Pasha) to Captain B. H. Liddell Hart and myself, 1963 and 1965.

narrative that were excluded from it, and declares that the reason for excluding them was that they 'were mere fabrications, which, if published, would prompt replies and denials from those familiar with the facts. He [Lawrence] therefore chose to keep them secret until after his death when, he hoped, many of those in a position to deny them would have died as well.' It is, however, common knowledge that copies of *S.P.* were immediately distributed to virtually every British official and officer who had been concerned with the events covered. Apart from Arabs, not all of whom were ignorant of the contents, and two Frenchmen, who else could have been familiar with the facts?

Antonius, an Arab nationalist equally at home in European affairs, dispassionately set forth critical conclusions in 1938 on the field which M. has aspired to cover more extensively. The leaders of the revolt and their British helpers were still living and answered his interrogations; he also interrogated persons, both Arab and British, fully cognizant of the post-war political struggles. His estimate of my brother's part in each sphere is very different from M.'s; almost the only point in which they concur is that Arab views of events were sometimes opposed, in particular as regards the capture of Aqaba. Knowing nothing of the events myself at first-hand, I am none the less entitled to criticize M.'s judgement of T. E. Lawrence's character. The opinions I personally gathered in conversations with Colonels Joyce, Newcombe and Stirling—all of whom have since died—and others of lesser rank who served in Arabia, together with a great body of material published by them, coincide with my own knowledge of the man and contradict Mr. Mousa's portrayal. Since there are now very few survivors of the campaign able to protest, I feel it is my business to do my inadequate best by pointing out some inconsistencies with written evidence on matters of detail. Any reader of the sources can judge for himself whether this book's general assessment is reconcilable with them, upon which the verdict of history must chiefly depend.

With due respect to Mr. A. W. Lawrence and the views he expresses, I wish to state again that I was not intent on minimizing the services rendered to the Arabs by T. E. Lawrence. My main concern was to shed new light on the whole story, by providing an honest and fair representation reflecting my findings on the subject. I do not wish to go into a detailed argument with Mr. Lawrence, but I think it my duty to record the following brief notes on his comments:

1. I am convinced that the journey into Syria did not take place. Antonius must have relied on the accounts published by Lowell Thomas, Graves and Liddell Hart. He is wrong when he gives us to understand that Naseeb left for Jebel Druze early in June 1917 and he differs from T. E. L. when he says that Lawrence and Nassir spent ten days visiting tribal chiefs after Lawrence's return from the supposed journey on 18 June. Had Antonius checked his information with Rikabi or Naseeb, he would have at least avoided describing Rikabi (who was at the time the civilian Mayor of Damascus) as a 'general officer commanding the city'. Leaving all evidence aside, it was impossible for Lawrence to have performed the journey at a time when the Bedouins would have gladly handed him over to the Turks. Nuri al-Sha'alan himself had the previous year handed over four Arab patriots, one of whom was subsequently hanged.

2. My authority for the account of the hasty crossing of the railway on 30 June, is Qasim ibn Eid (see p. 69) and several other Bedouins who participated in those activities.

3. The Arabs did not enter Wadi Musa and Shobek until September 1917, and Tafileh until 15 January 1918.

4. The statement that 'seven hundred men, women and children' were slaughtered at Salt, is far from true. The Turks executed two persons only for co-operating with the British after their raid in April 1918.

5. A detailed analysis of the discrepancies between *S.P.* and *Revolt in the Desert* and of the inconsistencies and errors in *S.P.* itself were not the aim of this book.

6. Mr. Lawrence relies on Antonius far too much. In fact Antonius pointed more than once to the 'errors of fact and interpretation' in *Seven Pillars* and to the 'often incomplete and faulty' knowledge of T. E. L. (pp. 320-324).

S.M.

BIBLIOGRAPHY

ABDULLAH, KING. *Memoirs of King Abdullah of Transjordan,* Edited by Philip Graves, with an introduction by R. J. C. Broadhurst (Jonathan Cape 1950)

ALDINGTON, RICHARD. *Lawrence of Arabia,* A Biographical Enquiry (Collins 1955)

ANTONIUS, GEORGE. *The Arab Awakening* (Hamish Hamilton 1938)

Arab Bulletin (Secret, Issued by the Arab Bureau, Cairo 1916–1919)

ARMITAGE, FLORA. *The Desert and the Stars,* A portrait of T. E. Lawrence (Faber 1956)

BIRDWOOD, LORD. *Nuri as-Said,* A Study in Arab Leadership (Cassell 1959)

BRÉMOND, EDOUARD. *Le Hedjaz dans la Guerre Mondiale* (Paris 1931)

BULLARD, SIR READER. *The Camels Must Go,* An Autobiography (Faber 1961)

ERSKINE, BEATRICE CAROLINE. *King Faisal of Iraq* (Hutchinson 1933)

GEORGE, DAVID LLOYD. *The Truth about the Peace Treaties* (Gollancz 1938)

GRAVES, ROBERT. *Lawrence and the Arabs* (Jonathan Cape 1928)

HART, LIDDELL. *'T. E. Lawrence' in Arabia and After* (Jonathan Cape 1945)

JARVIS, MAJOR C. S. *Arab Command,* The Biography of Lt. Col. F. G. Peake Pasha, C.M.G., C.B.E. (Hutchinson 1946)

KIRKBRIDE, SIR ALEC SEATH. *A Crackle of Thorns* (Murray 1956)

LAWRENCE, A. W. (editor) *T. E. Lawrence by his Friends* (Jonathan Cape 1937)

LAWRENCE, T. E. *Revolt in the Desert* (Jonathan Cape 1927)

— — *Seven Pillars of Wisdom* (Jonathan Cape 1935)

— — *Selected Letters of T. E. Lawrence,* Edited by David Garnett (Jonathan Cape 1938)

— — *Letters of T. E. Lawrence,* Edited by David Garnett (Jonathan Cape 1938)

— — *Oriental Assembly,* Edited by A. W. Lawrence with photographs by the author (Williams & Norgate 1939)

— — *Secret Despatches from Arabia,* Published by permission of the

Foreign Office. Foreword by A. W. Lawrence (Golden Cockerel Press 1939) (Edition limited to 1,000 numbered copies)

—— *T. E. Lawrence to his Biographers, Robert Graves and Liddell Hart* (Cassell 1936)

—— *The Home Letters of T. E. Lawrence and his Brothers*, Edited by M. R. Lawrence (Oxford University Press 1954)

Military Operations, Egypt and Palestine, Vol. 1, 1928, Vol. 2, Parts 1 & 2 (H.M. Stationery Office)

NUTTING, ANTHONY. *Lawrence of Arabia* (Hollis & Carter 1961)

PAYNE, ROBERT. *Lawrence of Arabia* (Pyramid Books, New York 1962)

PHILBY, H. ST. JOHN. *Arabian Days*, An Autobiography (Robert Hale 1948)

—— *Forty Years in the Wilderness* (Robert Hale 1957)

RICHARDS, VYVYAN. *T. E. Lawrence* (Duckworth 1939)

STORRS, SIR RONALD. *Orientations* (Ivor Nicholson & Watson 1939)

THOMAS, LOWELL. *With Lawrence in Arabia* (Hutchinson 1924)

WAVELL, COLONEL A. P. *The Palestine Campaigns*: Campaigns and their Lessons. Edited by Major General Sir Charles Callwell, K.C.B. (Constable 1936)

WEIZMANN, CHAIM. *Trial and Error* (Hamish Hamilton 1950)

ZEINE N. ZEINE, *The Struggle for Arab Independence* (Khayat, Beirut 1960)

ARABIC SOURCES

ABDULLAH IBN AL-HUSSEIN. *Muthakkarati* (My Memoirs) (Jerusalem 1945)

—— *al-'Amali al-Siyasyyah* (Political Dictates) (Amman 1939)

AJLUNI, MOHAMMED ALI. *Thikrayati 'an al-Thawret al-'Arabiyyet al-Kubra* (My Recollections of the Great Arab Revolt) (Amman 1956)

AL-GHUSSEIN, FA'IZ *Muthakkaratı 'an al-Thawret al-'Arabiyyeh* (My Memoirs of the Arab Revolt (1956)

SHAHBENDER, ABDUL RAHMAN. 'Lawrence in the Balance' *Al-Muqtataf* (March–July) (Cairo 1931)

AL-UMARI, MOHAMMED TAHER. *Tarikh Muqaddarat al-'Iraq al-Siyasyyah* (History of the Political Destinies of Iraq) 2 Vols. (Baghdad 1924)

AS-SAID, NURI. *Muhadarat 'an al-Herakat al-'Askariyyeh Lil-Jaysh al'-Arabi fi al-Hijaz wa Suriyya* (Lectures on the Military Operations of the Arab Army in Hejaz and Syria) 1916–18 (1947)

MOUSA, SULEIMAN. *al-Hussein ibn 'Ali wa al-Thawret al-'Arabiyyet al-Kubra* (Hussein bin Ali and the Great Arab Revolt) (Amman 1957)

MOUSA, SULEIMAN AND MADI, MUNIB. *Tarikh al-Urdun fi al-Qarn al'Ishrin* (History of Jordan in the Twentieth Century) (Amman 1957)

Mu'arrokh al-Thawret al-Arabiyyeh (Historian of the Arab Revolt) *Al-Malik Faisal al-Awwal* (King Feisal I) (Beirut n.d.)

Qadri, Ahemed. *Muthakkarati 'an al-Thawret al' Arabiyyet al-Kubra* (My Memoirs of the Great Arab Revolt) (Damascus 1956)

Sa'id, Amin. *Al-Thawret al-'Arabiyyet al-Kubra* (The Great Arab Revolt) 3 Vols. (Cairo 1934)

Wahba, Hafeth, *Jazairet fi al-'Arab al-Qarn al-'Ishrin* (The Arab Peninsula in the Twentieth Century) (Cairo 1935)

INDEX

NOTE:—In general, persons are indexed under their last name. The principal exceptions are members of the Sherifian Royal Family, as Hussein, King; Zeid ibn Hussein, Emir. Alternative spellings, found in quotations from other works, are given in brackets, with cross-references where necessary. The alphabetical order is on the 'word by word' system, ignoring the article *al*.

Abbas Hilmi, Khedive, 13, 106
Abdul Hadi, Awni, 64, 223, 225–30, 241
Abdul Mu'in, Sherif, 120, 122, 124, 126–7, 148, 150
Abdul Rahman, Sheikh, 77
Abdullah, Capt., Effendi, *see* al-Dleimi, Abdullah
Abdullah ibn Hussein, Emir (*later* King), 13, 19, 21, 27–32, 49–50, 55, 57–9, 61; military activity, 16, 22, 46–6, 122, 154, 206–7; *Memoirs*, 22–3 n., 32, 46, 55, 63, 247; TEL on, 29; on TEL, 55–6, 247, 256; strategy, 63, 92; proposed King of Iraq, 214, 238–9; and draft Hejaz Treaty, 243–4; becomes ruler of Transjordan, 239–40, 255–6, 259; war subsidy to, 258
Abu al-Lissan, 86, 95, 121, 125, 147, 167, 173–4, 178–9, 182, 188; battle of, 36, 70, 73, 274
Abu al-Na'am, 46, 56–7, 122
Abu Skour, Deifalla, 53, 85
Abu Suleiman, Sa'ad al-Din, *see* Ali, Sa'ad al-Din
Abu Tageiga, 53
Abu Tayeh (Tawaiha) (clan), 66, 96, 103, 126, 164
Abu Tayeh, Auda, 51, 74–6, 107–8, 162, 164, 175; joins revolt, 64–5; in the Aqaba campaign, 66–71, 78–9, 272; correspondence with Turks, 85–9; at Gueira, 95–7, 121; at Tafileh, 127–9; in final campaign, 198–9, 201–2; in Damascus, 210–11; his loan to Emir Abdullah, 259
Abu Tayeh, Mohammed, 74
Aden, 241

Adhoub, *see* al-Zebn
Afghanistan, 252
Ageyl, 20, 25, 68, 86, 160; deserters from Turks, 47; demolitions by, 73–4, 130, 169; at Tafileh, 141; at Damascus, 259
Aid, Sherif, 98
Aima, 134, 136, 138–9, 141
Ain al-Barrida, 72
Aircraft, Arab demands for, 23–4, 28, 31–2; British—in Hejaz, 40 n., 49, 58; Turkish air raids, 87, 95, 121, 193–5; British—at Quntilla, 95; British air support, 145, 164, 171–3, 176, 197; German, 171
al-Ajluni, Gen. Mohammed Ali, cited, 129, 131, 142, 144, 155
al-Akle, Miss Fareedah, 5
Ala, 27, 38
Alayan, Sheikh Salem, 99
Aleppo, 66 n., 73, 153, 206, 232
Alexandretta, 12, 14–15, 221, 266
Algerian troops with Brémond, 18
Ali Aziz, *see* al-Misri, Ali Aziz
Ali ibn Hussein, Emir, 15; military activity in Hejaz, 20, 22–3, 25–6, 43–5, 58–9, 92; TEL visits at Rabegh, 30, 32–4; and surrender of Medina, 206–7; his war subsidy, 258
Ali, Sa'ad al-Din (Abu Suleiman), 72, 75
Ali, Gen. Sayyid, 16
Ali, Tahsin, 188
All Souls College, 235
Allenby, Gen., first meeting with TEL, 79–82; command of Feisal's army, 83–4; and Yarmuk raid, 100–3, 118; capture of Jerusalem, 119; advance on Jericho, 126, 144, 159; plans for

final offensive, 153, 185–6; grant of political funds to TEL, 153, 260–1; requests attack on Ma'an, 155; 2,000 camels for Feisal, 168, 187; reassures Feisal, 172; requests King Hussein for reinforcements, 177–8; warns Feisal on Damascus, 179–80; decorates al-Askari, 182–3; final offensive, 193–5; in Damascus, 205, 213, 215; advance on Aleppo, 205–6; grants TEL leave, 213; supports Arab presence at Peace Conference, 216; meets Feisal in London, 232

Allenby, Lady, 98

Amman, 156, 176–7, 182; British plans to attack, 152–3, 155, 159–61, 165–7, 194; TEL's visit in disguise, 160–1, 276–7; Turkish strength at, 185; isolated by railway demolitions, 189; Turkish retreat from, 195, 204; Emir Abdullah at, 240; TEL at, 243–4

Aneyza station, see Uneiza

Aneza tribe, 72, 206

Aqaba (see also Aqaba campaign, Aqaba Station), 7, 19; British landing at, 67; supplies for, 79–80; consolidation, 83–5; Turkish plans for counter-action, 85–9, 121; TEL at 119, 129–30, 152–3, 159, 166, 177–9; Feisal at, 121; his headquarters moved from, 125

Aqaba campaign, origins of, 45, 51–3, 66; Abu Tayeh's role, 65–6; TEL's role, 65, 67–8; leadership, 68; execution, 68–72, 89

Aqaba Station, 165

Arab administration: in Dera'a, 200; in Damascus, 202, 204–5, 209–12; in Beirut, 204–5, 209

Arab Army, see Army, Arab

Arab Bulletin, 10, 41, 122, 154–5, 166, 171–2, 174, 176, 183, 234; compared with Seven Pillars, 54, 64–5, 74, 96–100; 117, 202–3; cited: on Aqaba campaign, 68, 72–4; on secret Syrian journey, 72; on Abu Tayeh, 86–7, 89; 'How to treat the Arabs', 90–1; on Yarmuk raid, 103–5; on TEL's bodyguard, 132; on battle of Tafileh, 140–2; on King Hussein, 246, 258–9

Arab Bureau, 9–10, 18

Arab casualties, see Casualties, Arab

Arab deserters, from Turkish forces, 114, 122, 134 n.

Arab Revolt, outbreak of, 14–16; British attitudes to, 17–18, 262; the critical stage, 23–4; TEL's confidence in, 28; French attitude to, 44–5; TEL on strategy for, 56, 62;

TEL's role in, 75, 78–9, 81; Arab record of—lost, 79; contribution to Palestine campaign, 101–2, 153, 166–7, 186–7, 258–9, 261–2; cost of—to Britain, 257–8

Arab unity, TEL and, 214–15; Feisal's call for, 225

Archaeology, 2–5

Areid, Sherif Ali ibn, 67 n., 120

Armenians, 114, 117, 191

Armoured cars, 58, 83, 129–30

Army, Arab (see also Ageyl), 16–18, 20–1; arms supply for, 16–17, 24, 35, 40 n., 52; organization of, 58; achievements of—belittled by foreign writers, 61; Feisal's section under Allenby's command, 83–5; weakness of southern sections, 92; command, 120; dispositions in Aqaba sector, 121, 123; strength of Feisal's section Jan. 1918, 146; Sept. 1918, 186; officers' suspicions of British, 154; strength in battle of Ma'an, 162; call for recruits, 172; transfer of units from southern sectors refused, 177–8; arrears of pay, 258

al-Asali (Aseli), Lutfi, 98–9, 141

al-Asbali, Mohammed, 148 and n., 273

Asir, 16

al-Askari, Ja'afar, 9, 120, 121, 123, 154, 162, 180, 188, 194; volunteers for Arab army, 18, 60; action in Hejaz, 60–1; moves to Aqaba sector, 95; at Tafileh, 128, 132, 150; decorated by Allenby, 182–3

Atef Bey, 59

al-Atrash, Hussein, 69, 72–3

al-Atrash, Hasan, 69 n.

al-Atrash, Salim, 69 n.

al-Atrash, Sultan, 69 and n., 211

Atwi (Tway) station, 69, 72–3

Auda abu Tayeh, see Abu Tayeh, Auda

al-Auran, Dhiab (Diab), 85, 128–9, 135, 142, 149, 158

al-Awar, Motlog, 146, 147, 149

Ayesha, see Jellal al-Leil

al-Ayyubi, Ali Jawdat, 188, 206

al-Ayyubi, Gen. Shukri, 205, 209–12

Azraq, 72, 100, 103, 106–8, 115, 117, 176–7; a front line base, 114, 187, 189, 194–7

Baalbek, 72–5, 192, 276–7

Bair, 68–70, 72–6, 103, 108, 113 n., 118, 176–7, 182, 188, 276

Baldwin, Stanley, 252

Balfour Declaration, 154, 221, 229, 234; TEL's views on, 214; Emir Abdullah's protest, 241, 244

Balqa, 75, 113, 167
Barrow, Gen., 194, 200–1, 203
Basra, 10; King Hussein's claim to, 259
Basri Pasha, 59
Batn al-Ghul, 87, 165
Beach, Col., 10
Beersheba, 7, 100, 118–19, 148, 152–3, 159, 177; area, 122, 144
Behjat Pasha, 95 n.
Behjet Bey, Brig. Gen., 209
Beidawi, Abdul Kerim, 43
Beidawi, Sherif Muhammad Ali, 54, 131, 145
Beirut, 4, 204–5, 209, 214
al-Bekri, Naseeb, 66 and n., 67–9, 72, 78, 179, 188, 197; cited 66–7, 74, 75–6
Bell, Gertrude, 8, 90, 235, 238, 247, 272 n.
Beni Atiyeh, 51–2, 96, 122–3, 131, 145, 172
Beni Hassan, 72, 75, 196
Beni Sakhr (Sukhur), 64, 76, 103–4, 108–14, 125–7, 156, 160, 165–7, 169, 276
Bertrand, M., 218
Besta, 124, 125, 147
Billi, 49, 52, 130
Bir Abbas, 26, 38, 58
Bir Derwish (Darwish), 23, 26, 38, 58–9, 207
Bir Hirmas, 122
Bir (al-) Mashi, 20, 26, 58–9, 207
Bir Said, 23, 25, 37, 42, 44, 49
Bir (al-) Shedia, 103, 119, 165
Bosra, 197
Brémond, Col. E., 18, 28–9, 44, 106; relations with TEL, 40, 219–20; cited, 45, 61, 66 n., 123, 125, 157–8, 218, 224; fabrications 158, 219
Britain, and British: guarantee to Sherif Hussein, 13; attitudes to Arab Revolt, 17–18; troops for Hejaz, 23, 27–8, 32, 39, 49; supply of arms to Arabs, see under Army, Arab; Military Mission in Hejaz, 47; at Aqaba, 121, 145, 164; troops attack Mudawwara, 175–7; Anglo-French territorial settlement, 233; evacuation of Syria and Lebanon, 233; military strength in Iraq 1921, 236; offer of Treaty to King Hussein, 241–3; see also Balfour Declaration, Peace Conference, Royal Navy, subsidies, Sykes-Picot Agreement
Brook, Mrs., 230
Bullard, Sir Reader, 237–8
Burga, 72
Bursa, 107
Burton, Percy, 264

Buwat Station, 25, 37, 122
Buxton, Major, 175–7, 179, 182

Cairo, see Arab Bureau
Cairo Conference, 238, 253–5, 270
Camel Corps, Arab, 173; British, 153–4, 168, 175–7, 178, 182; Egyptian, 164, 169, 170, 187
Camels, Allenby's gift to Feisal, 168, 187
Campbell Thompson, R., 5
Carchemish (Jerablus), 5–6, 7, 12, 77
Casualties, Arab: at Munifa, 104, 112; at Wadi Musa, 124; at Tafileh, 143; at Ma'an, 163; at Jerdun, 170, 174; at Haret al-Amarch, 172; total in campaign, 260; Turkish: in Aqaba campaign, 70–1; at Mudowwara, 97, 176; in Tebuk sector, 123; at Wadi Musa, 124; at Jurf al-Darawish, 127; at Tafileh, 138; in Damascus campaign, 203; totals, 186–7, 261–2
Cecil, Lord, 261
Chapman, Sir Thomas, 1
Chase, Mr., 265
Chauvel, Gen., 194
Chaytor, Maj. Gen., 186, 194, 208
Churchill, Winston, 237–41, 243, 248–53, 255
Clayton, Gen. G., 8, 10–11, 28, 32, 40–1, 53, 65, 72, 79–80, 82–3, 119, 152, 201
Clemenceau, Georges, 220, 224, 226–7, 233
Colonial Office, TEL at, 237, 241, 251
Committee of Union and Progress (Turkish), 13, 14
Cornwallis, Col., 19, 33, 237
Cox, Sir Percy, 238
Curon, Lord, 3, 224, 235, 236, 244, 247, 253

Dahoum, Ahmed, 6, 7
Damascus, 4, 7, 72, 75, 77; the Arab goal, 34–5, 44, 63, 168; Arab entry into, 180, 194–5 202; TEL at, 203–4, 209; Arab administration in, 204–5, 209–12; King-Crane Commission at, 232; French occupation of, 234
Dar al-Hamra, 60
Darawsheh clan, 70, 96, 99, 100, 169
Davenport, 39
Dawnay, Alan, Col., 146, 155, 162, 164, 175, 177–9
Dead Sea, 126, 144, 150, 153, 159
Deeds, Wyndham, 241, 250
Delagha, 71, 95, 121, 123
Dera'a, 101–2, 168, 178, 187–96; the legend of, 115–18, 276–7; Turkish withdrawal, 198; capture of, 200

Dghaithir, Nassir ibn, 68
Dhaba, 51, 53–4, 74–5
Dhami, Sheikh, 72
Dhat al-Haj, 122
al-Dheilan, Mohammed, 70, 87, 100, 165, 179
Dhiab al-Auran, see al-Auran, Dhiab
Dhiabat clan, 70
Dhumaniyeh, see Dumaniyeh
al-Dhuweibi, Nahis, 55
Disa'ad station, 68
Dixon, Alec, 256
al-Dleimi, Capt. Abdullah (Abdullah Effendi), 135–6, 140–3
Doughty, C. M., 2 n., 3, 241
Drubi, Major Zaki, 68–9, 75
Druze, Jebel, 67, 69 and n., 74–5, 100–2, 106, 109, 114, 118, 196–7, 276
Druzes, 69, 73, 102, 202, 205
Dumaniyeh (Dhumaniyeh) clan, 70, 96, 99, 138

Egypt and Egyptian: Survey Dept., 9; Units with Arab Army, 16, 26, 39, 42–3, 47, 95, 164, 169–70, 187
Eid, Qasim ibn, 69 and n., 74
Erskine, Mrs. Steuart, 256
Erzerum, 11
Eshref Bey, 22, 273

Fahad al-Zebn, see al-Zebn, Fahad
Faiz clan, 76 n.
al-Faiz, Fawaz, 72–3, 76, 276
al-Faiz, Mithqal, 76
al-Faiz, Nawaf, 76
Fakhri, Brig. Hamid, 132–3, 137–8, 140, 144
Fakhri Pasha, 15, 20, 22, 25–7, 35, 43–5, 50, 53, 59, 92–5, 101, 207, 262
Falkenhausen, von, 158
Falkenhayn, Marshal von, 95
Faraun Island, 7
Fareifra, 170, 171, 175
Faris, 115, 116, 118
Farraj, 100, 160, 274
Faruki, 19, 24, 31
Fassua', 154 and n.
al-Fawaz, Sayyid Nassir, cited 118, 199 n.
Feisal ibn Hussein, Emir (later King), escape from Damascus, 15; activities in Hejaz, 20–7, 37–8, 42–4, 47–9, 52–3, 58; TEL's first visit to, 30, 33–7; relations with TEL, 35–6, 54, 101, 120, 153, 212, 219, 223, 226–8, 230–1, 235, 256; TEL on, 41, 179; capture of Wejh, 49–52; subsidies to, 64, 258; the Aqaba campaign, 66–9, 72; moves to Aqaba, 83–4, 95; attacks Mudowwara,

145; arrests Tafileh tribesmen, 158; attacks Ma'an, 162–4; gets 2000 camels from Allenby, 168; plea to Allenby, 172; seeks reinforcements from southern armies, 177–8; correspondence with Turks, 180–2; offers resignation, 183; command of Dera'a campaign, 188, 195–6, 201; manifesto to Syrians, 188; enters Damascus, 205; sets up govt. in Damascus, 211; TEL recommends as ruler of Syria, 214; TEL recommends for Peace Conference, 216; French coolness towards, 217–19; in England, 219–20, 232–3, 235–6; at Peace Conference, 222–6; alleged agreement with Zionists, 228–9; negotiations with France, 231, 233; return to Syria, 231; King of Syria, 234; King of Iraq, 237–8, 239; loyalty to Britain, 267; death, 228
Fejeij, 169, 170
Fetat secret society, 66 n., 76, 200 n.
Foch, Marshal, 56
Foreign Office, TEL's connexions with, 214, 217, 222
France, Anatole, 233 n.
France, and French: TEL'S early visits to, 1, 2; opposes Alexandretta landing, 12, 15; military mission, 18, 40, 57, 95, 131, 145, 157; TEL's antipathy to, 40, 213, 254, 265–6; policies towards Arabs, 44, 45; Feisal's distrust of, 68; decoration for TEL, 218; units with Arabs, 162–5, 169, 171, 187, 194, 206; TEL on French claims in Syria, 214; opposition to Arabs at Peace Conference, 215, 217–18, 223, 225–6; distrust of TEL, 218; attitude on Palestine, 231; Anglo-French territorial agreement, 232–3; Arab rising in Syria against, 233; military strength in Syria, 236; precautions against Emir Abdullah, 239; occupation of Damascus, 234, 259; see also Brémond, Clemenceau, Pisani, Sykes-Picot Agreement
Frankfurter, Felix, 229
Fuweila, 68, 70, 73, 86–7, 95, 121

al-Gabbon (Qabun), 72, 77
Garland, Capt., 41, 43, 57, 59, 65
German, military mission, 15; units with Turks, 156–7, 171, 198, 202
Ghabrit, Qaddour ibn, 18
Ghadir al-Abyadh, 109, 113
Ghadir al-Haj, 70, 87, 122, 162, 165, 192
Ghair, 25, 49

Ghalib Pasha, 16
Ghanamat tribe, 166
Ghor al-Mazra'a, *see* Mazra'a
Ghor al-Safi, 149
Ghoraniyeh, 159
Ghrandal, 121, 123
al-Ghussein, Faiz, 32, 52, 180, 217, 228;
    cited, 21, 22 n., 41 n., 49, 53 n., 74,
    118, 210, 273
Ghuta, 72
Gibla (Hejaz gazette), 182
Glubb, Gen., 261–2, 268, 272 n.
Gouraud, Gen., 218, 233
Gout, Jean, 218, 223, 225
Graves, Robert, 3, 77–8, 132, 237, 243,
    247, 266, 275, 277
Greece, TEL visits, 9
Gueira (Guweira), capture of, 71;
    abu Tayeh's headquarters, 87, 95,
    121; Feisal's Headquarters, 125, 146,
    153

Haddad Pasha, Gen., 235, 236, 241,
    244
Hadiyya station, 46, 56, 57
Hadley, H. R. 272
Hail, 21
Haifa, 101
al-Halabi, Tawfiq, 9
al-Halabi, Capt. Zeki, 128, 129
Haldein, Gen., 238
Hama, 206
Hamed the Moor, 274
Hammoudi, 6
Hamzeh, Sherif Abdullah ibn, 96, 122,
    144
Harb tribe, 25
al-Hareidhin, Talal, *see* al-Hreidhin
Haret al-Amareh (Ammar) 96–7, 119,
    172, 276
al-Harith, Sherif Fauzan, 22 and n., 57
al-Harith, Nasir, 97, 98
al-Harithi, Sherif Abdullah ibn
    Thawab, 22
al-Harithi, Sherif Ali ibn al-Hussein,
    54, 100, 103–10, 112–15, 117–18, 123,
    131
Hart, Liddell, 11, 89, 178, 234, 238,
    247, 268
Hashem, Sherif, 99, 145
Hauran, 101–2, 114, 118, 197–9, 239
Hazzaa, Sherif, 145, 164
Hebron, 119, 159
Heidar, Ali, Sherif, 25, 56
Heidar, Rustom, 217, 224, 225
Hejaya tribe, 156, 166
Hejaz: TEL recommends
    independence, 214; draft British
    treaty with 241–5
Henakiyeh, 21, 22, 43, 45, 46, 59

Herbert, Aubrey, 8, 10
Hesa (Hasa) station, 125, 140, 156, 158,
    170, 188, *see also* Wadi Hesa
Hezm station, 123
Higris (Hejris), 42, 168
Himma bridge (Jisr el-Hemmi), 103,
    106–7, 109
Hisheh (Hisha), 73, 122, 127
Hogarth, D. G., 3–5, 8, 10–12, 16, 19,
    65, 226, 229, 235, 246, 259, 266, 271
Holdich, Col., 10
Homs, 206
Hornby, Major, 57, 65, 169, 177, 188
al-Hreidin (Hareidhin) Talal, 101–3,
    115–16, 117–18, 191, 196, 198–9 n.
Huleh, Lake, 73
al-Hussein al-Harithi, Ali ibn, *see*
    al-Harithi
Hussein, King (Sherif), 8, 12; early
    loyalty to Turks, 13–14; McMahon
    letters, 14; declares Arab Revolt,
    15–16; requests British aid, 23, 31, 40,
    64; refuses separate peace offers, 24,
    180–1; his leadership, 31–2, 44, 78,
    183; TEL on, 38, 246–8; transfer of
    Feisal's army to Allenby, 83–5;
    attitude to TEL, 84, 256; welcome to
    Abdul Kader al-Jezairi, 106–7; anger
    at British pretensions, 182–3; TEL's
    grudge against, 183, 243, 248; head
    of Arab govt. in Syria, 209; reliance
    on Britain before Peace Conference,
    215–17; French message to, 217–18;
    condemns Versailles Treaty, 235;
    contributes to Iraq revolution, 239,
    259; nominates Feisal ruler of Iraq,
    239; declines British treaty, 241–6;
    meetings with TEL, 242–4; the
    British subsidies, 243, 258–9; his
    obstinacy, 242, 247; disillusion with
    Britain, 245–6; view on Jewish
    immigration, 246; Emir Abdullah's
    loyalty to, 247; defeat and exile, 248,
    259
Huweitat, 51, 53, 64, 68, 85, 108, 126,
    138, 169, 172, 176, *see also* Abu
    Tayeh, Auda; Darawsheh;
    Dumaniyeh; Jazi; Togatga; Zelebani;
    Zuweida

Ibn Dakhil, 20
Ibn Dughmi, 53
Ibn Jad, 87
Ibn Jazi, *see* Jazi
Ibn Luayy, 55
Ibn Muhanna, 54
Ibn Rasheed, Emir, 21
Ibn Sa'ud, King, 52, 243, 246, 250
Ibn Za'al, 53
Imran, 64, 145

India, TEL in, 252
Indian unit with Arab army, 103–4, 107, 109, 111, 114, 118, 200–2
Intelligence Branch, Cairo, 8, 9, 39
Iraq: TEL's visit, 10; partition under Sykes-Picot Agreement, 221; draft Mandate for, 235; rebellion 1920, 236, 237, 239, 259; independence proposed, 237; see also Feisal, King
Irbid, 103, 106
Isa tribe, 166
Isawiya, 68
Isham, Ralph H., 274
Ismailia, 79

Jabir station, 189, 194
Jarvis, Major, cited 261
Jauf, 52, 64
(ibn) Jazi clan, 73, 126–7, 136, 139, 141–3, 149, 156
Jazi, Hamad ibn, 65, 126, 128, 142, 143
al-Jazi, Metaab, 143
Jebail, 5
Jebel Druze, see Druze, Jebel
Jebel Mani', 202
Jebel al-Musalla, 156
Jebel Semna, 162, see also Semna
Jedda, 16–18, 28, 38, 46, 178, 241
Jefer, 70, 73, 103, 107–8, 118, 128, 176, 179, 182, 188
Jeida, 58, 61, 83, 95
Jellal al-Leil, Ayesha, 98, 276
Jemal Pasha, Ahmed (the Butcher), 14–15, 60, 106, 180–2, 209
Jemal Pasha, Mehmed, 59, 85–6, 95, 112, 114, 124, 157, 181 and n.
Jemal Pasha, the lesser, 59, 181 and n., 185, 209–10
Jerablus, see Carchemish
Jerdun, 162, 165, 169, 171–3, 203; Arab defeats at, 170, 173–4, 179
Jericho, 126, 144, 149, 158–9, 166, 208
Jerusalem, 80, 101, 119, 126, 166, 240–1, 264
Jesus College, 3
Jewad Pasha, 185
Jews, and Jewish, see under Zionism
al-Jezairi, Abdul Kader, 106–9, 204, 210, 212
al-Jazairi, Mohammed Said, Emir, 107, 180, 182, 204, 209, 210–12
Jordan, river and valley, 149, 153, 159, 161, 166, 194
Joyce, Col., 39, 42, 171, 179; at Wejh, 58; at Aqaba, 95, 121, 123; raid on Tell al-Shahm 129–30; on Mudowwara, 145; suspected by Arab officers, 154; on Jerdun defeat, 174; opposed to use of British troops, 175; in final campaign, 188–9, 191, 194

Juheina, 22, 25, 37, 42–3, 57
Jurf al-Darawish, 126–7, 156–8, 170–1
Juwabra tribe, 169

Kaabar al-Abid, 147
al-Kadi, Dakhil Allah, 57
Kaf, 72, 74, 75
Karachi, 252
Kasim, 47
Kawakiba Aneza, 72
Kemal, Mustapha, 182, 185, 199, 206
Kennington, Eric, 249
Kerak, 64, 73, 77, 86, 126, 132–3, 138, 142, 146, 156, 159
Kethara, 71
Khadra, 71
al-Khadra, Subhi, cited 123
Khalil Pasha, 10
al-Khatib, Faud, 242
Kheiri Bey, 15, 16, 20, 37
Khirbet Nokheh, 136, 137, 143
Khirbet al-Tuwaneh, 156
al-Khouri, Faris, cited 211
al-Khreisheh, Rafe', 76
King-Crane Commission, 225–6, 231–2, 234
Kirkbride, Sir Alec, 148–9, 150–1, 188, 200
Kirkuk, 221
Kiswe, 201
Kitchener, Lord, 6, 7, 12, 13
Kreishan, Hussein, 85
Kseir al-Hallabat, 103, 104
Kuneitra, 194
Kura, 250
Kut al-Amara, 10
Kutrani, 72 n., 170, 173

Lange, H. 226
Lawrence, A. W., 256
Lawrence, T. E.:
    Biographical:
        birth and upbringing, 1–3; archaeology, 3–6; service in Royal Artillery, 3; visit to Syria, 3–5; degree at Oxford, 5; survey in Sinai, 6–8; in War Office, 8; promoted Captain, 8; in Intelligence Branch, Cairo, 8–9, 10, 27; mission to Iraq, 10; in Arab Bureau, 11; first visit to Jedda, 28–30; meets Feisal, 34–7; posted to Hejaz, 40–1; capture of Wejh, 51–2; visit to Emir Abdullah, 54–8; first railway demolition, 57; and the Aqaba campaign, 65–72; the Abu al-Lissan battle, 70; secret visit to Syria, 72–3, 74, 75, 77–8; meets Allenby, 79–82; promoted Major, 82; Colonel, 142, 154; decorations,

Lawrence, T. E. *cont.*:
 C. B., 82, *Croix de Guerre*, 218; D.S.O., 142, 144, 154, 241; meets King Hussein, 83–4; raids on railway, 96–100; Yarmuk raid, 103–10, 113; the Munifa (Minifir) train, 110–12, 114; the legend of Dera'a, 115–18; movements July–Dec. 1917, 119; his bodyguard, 131–2; battle of Tafileh, 135–44; winter journey, 146–8; allotment of political funds to, 150, 153–4, 257, 260–1; offers to leave Arab revolt, 150–2; attack on Ma'an, 163; obtains camels for Feisal, 168; abortive mission to King Hussein, 177–8; in final campaign, 188–92, 194–7, 200–2; his record of railway demolitions, 192; at Tafas, 199, 203; at Damascus, 203–4, 205, 209–12; to Cairo and England, 213–14; preparations for Peace Conference, 216–17; expelled from France, 218; with Feisal in England, 220; at Peace Conference, 224–8; air crashes, 234, 272; achieves fame, 234–5, 263–5; Fellow of All Souls, 235; in Colonial Office, 237–8; at Cairo Conference, 238, 255; missions to Emir Abdullah, 240–1, 243–4, 247–51; mission to King Hussein, 241–8, 256; leaves Colonial Office, 251; in R.A.F., 251–2; changes of name: Ross, Shaw, 251; in Tank Corps, 251–2; in India, 252; death 252
 Character: 2, 64, 270–5; ambition, 272; celibacy, 274–5; conceit, 34, 54, 56, 103, 263; endurance, 3, 4, 5, 105, 118, 148, 271–2; hate of soldiering, 40; luck, 12, 64; mendacity, instances of, 7, 11–12, 46, 72, 89, 98, 160–1, 181–2, 192, 212, 265, 276–8; the Syrian journey, 74–8; the Dera'a legend, 116–18; the battle of Tafileh, 142–4; visit to Mecca, 272–3; remorse, 274, 278; sadism, 274
 Disguises, 36, 57, 160–1, 273, 276–7
 Dress, Arab, 6, 41–2, 90–1, 139, 218, 220, 222, 225, 263
 Languages, proficiency in, 3; Arabic, 3, 5–6, 29, 139, 224, 227, 268; French, 3, 223
 Opinions of Arabs on TEL: Emir Abdullah, 55–6; al-Ajluni, 142; al-Asbali, 273; al-Bekri, 75–6; Feisal, 256; al-Jezairi, Abdul Kader, 107; as-Said, 33; Shagrani, 61;

 Shahbender, 9, 64; al-Sheibani, 148
 Relations: with Arabs, 4–6, 89–90, 200 nn., 252–6; with colleagues, 10, 27–8, 47 n., 49 n., 165, 196–7, 238; with Emir Abdullah, 240, 247; with Feisal, 101, 183–4, 213–14, 219, 223–4, 226–8, 230–1, 273; with the French, 40, 213, 218, 254, 266; with King Hussein, 84, 183, 243, 246–7
 Role in Arab Revolt, 43, 65, 78–9, 81, 119–20, 138–40, 178–9, 203, 262–3
 Views on Arabs, 6, 90–91, 253–4, 266–8
 Zionist leanings, 226–7, 229, 230, 241, 255–6, 268–70
Leachman, Col., 65, 66
League of Nations, 235
Leith, 16
Lejah, 72, 73, 75, 276
Lloyd, George (Lord Lloyd), 8, 45, 66, 103, 107, 108
Lloyd George, 220, 223–4, 232–5, 238
London Conference, 1921, 235–6

Maadi prison camp, 18
Ma'an, 7, 73; Turkish strength at, 50, 165, 185, 186; Turkish command, 59, 95 and n.; railway demolitions near, 84, 96, 99, 169–71, 173; Arab plans to attack, 101, 152–5, 157, 159, 161; loyal to Turks, 102, 163 n.; Arab threat to, 129, 172, 188; attack on, 162–3, 179; Turkish retreat from, 195, 204; Emir Abdullah's arrival, 239
McMahon correspondence, 14, 31, 215, 246, 248
McMahon, Sir Henry, 12, 14, 18, 39, 226, 253, 259
Madaba, 160
Maden, Sarah, 1–2
al-Madfai, Jemil, 188, 195
al-Madfai, Col. Rashid, 95, 123, 174
Madraj station, 57
Mafraq (Mafrak), 72, 109, 189, 195, 196
Magdalen College, 5
Mahamid tribe, 45
Mahtab station, 123
al-Majali, Qader, 77
Mandates, *see under* Syria, Palestine, Iraq
Mansur, Muhsin, Sherif, 16
Maronites, 73
Marshall, Dr., 150
Masmieh, 201
Mastur, Sherif, 53–4, 120, 127–9, 132–3, 141
Matawala, 73
Maulud, *see* Mukhlis
Maynard, Major, 145
Mazra'a, 144, 146, 166

Mbeirik, Hussein ibn, 20, 22
Mecca: Arab capture of, 16; Turkish threat to, 21, 23, 26–7, 40, 50; loss of Arab records at, 79; King Hussein's refuge from TEL, 178; TEL's supposed visit, 272–3
Medain Saleh, 60, 207
Medina, 15; Turkish strength at, 16, 50, 186, 261–2; Arab attacks on, 19–20, 32, 37, 49, 58–9; seige of, 21–6, 38, 44–6, 59–63, 92–5, 206–7; massacre at, 35; Turkish dispositions, 50, 51–2; Turkish withdrawal proposed, 53, 84, 92–5, 262; rail reserves at, 164 n.; railway closed, 165, 169; surrender of, 207
Meinertzhagen, Col., 237
Mejezz, 20, 23, 25, 49, 59
Menain tribe, 156, 169
Merzuk (Mirzuk), see al-Tekheimi
Meyer (German officer), 157
Mheisin clan, 128, 142–3, 158
Middle East Department, 237, 241
Mifleh, see al-Zebn
Military Operations in Egypt and Palestine, 186
Miranshah, 252
Mjrri, Sheikh, 148
al-Misri, Aziz Ali, 20–4, 28–9, 32–3, 85
al-Moayyad, Badri, 98
al Moayyad, Faiz, 98–9 n.
Moroccan, troops with Brémond, 18
Mosul, 220, 221, 233, 234
Matalga (Motalga), 139, 141
Motleg (Mutlaq), Za'al ibn, 69–70, 87, 96–8, 107–8, 276
Mreigha, 70, 125, 129
Muadhdham station, 27, 51, 54, 59
Muaggar, 176, 182
Mudowwara, 96–7, 129, 131, 164, 165, 166, 169; Arab attack on, 145–6; British troops destroy, 175–6, 178, 182, 207
Muhyi al-Din Bey, Hajem, 118
Mukhis, Maulud, 22, 35–6, 41, 60–1, 96, 120, 123–5, 129, 159; praised by TEL, 147; arrested and reinstated, 154–5; wounded, 162
Munifa (Minifir), 70, 73–4, 103–4, 111–14
Murray, Gen. Sir Archibald, 17, 30, 39, 52, 102
Muslimmieh, 66 n., 206
Muweileh, 51, 53
Muzeirib (Mezerib), 115, 117, 190, 191, 198

Nablus, 157, 171, 185, 193
al-Nahabi, Abdullah, 131
Nahi bey, 116–17
Naimat tribe, 169

Nakhl Mubarak, 41, 42
Namek, Capt. Ismail, 135
Namier, Sir Lewis, 255, 270.
Naqab Ashtar (el-Star), 71, 87
Nassir (Nasir), Sherif: military activity in Hejaz, 44, 49, 54, 60; TEL's praise, 66 n., 202; in Aqaba campaign, 66–9, 71–6, 78, 80, 87–8, 113, 121; attacks on railway, 126–7, 169–70, 173, 175, 177; capture of Tafileh, 128; at Tafileh, 132, 149–50, 157; at Wadi Hesa, 172, 178; in final campaign, 188, 190–1, 195–8, 200, 201, 206; at Damascus, 202, 209–11
Nazareth, 185
Nebk, 69, 72, 74–6, 78
Negev, 221
Nejd, 47
Newcombe, Col. S. F., 6, 8, 47, 53, 57, 60, 65–6, 105, 119; relations with TEL, 49 n.
Niazi Bey, 70
Nicholas, Duke, 11
Nisib, 116, 117, 189, 191–2
Numan, Dr. Thabet, 233
Nuri as-Said, see as-Said, Nuri
Nutting, Anthony, 213–14, 219
Nuweimeh, 197

Odeh, Rev. N., 3
Odroh, 146, 147, 169
Odyssey, TEL's translation, 252
Oil, Iraq, 221, 222, 234
Ottoman, see Turkey, and Turkish
Oxford, 1, 3, 5

Palestine: the Arab catastrophe, 215, 254; British demand for control of, 220–1; in Sykes-Picot agreement, 221; the Mandate, 234; proposed Arab Agency for, 238; King Hussein demands independence for, 242;
— Arabs influence Hussein, 244, 246; see also Balfour Declaration, Zionism
— campaign: plans for, 101–3, 152–3, 178, 187; Arab contribution to, 155–6, 208; British divisions withdrawn, 167; the opposing forces, 185–6; the final battle, 193, 194
Palmyra (Tudmor), 72, 74, 75, 276, 277
Paris, see Peace Conference
Parker, Col., 32
Partition of Arab homeland, 215, 254
Peace conference: 222–8; Arab representation at, 215–16; British and French ambitions, 221–2
Peake, Col., 164, 169, 171, 177, 187–90 n., 213, 258, 261 cited, 249–50
Petra, 7, 96, 124, 132

Philby, St. John, cited 244, 245, 248, 250–1, 268, 272
Pichon, M., 231
Picot, Georges, 66, 218, 232; *see also* Sykes-Picot Agreement
Pisani, Capt., 95, 98, 99, 131, 163, 187
Plebiscite, agreed for Arabs, 224
Port Sudan, 16, 38–9
Prisoner of War Camps, volunteers from, 17, 18, 60, 172, 207

Qabun (el Gabbon), 72, 77
Qadri, Dr. Ahmed, 180, 200, 217; cited, 138 n., 181, 210, 220
Qadri, Tahsin, 217
Qasr Amrah, 108
Quntilla, 95, 96
Qusus, Auda, 86 and n.

Rabegh, 16, 25, 32–3, 44, 45, 47, 58; supply base, 20–1; request for British force at, 23, 27, 39
Rafadeh, Suleiman ibn, 52, 130
Raglan, Lord, 273
Raheil, 118
Rahu, Capt., 57
Railway: demolitions Maan to Medina, 19, 20, 22, 41, 55–9, 96–100, 122–3, 129–31; demolitions north of Maan, 69, 72–4, 110–12, 127, 169–71, 173–4, 177; Turkish defence of, 50, 52; the Yarmuk bridge, 103–5, 113–14; reserves of rails, 164 n.; Medina line closed, 165, 169, 207; demolitions in Dera'a sector, 187–94, 197; TEL's demolition claims, 192
Raji, Kassem, 126 n.
Rameid, 146–8
Ramle (Palestine), 180
Ramleh station, 164–5
Ras Baalbek, *see* Baalbeck
Rashadieh, 146, 157
Rasim, *see* Sardast
Ramtha, 106, 110, 191, 198, 200
Revolt in the Desert, Arabic translation, 33; suppressions in 275–7
Richards, V. W., 271, 273
al-Rikabi, Akram, 77, 212
al-Rikabi, Ali Rida, 12, 72, 77 and n., 204, 210
Rome, TEL at, 234
Ross, Major, 40 n., 58
Ross (TEL), 251
Royal Air Force, TEL in, 251–2, 278
Royal Artillery, TEL enlists in, 3
Royal Navy, in Red Sea, 17, 25, 38, 43–4, 47, 49, 67, 72, 79, 83, 87; *see also* Wemyss, Admiral
Rujom Keraka, 134, 136, 143
Rumm (Rum), 96, 98–9, 103, 118, 176

Russia, and Sykes-Picot Agreement, 180, 220–1; TEL accused of spying against, 252
Ruwalla (Rualla), 51, 53, 64, 72, 114, 123, 179, 195, 197, 200

Sabin, 197; *see also* Young
Said, Amin, 219
as-Said, Nuri: British suspicions of, 17; in Hejaz, 20; cited, 17, 21–2, 23, 26, 89, 124, 126, 161, 163, 175–6, 196, 199, 205; on TEL, 33, 163; attacks on railway, 126–7, 145, 169, 174; in battle of Ma'an, 162–3; in final campaign, 187–92, 194, 196, 198–201; at Damascus, 205, 209, 212; in Peace Conference, 217, 225
Saladin's tomb, 203
Salem, 98, 100
Salkhad, 72, 106
Salmond, Air Marshal, 240
Salt, 152–3, 155, 159–60, 165–7, 179, 181, 195, 240
Samuel, Sir Herbert, 238, 241, 250
San Remo Conference, 234–5
Sanders, Gen. Liman von, 157–8, 185, 191, 193, 209
Sanussi, 9, 60
Sardast, Capt. Rasim, 42–3, 53, 127–8, 135–6, 141, 169
Scott, Major R. H., 214
Semna, 125, 129, 162, 173, 188, 204
Serahin (Serhan tribe), 101, 104, 108–10, 160
Serhan, *see* Serahin
Serdyeh (Serdiyeh), 69, 101, 116
Serj, 146, 147, 148
Seven Pillars of Wisdom: compared with Arab Bulletin, 54, 72–5, 98–100, 105, 117, 142, 202–3; and with Intelligence Report, 72, 76; the omissions in *Revolt in the Desert*, 275–7
al-Sha'alan, Khalid, 200
al-Sha'alan, Nawwaf ibn Nuri, 52, 72
al-Sha'alan, Nuri, 51–2, 53 n., 67, 69, 72, 100, 114, 179, 188, 194–202
al-Sha'alan, Terad, 200 and n.
Shefia, Saleh ibn, 47, 147, 164
Shahbender, Dr. A. R.; cited, 18, 255, 262; on TEL, 9–10, 64
Shakir, Sherif, 19, 27, 38, 50, 57
al-Shakrani Sherif Hussein, 61, 120, 125, 150
al-Shaliji, Abdul Hamid, 188
Sharaf, Sherif, 41, 49, 59, 95
Shararat (Sherarat), 64, 72, 75, 123
Shaw (TEL), 251
Shaw, G. B., 117, 252, 263

Shaw, Mrs., 117
al-Sheheri, Mohammed, see al-Asbali
al-Sheibani, Ghweileb, 148
Sheikh Sa'ad, 115, 117, 196, 198, 203
Sherif Bey, 203
Shobek, 73–4, 126–7, 146, 148, 150, 157, 159
Shobek forest (Hisheh), 122, 124, 127
Shunet Nimrin, 160, 166, 167
al-Sikeini, Sa'ad, 130–1
Simpson, Col., 18
Sinai, 6, 8, 12
Sirhan, see Wadi Sirhan
Stanton, Mr., 235
Stirling, Major W. F., 176, 201
Storrs, Sir Ronald, 8, 11, 13, 28–30, 32, 37, 46–7, 57, 250, 264; cited, 19, 31, 85, 256, 257, 259
Stotzingen, Baron von, 15, 16
Subsidies to Arab leaders, 64, 80, 243, 246, 257–8, 259, 261
Suez, 23, 39, 71–2, 166
Suez canal, 14, 221
Sukhur, see Beni Sakhr
Sultani station, 73, 75
Survey Department of Egypt, 9
Sykes, Sir Mark, 65–6
Sykes-Picot Agreement, 66, 180, 181, 214, 220–1, 253
Syria, and Syrian, see also Damascus: TEL's first visits, 3–5; measures against Arab nationalists, 14–15; Arab request for British diversion in, 19; Feisal's plans for, 67; TEL's secret visit, 72–3, 74–5, 77–8, 276–7; nationalists join Feisal, 100, 114, 121–2; the dilemma of a rising in, 101–3; officers meddling with politics, 154; TEL recommends independence for, 214; partition of Greater Syria, 215; French demand Mandate, 220–1; King-Crane Commission visits, 232; National Congress, 233; end of independence, 234; appeal to King Hussein, 239; TEL on, 266, 268

Tafas, 115, 117, 118, 198–9; reported massacre at, 203
Tafileh, 73, 74, 146, 148–51, 166–7; Arabs capture, 126–9; Battle of, 132–44; Turkish counter-offensives, 156–9, 204
Taibeh, 194
Taif, 16, 17, 21
Talal, see al-Hreidhin, Talal
Tank Corps, TEL enlists, 251–2
Tawaiha, see Abu Tayeh (clan)
Tebuk, 27, 50, 51, 54, 122–3, 124, 207
al-Tekheimi, Merzuk, 120, 122, 159–61, 165, 167, 168, 173

Tell Arar, 115, 117, 189–90, 191, 194, 197
Tell al-Shahm (Shahim), 129–30, 164
Tell Shehab, 103–4, 109–10, 113, 191
Terabin, 144
Thamad, 166
Thomas, Lowell, 234–5, 252, 263–5, 267, 275, 277
Thompson, R. Campbell, 5
Togatga clan, 96
Townshend, Gen., 10
Transjordan, 221, 239, 254; Emir Abdullah becomes ruler of, 239–41; TEL posted in, 248–9
Trenchard, Lord, 238
Tudmor, see Palmyra
Tulkarm, 185
Turki, see al-Zebn
Turkey, and Turkish: army, Arab personnel in, 11–12, 122; outbreak of war, 13; measure against Arab nationalists, 14–15; Arab advantages against, 24–5; armistice, 66 n., 206; army strength, 102, 185, 208, 261–2; weakness in Palestine, 158; peace offers to Arabs, 180–2; atrocities, 35, 203; peace settlement with, 224; see also, Committee of Union and Progress; Medina
Turra, 199, 203
Tuweira, 59
Tway, see Atwi

al-Ula, 54, 59, 60, 105, 207
Um Keis, 72, 74, 75, 76, 276
Um Lejj, 16, 38, 44, 47, 49, 168
Um al-Surab, 194, 195
al-Umari, Lieut. Subhi, 134–5 n., 138; cited, 136–7, 139, 268
Umtaiye, 115, 189, 191, 194, 195, 197
Uneiza (Aneiza) station, 73–4, 87, 122, 127, 170–3
Unionists, see Committee of Union and Progress
United States, TEL publicized in, 263–4
Uteiba, 57

Versailles Treaty, 235; see also under Peace Conference
Vickery, Major C. E., 47, 49, 52

Wadi Ais, 22–3, 26–7, 45–6, 49–50, 54–5, 57–9
Wadi Araba, 123, 127, 144, 157
Wadi al-Hesa (Seil al-Hasa), 132–3, 142–3, 149, 171, 172, 173, 177–8; see also Hesa station
Wadi Itm, 71, 87 and n., 123, 176
Wadi Musa, 73–4, 96, 121–5, 127, 135

Wadi Safra, 22–3, 25–6, 34, 37, 41–2, 45, 49
Wadi al-Seer, 166, 167
Wadi Sirhan, 52, 65, 68–9, 74, 76, 80, 100
Wadi Yarmuk, see Yarmuk
Wahbeh, Sheikh Hafez, 79
Wahbi Bey, Ali, 204
Wahida, 71, 86, 121, 125, 163, 173–4
Wahhabis, 55
Walad (Wald) Ali, 72, 202
War Office, TEL in, 8
Wavell, Gen. Sir Archibald, cited, 159, 167, 212 n., 272
Weizmann, Chaim, 228–9, 269–70
Wejh, 21, 25, 27, 38, 53–4, 58–60, 62, 64–5, 72, 83, 95; advance on, 44–5, 47; capture of, 49–50; TEL on campaign, 51–2
Wemyss, Admiral, 38–9, 80, 83
Wilson, Col. C. E., 17, 18, 28, 32, 35, 42, 44, 61, 83–5, 87, 273
Wilson, President, 215, 224, 225–6, 231–2
Wingate, Sir Reginald, 18, 38–9, 41, 45, 79 n., 83–4, 177–8, 216, 246
Winterton, Lord, 188, 189, 195, 239
Wood, Lieut., 103, 107, 109, 111
Woolley, Sir Leonard, 5, 6, 7, 8

Yanbo', 16, 21, 25–6, 37–8, 41–7, 49–50, 58, 207
Yanbo' al-Nakhl, 20, 22, 23
Yarmuk, 72, 74, 118, 276; the bridge raid, 103–10
Yehya, Imam, 273
Yemen, 15, 16, 208, 273

Young, Sir Hubert, 10, 165, 168, 175, 187–8, 191, 196–7, 205, 237–8, 267–8, 271

al-Za'agi, Abdullah, 131, 146
Za'al, Auda ibn, 87
Zaal ibn Mutlaq, see Motleg
al-Zebn, Adhoub, 76, 108–10, 112–14, 160–1
al-Zebn clan, 76 and n., 108–9, 113
al-Zebn, Fahad, 108–9, 112–13, 160, 166
al-Zebn, Mifleh, 103, 108–10, 112–13, 160
al-Zebn, Turki ibn Mifleh, 108, 111–14, 161
Zeid ibn Hussein, Emir, 19; military activity in Hejaz, 20, 25, 41, 44, 49, 58–9; TEL on, 33; with northern army, 120, 125–6; at Tafileh, 128, 132, 134–41, 143, 146, 148, 156–9; his expenditure of £24,000, 149–52, 276; attacks on Ma'an railway, 165, 169, 188; enters Ma'an, 204; TEL recommends as ruler of north Iraq, 214; in charge at Damascus, 219; French hostility to, 240; at Jedda, 242; share of war subsidies, 258
Zelebani clan, 96
Zerqa, 69, 72, 189
Zionism, and Zionists: 154, 226–7, 244–6, 268–70; Jewish influence in U.S.A., 221; Feisal's alleged agreement with, 228
Zizia (Ziza), 72, 74, 76, 160, 204
Zumorrod, 60, 61
Zuweida clan, 96

B
Lawrence
        Mousa, Suleiman
            T. E. Lawrence; an
        Arab view.

        15 MAY 67   WP   2149

B   Mousa, Suleiman
Lawrence   T. E. Lawrence; an
        Arab view.
                                4-67

Wilmington Public Library
Wilmington, N. C.

RULES

1.   Books marked 7 days may be kept one
week. Books marked 14 days, two weeks. The
latter may be renewed, if more than 6 months old.

2.   A fine of two cents a day will be charged
on each book which is not returned according
to the above rule.   No book will be issued to
any person having a fine of 25 cents or over.

3.   A charge of ten cents will be made for
mutilated plastic jackets. All injuries books
beyond reasonable wear and all losses shall be
made good to the satisfaction of the Librarian.

4.   Each borrower is held responsible for all
books drawn on his card and for all fines ac-
ing on the same.